GOOD
HOUSEKEEPING

FREEZER
—— TO ——
MICROWAVE
ENCYCLOPEDIA

GOOD HOUSEKEEPING

FREEZER

—— TO ——

MICROWAVE
ENCYCLOPEDIA

GUILD PUBLISHING
LONDON · NEW YORK · SYDNEY · TORONTO

This edition published 1990 by
Guild Publishing by arrangement with Ebury Press

Editors: Barbara Croxford and Felicity Jackson
Photographers: Sue Atkinson, Laurie Evans, Don Last,
James Murphy, Grant Symon and Paul Williams
Home Economists: Sarah Maxwell and Jane Lawrie
Design: Peartree Design Associates

Phototypeset in Century Old Style by
Rowland Phototypesetting Limited, Bury St Edmunds, Suffolk

Printed and bound in Great Britain by
Butler & Tanner Limited, Frome and London

CN 2965

CONTENTS

INTRODUCTION

The freezer and the microwave are the perfect kitchen partners, enabling you to produce delicious meals in minutes rather than hours. The *Good Housekeeping Freezer to Microwave Encyclopedia* is the essential reference book to help you get the best from this partnership.

A complete guide to installing and running a freezer tells you everything from where to site the freezer to how to cope with a power cut, as well as explaining the freezing techniques for meat, poultry, game, fish, vegetables, fruit, dairy produce, breads, cakes and biscuits.

The microwave techniques section of the book explains how a microwave cooker works, the basic equipment needed and the various cooking techniques that help you get perfect results every time.

The comprehensive reference section is arranged in alphabetical order with each entry including freezing and storage instructions plus advice on thawing conventionally or in the microwave where appropriate.

Over 150 mouthwatering recipes – everything from soups and starters, fish and meat dishes, light meals and snacks, to sumptuous cakes and desserts – complete the book. Every recipe has both conventional and microwave instructions for cooking the dish, plus instructions on freezing, thawing and reheating both conventionally or in the microwave.

FREEZING TECHNIQUES

Owning a freezer means you can shop less often, cook only when you feel like it, preserve produce straight from the garden (and any you might buy cheaply at the height of the season) and you will always have meals at the ready for unexpected occasions.

Frozen food is one of the miracles of modern life. Freezing retains more of the quality, character and nutritive value of the food than other preserving methods, and takes only a fraction of the time that curing, smoking, pickling and bottling take.

How freezing works
Food spoilage is caused by micro-organisms and enzymes naturally present in foods and the surrounding air. In the right conditions, they rapidly cause deterioration and decay in food. Freezing takes away one of the most vital requirements for their existence – temperature.

The pathogenic or food poisoning bacteria are inactive below 4°C, whereas some of the food spoilage bacteria, yeasts and moulds are more resistant and will grow very slowly even at −12°C. However, both pathogenic and spoilage micro-organisms are completely dormant at −18°C, the temperature of the home freezer. A small amount of enzyme activity can still take place and it is this which causes loss of quality in long-term storage and eventually makes the food unacceptable.

BUYING A FREEZER
The type of freezer you choose will depend on the amount of space you have to put it in, and what kind of food you plan to freeze. All freezers must carry the star symbol ★ ★★★ which indicates that they are capable of freezing fresh food. An appliance with three stars or less is suitable only for storing ready-frozen food:

★ for 1 week ★★ for 1 month ★★★ for 3 months

Upright freezers
These are the same shape as a full-size refrigerator and range in size from small table-top models to large upright ones. They have front opening doors – large freezers sometimes have two doors – take up less floor space than chest freezers and are less obtrusive.

Upright freezers, fitted with shelves and/or pull-out baskets, are easy to load and unload. In some models, each shelf or basket is fronted by its own flap which shuts out warm air when the door is opened. Upright freezers need defrosting more often than the chest type: frost-free models are available, though they are more expensive both to buy and to run.

Chest freezers
Size for size, chest freezers are cheaper than upright models, and running costs are lower. They have an additional advantage too: more food will fit into the same amount of space since large items can be accommodated with small ones tucked in around them, unrestricted by shelves and baskets. However, they do take up considerably more floor space and are more difficult to keep organised. Small people and those with bad backs will find it difficult to reach down to the bottom of the freezer cabinet.

Refrigerators/freezers
A unit that incorporates both a refrigerator and freezer, one above the other, is popular in small kitchens. The refrigeration and freezing capacities are roughly equal in many models, although it is also possible to buy units which have larger freezers than refrigerators, and vice versa.

Freezer size

Freezer capacity is quoted in either cubic litres or feet. (To make a rough comparison, divide the number of litres by 30 to give the number of cubic feet: the precise measurement is 1 cubic foot = 28.3 litres.) Some manufacturers quote capacity in gross volume and some not, so watch out for this.

How large a freezer you need depends on a number of factors: for instance, how often you shop; whether you plan to cook for your freezer or merely to store basic ingredients; how many people there are in the household, and whether you will be freezing your own produce.

It is generally suggested that you should allow 56 litres (2 cubic feet) per person plus an extra 56 litres, but do think carefully about your particular needs before deciding. Talk to friends who own freezers to see whether they are satisfied with the size they have. If in doubt, buy a model that is 28–56 litres (1–2 cubic feet) larger than you think you need – you will undoubtably use the extra capacity.

Points to look for

Before buying, check the models you are interested in. See how easy it will be to open the door when the freezer is in position in your home – it is sometimes possible to buy a model with a door which can be hung either side.

Check that you can reach the top shelf of an upright model, or the bottom corners of a chest freezer. Look at the position of the controls: are they simple to use and understand? Could they be altered by an inquisitive child?

See if the freezer has a lock – this may be necessary if you are going to keep the freezer in a garage or shed – and do you need an interior light? A drainage hole is useful in a chest freezer so you do not have to bale out when defrosting.

Look too for rollers, which enable you to slide the freezer out to clean behind and underneath it, and also for adjustable levelling feet if your floor is uneven. Finally, check what is the maximum amount of fresh food that can be frozen in 24 hours.

Buying a secondhand freezer

A secondhand freezer can be a good buy but you should check it carefully first. Make sure it can freeze down food and not simply store frozen food, check how old it is – if over five years it may just be reaching the point where things start to go wrong. Look for signs of rust; check all the controls work and test whether the door seal is tight by shutting a piece of paper in the door and seeing whether it moves easily or not. Some shops sell reconditioned freezers which are often very good value and usually come with a three- or six-month guarantee.

Siting a freezer

The most convenient place for a freezer is obviously in or near the kitchen, but it can be sited anywhere in the home, or even in a garage or shed. Bear in mind, though, that it does make a certain amount of noise which may rule out a dining room or bedroom. Chest freezers take up a lot of space but are unlikely to provide the same amount of worktop area as you will need to be able to open it. Upright freezers may need more than their width in order to be able to open the door properly: on some models the door must be opened more than 90° before you can pull out the baskets. Also you need to allow about 5cm (2 inches) at the back for ventilation.

If siting a freezer upstairs be careful that it is not tilted to an angle of more than 30° from upright while it is being moved or you may get an airlock in the coolant. A chest freezer should always be positioned across the joists if upstairs otherwise it may damage the floorboards as it will be very heavy when full.

If the freezer is to be sited in a garage or shed, it is best to put it on strong bricks or solid pieces of wood to prevent it getting damp and rusting. Any freezer which is kept in an out-of-the-way place should be fitted with a freezer alarm so that you get a warning if anything goes wrong, such as a blown fuse.

FREEZER MAINTENANCE

Running costs

Running costs are hard to estimate as they will vary according to the warmth of the room the freezer is sited in. It is possible to get a rough idea of the running costs by checking the wattage on the rating plate at the back of the freezer. Look at the figure before the 'w' or 'kW'. If it is in watts divide it by 1000 to give the kW rating, then multiply this figure by the current cost of a unit of electricity – this will give you the running cost for an hour. However, the freezer is only using electricity when the compressor is pumping the coolant round the system, so the actual running cost will be much lower than this.

You can keep the costs down by following a few simple measures:

• Do not site the freezer near a central heating boiler, hob or oven, or where direct sunlight will fall on it.

• Open the freezer door/lid as little as possible.

• Only put cold food into the freezer.

It may be worth buying a freezer alarm, which sounds if the door has not been shut properly.

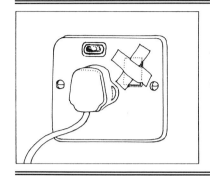

Cover the switch of your freezer with adhesive tape to prevent it being accidentally switched off.

Breakdowns
Freezers are generally reliable but they may break down from time to time. Before you call a service engineer, check the following points:

• Is there a power cut?
Check by switching on a light.

• Is the socket outlet working?
Plug in another appliance and check.

• Has the fuse in the plug blown?
Change it and see.

• Is the compressor working?
Switch to fast-freeze and listen, if there is no noise it is not working.

If the freezer seems very cold you may have left the fast-freeze switch on, or accidentally knocked the thermostat setting. If it sounds very noisy, check that the freezer has not been pushed too close to the wall and that it is level.

You may be able to repair a faulty door seal or perished rubber pads by the compressor – you should be able to buy the spare parts from the manufacturer.

Power cuts
Provided you take certain precautions, food in a chest freezer will remain undamaged for about 48 hours without power if you have had advanced warning and 30–35 hours without. An upright freezer will keep the contents safe for about 26 hours with advance warning, 30 hours without.

If there is advance warning of a power cut at least 6 hours before it occurs, turn on the fast-freeze switch, but first make sure the freezer is full – fill any gaps with rolled-up newspaper, old towels or plastic boxes filled with water.

Do not open the door during a power cut as this will let warm air into the freezer.

Cover the freezer with a blanket to increase its insulation but make sure the condensor and pipes at the back are left clear.

Once the power has been restored, leave the freezer on fast-freeze (or switch to it if there has been no advance warning) for at least 2 hours.

The contents of your freezer can be worth a considerable amount of money and it is worth looking into freezer insurance. Several insurance companies offer freezer insurance as part of a household contents policy while others issue a separate policy. In either case, check exactly what is covered.

Moving house
If possible it is best to empty the freezer if it is to be moved, as a full freezer is very heavy. Some removal firms do have the facility to plug a loaded freezer into an electrical supply in their van; if you want to do this, the freezer should be the last item into the van and the first one into your new home.

When moving a freezer it should be kept as upright as possible and never tipped at an angle of more than 30° as this could cause an airlock in the cooling system. When it is unloaded and installed, switch the freezer on to check that all the lights work, then turn it off and let the oil in the compressor settle down for 2 or 3 hours before running it. When you sign the removal firm's document stating that the job has been completed, write a note to the effect that the freezer has not been tested, so that you can take action if you find it has been damaged.

Defrosting
Freezers need defrosting when the frost on the shelves reaches a thickness of 0.5cm (¼ inch). Try to defrost when stocks are low or when it is a cold day. Put the contents of the freezer into the refrigerator, a cool box or wrap it in newspapers or an old blanket.

You will need a plastic spatula to tap the frost free as it melts, old towels to mop up the water and bowls of hot water to speed up the process. Follow

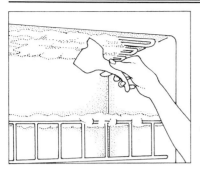

Use a plastic spatula to defrost. Never use a metal implement as this will damage the freezer surface.

Avoid a flood by using a sheet of foil to funnel melting ice into a bowl.

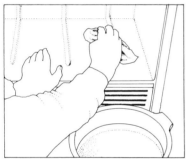

When the freezer is defrosted, wash out with a solution of 15 ml (1 tbsp) bicarbonate of soda to 1 litre (1¾ pints) water.

the manufacturer's instructions for the procedure. When the freezer is free of frost, wash it out with a solution of 15ml (1 tbsp) bicarbonate of soda to 1 litre (1¾ pints) warm water. Dry the freezer thoroughly before switching on again.

Maintain the outside of the freezer by wiping it with a solution of washing up liquid and warm water, then dry thoroughly. Use the crevice tool on the vacuum cleaner to remove dust from the pipes at the back. If the freezer is sited in a garage or shed, polish it from time to time with a silicon all-purpose polish to help it resist damp.

STOCKING A FREEZER

A greater variety of foods can be preserved by freezing than by any other method – everything from fresh or cooked fruit, vegetables and meat to baked goods and complete meals. However, it is worth remembering that it is only worth storing the kinds of foods you would normally buy and eat.

There is no point in filling the freezer with cheap cuts of meat if you never cook these.

Buying in bulk for the freezer can save time and money. You can shop less often and the cost of the food is lower. Some of the biggest savings can be made on the bulk purchase of meat, by buying a whole, half or quarter animal, or large quantities of one particular cut.

In order to save money by buying a carcass and freezing it yourself, you need to have a very large freezer. A hind or forequarter of beef, for instance, weighs about 68kg (150lb) and is enough to half-fill a 340 litres (12 cubic foot) freezer. Also, to make it economical, you need to use all the animal, so do consider your family's likes and dislikes. If they only eat certain cuts it may be better to buy ready-butchered frozen meat in the joints that you eat most often.

Look for good quality products – there is no point saving money only to find that the food is inferior. Savings can also be made on large sizes of everything, from ice cream and beefburgers to complete meals from freezer centres.

PACKAGING

Careful packaging is essential if food is to remain in good condition. The water content in food, that is converted to ice crystals when the food is frozen, must be retained so that it can be converted back to moisture when the food is thawed. Badly packed food that is not properly protected from the cold dry air in the freezer will dry out causing white patches known as freezer burn. Although it is perfectly safe to eat, the food looks unattractive after cooking and it may taste dry.

Packing materials
Aluminium foil This is very useful for wrapping because it can be shaped to cover awkward shapes and pressed against the food to ensure air does not

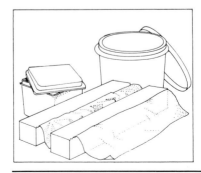

Careful packaging is essential if food is to remain in good condition.

Keep a supply of moisture and vapour-proof containers suitable for the freezer.

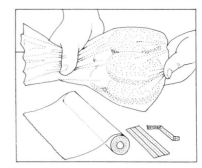

Exclude air from polythene bags before the food is frozen.

Foil is useful for lining casserole dishes when preparing food for the freezer.

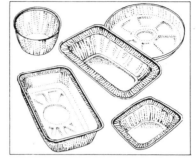

Foil containers come in a range of shapes and sizes.

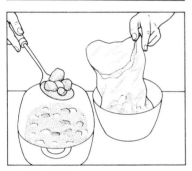

Freeze casseroles in a polythene bag inside a rigid container. Remove the container when the food is solid.

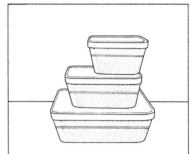

Plastic containers should have airtight lids.

get in. If using standard thickness foil, use a single layer; if thin kitchen foil, use a double layer. Seal it by folding the edges closely over each other, using freezer tape to hold it in place if necessary. Do not use foil with acidic fruits as they may react with it. If you think the foil may become punctured in the freezer, overwrap it in a polythene bag.

Foil is also useful for lining casserole dishes when preparing food for the freezer. Once the dish has been cooked and frozen, the foil lining containing the food can be removed from the casserole and used to wrap the food. The food can be unwrapped and replaced in the casserole, without the foil, for reheating.

Polythene bags Both polythene bags and sheeting are useful for wrapping foods for freezing. Use heavy-duty polythene which will protect the food rather than the thin bags used for packing sandwiches. Liquids and solids such as stews, should be frozen in a polythene bag placed in a container – the regular shape is easier to store in the freezer.

Squeeze out as much air as possible from the bags before they are put in the freezer; or suck it out with a straw or vacuum pump. Seal the bags with freezer tape or twist ties.

Plastic wrap/cling film/freezer wrap This plastic film clings to itself and also to plastic and metal, so it is very useful for wrapping food for the freezer. Use it as a lining if you want to pack acidic fruits in foil and also for wrapping individual portions of foods which can then be stored together in a polythene bag and removed one at a time. Always overwrap in polythene bags in case the film becomes loose. Use freezer and microwave plastic wrap and freezer plastic wrap if thawing the food in the microwave as the plasticiser in ordinary cling film can migrate into the food if it is used in the microwave.

Note: Throughout the book we have used the term plastic wrap. Use whichever type is required.

Foil dishes These come in a range of sizes and shapes and you can cook, freeze and reheat in them, but you cannot use them in the microwave. If cleaned carefully they can be used several times for freezing, but the lids should only be used once.

Plastic containers These are more expensive than other types of freezer packaging but will last for years. Some varieties may lose their airtight seal after a while and need sealing with freezer tape to prevent air affecting the contents – good quality brands of containers usually carry a guarantee.

Glass Most glass is unsuitable for use in the freezer because it is likely to shatter. Special toughened glass dishes are handy for mousses and desserts which are to be served in the dish, but do make sure they are freezerproof. If you are attempting to chill a bottle of wine or beer in an emergency, if you leave it too long it will be splattered around the freezer by the time you get to it. Never do this with any fizzy drinks.

If you do use a glass container, make sure it has straight sides, as these make it easier to get the contents out again, and leave 2.5–5cm (1–2 inches) headspace.

Other packaging The containers from some bought foods are useful for using in the freezer (though not in the microwave), particularly margarine tubs, yogurt and cream pots and foil dishes. Make sure they are clean and do not expect them to last more than two or three sessions in the freezer.

Dishes for freezer and microwave Where possible, pack food in containers that are suitable for both the freezer and the microwave cooker. Freezer-to-oven microwave, designed especially for freezing conventionally cooked foods to be reheated in a microwave, is now increasingly available. Cardboard-type cartons are ideal for pies, flans and non-liquid dishes which need microwaving only for a short time, but it can only be used once. Boil in the bags and roasting bags, which are ideal for freezing casseroles, vegetables and small joints, can both be put directly into the microwave.

HOW TO FREEZE

Freezing is a very simple process, based on how quickly heat can be taken out of food (not cold air pumped in), but unless you grasp the basics, it is possible to make some equally simple mistakes. These rarely make the food inedible, but they may affect its taste, texture, colour and – most vital of all if you are feeding a young growing family – its food value.

Most foods are largely made up of water, even something as seemingly solid as lean meat contains about 70 per cent water. All freezing does is convert this water to ice crystals. Quick freezing results in tiny ice crystals, retained within the cell structure of the food, so that on thawing the structure is undamaged and the food value unchanged. Slow freezing, on the other hand, results in the formation of large ice crystals, which damage the cell structure and cause loss of nutrients. This damage is irreversible, and slow-frozen food shows loss of texture, colour and flavour when thawed. Foods like cucumber and strawberries, which have a high water content and delicate structure, never freeze successfully because the tiniest crystal formation breaks them down.

In order to avoid slow freezing, it is important to only freeze one-tenth of your freezer's capacity in any 24 hours or else not only will heat be absorbed by the freezer's refrigeration system, but also by food already frozen. If, for instance, you have a 50kg (110lb) freezer (approximately 170 litres or 6 cubic feet) you should only freeze about 5kg (11lb) food at a time. If you freeze more, the addition of the unfrozen food will push up the freezer temperature and the result will be slow-frozen food – the very thing you want to avoid.

Small fluctuations of temperature in the freezer are harmless – every time you add an unfrozen product, you are going to create a small temperature change – though you can keep it to the minimum by chilling food in the refrigerator first. Larger swings in temperature are more harmful because even if you have quick-frozen the food, any pronounced fluctuation is still going to affect ice crystal formation – with possible loss of quality.

Fast-freeze switch

To enable you to fast-freeze food, most freezers have a fast or super freeze switch which overrides the freezer thermostat and takes the temperature down below −18°C. The newly introduced food, preferably already cooled in the refrigerator (made-up dishes should have been quickly cooled by standing the dish in cold water and then chilled in the refrigerator), can be frozen quickly without affecting the temperature of the food already in the freezer. If your freezer does not have a fast-freeze switch, turn down the thermostat to its lowest setting 2 hours before the food is put in.

It is not necessary to use the switch for small items like the odd loaf of bread or fruit pie. For a fairly small amount, such a four casseroles or three or four pies, put on the switch for about 2 hours before putting the food in and leave it on for about 4 hours afterwards. For a large amount, such as half a carcass of meat, switch on 6 hours beforehand and leave on for a further 20–40 hours after putting the food in.

FREEZING MEAT

Ready-butchered meat needs very little preparation before freezing. Excess fat should be removed as it tends to go rancid more quickly than the flesh during storage. Wherever possible, it is a good idea to remove any bones as well – they take up valuable space without giving any return for your money. It is better to make stock or soup with the bones and freeze that instead, therefore using up much less freezer space.

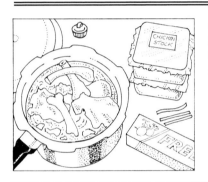

It saves space if you freeze stock rather than bones.

FREEZING POULTRY

It is only worth freezing young, plump, tender birds. Commercially frozen raw poultry is so readily available it is only an advantage to freeze poultry at home when the price is very favourable.

Turn the freezer temperature control down low at least 24 hours before planning to freeze a bird – you need to freeze it at the lowest possible temperature for your freezer – ideally −32°C (−26°F). Once the chicken is frozen, return to the normal freezer temperature.

Whole birds

After plucking and drawing, wipe the bird. Do not stuff the chicken, as it takes too long to freeze and thaw; freeze any stuffing separately. Pack the giblets separately because they will only keep for a quarter of the time the chicken can be stored.

To truss the bird, place it on the table with the breast uppermost and the legs on the right-hand side ready for trussing. Insert the trussing needle, threaded with fine string, through the top joint of one leg, through the body and out through the other leg, leaving an end of string. Catch in the wing, then pass the needle through the body and catch in the bottom of the opposite leg. Again, insert the needle through the bottom end of the leg, pass the needle through the body and through the bottom of the opposite leg. Finally, pass the needle diagonally through the body and catch in the

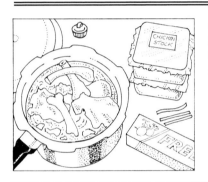

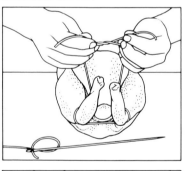

Trussing the legs of a chicken.

Using a trussing needle to truss a chicken.

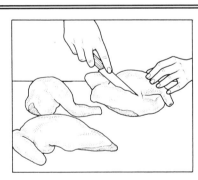

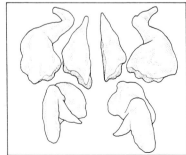

Dividing poultry into portions.

Poultry divided into six portions.

remaining wing. Tie the string tightly and securely.

To truss the bird without using a special needle, insert a skewer through the body just below the thigh bone and turn the chicken over on its breast. Catching in the wing tips, pass the string under the ends of the skewer and cross it over the back. Turn the bird over and tie the ends of the string round the tail, at the same time securing the drumsticks.

Portions

Divide small birds, around 1–1.4kg (2–3lb), into quarters, using poultry shears or a sharp knife. Cut the bird in half, through and along the breastbone. Open the bird out, then cut along the length of the backbone, using a knife or poultry shears.

If you want to remove the backbone entirely, cut along either side of it, then lift out. If you are using a knife, you will have to tap the back sharply with a heavy weight to cut through the bony sections. Once the bird is in two halves, lay them skin side up and divide each in half again by cutting diagonally across between wing and thigh – allocating more breast meat to the wing than to the thigh, to even out the amount of meat per portion.

Smaller chicken joints

For smaller joints for casseroles, use a larger bird. Cut the thigh loose along the rounded edge and pull the leg away from the body to isolate the joint. Break the thigh backwards so that the knife can cut through the socket of each thigh joint, and loosen the wings from the breast meat in the same way. Divide the legs into two pieces in the centre of the joint. Turn over the body of the bird on its back and carve the breast meat from the breastbone. Both breast portions may be halved, and the back divided into two or three pieces or used to supplement the stock pot.

FREEZING FISH

Fish for freezing must be really fresh – it should be frozen within 12 hours of being caught. Wash, then remove the scale, scrape tail-to-head with the back of a knife.

To gut round fish, make a slit along the abdomen from the gills to the tail vent and remove the insides. Clean away any blood by rubbing with a little salt to remove the black skin and blood. Rinse under cold running water. Drain and pat dry with absorbent kitchen paper.

To gut flat fish, open the cavity which lies in the upper part of the body under the gills and clean out

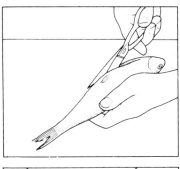

Slitting the belly of a round fish.

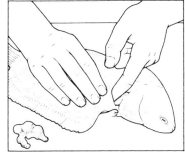

Gutting a flat fish.

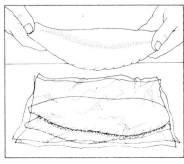

Interleave fish fillets with plastic wrap for freezing.

the entrails in the same way. Rinse under cold running water. Drain and dry with kitchen paper.

To freeze a whole fish, for best results, place the fish unwrapped in the freezer until solid. Remove and dip in cold water: this will form a layer of thin ice over the fish and is known as 'ice glazing'. Return the fish to the freezer and repeat the process until the ice glaze is 0.5cm (¼ inch) thick. Wrap in plastic wrap and support with a thin board.

To freeze fish steaks, separate them with a double layer of plastic wrap, then overwrap in foil or plastic wrap.

Shellfish should only be frozen if you can freeze them within 12 hours of being caught.

Cooked fish, in pies, fish cakes, croquettes, kedgeree or paella, should be prepared according to the recipe, but be absolutely sure the fish is very fresh. Freeze the prepared dishes in foil-lined containers. Remove when hard, then pack in polythene bags.

FREEZING VEGETABLES

Most vegetables freeze well, the exceptions are tomatoes and salad vegetables like lettuce and cucumber. Vegetables for freezing should just have reached maturity.

Vegetables need to be blanched before freezing to destroy the enzymes present which cause the food to deteriorate quickly; also to preserve the colour, flavour and texture of food. It also helps to retain their vitamin C content which these enzymes destroy.

The vegetables should be prepared as if for cooking, then blanched in not less than 4 litres (7 pints) boiling water to each 450g (1lb), with 10ml (2 tsp) salt. The water must return to the boil in 1 minute after the vegetables are added. The blanching water can be used six or seven times, then must be replaced with fresh water. Do not blanch more than 450g (1lb) at a time. Calculate the blanching time from when the water re-boils.

After blanching, remove the vegetables at once (a blanching basket makes this much easier) and plunge them into ice cold water (add ice cubes to the water) to prevent overcooking and to cool the vegetables as quickly as possible. Cooling time is usually the same as the blanching time. For each batch, use fresh iced water. Drain in a colander as soon as the vegetables are cool. Careful timing is essential so use a watch with a second hand or a kitchen timer.

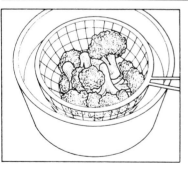

A blanching basket makes blanching easier.

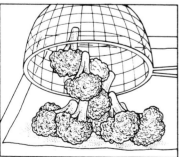

Drain cooled, blanched vegetables on a clean tea towel.

Blanching in the microwave

Vegetables can be blanched very successfully in the microwave and in much smaller amounts of water. Small quantities of vegetables blanch more evenly than large – if necessary blanch in batches, microwaving the first batch while preparing the next batch. A 2 litre (3½ pint) casserole is suitable for most vegetables.

FREEZING FRUIT

Fruits should be frozen just as they become ready for eating, though slightly over-ripe fruits can be frozen as purées. It is best to choose unblemished, fresh fruit. Lightly wash and dry well, if necessary. Do not freeze in contact with any metal, including aluminium foil. If blanching, blanch as vegetables, without the salt. There are four basic methods for freezing fruit: dry (free flow) pack, dry sugar pack, syrup pack and purée.

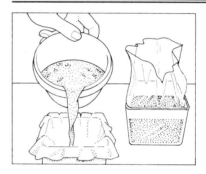

Freeze fruit purées in a polythene bag placed inside a rigid container. Remove the container when the food is solid.

Dry pack

Fruits like blackcurrants, gooseberries, blackberries and raspberries, which do not discolour easily, can be frozen just as they are. Spread the fruit on baking trays or sheets lined with non-stick or greaseproof paper and put into the freezer until frozen – this is known as open freezing. Pack the frozen fruit in polythene bags. The fruit will stay separate or 'free-flow', so that small amounts can be used as required.

Dry sugar pack

Fruits like the above can be sprinkled with sugar before freezing, then as they thaw the liquid and sugar make a syrup. Spread the fruit in a shallow dish and sprinkle with caster sugar, allowing 50g (2oz) sugar to each 450g (1lb) fruit (unless individual A–Z entry states otherwise). Gently mix. Pack in rigid containers, leaving 1–2cm (½–¾ inch) headspace.

Syrup pack

Firm-textured fruits like peaches and apricots which are likely to discolour easily, particularly on thawing, are best frozen in a sugar syrup.

As a rough guide, allow 300ml (½ pint) syrup (made up to the strength indicated in the A–Z entries) for every 450g (1lb) fruit. Dissolve the sugar in the water, bring to the boil and remove from the heat. Add lemon juice where indicated, then cover and leave to cool. Pour the syrup over the fruit or place the fruit in a container with the syrup. Light fruits which tend to rise in liquids can be held below the surface by using a dampened and crumpled piece of non-absorbent paper, such as greaseproof, on top of the mixture. Leave 1–2cm (½–¾ inch) headspace for expansion.

Fruits that discolour, such as apples and pears, should first be soaked in a solution of lemon juice. Use the juice of 1 lemon to each 1 litre (1¾ pints) water used. When preparing large quantities of fruit, make the syrup the day before and leave to chill overnight, as it has to be used cold.

Purée

Over-ripe fruit can be puréed in a blender or food processor, then sieved to remove seeds if necessary. Pack in rigid containers, leaving 1–2cm (½–¾ inch) headspace for expansion. Cover purées with a layer of plastic wrap if they are likely to discolour. Purées make good stand-by sauces and desserts.

FREEZING LIQUIDS

Unlike solid foods, where you must expel as much air as possible, when freezing liquids you must leave at least 1cm (½ inch) headspace in containers – for 600ml (1 pint) liquid you need to leave up to 2.5cm (1 inch). This is because water expands one-tenth on freezing.

Unless you leave room for expansion, items such as soups, sauces, and fruits packed in syrup, will push off their lids (see also Glass on page 13).

Liquids and solids

A combination of solids and liquid, such as stews and casseroles or fruit in syrup, should if possible have a layer of liquid on the top with no pieces of food sticking out. Leave 1cm (½ inch) headspace. Solids which rise above the surface of the liquid, such as fruit salad, need an inner covering of crumpled non-stick paper or plastic wrap before completing the wrapping to prevent any dehydration.

SEALING AND LABELLING

Once you have extracted all the air from polythene bags of food for freezing, the bags should be sealed with twist ties or freezer tape. Twist ties with metal closures should be removed before putting food in the microwave. Freezer tape has a special adhesive that sticks at low temperatures – unlike ordinary sticky tape – and is available in white so

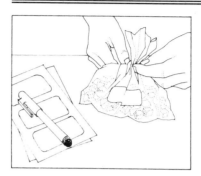

Pack and label food carefully before freezing.

that you can write on it and save the extra cost of labels.

Another very secure way of sealing bags is by heat sealing and this is particularly useful if you want to use the bag as a boil-in-the-bag packet. You can buy special electric sealers for freezer bags. It is probably not worth investing in a special sealer unless you think you will use it regularly.

Labelling is essential, unless the food is a commercial packet that states clearly what it is, as once the food is frozen and has been in the freezer for a couple of months it is very hard to identify. Use a chinagraph pencil or waterproof felt-tipped pen for labelling, so that the information is not rubbed off while the package is in the freezer. Some polythene bags have a white printed label on them. On each packet write the contents, quantity and date of freezing. If other people are going to use the food, it is worth including brief instructions about thawing, reheating and any extra ingredients which should be added. You can buy freezer labels in different colours so that you can code foods for easier finding – such as red labels for meat, green for vegetables and so on.

STORING FOOD

If food is stored in the freezer at a constant temperature of −18°C (0°F) it will keep almost indefinitely, however there will be some deterioration in the flavour, colour, texture and taste. Food is perfectly safe to eat after long periods of freezing because at this temperature food poisoning bacteria cannot multiply in or on the frozen food. However, food contaminated before it is frozen will still be contaminated when thawed. If frozen food is allowed to thaw out and is kept at room temperature (rather than in the refrigerator), bacteria will develop and the food will become a health hazard. This is because micro-organisms require a temperature above 7°C (45°F) to multiply.

Different foods have different storage times and these are determined by the length of time foods can be stored without any detectable change in eating quality. These are determined by the composition of the food, for example how much fat and water the food contains and whether the food is strongly flavoured.

Maximum recommended storage time for most vegetables is 10–12 months; for most fruits packed in syrup or sugar, 9–12 months; for fruits packed alone or as purées, 6–8 months; fruit juices, 4–6 months. Meats like beef and lamb can be stored for up to 8 months, but fattier meats like pork should preferably be kept for no longer than 6 months. This is because the fat tends to oxidise and go rancid, destroying fat-soluble vitamins such as vitamin A, as well as spoiling flavour. Oxidation can take place in oily fish like mackerel, too, which is why they can only be kept for 2 months as opposed to 3 months for white fish.

THAWING FOOD
Some foods can be cooked or reheated straight from the freezer, others need to thaw first. (For thawing in the microwave, see pages 28–31.)

Meat
The quickest way to thaw meat is to cook it from frozen. This is usually determined by the size and thickness of the piece of meat, so chops, steaks, liver slices and kidneys can be cooked from frozen, as well as cubed meat for stews and kebabs. But, boned and rolled cuts of meat should not be cooked from frozen, but thawed first. Cooking times for joints over 2.7kg (6lb) are very difficult to calculate, so to prevent the outside being overcooked before the inside is thawed, it is better to thaw large joints before cooking. If you have to roast from frozen, it is essential to use a meat thermometer. To test if cooked, shortly before the estimated cooking time, insert the thermometer into the centre of the meat or, if applicable, as near the bone as possible, making sure that the point of the thermometer does not touch the bone. The temperature on the

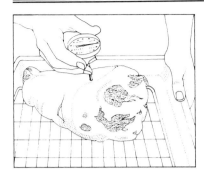

Testing a joint of meat with a thermometer.

thermometer should read at least 70°C/160°F.

Stews, pre-cooked pies and casseroles can be reheated from frozen, but unless you freeze them in fairly shallow dishes to begin with, there is always the danger they will not have reheated right through. Ideally thaw at cool room temperature.

Poultry
All frozen poultry must be completely thawed before cooking. It is then as perishable as fresh meat and should be cooked as soon as possible.

In the light of recent research, it is recommended that poultry is thawed in its wrapping at cool room temperature of 16–17°C (65–70°F) rather than in the refrigerator.

Fish
To retain their juiciness and texture, whole fish are best thawed before cooking, as are large portions for deep frying. Small fish and cuts such as fillets can be cooked from frozen.

RE-FREEZING PARTLY THAWED FOOD
Some partly thawed food may be refrozen without danger to health. If you can crunch a pack of food this indicates the presence of ice crystals and means it is generally safe to re-freeze, but the quality of the food will have deteriorated.

It is best not to re-freeze food that has been thawed and kept at room temperature for more than a few hours but if it has only softened on the outside, it can be re-frozen but will suffer loss of colour, texture, flavour and food value.

If you return home from holiday and find the freezer off and food lying in a puddle, the safest thing is to discard the whole lot (unless some articles are still partly frozen).

It is perfectly safe to thaw uncooked frozen food, cook it and re-freeze it.

MICROWAVE TECHNIQUES

The great advantage of the microwave cooker is its speed – it can cook, thaw and reheat food in a fraction of the time it takes conventionally and is the perfect partner for the freezer.

Microwave cookers are very compact: even the largest model will sit on a work surface, and the small models are still large enough to cook reasonable quantities of food while occupying very little space.

Cooking times are so short with the microwave cooker that they are energy-saving. Most cookers run off a 13 amp socket outlet and cost only a few pence per hour to run on full power.

Microwaving is a very clean form of cooking. The cooker walls never get very hot so that any food which spills and splatters does not burn on to them. Cooking smells and steam are minimal.

It also can be a more healthy way of cooking many foods: as little or no fat is needed in the cooking.

The microwave and the freezer are perfect partners – the frozen food can be thawed and reheated in minutes in the microwave. When reheating ready-made dishes in the microwave, the texture of the food remains unchanged. Whole joints of meat can be thawed in the microwave ready for microwave or conventional cooking.

How a Microwave Cooker Works

A microwave cooker is very simple: it is basically a metal-lined box which converts the electric current into microwaves using a device called a magnetron. Microwaves are high frequency, short-length, electro-magnetic waves, similar to TV radio waves. They have three very important characteristics: they are reflected by metal, they are able to pass through most other materials and they are attracted to moisture.

As soon as the cooker is switched on, microwaves are generated and enter the cooking cavity where they are reflected off the metal walls. As they bounce off the walls in a regular pattern, they pass through the food containers and into the food. Once in the food, they make the water molecules vibrate millions of times per second, causing friction and thus generating a great amount of heat. The heat spreads through the food by conduction, so cooking it.

The microwaves are only generated when the cooker door is closed and the correct controls have been operated, and then only for the duration of the pre-selected time, so that as soon as the timer switches off or the cooker door is opened,

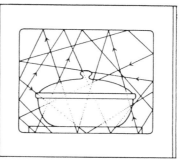

Microwaves bounce off the walls in a regular pattern. They pass through food containers into the food.

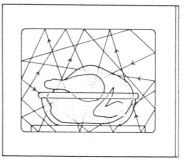

Once in the food, microwaves make water molecules vibrate, causing friction and generating heat.

microwaves cease to be generated. The food continues to cook after the microwave is switched off, not by the action of microwaves, but by the conduction of heat within the food. This is why many microwaved dishes require standing time after being removed from the cooker.

Power settings

Unlike conventional ovens, the power output and heat controls on microwave cookers do not follow a standard formula. When manufacturers refer to a 700-watt cooker they are referring to the cooker's power output; its input, which is indicated on the back of the cooker, is usually about double that figure. The higher the wattage of a cooker, the faster the rate of cooking – food cooked at 700 watts on full power will cook in half the time of food cooked at 350 watts. The vast majority of microwave cookers sold today are either 600, 650 or 700 watts, but there are many cookers still in use which may be 400 or 500 watts.

In this book HIGH refers to 100% full power output of 650 watts; MEDIUM refers to 60% of full power; LOW is 35% of full power.

Whatever the wattage of your cooker, the HIGH/FULL setting will always be 100% of the cooker's output. Thus your highest setting will correspond to HIGH. However, the MEDIUM and LOW settings used in this book may not be equivalent to the MEDIUM and LOW settings marked on your cooker. As these settings vary according to power input, use the following calculation to estimate the correct setting for your cooker.

Multiply the percentage power required by the total number of settings on your cooker and divide by 100. To work out what setting MEDIUM and LOW correspond to on your cooker, calculate:

MEDIUM (60%) = % Power required
× Total number of cooker
settings ÷ 100
= Correct setting
$$\frac{60 \times 9}{100} = 5$$

LOW (35%) = % Power required
× Total number of cooker
settings ÷ 100
= Correct setting
$$\frac{35 \times 9}{100} = 3$$

If your cooker output is lower than 600 watts, you must allow a longer cooking and thawing time than those given in the book. Add approximately 10–15 seconds per minute for a 500 watt cooker, and 15–20 seconds per minute for a 400 watt cooker.

No matter what the wattage of your cooker is, you should always check food before the end of the cooking time to make sure that it does not overcook, and allow for the standing time which is when many foods finish cooking. Food should always be piping hot before it is ready to serve.

TYPES OF COOKERS

A wide range of microwave cookers is available, from small models with two or three power settings, to large, more sophisticated versions with a number of different settings. They fall into three main categories: countertop microwave cookers, double oven microwave cookers and combination ovens. Your choice will depend on what you want to pay and what you want the microwave to do, as well as the size of your kitchen.

Countertop microwave cookers These take up little space and are the most popular. Some have a rack or shelf inside, offering two cooking positions, though this makes them more complicated to use. Usually the food on the shelf gets more of the microwave energy than that on the base so you have to choose foods that will cook together satisfactorily.

Double oven microwave cookers These are available as either free-standing cookers with a hob, or as a double oven unit, housing a separate microwave and conventional oven, but no hob. Both have the advantage of complementary cooking in one unit – you can start cooking a joint of meat in the microwave, then brown it in the conventional oven.

Combination ovens These have both microwave and conventional cooking facilities in the same oven. Although microwave cookers work fast they cannot brown or crisp foods. A combination oven has the advantage that it cooks food in about half the normal time and browns it as well. It combines several cooking methods in one unit; these are usually convection cooking, microwave cooking and a combination of the two, known as 'combination' cooking. A grill is sometimes included as well, and one model even has a ceramic hob on the top. These different methods of cooking can be used on their own or in combination with one another.

Convection cooking (also known as turbo or convectional heat) is the same as cooking in an ordinary electric oven. The convection system in most combination ovens is fan assisted – the hot air is circulated in the oven by a fan – and this speeds up the cooking process (if you are cooking recipes designed for cooking in an ordinary oven, you will need to reduce the temperature by 10°C).

The microwave system in a combination oven is the same as in a microwave cooker.

To cook on combination, you must first set the temperature in °C for the convection system, and then set the microwave level. Some books and manufacturers recommend cooking at 250°C and on a HIGH microwave setting. This cooks the food quickly but the food can dry out and burn on the outside at these settings – the best combination is 200°C/MEDIUM LOW. Consult individual recipes or the manufacturer's handbook for more accurate results.

Standard features
On/off control All standard microwave cookers have an on/off control or button which switches on the power and, in most basic cookers, also activates the interior light and cooling fans. They also have a Cook or Start button which switches on the microwave energy for cooking, heating and thawing food. This will only work when the cooker door is completely closed. (When the door is opened, the microwave energy is automatically switched off. To continue cooking, the door must be closed and this control switched on again.)
Timer The cooking time is controlled by a timer which may be mechanical or digital. When the pre-set time is reached, a buzzer or 'beeper' sounds and the cooker will switch off automatically. Some models have a facility which reminds you that the food is still standing in the microwave. The buzzer or 'beeper' sounds at a pre-set interval after the cooking period is over, usually 1 minute.
Door The design varies from model to model, most have side-opening doors, although drop-down and slide-up types are available. There is usually a transparent mesh panel in the door that enables you to see into the oven as the food cooks.
Cavity The cooker cavity is a smooth, metal-lined box which may have a plastic or paint coating. Some models have removable glass floors or shelves and many have removable turntables; these models are the easiest to clean. Some now have non-stick linings on the top under the grill element.
Vents and filters All cookers have some sort of vent to allow moisture to escape during cooking. Some models also have air filters through which cooling air for the components will pass into the cooker

cavity and cool the inner components. These filters are removable and should be checked and cleaned from time to time according to the manufacturer's instructions.

Special features
In addition to the standard fittings, some microwave cookers have more sophisticated features which may be worth considering.
Automatic programming This allows more than one power setting to be programmed at once, so that a number of cooking sequences can be carried out on the one setting. The cooker can be programmed to start off cooking the food at HIGH, then to complete the cooking on LOW; to come on at a set time and cook the food so that it is ready when you come home; or thaw food, then automatically switch to a setting for cooking.
Browning element or integral grill This provides a convenient way of giving microwaved food a traditional brown appearance, either before or after cooking. It is usually situated at the top of the cooker and works in the same way as a conventional grill. It is useful if the microwave is your main cooking appliance.
Defrost control This is an automatic control which provides even thawing of frozen foods. When used with the timer, the microwave energy is automatically turned on and off to allow rest periods in between short bursts of microwave energy. These short bursts ensure that thawing is carried out at an even rate so that the food thaws without cooking. In microwaves without this control, this will have to be done by hand allowing periods of standing time between microwaving.
Temperature probe This is an instrument which allows cooking to be determined by the internal temperature of the food being cooked, rather than by time. One end of the probe is inserted into the thickest part of the food and the other end is plugged into a special socket in the cooker cavity. The required internal temperature is then selected and when the food reaches the required point, the microwave energy is automatically switched off or reduced to a lower setting. This probe is particularly useful when cooking large, dense foods such as joints of meat and whole poultry.
Turntable This is a rotating platform which automatically moves the food around the cooking cavity and helps it to cook evenly, though some foods will still need repositioning by hand.
Variable power This enables the cooking speed to be varied in much the same way as changing

temperature in a conventional oven. Settings vary according to the different models, and are described as HIGH, MEDIUM and LOW, or graduated numbers, or terms such as Roast, Bake, Simmer, Defrost and Reheat.

COOKING CONTAINERS

Many of the bowls and dishes you normally use in the kitchen are perfectly suitable for microwave cooking. In order to be used in a microwave cooker, the container must be made of a material which allows the microwaves to pass through it into the food, absorbing little or no microwave energy itself. It must be resistant to the heat of the food and it should be the right shape and size. Metal dishes or foil containers should never be used unless specified otherwise by the cooker manufacturer, as metal reflects microwaves so

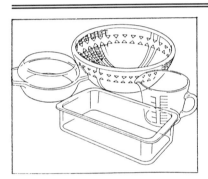

China, glass and pottery can be used in the microwave. Avoid anything with a metallic finish.

preventing them reaching the food and heating it. More importantly, metal containers will cause sparking (arcing) which can pit the cooker walls, distorting the microwave pattern, and may even damage the magnetron.

China and pottery Glazed china plates, cups, saucers, bowls and mugs can all be used. Avoid using china that has a metallic decoration or

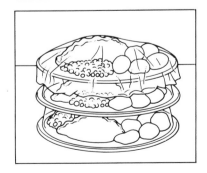

Use plate rings to reheat several plates of food.

marking, such as gold or gold leaf, as this might cause sparking. Fine bone china should only be used for reheating foods for short periods as it could crack with excessive heat. Unglazed pottery and earthenware are porous and, although they can be used, they absorb some of the microwave energy and slow down cooking, so they are best avoided.

Glass Ovenproof glass and glass ceramic dishes are the most useful microwave containers. Clear glass dishes are particularly good as you can see the food cooking. Ovenproof glass measuring jugs are also very useful, as they can be used for measuring and mixing as well as cooking. Ordinary glasses and glass dishes are only suitable for heating foods for a short time as they could crack from the heat of the food. Do not use cut glass or leaded glass.

Plastic An increasing range of plasticware is available specially for use in the microwave cooker. Boilable, rigid plastic containers that are dishwasher proof are normally suitable for microwave cooking, though preferably only for short cooking times. It is not always easy to tell what sort of plastic a container is made from, so if you are not sure if it is suitable, use the container test (see right). Cream and yogurt cartons will melt in the microwave, as will ordinary polythene bags. Polythene freezer bags and freezer containers can be used for short periods of thawing or reheating if a slit is made in the top of the bag before reheating. Boiling bags, roasting bags and microwave cling film (plastic wrap) can all be used, but they must be slit or vented to allow steam to escape, otherwise the build-up of steam may make the bag burst.

Paper Paper cups and cartons, plain white plates, napkins and cardboard can all be used in the microwave for short cooking times, although longer cooking may cause them to burn. Coloured plates and napkins should be avoided as the dye may run into the food. Greaseproof paper and absorbent kitchen paper can be used as coverings for fatty foods to prevent them spattering, or they can be placed underneath bread and pastries when they are reheated to prevent them becoming soggy. Do not use absorbent kitchen paper made from recycled paper as it contains impurities such as tiny particles of metal that could cause sparking in the microwave. Follow the manufacturer's recommendations about using waxed and plastic-coated cups as some may melt if used in the microwave.

Wood and wicker These can be used for short

periods of heating, but will dry out and crack if used for a long time. Wooden bowls or spoons used in the microwave should be rubbed occasionally with vegetable oil to keep them in good condition.
Microwave cookware There is an enormous range of cookware specially designed for the microwave. Some containers, such as those made of soft plastics and pressed polystyrene, are disposable, others are designed for permanent use. Many can be used in conventional ovens as well, or can be placed in the freezer as well as the microwave.

Container test
To test that a container is suitable for use in a microwave cooker, carry out this simple test. Place the dish or container in the cooker together with a glass half full of water. Microwave on HIGH for 1½ –2 minutes. At the end of this time, the water should be hot but the dish still cool. If both are hot the dish can be used, but food will take longer to cook in it. But if the container is hot and the water cold, this means the dish has absorbed microwave energy, and should not be used in the cooker.

When testing plastic containers, microwave on HIGH for 10–15 seconds just in case they start to melt.

Shape
Food cooks more evenly in a round dish than a square, oval or rectangular one. If you have to use a container with corners use one with rounded corners; avoid square corners, as microwaves will cluster in these making the food in the corners overcook.

Non-metal ring moulds are ideal for cooking or heating foods that cannot be stirred during cooking to equalize temperature. They are especially good for cakes and desserts, as they allow microwaves to penetrate the food from the centre as well as the sides, top and bottom. If you do not have a ring

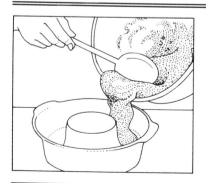

Ring moulds are ideal for cakes and desserts. They allow microwaves to penetrate from the centre as well as the sides.

mould, you can improvise by placing a glass tumbler in the centre of a round dish.

Straight-sided containers cook food more evenly than those with sloping or curved sides. This is because in the very areas where most of the microwave energy is received, on the outside, the food is less deep and is therefore in greater danger of overcooking. Straight-sided dishes provide a uniform depth of food.

The depth of the dish affects how the food cooks and the length of time required. Large, shallow dishes will cook food more quickly than deep, narrow ones as the food can be spread out, giving it maximum exposure to the microwaves.

Use a deeper casserole when cooking large quantities of food which need to be simmered or require stirring during cooking, and a shallow dish for foods which do not require to be stirred, or for heating leftovers which cannot be stirred or re-arranged during reheating.

Size
The size of the container is extremely important with microwave cooking. You need to use larger containers for microwave cooking than you would for conventional cooking, and never fill the dish or container more than two-thirds full. This allows for liquids boiling up during cooking and provides space for stirring mixtures, if necessary. Light cakes and

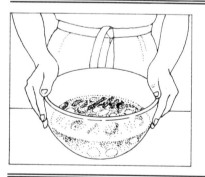

Never fill a container more than two-thirds full to allow for liquids to boil up during cooking.

puddings should only come about halfway up the sides of the dish as they rise so much during cooking.

Special accessories
Browning dishes These look like ordinary ceramic or ovenproof glass but have a tin oxide coating on the base which absorbs microwave energy. They are used to sear and brown foods which are normally grilled or fried, such as steak, chops,

Use a browning dish to sear and brown foods.

beefburgers, sausages and chicken portions. The dish must be preheated according to the manufacturer's instructions and must be reheated in between cooking batches of food. Do not place browning dishes on work surfaces and wear oven gloves when handling them as they get very hot.

Microwave thermometers Ordinary meat and sugar thermometers cannot be used in a microwave, as the mercury in them is affected by the microwaves. Microwave thermometers do not contain mercury. They are particularly useful for roasting joints.

Roasting rack This is useful for raising meat or poultry above its own juices during cooking, or for thawing large, solid items like turkeys, or for thawing or reheating rolls, pastries, cakes and

A roasting rack is useful for cooking meat or poultry and for thawing cakes, pastries and breads.

breads. They are usually made of a hard plastic or ceramic material, and allow the microwaves to completely circulate around the food.

FACTORS THAT AFFECT COOKING

Several factors will affect the timings and results of food cooked in the microwave.

Amount of food

The larger the amount of food being cooked, the longer it will take to cook. As a general guideline,

allow about one third to one half extra cooking time when doubling the ingredients. When cooking quantities are halved, decrease the cooking time by slightly more than half the time allowed for the full quantity of that food. Always underestimate, rather than overestimate, cooking time in the microwave – food which is undercooked can always be returned to the cooker for a further minute or so, but once it is overcooked nothing can be done.

Composition of food

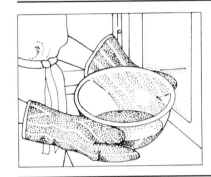

Foods high in sugar or fat become very hot. Use oven gloves when removing the bowl from the cooker.

Foods with a high moisture content will take longer to cook than dry foods, and foods high in fat or sugar will cook or reheat more quickly than those that are low in these ingredients. Jam fillings and sugary coatings on cakes and puddings heat up much more quickly than the dough or pastry in these foods and can become extremely hot. Do not attempt to eat them straight from the microwave. Always leave to cool.

Foods such as cheese, eggs, cream, mushrooms and seafood are easily overcooked, and should always be cooked for the minimum time recommended. Where possible, cook them on LOW.

Density and texture

Dense foods such as joints of meat take longer to cook than light, open-textured foods such as breads

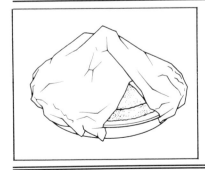

Standing time is important to allow the heat to be conducted to the centre of the food. Cover with foil to keep the heat in.

and cakes. Standing time is particularly important with dense foods like meat to allow the heat to be conducted to the centre of the food. A microwave thermometer or temperature probe is useful for checking food is sufficiently cooked.

Size and shape
Food cut into pieces will cook more quickly than the same amount of food cooked in one piece. The pieces should all be the same size so that they cook evenly.

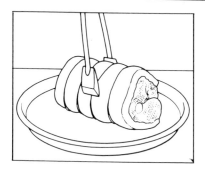

Turn thick pieces of food during cooking.

Temperature of food
The colder the temperature of the food going into the microwave, the longer it will take to heat up. Extra time must be allowed for the centre of cold food to become hot, especially important when cooking poultry and game.

PREPARING FOOD FOR COOKING
Meat
Larger joints of meat will cook more evenly if boned and rolled. Small joints, less than 1.4kg (3lb), do not have time to brown during microwaving. If you do not like the paler appearance of microwaved meats, use a browning dish or glaze the meat by basting with a preparatory microwave browning liquid, soy sauce, paprika, turmeric, brown sugar, honey or other dark-coloured flavourings to give the meat a browned appearance. Arrange the thinner ends of chops in the centre of the dish and the thicker ends at the edge for cooking. Prick sausages, liver and kidneys before cooking to prevent bursting.

Poultry
Whole poultry will cook more evenly if it is tightly trussed into a compact shape. Arrange poultry pieces, such as drumsticks, with the thickest parts to the outside of the dish. Prick giblets and livers to prevent them bursting.

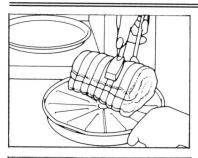

Re-position even-sized pieces of food.

Fish
Slash the skin of whole fish in two or three places to prevent it bursting during cooking. Arrange fillets with the thinner ends to the centre.

Eggs
Do not cook eggs in their shells or they will burst. Prick egg yolks with the tip of a knife or a cocktail stick.

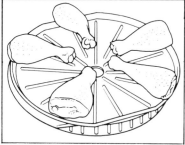

Start cooking meat fat side down and turn during cooking.

Place thinner parts of food towards the centre of the dish. Leave the centre empty.

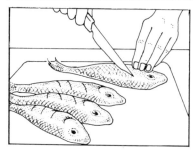

Whole fish should be slashed to prevent them bursting.

Prick whole vegetables to prevent them bursting.

COOKING TECHNIQUES

There are certain cooking techniques that need to be followed to get the best results with microwave cooking.

Arranging the food

Correct arrangement of the food is essential to make sure that it cooks, reheats or thaws evenly. The thicker parts of the food should always be placed at the edges of the dish and the more

Vegetables

Trim vegetables to a uniform size where possible. Large or uneven vegetables should be arranged with the thinner part to the centre of the dish. Pierce any vegetables that have tight skins, such as aubergines or potatoes, before cooking.

Arrange small items, in a ring around the edge of the plate.

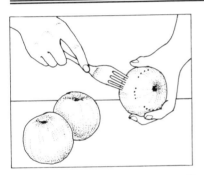

Pierce whole fruits to prevent them bursting.

Reposition foods during cooking, moving foods from the outside of the dish to the middle.

If you require more than 300ml (½ pint) water, it is quicker to boil it in a kettle.

delicate, thinner areas near the centre, overlapping them where necessary.

When cooking several small items, like baked apples, potatoes or cup cakes, arrange them in a ring around the edge of a plate, or directly on the oven shelf. This allows the microwaves to penetrate from the centre as well as the outside.

Fruit

Pierce fruits that have tight skins, such as apples and pears.

Seasoning

Salt has a toughening effect on meats, fish and vegetables, so do not sprinkle it over foods without any liquid until cooking is complete. It is always best to add seasoning at the end of the cooking time.

Season meat at the end of cooking.

The more surface area of food that can be exposed to the microwaves, the quicker and more even the cooking, thawing or reheating will be. If this is not possible, re-arrange the items during the cooking, placing the outer items in the centre and vice versa, removing them as soon as they are cooked or thawed. Arrange foods such as peas in a single layer rather than in a pile.

Browning

Because foods do not brown as they would in a conventional oven, meat and poultry can either be browned in a browning dish (see page 23), browned conventionally under the grill, or they can be sprinkled with paprika or browned breadcrumbs, brushed with sauces such as tomato, brown sauce, soy or Worcestershire sauce, or glazed with honey, marmalade or apricot jam.

Cakes cooked in the microwave do not brown because the sugar in them does not caramelise and form a crust on the surface. To give a more attractive appearance, use dark ingredients such as dark brown sugar, molasses, treacle, coffee, chocolate or cocoa powder.

Covering

Covering foods in the microwave prevents the surface of moist foods such as vegetables from drying out, and speeds up the cooking by trapping moisture underneath the cover. The covering can be of any material that is suitable for use in the microwave (see page 22). If using microwave cling film (plastic wrap) or polythene bags, make a slit in them to allow steam to escape. Fold back one corner of a cling film covering so that foods can be stirred if necessary (there is no need to make a slit as well in this case). A plate makes a good cover, acting like a saucepan lid.

Fatty foods like bacon that are likely to splatter can be covered with absorbent kitchen paper which will soak up the fat and prevent it splattering over the inside of the cooker. Unevenly shaped foods such as chicken joints may need to have the thinner parts partially covered during cooking to prevent them overcooking. Breads and pastries do not require covering.

Stirring and turning food

Because microwaves only penetrate food to a depth of about 2.5cm (1 inch) and then it is the molecules rubbing together which cook the food, stirring is very important to ensure even cooking. Foods that cannot be stirred should be turned over during the

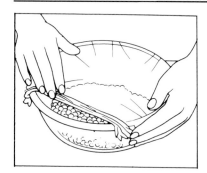

Fold back one corner of a cling film cover so that foods can be stirred.

A plate makes a good cover.

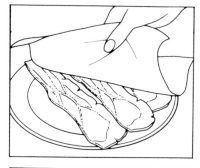

Fatty foods that are likely to splatter can be covered with absorbent kitchen paper.

Stir foods at intervals to speed up cooking.

Foods that cannot be stirred should be turned during cooking.

cooking time. Foods, such as cakes that cannot be stirred or turned over, need the dish or container turned several times during cooking. Even if the cooker has a turntable, it is advisable to turn cakes.

Standing time

Food continues to cook after it is removed from the cooker (or when the power is switched off) because of the conduction of heat, and the period of time during which this happens is known as the standing time. The standing time varies according to the size and density of the food. If in doubt about estimating the cooking time, it is better to undercook the food, test it at the end of the standing time and then cook it for a few seconds more if necessary. Cakes, for instance, may still look uncooked when they come out of the microwave but will firm up and dry out as they finish cooking during the standing time.

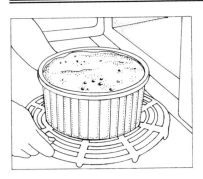

Food continues to cook during standing time because of the conduction of heat.

Cooking techniques for combination ovens

The cooking techniques are the same for a combination oven as for an ordinary microwave cooking, but do not cover food with plastic wrap or foil when cooking in a combination oven.

THAWING FROZEN FOOD

Food can be thawed in the microwave in a fraction of the time it would take to thaw conventionally, but it is essential that it thaws gently and evenly. When food is thawed, the small ice crystals melt first and if thawing in the microwave is too rapid, parts of the food will start to cook before the areas of larger ice crystals have thawed. It is best to thaw food on LOW or DEFROST. Some cookers will thaw food by automatically switching on and off at a high setting, allowing rest periods in between.

If your microwave does not have a LOW or DEFROST setting, you can thaw manually by turning off the cooker every 30 seconds and allowing the

food to stand for 1½ minutes before turning the cooker on again for another 30 seconds. The number of microwaving and resting times will depend on the size and amount of food being thawed – the larger the item the longer the periods of heating and resting. Dense foods like joints of meat need a standing time of at least 15–20

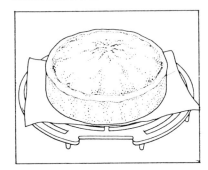

Stand foods such as breads, cakes and pastries on absorbent kitchen paper on a rack.

minutes at the end of the thawing time.

Turn foods over during thawing and separate small items as soon as possible. Break up liquid or semi-liquid foods with a fork and shake or fork apart vegetables and small fruit. Stand foods such as breads, cakes and pastries on absorbent kitchen paper to absorb the moisture.

Containers for thawing

Foods should be put into containers or dishes of an appropriate size and shape for thawing: stews, casseroles and liquid foods will thaw more evenly if put into a deeper dish that keeps their contents together. If the dish is too large, the liquid will start to heat before the rest of the food has begun to thaw.

Frozen food in polythene bags can be thawed in the bags as long as any metal ties are removed and replaced with elastic bands or string. Food frozen in foil containers must be transferred to another container before thawing in the microwave.

Thawing meat

Meat can be thawed very successfully in the microwave. Start thawing a joint in its wrapper, first piercing it, and remove it as soon as possible – usually after one-quarter of the thawing. Place the joint on a microwave roasting rack so that it does not stand in liquid during thawing. Frozen meat exudes a lot of liquid during thawing and because microwaves are attracted to water, the liquid should be poured off or mopped with absorbent kitchen paper when it collects, otherwise thawing will take longer.

Remember to turn over a large piece of meat and, if it shows signs of cooking, give the meat a rest period of 20 minutes. A joint is thawed when a skewer can easily pass through the thickest part of the meat. Chops and steaks should be re-arranged during thawing; test them by pressing the surface with your fingers – the meat should feel cold to the touch and soft in the thickest part.

Thawing poultry
Poultry should be thawed in its freezer wrapping, which should be pierced first and any metal ties or tags removed. Pour off the liquid that collects in the wrapping during thawing. Finish thawing in a bowl of cold water with the bird still in its wrapping. Chicken portions can be thawed in their polystyrene trays where applicable.

Thawing fish and shellfish
Separate cutlets, fillets or steaks as soon as possible during thawing. Like poultry, it is best to finish thawing small whole fish or flat fish in cold

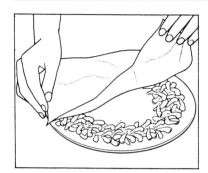

Arrange prawns and scallops in a circle and cover with absorbent kitchen paper to help absorb liquid.

water to prevent the surface drying out. Arrange scallops and prawns in a circle, cover with absorbent kitchen paper to help absorb liquid and remove shellfish as soon as they thaw.

Thawing vegetables
There is no need to thaw frozen vegetables, they can be cooked straight from the freezer in their original plastic packaging, as long as it is first slit, and then placed on a plate. Alternatively, transfer the contents to a shallow dish or bowl and cover.

THAWING MEAT IN THE MICROWAVE

Frozen meat exudes a lot of liquid during thawing and because microwaves are attracted to water, the liquid should be poured off or mopped up with absorbent kitchen paper when it collects, otherwise thawing will take longer. Start thawing a joint in its wrapper, first piercing it, and remove it as soon as possible – usually after one quarter of the thawing time. Place the joint on a microwave roasting rack.

Remember to turn over a large piece of meat. If the joint shows signs of cooking, give the meat a 'rest' period of 20 minutes. A joint is thawed when a skewer can easily pass through the thickest part of the meat. Chops and steaks should be re-positioned during thawing; test them by pressing the surface with your fingers – the meat should feel cold to the touch and give in the thickest part.

Type	Approximate time on LOW	Special instructions
Beef		
Boned roasting joints (sirloin, topside)	8–10 minutes per 450g (1lb)	Turn over regularly during thawing and rest if the meat shows signs of cooking. Stand for 1 hour.
Joints on bone (ribs of beef)	10–12 minutes per 450g (1lb)	Turn over joint during thawing. The meat will still be icy in the centre but will complete thawing if left to stand for 1 hour.
Minced beef	8–10 minutes per 450g (1lb)	Stand for 10 minutes.
Cubed steak	6–8 minutes per 450g (1lb)	Stand for 10 minutes.
Steak (sirloin, rump)	8–10 minutes per 450g (1lb)	Stand for 10 minutes.
Beefburgers standard (50g/2oz) quarter-pounder	2 burgers: 2 minutes 4 burgers: 2–3 minutes 2 burgers: 2–3 minutes 4 burgers: 5 minutes	Can be cooked from frozen without thawing, if preferred.

THAWING POULTRY AND GAME

Poultry and game should be thawed in its freezer wrapping, which should be pierced first and any metal tag removed. During thawing, pour off liquid that collects in the wrapping. Finish thawing in a bowl of cold water with the bird still in its wrapping. Chicken portions can be thawed in their polystyrene trays if shop-bought.

Type	Approximate time on LOW	Special instructions
Whole chicken or duckling	6–8 minutes per 450 g (1lb)	Remove giblets if necessary. Allow bird to stand in cold water for 30 minutes.
Whole turkey	10–18 minutes per 450 g (1lb)	Remove giblets if necessary. Allow bird to stand in cold water for 2–3 hours.
Chicken portions	5–7 minutes per 450g (1lb)	Separate during thawing. Stand for 10 minutes.

Type	Approximate time on LOW	Special instructions
Lamb/Veal		
Boned, rolled joint (loin, leg, shoulder)	5–6 minutes per 450g (1lb)	As for boned roasting joints of beef.
On the bone (leg and shoulder)	5–6 minutes per 450g (1lb)	As for beef joints on the bone.
Minced lamb or veal	8–10 minutes per 450g (1lb)	Stand for 10 minutes.
Chops	8–10 minutes per 450g (1lb)	Separate during thawing. Stand for 10 minutes.
Pork		
Boned, rolled joint (loin, leg)	7–8 minutes per 450g (1lb)	As for boned roasting joints of beef.
On the bone (leg, hand)	7–8 minutes per 450g (1lb)	As for beef joints on bone.
Tenderloin	8–10 minutes per 450g (1lb)	Stand for 10 minutes.
Chops	8–10 minutes per 450g (1lb)	Separate during thawing and arrange 'spoke' fashion. Stand for 10 minutes.
Sausages	5–6 minutes per 450g (1lb)	Separate during thawing. Stand for 5 minutes.
Offal		
Liver	8–10 minutes per 450g (1lb)	Separate during thawing. Stand for 5 minutes.
Kidney	6–9 minutes per 450g (1lb)	Separate during thawing. Stand for 5 minutes.

THAWING FISH

Separate cutlets, fillets or steaks as soon as possible during thawing. Finish thawing whole fish like plaice and sole in cold water for 30 minutes to prevent drying out of the surface.

Type	Approximate time on LOW	Special instructions
White fish fillets or cutlets, eg cod, haddock, halibut, or whole plaice or sole	3–4 minutes per 450g (1lb) plus 2–3 minutes	Stand for 5 minutes after each 2 minutes.
Oily fish, eg whole mackerel	2–3 minutes per 225g (8oz) plus 3–4 minutes	Stand for 5 minutes after each 2 minutes.
Kipper fillets	2–3 minutes per 225g (8oz)	As for oily fish above.
Lobster tails, crab claws etc.	3–4 minutes per 225g (8oz)	As for oily fish above.
Prawns, shrimps, scampi	2½ minutes per 100g (4oz) 3–4 minutes per 225g (8oz)	Pierce bag if necessary. (See page 70.)

REHEATING FOOD

Foods can be reheated in the microwave with no loss of quality, flavour and colour, and usually less loss of nutrients than if reheated conventionally.

Reheating times will depend on the quantity of food and its density and the starting temperature of the food – food taken from the freezer may need a thawing time, a standing time and then a reheating time. Timing is largely a matter of experimenting: check the food regularly, it is better to microwave for too short a time than for too long. Always return food to the microwave for a little longer if it is not piping hot.

Arrange foods on a plate for reheating so that the thicker, denser and meatier portions are to the outer edge. Re-arrange food during cooking time. Cover foods with microwave plastic wrap (cling film), pierced to allow steam to escape.

Stir soups, sauces, casseroles and other liquids during reheating and again at the end of the microwaving time to make sure the food is heated right through. If food cannot be stirred, then rotate the dish or re-arrange the food several times until the food is piping hot. It is important to do this to ensure that all the food is heated, particularly if your microwave has cold spots (i.e. where it does not heat the food to as high a temperature as other spots in the microwave cavity).

Vegetable casseroles or vegetables in a sauce reheat better than vegetables on their own. For best results, food in a sauce or gravy should be reheated in a narrow, deep dish rather than a shallow wide one so that the sauce doesn't spread and dry out at the edges. Any foods in a sauce should be loosely covered during reheating.

Soups are easy to reheat in individual portions, either in a mug or a bowl, and take only a few minutes depending on the thickness of the soup. Stir the soup when it starts bubbling up at the edge of the container, then cook for another minute or so to allow it to heat through to the centre.

Dry foods with a crisp finish can be reheated on, or covered with, absorbent kitchen paper. Reheating in the microwave is extremely quick so special attention should be given to small items of food to avoid overcooking, especially pastry and bread. Place them on absorbent kitchen paper to absorb moisture during reheating and prevent the bottom becoming soggy. Microwaves are attracted to the moist fillings in pies and pastries, so that the liquid will heat up quickly. The steam produced by this is often absorbed into the pastry covering leaving it less crisp than when reheated in a conventional oven.

One of the advantages of a combination oven is that it is ideal for reheating the things that don't reheat well in the microwave alone. Pies, pastries and breads can be reheated without any danger of becoming soggy. Reheat at a temperature of 200–250°C combined with a MEDIUM/LOW microwave setting.

Always take care when reheating anything with a jam or other high sugar filling in the microwave as this will become extremely hot very quickly while the outside may still feel cool.

To test whether the food is hot enough, feel the underneath of the dish – if it feels warm the food will be hot. With pastry foods such as fruit pies, the outer pastry should feel just warm. The temperature of pastry and filling will equalize if given a few minutes standing time.

Note: All food must be piping hot before serving. If in any doubt, return it to the microwave for a little longer.

A–Z

This comprehensive alphabetical section provides complete information on how to freeze and package foods, how long they can be stored in the freezer, then detailed instructions are given for thawing. Where possible, microwave information is included for blanching and thawing.

ALMOND PASTE (Marzipan)
Because of high oil content of almond paste its freezer life is limited to around 3 months. After this time the oil begins to separate out and makes the marzipan tough and unsuitable for use, especially for cake decorating purposes as the oil will quickly seep through and colour white icing. It will store equally well in a cool cupboard for up to 3 months, or see label for 'best before date'.

To freeze: Wrap almond paste in foil and overwrap in a polythene bag. Seal, label and freeze.

Storage time: 3 months.

To thaw: Leave to thaw in wrapping overnight at room temperature, then use in the usual way.

ANCHOVY
Fresh anchovies can be frozen as long as they are very fresh. It is best not to freeze salted anchovies as they go rancid quite quickly. Pizzas are best frozen without anchovies, which can be added before serving.

To freeze: Clean (see page 15) and remove backbone and smaller bones. Pack in polythene bags, interleaving with plastic wrap. Seal, label and freeze.

Storage time: 3 months.

To thaw/cook: Grill or fry from frozen.

APPLE
As apples are available all year round, there is no point freezing whole apples. However, it is convenient to have prepared apple slices or purée in the freezer to use for pies and flans.

To freeze: Peel, core and drop apples into cold water. Cut into 0.5cm (¼ inch) slices. Blanch for 2–3 minutes (see page 16). To blanch in the microwave, put 450g (1lb) apple slices in a single layer in a dish with 45ml (3 tbsp) water, cover and microwave on HIGH for 1–2 minutes. Cool, drain and pack in rigid containers. To freeze purée, peel, core and stew apple in the minimum amount of water, sweetened or unsweetened. Purée and leave to cool. Pack in rigid containers. Cover, label and freeze.

Storage time: Slices, 6–8 months; purée, 6–8 months.

To thaw: Leave to thaw in unopened container for about 1 hour at room temperature. To thaw in the microwave, microwave on LOW for 8–9 minutes, stirring once. Allow to stand for 4–5 minutes.

APRICOT
These round stone fruits are about the size of a plum and have velvety, yellowish-orange skin and fairly soft, juicy flesh. Unripe apricots are hard and sour; over-ripe ones are mealy and tasteless. Choose firm, unwrinkled fruit for freezing.

To freeze: Plunge apricots into boiling water for 30 seconds to loosen the skins, then peel. Prepare in one of the following ways.
(a) Cut in half or slice into syrup (see page 17), made with 450g (1lb) sugar to 1 litre (2 pints) water, with some lemon juice added to prevent

FREEZER TO MICROWAVE ENCYCLOPEDIA

browning (allow 1 lemon to each 450g (1lb) pack). Immerse the apricots by placing a piece of clean crumpled, non-absorbent paper on the fruit under the lid.

(b) Leave the fruit whole and freeze in cold syrup. After long storage, an almond flavour may develop round the stone.

(c) Purée cooked apricots, sweetened or unsweetened. Pack in rigid containers. Cover, label and freeze.

Storage time: In syrup, 9–12 months; purée, 6–8 months.

To thaw: Leave to thaw in unopened container in the refrigerator for about 3 hours. To thaw in the microwave, put 450g (1lb) in a dish and microwave on HIGH for 4–6 minutes. Re-arrange during thawing time.

ARTICHOKE (Globe)
This thistle is native to North Africa but is now grown in Europe and America as a vegetable. Choose heads with a clear green colour and leaves with no dry edges. Look for ones that are tightly curled rather than wide open.

To freeze: Remove all outer coarse leaves and stalks, and the hairy purple 'choke' from the centre. Trim tops and stems. Wash well in cold water. Add a little lemon juice to the blanching water and blanch a few at a time, 5 minutes for small heads, 7 minutes for large heads (see page 16). To blanch in the microwave: arrange 3–4 artichokes upright in a large, shallow dish, cover and microwave on HIGH for 6–7 minutes. Cool quickly, drain well and dab dry. Pack in rigid containers. Cover, label and freeze.

Storage time: 6 months.

To thaw: Cook from frozen in acidulated water for 10–15 minutes or until a fork goes easily through the base. To thaw/cook in the microwave: arrange 3–4 frozen artichokes upright in a shallow, covered dish with 60ml (4 tbsp) water, microwave on HIGH for 6–7 minutes or until tender.

ARTICHOKE (Jerusalem)
This is a tuber with a nutty taste, which ranges in colour from beige to brownish-red. It is only suitable for freezing as a purée or soup. Choose the smoothest ones available as they are easier to peel.

To freeze: Scrub artichokes well and peel thinly. Cook in boiling salted water, with 15ml (1 tbsp) lemon juice or vinegar added to prevent discoloration, for 15–20 minutes. Purée or make into soup. Pack in rigid containers. Cover, label and freeze.

Storage time: 3 months.

To thaw: Heat through gently from frozen.

ASPARAGUS
There are two basic types: blanched (white) asparagus which is cut below the soil when the tips are 5cm (2 inches) above it, and green asparagus which is cut at soil level. Choose stems that look fresh and tender.

To freeze: Grade into thick and thin stems but do not tie into bunches yet. Wash in cold water, then blanch thick stems for 4 minutes, thin stems for 2 minutes (see page 16). To blanch in the microwave, put 450g (1lb) asparagus in a dish with 45ml (3 tbsp) water, cover and microwave on HIGH for 3 minutes for thick stems, 2 minutes for thin. Tie into small bundles. Pack in rigid containers or polythene bags. Cover or seal, label and freeze.

Storage time: 9 months.

To thaw: Leave to thaw until the stems can be separated, then cook in boiling salted water for 2–4 minutes.

AUBERGINE
Aubergines range in colour from white and whitish-green through dark green to yellowish purple to the more commonly available red purple or black. Choose firm, shiny aubergines free from blemishes.

To freeze: Peel and cut roughly into 2.5cm (1 inch) slices. Blanch for 3–4 minutes (see page 16). To blanch in the microwave, put 450g (1lb) slices in a dish with 45ml (3 tbsp) water, cover and microwave on HIGH for 2 minutes. Cool and dry on absorbent kitchen paper. Pack in rigid containers, separating the slices with non-stick paper. Cover, label and freeze.

Storage time: 12 months.

Right: Finnan Haddie Soup (page 84)

To thaw: Leave to thaw in container at room temperature or in the refrigerator. Pat dry when thawed and fry in hot oil.

AVOCADO

Whole avocados lose their flavour and texture when frozen, but they can be pulped and frozen for dips and soups. Choose just ripe avocados.

To freeze: Peel, stone and, removing any blemished areas, mash, adding 15ml (1 tbsp) lemon juice to each avocado. Pack in small containers. Cover, label and freeze.

Storage time: 2 months.

To thaw: Leave to thaw in unopened container at room temperature for about 2 hours. Use immediately.

BACON

Only freeze bacon that is perfectly fresh. If possible, it should be frozen on the day it is supplied to the retailer – the longer it has been kept in the shop, the shorter its storage life in the freezer. Do not exceed the recommended storage times, otherwise both flavour and texture will be disappointing.

To freeze: If possible buy bacon for freezing ready-packed as the maximum amount of air has already been extracted. Bacon that is not vacuum-packed should be closely wrapped in plastic wrap or foil and overwrapped in polythene bags. Do not pack more than 225g (8oz) rashers in a package. Rashers can be interleaved with waxed or non-stick paper for easier separation, if wished. Wrap bacon chops individually in foil, then pack together in a polythene bag. Joints up to 1.4–1.8kg (3–4lb) should be wrapped in foil, then overwrapped in a polythene bag. It is also a good idea to overwrap vacuum-packed bacon, and to check each pack carefully to make sure the vacuum is intact. Seal, label and freeze.

Storage time: Vacuum-packed bacon, 3 months; smoked rashers, chops, gammon steaks and joints, 2 months; unsmoked rashers, chops, gammon steaks and joints, 1 month.

To thaw: Leave to thaw in a cool place, preferably overnight in the refrigerator. Cook as soon as possible after thawing.

BASS

Bass is a round fish, similar to salmon in shape, that can weigh up to 4.5kg (10lb). It is sold whole or as steaks or fillets.

To freeze: Wash, remove scales and gut (see page 15). Ice glaze whole fish (see Bream page 38). Separate steaks and fillets with a double layer of plastic wrap, then overwrap in foil or plastic wrap. Seal, label and freeze.

Storage time: 3 months.

To thaw: Allow whole fish to thaw in a cool place for 24 hours. Once thawed, use promptly. Steaks or fillets can be cooked from frozen. To thaw fillets or steaks in the microwave, microwave on LOW for 3–4 minutes per 450g (1lb) plus 2–3 minutes. Allow to stand for 5 minutes after each 2 minutes.

BEAN (Broad, French and Runner)

Choose young, small, tender broad bean pods. Choose French and runner beans that break with a crisp snap.

To freeze: For broad beans, shell and blanch for 3 minutes (see page 16). For French beans, trim ends, then blanch for 2–3 minutes. For runner beans, slice thickly and blanch for 2 minutes. To blanch in the microwave, put 450g (1lb) beans in a bowl with 45ml (3 tbsp) water. Cover and microwave on HIGH for 2 minutes for broad beans, 2½ minutes for French beans, 1½ minutes for runner beans. Cool, drain and pack in rigid containers or polythene bags. Cover or seal, label and freeze.

Storage time: 12 months.

To thaw/cook: Cook from frozen.

BEAN SPROUT

Bean sprouts lose their crispness when they are frozen, but can be used for cooked dishes.

To freeze: Blanch for 1 minute (see page 16). Cool and drain. Pat dry and pack in rigid containers or polythene bags. Cover or seal, label and freeze.

Storage time: 2 months.

To thaw: Leave to thaw in the refrigerator if time, otherwise unwrap and thaw at room temperature.

BEEF

Use good quality fresh beef. Beef should look fresh and moist but not watery, with small flecks of fat through the lean – this fat or marbling helps to keep the meat moist and tender when it is cooked. Choose meat with little gristle between the fat and the lean. Removing bones will save space in the freezer; butcher in suitable quantities.

Joints can be roasted and frozen for serving cold, but take care not overcook them. Reheated whole joints are not very satisfactory. Sliced and frozen cooked meat tends to be dry when reheated.

To freeze: Pack carefully in heavy-duty polythene bags. Group in similar types, then overwrap with mutton cloth, stockinette, thin polythene or newspaper, to protect against puncturing and loss of quality. If freezing a cooked joint, best results are achieved by freezing the whole joint, but small pieces can be sliced and packed in polythene if required to serve cold, or put in foil containers (or plastic if thawing in the microwave) and covered with gravy if to be served hot.

Storage time: Raw, 8 months; cooked and sliced with gravy, 3 months; without gravy, 2 months.

To thaw: Joints of less than 1.4kg (3lb) take 6–8 hours per 450g (1lb) in the refrigerator, 1–2 hours per 450g (1lb) at room temperature. Joints over 1.4kg (3lb) take 14 hours per 450g (1lb) in the refrigerator, 2–3 hours per 450g (1lb) at room temperature. Steaks and stewing steak (not cubed) take 5–6 hours in the refrigerator, 2–4 hours at room temperature.

To thaw cooked meat, thaw in the wrapping and allow about 4 hours per 450g (1lb) at room temperature, or double that time in the refrigerator. Sliced meat requires less time.

To thaw in the microwave (see page 30), microwave on LOW for 8–10 minutes per 450g (1lb) for boned roasting joints. Turn over regularly during thawing and leave to rest if the meat shows signs of cooking. Allow to stand for 1 hour. For joints on the bone, microwave on LOW for 10–12 minutes per 450g (1lb). Turn over joint during thawing. The meat will still be icy in the centre but will complete thawing if left to stand for 1 hour.

For steak and minced beef, microwave on LOW for 8–10 minutes per 450g (1lb). Allow to stand for 10 minutes. For cubed steak, microwave on LOW 6–8 minutes per 450g (1lb). Allow to stand for 10 minutes. For beefburgers: 2 × 50g (2oz) beef burgers, 2 minutes; 4 × 50g (2oz), 2–3 minutes; 2 × 100g (4oz), 2–3 minutes; 4 × 100g (4oz), 5 minutes. They can be cooked from frozen without thawing, if preferred.

BEETROOT

It is worth freezing cooked beetroot, so that they can be thawed and used as required in salads or gently reheated as a vegetable. Choose small beetroot up to 5cm (2 inches) in diameter for freezing.

To freeze: Wash well, then cook small, whole beetroots for 30–40 minutes; large beetroot, cook for 40–50 minutes or until tender. To cook in the microwave, arrange 8–10 beetroot around the edge of a shallow dish with 45ml (3 tbsp) water, cover and microwave on HIGH for 10–12 minutes, 4 medium beetroot for 14–16 minutes or until tender. Beetroot under 2.5cm (1 inch) in diameter may be frozen whole, others should be sliced or diced. Pack in rigid containers. Cover, label and freeze.

Storage time: 6 months.

To thaw: Leave to thaw in container in the refrigerator or thaw more rapidly at room temperature. Thaw in the microwave on HIGH for 4–6 minutes for small beetroot, 6–8 minutes for medium beetroot.

BERRY

All berries, including currants and cherries, can be frozen by the dry pack method (see page 16), but the dry sugar pack method is suitable for soft fruits such as raspberries. Whole strawberries lose texture and flavour when frozen.

To freeze: Blackberries: (a) Dry pack. (b) Dry sugar pack, allowing 225g (8oz) sugar to 900g (2lb) fruit. Pack in rigid containers. Blackcurrants, blueberries or bilberries: wash in chilled water and drain thoroughly; (a) Dry pack. (b) Dry sugar pack, allowing 100g (4oz) sugar to 450–700g (1–1½lb) fruit; slightly crush berries, mix with sugar until dissolved, then pack in rigid containers. (c) Cold syrup pack (see page 17) made with 900g (2lb) sugar to 1 litre (2 pints) water. Gooseberries: wash and dry thoroughly; (a) Dry pack. (b) Cold syrup pack, made with 900g (2lb) sugar to 1 litre (2 pints) water. (c) Purée and sweeten to taste. Loganberries: remove stalks and freeze by dry pack method. Strawberries and raspberries: use firm, clean, dry fruit; (a) Dry pack, though strawberries can be disappointing. (b) Dry sugar pack, allowing 100g (4oz) sugar to each 450g (1lb) fruit. (c) Purée, sweetening to taste – about 50g (2oz) sugar per 225g (8oz) purée – and add a little lemon juice to strawberry purée. Freeze in small containers. Redcurrants: wash and dry whole fruit, then freeze by dry pack method. Pack in rigid containers. Cover, label and seal.

Storage time: Dry pack, 6–8 months; dry sugar pack or syrup pack, 9–12 months; purée, 6–8 months.

To thaw: Fruit that is to be eaten without further preparation needs the gentlest possible thawing. Thaw in unopened container, particularly ones that tend to discolour on contact with air. Some fruit tends to 'fall' and the juices leak out, so soft berries like strawberries and raspberries require only partial thawing and can be eaten while there is still some ice in it.

BREAD
Freshly baked bread, both bought and home-made, can be frozen. Crisp, crusty bread stores well for up to 1 week, then the crust begins to shell off. Breadcrumbs remain separate when frozen and are useful for coating food.

To freeze: Bought bread may be frozen in its original wrapper for up to 1 week; for longer periods, seal in foil or a polythene bag. Home-made bread: freeze in foil or polythene bags. To freeze bought part-baked loaves and rolls, leave loaves in the bags, pack rolls in polythene bags. Seal, label and freeze.

Storage time: Home-made and shop-bought bread, 6 months; bought part-baked bread and rolls, 4 months; breadcrumbs, 3 months. Enriched breads and rolls (milk, fruit, malt loaves and soft baps), 4 months.

To thaw: Leave to thaw in the wrapper or polythene bag at room temperature for 3–6 hours, or overnight in the refrigerator. Alternatively, leave foil-wrapped and crisp in the oven at 200°C (400°F) mark 6 for about 45 minutes. Sliced bought bread can be toasted from frozen. To thaw and cook part-baked bread, place the unwrapped loaf in the oven at 220°C (425°F) mark 7 for about 40 minutes. Cool before eating. Place frozen unwrapped rolls in

the oven at 200°C (400°F) mark 6 for 15 minutes. There is no need to thaw breadcrumbs if they are being sprinkled on food. If using for coating, thaw them for 30 minutes at room temperature.

To thaw bread in the microwave, uncover the loaf and place on absorbent kitchen paper. Microwave on LOW for 6–8 minutes for a whole large loaf, 4–6 minutes for a whole small loaf, turning over once during thawing. Allow to stand for 5–15 minutes. To thaw a large sliced loaf, leave in its original wrapper (but remove any metal tags) and microwave on LOW for 6–8 minutes, and a small sliced loaf for 4–6 minutes. Allow to stand for 10–15 minutes. Thaw a 25g (1oz) slice of bread on absorbent kitchen paper on LOW for 10–15 seconds. Allow to stand for 1–2 minutes. For bread rolls, place on absorbent kitchen paper and microwave on LOW for 15–20 seconds for 2 rolls, 25–35 seconds for 4 rolls. Stand for 2–3 minutes.

BREAM
Bream is a round, red-backed fish with a silvery belly and red fins. Usually sold whole, it has firm white flesh which has a mild flavour. Bream must be frozen within 12 hours of being caught.

To freeze: Wash, remove scales and gut (see page 15). Place whole fish unwrapped in the freezer until solid. Remove and dip in cold water. This forms thin ice over the fish. Return to the freezer; repeat process until the ice glaze is 0.5cm (¼ inch) thick. Wrap in plastic wrap and support with a thin board. Separate steaks with a double layer of plastic wrap, then overwrap in foil or plastic wrap. Seal, label and freeze.

Storage time: 3 months.

To thaw: Allow whole fish to thaw in a cool place for 24 hours. Once thawed, use promptly. Steaks can be cooked from frozen. To thaw fillets in the microwave, microwave on LOW for 3–4 minutes per 450g (1lb) plus 2–3 minutes. Allow to stand for 5 minutes after each 2 minutes.

BRILL
This is a flat fish with a good flavour and texture which resembles turbot. The flesh is firm and slightly yellowish, avoid any with a bluish tinge. It is sold whole or as fillets. Freeze as for BREAM.

Right: Autumn Pudding (page 197)

BROCCOLI

There are several types of broccoli; the sprouting ones which produce many purple, white or green shoots, and the heading type with one large close head like a cauliflower. Calabrese is another variety with green heads. Choose firm, tightly packed heads with strong stalks. The purple and green varieties have a more delicate flavour.

To freeze: Trim off any woody parts and large leaves. Wash in salted water and cut into small sprigs. Blanch thin stems for 3 minutes, medium stems for 4 minutes and thick stems for 5 minutes (see page 16). To blanch in the microwave, put 450g (1lb) broccoli in a dish with 45ml (3 tbsp) water, cover and microwave on HIGH for 3½ minutes for large stems, 2½ minutes for medium stems and 2 minutes for small stems. Cool and drain well. Pack in rigid containers in 1–2 layers, tips to stalks. Cover, label and freeze.

Storage time: 12 months.

To thaw/cook: Cook from frozen for 3–7 minutes, depending on the thickness of the stems.

BRUSSELS SPROUT

Choose small or medium, round sprouts with tightly packed heads and no wilted leaves.

To freeze: Remove the outer leaves and wash well. Make small cuts in stems. Blanch small sprouts for 3 minutes, medium for 4 minutes (see page 16). To blanch in the microwave, put 450g (1lb) sprouts in a dish with 45ml (3 tbsp) water. Cover and microwave on HIGH for 2½ minutes for small, 3 minutes for medium. Cool, drain and pack in polythene bags. Seal, label and freeze.

Storage time: 12 months.

To thaw/cook: Cook from frozen for 4–8 minutes, or until tender, depending on the size.

BUCKLING

This is a whole smoked herring, ready to eat. It is very good for making pâtés.

To freeze: Wrap each fish individually in plastic wrap and pack several together in a polythene bag. Seal, label and freeze.

Storage time: 3 months.

To thaw: Leave to thaw in wrapping in the refrigerator for 3 hours. Unwrap, skin and serve with horseradish and lemon, or make into pâté.

BUTTER (See FATS)

BUTTERMILK

Buttermilk is the liquid left after churning cream to make butter. Nowadays, most buttermilk is made from skimmed milk with a culture added to make it thicker and slightly acidic. It is not always readily available, so it is useful to have in the freezer.

To freeze: Freeze in the waxed cartons or in rigid containers, leaving headspace. Cover, label and freeze.

Storage time: 6 weeks.

To thaw: Leave to thaw in container in the refrigerator for about 8 hours. If the buttermilk has separated, whisk briefly.

CABBAGE

Crisp, well-hearted red, green and white cabbage can be frozen.

To freeze: Wash thoroughly and shred. Blanch for 1–2 minutes (see page 16). To blanch in the microwave, put 450g (1lb) cabbage in a dish with 45ml (3 tbsp) water, cover and microwave on HIGH for 2 minutes. Cool, drain and pack in small quantities in polythene bags. Seal, label and freeze.

Storage time: 6 months.

To thaw/cook: Cook from frozen for 5–8 minutes, according to taste.

CAKE

Both cooked cakes and uncooked cake mixture can be frozen. Iced cakes lose quality after 2 months.

To freeze: Bake in the usual way. Leave on a wire rack until cold. Swiss rolls are best rolled up in cornflour, not sugar, if to be frozen without a filling. Do not spread or layer with jam before freezing. Keep flavourings to a minimum and use spices carefully. Wrap plain cake layers separately, or together with plastic wrap or waxed paper between layers. Freeze iced cakes (whole or cut) unwrapped until icing has set. Wrap, seal and pack in boxes to protect icing.

Whisked sponge mixtures do not freeze well uncooked. Put rich creamed mixtures into containers, or line the tin to be used later with greased foil, add cake mixture and freeze uncovered. When frozen, remove from tin, pack in foil and overwrap. Return to freezer.

Storage time: Cooked cakes including sponge flans, Swiss rolls and layer cakes, 4 months; iced cakes, 2 months; uncooked cake mixtures, 2 months.

To thaw: Iced cakes: unwrap before thawing, then the wrapping will not stick to the icing when thawing. Cream cakes: may be sliced while frozen for a better shape and quick thawing. Plain cakes: leave in package and thaw at room temperature. Un-iced layer cakes and small cakes thaw in about 1–2 hours at room temperature; iced layer cakes take up to 4 hours. To thaw uncooked mixtures: leave at room temperature for 2–3 hours, then fill tins to bake. Pre-formed cake mixtures can be returned to original tins without wrapping. Remove foil lining if cooking in the microwave. Place frozen in preheated oven and bake in the usual way, but allow longer cooking time.

CARP

This freshwater fish has a muddy flavour so it is best soaked in salted water for 3–4 hours. Rinse well before freezing.

To freeze: Wash, remove scales and gut (see page 15). Ice glaze whole fish (see Bream page 38).

Storage time: 3 months.

To thaw: Leave to thaw in a cool place for up to 24 hours before cooking. Once thawed, use promptly.

CARROT

Freeze small, young carrots with smooth skins.

To freeze: If freezing whole, blanch for 3–5 minutes (see page 16), then scrape. Alternatively, slice or cut into small dice, then blanch. To blanch in the microwave, put 450g (1lb) carrots in a dish with 45ml (3 tbsp) water, cover and microwave on HIGH for 3 minutes. Cool, drain and pack in polythene bags. Seal, label and freeze.

Storage time: 12 months.

To thaw/cook: Cook from frozen.

CAULIFLOWER

Choose cauliflowers with firm, white heads surrounded by fresh green leaves.

To freeze: Wash, then break into small sprigs about 5 cm (2 inches) in diameter. Add the juice of 1 lemon to the blanching water and blanch for 3 minutes (see page 16). To blanch in the microwave, put 450 g (1 lb) cauliflower in a dish with 45 ml (3 tbsp) water, cover and microwave on HIGH for 2½ minutes. Cool, drain and pack in polythene bags. Seal, label and freeze.

Storage time: 10–12 months.

To thaw/cook: Cook from frozen for 4 minutes, or until tender.

CELERIAC

Sometimes known as turnip-rooted celery, celeriac is a large swollen root with a pronounced celery flavour.

To freeze: Wash and trim. Cook until just tender, then peel and slice. Cool, then pack in rigid containers or polythene bags. Cover or seal, label and freeze.

Storage time: 12 months.

To thaw: Leave to thaw in container or bag at room temperature, or unwrap and heat from frozen in soups and stews.

CELERY

Choose celery with thick unblemished sticks and fresh leafy tops. Celery that has been frozen is only suitable for cooked dishes.

To freeze: Trim, removing any strings, and scrub well. Cut into 2.5cm (1 inch) lengths. Blanch for 2 minutes (see page 16). To blanch in the microwave, put 450g (1lb) celery in a dish with 45ml (3 tbsp) water, cover and microwave on HIGH for 3 minutes. Cool, drain and pack in rigid containers or polythene bags. Cover or seal, label and freeze.

Storage time: 12 months.

To thaw/cook: Cook from frozen.

CHEESE

Hard cheeses, such as Cheddar, Cheshire, Double Gloucester and Edam, freeze well. The longer they remain in the freezer the more crumbly they become, but they can still be used for cooking without the need to grate them. Blue cheese does not freeze very successfully as it becomes extremely crumbly, but again it can be used for cooking. Hard cheeses can also be stored grated in polythene bags ready for using in sauces. Fully matured soft cheeses, such as Brie, Camembert, Mozzarella and Roquefort, can also be frozen.

Full fat soft cheese can only be frozen if it contain at least 40 per cent butterfat. Cottage, curd and low fat soft cheeses do not freeze well, though they can be frozen when combined with other ingredients in cooked dishes.

To freeze: Wrap hard and soft cheeses in plastic wrap or foil and overwrap in polythene bags. Freeze full fat soft cheese in cartons or other rigid containers. Cover or seal, label and freeze.

Storage time: 3–6 months.

To thaw: Leave to thaw for 24 hours in the refrigerator, then allow to come to room temperature before serving. Grated cheese can be used straight from the freezer.

CHERRY

Cherries vary in colour from white through red to black. Red and black cherries are the most suitable for freezing as they keep their colour once thawed. Avoid damaged, bruised or immature fruit.

To freeze: Remove stalks, then wash and dry the fruit. Freeze by (a) Dry pack (see page 16); (b) Dry sugar pack, allowing 225g (8oz) sugar to 900g (2lb) stoned cherries, cooked or uncooked; (c) Syrup pack, made with 450g (1lb) sugar to 1 litre (2 pints) water mixed with 2.5ml (½ tsp) ascorbic acid per 1 litre (2 pints) syrup. Pack in rigid containers, leaving headspace. Cover, label and freeze.

Storage time: Dry sugar pack or syrup pack, 9–12 months; dry pack, 6–8 months.

To thaw: Fruit that is to be eaten without further preparation needs the gentlest possible thawing. Thaw in unopened container for about 3 hours at room temperature, then use immediately or the fruit will discolour. Cherries in syrup can be gently reheated in a saucepan. To thaw in the microwave, put 450g (1lb) fruit in a bowl, cover and microwave on LOW for 6½–7½ minutes, stirring gently once or twice. Allow to stand for 3–4 minutes.

CHESTNUT

This is the fruit of the sweet chestnut tree which grows mainly in European countries.

To freeze: Chestnuts are sold in their skins and must be peeled before freezing. To peel, make a tiny slit in the skin near the pointed end. Put them in a saucepan of water, bring to the boil and simmer for 1–2 minutes. Remove from the water, one at a time, and peel off the thick outer skin and thin inner skin while warm.

Chestnuts can be cooked and frozen as a purée, if preferred. To cook, simmer the peeled nuts for 30–40 minutes. Alternatively, bake the nuts in their skins in the oven at 200°C (400°F) mark 6 for 20 minutes, then peel. Purée the nuts.

To prepare chestnuts in the microwave, slit the skins with a sharp knife and microwave on HIGH for 3 minutes per 225g (8oz), shaking halfway through, then peel.

Pack whole nuts or purée in rigid containers. Cover, label and freeze.

Storage time: 6 months.

To thaw: Leave to thaw in container at room temperature until whole nuts can be separated or purée can be whipped easily with a fork. Whole chestnuts can be cooked and used for soups and stuffings. Use purée for cakes and desserts.

CHICKEN

Only freeze young, plump, tender birds. For preparing birds, see Freezing poultry, page 14.

To freeze: Whole birds: wipe and dry the bird after plucking and drawing. Freeze the giblets separately as they will not keep as long as the chicken. Truss the bird (see page 14), then pad the legs with non-stick paper so that they do not pierce the wrapping. Pack in polythene bags. Portions: (see page 15 for portioning birds), pack individually in polythene bags, then combine into larger bags. Cold roast or poached chicken should be cooled as quickly as possible after cooking. Parcel small amounts in plastic wrap and overwrap in plastic wrap, with any stuffing packed separately. Seal, label and freeze at once.

Storage time: Chicken, 12 months; giblets, 3 months; cold cooked chicken, 2–3 months.

Right: Cherry and Almond Cake (page 213)

To thaw: All poultry must be completely thawed before cooking. Remember that once thawed poultry is as perishable as any fresh meat and should be cooked as soon as possible. In the light of new research, it is recommended that poultry is thawed in its wrapping at room temperature of 16–17°C (65–70°F) rather than in the refrigerator. A 1.4kg (3lb) bird takes about 9 hours; portions need only about 3 hours.

To thaw in the microwave, thaw in the wrapping, which should be pierced first and any metal tag removed. Microwave on LOW for 6–8 minutes per 450g (1lb). During thawing, pour off the liquid that collects in the wrapping. Finish thawing in a bowl of cold water for 30 minutes with the bird still in its wrapping. Chicken portions can be thawed in their polystyrene trays if shop-bought.

CHICORY
Chicory loses its crisp texture when frozen but it is worth freezing to use in cooked dishes.

To freeze: Wipe clean, then blanch for 5 minutes (see page 16). To blanch in the microwave, put 450g (1lb) chicory in a dish with 45ml (3 tbsp) water, cover and microwave on HIGH for 4–5 minutes. Cool, drain and pack in polythene bags. Seal, label and freeze.

Storage time: 6 months.

To thaw: Leave to thaw in wrapping at room temperature for 2 hours. Gently squeeze out any excess moisture from the chicory before using in cooked dishes.

CHILLI
The oils in chillies can make your skin tingle, so take care when preparing them.

To freeze: Remove stalks and scoop out the seeds and pithy part. Blanch for 2 minutes (see page 16). To blanch in the microwave, arrange 8–10 small chillies in a dish with the thickest parts to the outside, with 45ml (3 tbsp) water, cover and microwave on HIGH for 2–3 minutes. Cool, drain and pack in rigid containers or polythene bags. Cover or seal, label and freeze.

Storage time: 12 months.

To thaw: Leave to thaw at room temperature, or use frozen.

CHINESE CABBAGE
Chinese cabbage loses its crispness when frozen, but it can be used for adding to cooked dishes and soups.

To freeze: Shred, then blanch for 1 minute (see page 16). To blanch in the microwave, put 450g (1lb) in a dish with 45ml (3 tbsp) water, cover and microwave on HIGH for 1–2 minutes. Cool, drain and pat dry. Pack in polythene bags. Seal, label and freeze.

Storage time: 12 months.

To thaw: Unpack and leave to thaw at room temperature for a few minutes.

CHOCOLATE
It is well worth keeping chocolate decorations in the freezer for last minute decoration of cakes and mousses.

Squares: melt some plain chocolate. Using a palette knife, spread it in a thin, even layer over a sheet of non-stick paper, but do not take it quite to the edges. When firm, but not brittle, cut squares of the required size, using a sharp knife, with a ruler as a guide. When it is completely firm, place the paper over the edge of a table, pull it down, and ease the squares off one at a time.

Leaves: melt the chocolate. Collect some small rose leaves, preferably with the stem attached. Spread a little of the chocolate over the underside of each leaf, using a teaspoon. Place on non-stick paper and leave to set. When hard, pull the leaves away, starting from the stem. Work gently to avoid the chocolate melting.

Caraque: melt the chocolate in the usual way and spread it thinly on a cold work surface. When just on the point of setting, shave the chocolate off in curls with a thin, sharp knife. Some of the softer blocks of chocolate or special chocolate covering can be curled by using a potato peeler on the flat side of the block. Pack in rigid containers to prevent breakages. Cover, label and freeze.

Storage time: 2 months.

To thaw: Unpack and leave to thaw in the refrigerator or at room temperature.

CLAM
Clams are sold live in their shells. Small ones can be eaten raw, large ones can be cooked like

mussels. Freezing clams is only advisable if you can freeze them when really fresh, within 12 hours of being caught.

To freeze: Wash thoroughly. Open the shells and remove the clams. Put in a sieve over a bowl and leave to drain. Reserve the juice in the bowl. Wash the clams in salted water, allowing 15ml (1 tbsp) salt to 1 litre (2 pints) water. Pack in rigid containers, cover with the reserved liquid, leaving headspace. Cover, label and freeze.

Storage time: 3 months.

To thaw: Leave to thaw in container in the refrigerator for 2 hours.

CLEMENTINE
Prepare, freeze and thaw as for ORANGE.

COCKLE
Cockles are usually sold cooked and shelled. Only freeze fresh cockles if you can freeze them within 12 hours of being caught.

To freeze: Rinse well under cold running water, then leave to soak for 2–3 hours before cooking. Place in a saucepan with a little water and heat gently, shaking the pan for about 5 minutes until the shells open. Take the cockles out of their shells and cook for a further 4 minutes. Cool, then pack in rigid containers. Either freeze dry or pour some of the cooking liquid into the containers, leaving headspace. Cover, label and freeze.

Storage time: 1 month.

To thaw: Leave to thaw in container in the refrigerator for 2 hours.

COCONUT
Fresh coconut can be frozen and used in cakes, biscuits, puddings and curries.

To freeze: Grate the coconut and pack in rigid containers or polythene bags. Cover or seal, label and freeze.

Storage time: 6 months.

To thaw: Unwrap and place the frozen coconut in a colander to drain while it thaws. Leave at room temperature for about 2 hours.

COD
Cod is a large round fish with close white flesh. It is available all year but is best from October to May. It may be sold whole when young and small, or as fillets or steaks when large.

To freeze: Wash, remove scales and gut (see page 15). Place whole fish unwrapped in the freezer until solid. Remove and dip in cold water. This forms thin ice over the fish. Return to freezer; repeat process until the ice glaze is 0.5cm (¼ inch) thick. Wrap in plastic wrap and support with a thin board. Separate steaks and fillets with a double layer of plastic wrap, then overwrap in foil or plastic wrap.

Storage time: 3 months.

To thaw: Allow whole fish to thaw in a cool place for up to 24 hours. Once thawed, use promptly. Steaks and fillets can be cooked from frozen. To thaw steaks and fillets in the microwave, microwave on LOW for 3–4 minutes per 450g (1lb) plus 2–3 minutes. Allow to stand for 5 minutes after each 2 minutes.

COLEY
Coley is a member of the cod family with bluish-black skin. It is usually cheaper than cod and is sold as fillets or cutlets but may be sold whole. The well flavoured meaty flesh is pinkish-grey and turns white when cooked. It is drier than cod and needs more liquid adding during cooking.

To freeze: Freeze and thaw as for COD.

CORN-ON-THE-COB
Choose young yellow kernels, not over-ripe or shrunken ones.

To freeze: Remove husks and silks. Blanch small cobs for 4 minutes, medium for 6 minutes, large for 8 minutes (see page 16). To blanch in the microwave, place 4 cobs in a dish with 125ml (4fl oz) water, cover and microwave on HIGH for 10 minutes, turning each cob once. Cool, then pat dry. Pack individually in plastic wrap, then overwrap in polythene bags. Seal, label and freeze.

Storage time: 12 months.

To thaw/cook: Leave to thaw in wrapping at room temperature for about 2 hours. Cook in boiling water for 5–10 minutes, according to size. To thaw and cook in the microwave, dot the cobs with butter and wrap in greaseproof paper. Microwave on HIGH for 3–4 minutes for 1 cob, 6–7 minutes for 2 cobs.

COURGETTE

Choose young courgettes for freezing.

To freeze: Wash and cut into 1cm (½ inch) slices. Blanch for 1 minute (see page 16) or sauté in a little butter. To blanch in the microwave, put 450g (1lb) courgettes in a dish with 45ml (3 tbsp) water, cover and microwave on HIGH for 1½ minutes. Cool, drain and pack in rigid containers or polythene bags. Cover or seal, label and freeze.

Storage time: 6 months.

To thaw/cook: Cook from frozen in hot butter and oil or boiling water.

CRAB

Only freeze freshly cooked crab. If freezing fresh crab, it should be frozen within 12 hours of being caught. To cook crab, place it in a large saucepan with enough cold, salted water to cover. Add a bay leaf and 15ml (1 tbsp) lemon juice, then bring slowly to the boil. Cover and boil rapidly for 10–20 minutes. Allow to cool in the water.

To remove the meat, place the crab on its back on a chopping board. Take a claw in one hand and twist it off, holding the body with the other hand. Remove the other claw and legs the same way. Snap the claws in half by bending them backwards at the joint. Hold the claws at the top end and, with a hammer, tap the shell to crack open. Using a blunt knife, ease out the meat. Crack the large legs and scrape out the white meat. Place the crab on its back with the tail flap towards you. Hold the shell firmly and press the body section upwards from beneath the tail flap and ease out with your thumbs until the body is detached. Pull off the inedible, grey feathery gills from the body and discard. Use a spoon to remove the stomach bag and mouth which are attached to the back shell. Ease the brown meat out of the shell. Keep separate from the white meat. Discard any membrane and scrape out corners of the shell with the handle of a teaspoon.

To freeze: Pack white and brown meat separately in rigid containers. Alternatively, pack the meat in the shell, wrap in plastic wrap and overwrap in foil or a polythene bag. Cover or seal, label and freeze.

Storage time: 1 month.

To thaw: Leave to thaw in wrapping in the refrigerator for 3 hours. Use immediately after thawing.

CRAB APPLE

Crab apples are the original wild apples. The small fruit have a shiny red or yellow skin and firm flesh which is usually very sour. They are mostly used to make jelly and other preserves. If you have a glut of crab apples, it is worth freezing them to make jelly at a later date.

To freeze: Wash and pat dry, then pack in polythene bags. Seal, label and freeze.

Storage time: 8 months.

To thaw/cook: Use from frozen to make crab apple jelly, allowing a little extra cooking time.

CRANBERRY (See BERRY)

CRAWFISH

Often called the spiny lobster, the crawfish resembles a lobster without the big claws. Prepare and cook as for LOBSTER. Remove flesh and pack in rigid containers. Cover, label and freeze.

Storage time: 1–2 months.

To thaw: Leave to thaw in the refrigerator for 3 hours, then serve hot or cold. To thaw in the microwave, microwave on LOW for 3–4 minutes per 450g (1lb) plus 2–3 minutes. Allow to stand for 5 minutes after each 2 minutes.

CRAYFISH

The crayfish is a freshwater crustacean which looks like a miniature lobster. It varies in colour from dark purple to red.

To freeze: Rinse well, then remove the intestinal tube under the tail, using a pointed knife. Put into a saucepan of cold salted water, bring to the boil and cook for about 10 minutes. Leave to cool, then drain. Pack in polythene bags. Seal, label and freeze.

Storage time: 1–2 months.

Right: Celeriac with Tomato Sauce (page 180)

To thaw: Bring a pan of water to the boil, add the frozen crayfish and heat until thawed. To thaw in the microwave, arrange in a circle and cover with absorbent kitchen paper. Microwave on LOW for 2½ minutes per 100g (4oz), 3–4 minutes per 225g (8oz), separating with a fork after 2 minutes. Allow to stand for 2 minutes, then plunge into cold water and drain.

CREAM
Only freeze pasteurised cream with a butterfat content of at least 35 per cent, such as whipping or double cream. Whipped cream can be piped in rosettes on waxed paper; the best results are achieved with half-whipped cream with a little sugar added – 5ml (1 tsp) to 150ml (¼ pint) cream.

To freeze: Transfer the cream to a suitable container, leaving headspace for expansion. Leave commercially-frozen cream in its container. Freeze rosettes unwrapped, then pack in a single layer in foil. Cover or seal, label and freeze.

Storage time: Fresh cream, 3 months; commercially-frozen, up to 1 year.

To thaw: Leave to thaw in the refrigerator for 24 hours or at room temperature for 12 hours. Put frozen rosettes in position as decoration before thawing or they cannot be handled; these take less time to thaw. To thaw in the microwave, remove any foil and cover 250ml (9fl oz) cream with microwave cling film. Microwave on LOW for 2½–3 minutes. Allow to stand for 5 minutes.

CROISSANT
Baked or unbaked croissants can be frozen successfully. Unbaked can be stored for slightly longer.

To freeze: Unbaked: prepare to the stage when all the fat has been absorbed, but do not give the final rolling. Baked: bake as usual. Pack in polythene bags. Seal, label and freeze.

Storage time: Unbaked, 6 weeks; baked, 4 weeks.

To thaw: Unbaked: leave in polythene bag, but unseal and re-tie loosely, allowing space for the dough to rise. Preferably thaw overnight in the refrigerator, or leave for 5 hours at room temperature. Complete the final rolling and shaping and bake. Baked: loosen wrapping and thaw as for unbaked.

CUCUMBER
Cucumber contains too much water for it to be frozen as a vegetable but it can be frozen as a raw purée for use in iced soups and sauces.

To freeze: Peel, then purée in a blender or food processor. Pack in rigid containers, leaving headspace. Cover, label and freeze.

Storage time: 2 months.

To thaw: Leave to thaw in container at room temperature until thawed. To thaw in the microwave, thaw as SAUCE.

CURRANT (see BERRY)

CUTTLEFISH
The cuttlefish is a member of a group of aquatic creatures known as cephalopods – a name which comes from the Greek words for head and feet – so called because they have tentacles protruding from their heads. Cuttlefish are mostly sold frozen. If buying fresh, prepare and freeze as for SQUID.

DAMSON
Damsons are small dark blue or purple plums with yellow flesh. As they are sour, they need to be cooked and made into pies or preserves.

To freeze: Wash in cold water. The skins are inclined to toughen during freezing. Freeze (a) as a purée, (b) poach and sweeten, (c) halve, stone and pack in cold syrup made with 450g (1lb) sugar to 1 litre (2 pints) water; they will need cooking after freezing. Pack in rigid containers. Cover, label and freeze.

Storage time: 12 months.

To thaw: Leave to thaw in containers at room temperature for 2–3 hours, or cook from frozen to use as stewed fruit.

DOVER SOLE
The name sole is given to several species of flat fish. Dover sole is the only true sole and is considered one of the finest flat fish. It has dark brown-grey skin and pale, firm flesh with a delicious flavour. It is sold whole or as fillets.

To freeze: Wash, remove scales and gut (see page 15). Place whole fish unwrapped in freezer until solid. Remove and dip in cold water. This forms thin ice over the fish. Return to the freezer; repeat process until the ice glaze is 0.5cm (¼ inch) thick. Wrap in plastic wrap and support with a thin board. Separate fillets with a double layer of plastic wrap, then overwrap in foil or plastic wrap. Seal, label and freeze.

Storage time: 3 months.

To thaw: Allow whole fish to thaw in a cool place for 24 hours. Once thawed, use promptly. Fillets can be cooked from frozen. To thaw fillets or whole fish in the microwave, microwave on LOW for 3–4 minutes per 450g (1lb) plus 2–3 minutes. Allow to stand for 5 minutes after each 2 minutes. Finish thawing whole fish in a bowl of cold water for 30 minutes with the fish still in its wrapping.

DUCKLING

Duckling is sold both fresh and frozen, ready for the oven, and is also available as portions. Choose young birds without too much fat, which can go rancid during storage in the freezer. Duckling can be frozen whole, jointed or cut up (see page 15).

To freeze: Whole birds: wipe and dry the bird. Pad the legs with non-stick paper so that they do not pierce the wrapping. Pack in polythene bags. Portions: pack individually in polythene bags, then combine into larger bags. Cold roast duckling should be cooled as quickly as possible after cooking. Parcel small amounts in plastic wrap and overwrap in plastic wrap, with any stuffing packed separately. Seal, label and freeze at once.

Storage time: Duckling, 12 months; cold cooked duckling, 2–3 months.

To thaw: In the light of new research, it is recommended that poultry is thawed in its wrapping at room temperature of 16–17°C (65–70°F) rather than in the refrigerator. A 1.4kg (3lb) bird takes about 9 hours; portions need only about 3 hours. To thaw in the microwave, thaw in the wrapping, removing any metal tags, and piercing the wrapping. Microwave on LOW for 6–8 minutes per 450g (1lb). During thawing, pour off the liquid that collects in the wrapping. Finish thawing in a bowl of cold water for 30 minutes with the bird still in the wrapping.

DUXELLES (See MUSHROOM)

EEL

Both conger and freshwater eels can be frozen. The conger eel is a sea fish which is a greyish-brown colour on top and silver underneath. The full-flavoured flesh is white and firm; larger eels have a coarser texture than small ones. The conger eel is larger than the common (freshwater) eel, but both are prepared and cooked in the same way. They can be baked or poached. Tiny eels (elvers) can be deep fried.

To freeze: Skin, clean and remove the head. Cut into 7.5cm (3 inch) lengths. Wash thoroughly and leave to soak briefly in lightly salted water. Drain, pat dry and pack in polythene bags. Tiny eels (elvers) just need to be washed and can be frozen in 450g (1lb) batches. Seal, label and freeze.

Storage time: 3 months.

To thaw/cook: Cook from frozen.

EGG

Eggs cannot be frozen in their shells as they would burst. Hard-boiled eggs cannot be frozen as the whites become leathery. However, very fresh yolks and whites can be frozen separately.

To freeze: Pack yolks and whites in rigid containers. For single egg yolks, add 2.5ml (½ tsp) salt or sugar; for every 6 yolks, add 5ml (1 tsp) salt or 10ml (2 tsp) sugar. Cover, label and freeze.

Storage time: 8–10 months.

To thaw: Leave to thaw in the refrigerator or at room temperature.

FATS

Only freeze fresh butter, margarine or suet. Farmhouse butter must be made from pasteurised cream.

To freeze: Overwrap in foil in 225–450g (8oz–1lb) quantities.

Storage time: Unsalted butter, 6 months; salted butter and margarine, 3 months; suet, 6 months.

To thaw: Leave to thaw in the refrigerator for 4 hours for a 225g (8oz) block. To thaw in the microwave, for 225g (8oz), microwave on LOW for 1½–2 minutes. Allow to stand for 5 minutes.

FENNEL

Fennel root can be frozen for use as a cooked vegetable. It cannot be used for salads after freezing as it loses its crispness.

To freeze: Trim and cut into short lengths. Blanch for 2 minutes (see page 16). To blanch in the microwave, put 450g (1lb) in a dish with 45ml (3 tbsp) water, cover and microwave on HIGH for 3–4 minutes. Cool, drain and pack in rigid containers or polythene bags. Cover or seal, label and freeze.

Storage time: 6 months.

To thaw/cook: Cook from frozen.

FIG

Only fresh ripe, undamaged figs should be frozen.

To freeze: Wash gently to avoid bruising. Remove stems. Freeze (a) Unsweetened, either whole or peeled, in polythene bags. (b) Peel and pack in cold syrup (see page 17), made with 450g (1lb) sugar to 1 litre (2 pints) water. (c) Leave whole and wrap in foil. Cover or seal, label and freeze.

Storage time: 12 months.

To thaw: Leave to thaw in container at room temperature for about 1½ hours.

FLOUNDER

Flounder is a flat fish resembling plaice but without such a good texture and taste. It is sold whole or as fillets and can be cooked like plaice.

To freeze: Wash, remove scales and gut (see page 15). Place whole fish unwrapped in the freezer until solid. Remove and dip in cold water. This forms thin ice over the fish. Return to the freezer; repeat process until the ice glaze is 0.5cm (¼ inch) thick. Wrap in plastic wrap and support with a thin board. Separate fillets with a double layer of plastic wrap, then overwrap in foil or plastic wrap. Seal, label and freeze.

Storage time: 3 months.

To thaw: Allow whole fish to thaw in a cool place for 24 hours. Once thawed, use promptly. Fillets can be cooked from frozen. To thaw fillets or whole fish in the microwave, microwave on LOW for 3–4 minutes per 450g (1lb) plus 2–3 minutes. Allow to stand for 5 minutes after each 2 minutes. Finish thawing whole fish in a bowl of cold water for 30 minutes with the fish still in its wrapping.

FRANKFURTER

Frankfurters are a useful stand-by to have in the freezer.

To freeze: Pack in polythene bags. Seal, label and freeze. Vacuum packs of frankfurters can be frozen as they are.

Storage time: 3 months.

To thaw: Leave to thaw in wrapping in the refrigerator overnight, then cook as for fresh frankfurters. To thaw in the microwave, microwave on LOW for 1½–2 minutes for 4 frankfurters, then allow to stand for 2 minutes. For 8 frankfurters, microwave for 3–3½ minutes, then stand for 4 minutes.

GAME

When choosing game for freezing, select young, plump animals and birds. Do not freeze a bird that has been damaged by shot. Most game birds need to be hung, so ask the butcher or poulterer if the bird has been hung and for how long – if it is not hung the flesh will be tough and tasteless. Alternatively, order game from your butcher or poulterer and he will hang the bird for the specified time. If you are given game, you can hang it yourself for the time specified in the chart overleaf. The birds should be hung by the neck without being plucked or drawn.

Hares are available from late autumn to early spring. They should be hung by the hind feet, without the entrails being removed, for 5–7 days. During this time, the blood collects in the chest cavity. When paunching (removing entrails), collect the blood, if wished, for use in Jugged hare. Add 5ml (1 tsp) malt vinegar to it and store, covered, in the refrigerator for 2–3 days. Rabbits are available fresh or frozen and, unlike hares, they are paunched within hours of killing and are not hung.

Venison is the meat of the red, fallow or roe deer. The meat needs to be hung for 1–2 weeks before freezing or cooking.

To freeze: Prepare and draw game birds as for poultry (see Freezing poultry, page 14). Do not

Right: Individual Apple Soufflés (page 204)

HANGING TIMES FOR GAME BIRDS	
Bird	*Hanging (days)*
Blackgame (Black Grouse)	3–10
Capercaillie	7–14
Grouse	2–4
Partridge (Grey and Red-legged)	3–5
Pheasant	3–10
Ptarmigan	2–4
Quail	requires no hanging
Snipe	3–4
Wild Duck, Teal and Wigeon	2–3 (may be drawn before hanging)
Wild Geese (Pink-footed and Greylag)	2–9
Woodcock	3–5
Wood pigeon	requires no hanging

stuff before freezing. Cover protruding bones with non-stick paper or foil. Pack in polythene bags; freeze giblets separately. Hare and rabbit can be frozen whole or jointed. Wrap hare, rabbit and venison joints individually, then overwrap in plastic wrap. Seal, label and freeze.

Storage time: Game birds, 9 months; hare and rabbit, 8 months; venison, 12 months.

To thaw: In the light of new research, it is recommended that birds are thawed in their wrapping at room temperature of 16–17°C (65–70°F) rather than in the refrigerator. A 1.4kg (3lb) bird takes about 9 hours. Thaw whole hare or rabbit for 24 hours in the refrigerator if under 3.6kg (8lb), or 48 hours if over 3.6kg (8lb). Joints take 12–15 hours in the refrigerator. For venison joints under 3.6kg (8lb), thaw in the refrigerator for 24 hours, or 48 hours for joints over 3.6kg (8lb).

To thaw in the microwave, thaw in the wrapping, which should be pierced first. Microwave on LOW for 5–7 minutes per 450g (1lb).

Thaw whole rabbit or hare in the microwave on LOW for 6–8 minutes per 450g (1lb), stand in cold water for 30 minutes. Jointed rabbit or hare, microwave on LOW for 5–7 minutes per 450g (1lb). Separate during thawing time. Stand for 10–15 minutes.

To thaw venison joints on the bone, microwave on LOW for 10–12 minutes per 450g (1lb). Turn

over the joint during thawing. The meat will still be icy at the centre, but will complete thawing if left to stand for 1 hour at room temperature. Microwave boned and rolled joints on LOW for 5–6 minutes per 450g (1lb). Stand for 30–45 minutes.

GAMMON (See Bacon)

GARLIC

Garlic keeps just as well in a cool, dry place so there is no need to freeze it. However, it can be frozen if wished, but remove it from the freezer if you can smell garlic when you open the freezer door.

To freeze: Wrap whole bulbs in foil or plastic wrap, then overwrap in a polythene bag. Seal, label and freeze.

Storage time: 3 months.

To thaw: Break off cloves as you need them, they will thaw in a few minutes.

GOOSE

Although fresh geese are available all year, you may need to order one from your butcher. Geese may be oven-ready or 'rough plucked' with head and feet on and not drawn. They are also sold frozen ready for the oven.

To freeze: Wipe and dry the bird. Pad the legs with foil so that they can not spike their way through the wrapping. Pack in a large polythene bag. Seal, label and freeze.

Storage time: 4–5 months.

To thaw: In the light of new research, it is recommended that poultry is thawed in its wrapping at room temperature of 16–17°C (65–70°F) rather than in the refrigerator. A 1.4kg (3lb) bird takes about 9 hours, a 6.8kg (15lb) bird 24 hours.

GRAPE

Choose plump, unbruised grapes with a distinct bloom to them. Buy in bunches if possible and avoid shrivelled or squashed ones. When thawed, grapes can become mushy and collapse easily.

To freeze: Seedless grapes can be packed whole, others should be skinned, pipped and halved. Pack in cold syrup (see page 17), made with 450g (1lb) sugar to 1 litre (2 pints) water. Pack in rigid containers, leaving headspace. Cover, label and freeze.

Storage time: 12 months.

To thaw: Leave to thaw at room temperature for 2 hours.

GRAPEFRUIT
Both yellow and pink fleshed varieties can be frozen. Pink grapefruit are sweeter.

To freeze: Peel the fruit, removing all pith, and divide into segments. Freeze by (a) Dry sugar pack using 225g (8oz) sugar to 450g (1lb) fruit. Sprinkle sugar over the fruit. When juices start to run, pack in rigid containers. (b) Cold syrup pack (see page 17), made with equal quantities of sugar and water. Use any juice from the fruit to make up the syrup. Cover, label and freeze.

Storage time: 12 months.

To thaw: Leave to thaw in container at room temperature for 2 hours.

GREENGAGE (See PLUM)

GREY MULLET (See MULLET)

GUAVA
Tropical fruit of South American and Indian origin which may be round or pear-shaped. They have whitish yellow to red skins and musky smelling flesh. They can be eaten raw or cooked.

To freeze: Peel, halve and scoop out seeds. Leave in halves or slice. Freeze by (a) Dry pack (see page 16). (b) Syrup pack (see page 17), made with 450g (1lb) sugar to 1 litre (2 pints) water. Pack in rigid containers, leaving headspace. Cover, label and freeze.

Storage time: 12 months.

To thaw: Leave to thaw in container at room temperature for 2 hours.

GUINEA FOWL
These are available all year round but are at their best from February to June. An average-sized bird will serve 3–4 people. They have a more gamey flavour than chicken and are not usually available jointed. They can be frozen like chickens.

To freeze: Prepare and draw like chicken (see Freezing poultry, page 14). Do not stuff before freezing. Cover protruding bones with non-stick paper. Pack bird in a polythene bag and exclude as much air as possible. Seal, label and freeze. Freeze giblets separately.

Storage time: 9 months; giblets, 3 months.

To thaw: Guinea fowl must be completely thawed before cooking. In the light of new research, it is recommended that guinea fowl is thawed in its wrapping at room temperature of 16–17°C (65–70°F) rather than in the refrigerator. A 1.4kg (3lb) bird takes about 9 hours. To thaw in the microwave, thaw in the wrapping which should be pierced first and any metal tag removed. Microwave on LOW for 6–8 minutes per 450g (1lb). During thawing, pour off the liquid that collects in the wrapping. Finish thawing in a bowl of cold water for 30 minutes with the bird still in its wrapping.

HADDOCK
This round fish, a cousin of the cod, has firm white flesh. It is sold as fillets or cutlets. Both fresh and smoked haddock can be frozen.

To freeze: Separate fillets or cutlets with a double layer of plastic wrap and overwrap in foil or plastic wrap. Seal, label and freeze.

Storage time: 3 months.

To thaw/cook: Can be cooked from frozen. To thaw in the microwave, microwave on LOW for 3–4 minutes per 450g (1lb) plus 2–3 minutes. Allow to stand for 5 minutes after each 2 minutes.

HAKE
Hake belongs to the same family as cod and is similar in shape, but has a closer white flesh and a better flavour. Small hake are sold whole, large ones are sold as fillets, steaks or cutlets.

To freeze: Wash, remove scales and gut (see page 15). Place whole fish unwrapped in the freezer until solid. Remove and dip in cold water. This forms thin ice over the fish. Return to the freezer; repeat process until the ice glaze is 0.5cm (¼ inch) thick.

Wrap in plastic wrap and support with a thin board. Separate steaks, fillets and cutlets with a double layer of plastic wrap, then overwrap in foil or plastic wrap. Seal, label and freeze.

Storage time: 3 months.

To thaw: Allow whole fish to thaw in a cool place for up to 24 hours. Once thawed, use promptly. Steaks, fillets and cutlets can be cooked from frozen. To thaw steaks and fillets in the microwave, microwave on LOW for 3–4 minutes per 450g (1lb) plus 2–3 minutes. Allow to stand for 5 minutes after each 2 minutes.

HALIBUT

Halibut is a very large flat fish and, like turbot, is regarded as one of the best flavoured fish. It is sold as fillets or steaks. Freeze and thaw as for HAKE.

HAM

Both raw and cooked ham may be frozen but due to their high salt and fat content they cannot be stored for long because they quickly became rancid.

To freeze: Raw ham: leave in a piece, wrap in plastic wrap, then overwrap in a polythene bag. Cooked ham: pack joints as for raw ham. Pack sliced ham in polythene bags, interleaving slices with plastic wrap. Seal, label and freeze.

Storage time: Raw, 2 months; cooked, 1 month.

To thaw: Thaw joints in wrapping overnight in the refrigerator. Thaw slices in wrapping for about 3 hours in the refrigerator.

HARE (See GAME)

HERBS

Freeze young and tender herbs.

To freeze: Wash and trim if necessary. Dry thoroughly. Freeze in small bunches in a rigid container or polythene bag. Alternatively, herbs – especially parsley – can be chopped and frozen in ice cube trays. Transfer to polythene bags when solid. Cover or seal, label and freeze.

Storage time: Up to 6 months.

To thaw: Can be used from frozen. Crumble them, or add frozen cubes to cooked dishes.

HERRING

Herring is a fairly small, round, oily fish with cream-coloured flesh.

To freeze: Wash, remove scales and gut (see page 15). Remove backbone and as many smaller bones as possible. Open out and pack in pairs in polythene bags, interleaving each herring with plastic wrap. Seal, label and freeze.

Storage time: 3 months.

To thaw: Grill or fry from frozen. To thaw in the microwave, microwave on LOW for 2–3 minutes per 225g (8oz) plus 3–4 minutes. Allow to stand for 5 minutes after each 2 minutes.

HORSERADISH

This root of the mustard family has a hot, pungent taste. Freeze young roots.

To freeze: Grate or mince, then sprinkle with white wine vinegar to prevent discoloration. Pack in small rigid containers. Cover, label and freeze.

Storage time: 6 months.

To thaw: Leave to thaw in container in the refrigerator or, for more rapid thawing, remove from container and thaw at room temperature. To thaw in the microwave, microwave on LOW for 8–10 minutes.

ICE CREAM

Either home-made or bought ice creams can be stored in the freezer. Bought ice creams should be rewrapped in moisture-proof bags before storing. Home-made ones should be frozen in moulds or rigid containers and overwrapped. Cover or seal, label and freeze.

Storage time: Home-made, 3 months; commercially-made, 3 months or as directed on pack.

To thaw/serve: Transfer to the refrigerator for a short time to soften a little. Most bought 'soft-scoop' ice cream can be used straight from the freezer, provided it is not kept in the coldest part. (Warn children that ice lollipops and water ices eaten straight from the freezer may burn their mouths.)

Right: Marmalade Teabread (page 217) and Marbled Chocolate Teabread (page 212)

JAM

Low sugar jam, the sort that has to be kept in the refrigerator after opening, can be frozen.

To freeze: Pack in small rigid containers. Cover, label and freeze.

Storage time: 3 months.

To thaw: Leave overnight in the container at cool room temperature. To thaw in the microwave, microwave on HIGH for 6–7 minutes, breaking up the block as it thaws. Stand for 10–15 minutes. Use quickly after thawing.

JOHN DORY

This ugly, flat fish has very large jaws and a nearly oval body. It is sold whole or as fillets.

To freeze: Wash, remove scales and gut (see page 15). Place whole fish unwrapped in the freezer until solid. Remove and dip in cold water. This forms thin ice over the fish. Return to the freezer; repeat process until the ice glaze is 0.5cm (¼ inch) thick. Wrap in plastic wrap and support with a thin board. Separate fillets with a double layer of plastic wrap, then overwrap in foil or plastic wrap. Seal, label and freeze.

Storage time: 3 months.

To thaw: Allow whole fish to thaw in a cool place for up to 24 hours. Once thawed, use promptly. Fillets can be cooked from frozen. To thaw fillets in the microwave, microwave on LOW for 3–4 minutes per 450g (1lb) plus 2–3 minutes. Allow to stand for 5 minutes after each 2 minutes.

JUICE, FRUIT

Freshly squeezed juice keeps well in the freezer. It is useful for sauces as well as drinks.

To freeze: Pour into rigid containers leaving 1cm (½ inch) headspace. Cover, label and freeze. Alternatively, freeze in ice cube trays, then pack in polythene bags. Seal, label and freeze.

Storage time: 4 months.

To thaw: Leave to thaw in container in the refrigerator overnight or at room temperature for several hours. Bought concentrated fruit juice can be used from frozen, diluted with water.

KALE

There are many varieties, both flat and curly. Frozen kale is only suitable for using for soups and purées.

To freeze: Wash, then blanch for 1 minute (see page 16). To blanch in the microwave, put 450g (1lb) kale in a dish with 45ml (3 tbsp) water, cover and microwave on HIGH for 4–5 minutes. Cool, drain and pack the kale in polythene bags. Seal, label and freeze.

Storage time: 12 months.

To thaw/cook: Cook from frozen.

KIDNEY (See OFFAL)

KIPPER

Kippers are herrings, split, lightly brined, then cold-smoked.

To freeze: Wrap individually in a double layer of plastic wrap, then overwrap in foil or plastic wrap. Seal, label and freeze.

Storage time: 2–3 months.

To thaw/cook: Can be cooked from frozen. To thaw in the microwave, microwave on LOW for 2–3 minutes per 225g (8oz) plus 3–4 minutes. Allow to stand for 5 minutes after each 2 minutes.

KOHLRABI

This unusual looking vegetable is a swollen stalk not a root. It can be white or purple-skinned. Choose young, tender kohlrabi no more than 5cm (2 inches) in diameter.

To freeze: Trim the base, leaves and stalks. Wash, then blanch whole for 3 minutes (see page 16). To blanch in the microwave, put 450g (1lb) kohlrabi in a shallow dish, thicker parts towards the outside, with 45ml (3 tbsp) water, cover and microwave on HIGH for 4–6 minutes. Cool, drain and pack in rigid containers or polythene bags. Seal, label and freeze.

Storage time: 12 months.

To thaw/cook: Leave to partially thaw at room temperature, then cook until tender. To thaw in the microwave, microwave on LOW for 4–6 minutes.

KUMQUAT

Kumquats are tiny oranges about half the size of plums which are eaten whole, peel and pips included. They can be frozen for use in desserts or for making preserves.

To freeze: Leave whole. Freeze by (a) Dry pack (see page 16). (b) Syrup pack (see page 17) made with 450g (1lb) sugar to 1 litre (2 pints) water. (c) If using for preserves, they can be sliced or chopped and packed by the dry sugar method. Pack in rigid containers. Cover, label and freeze.

Storage time: 12 months.

To thaw: Leave to thaw in wrapping at room temperature for about 2 hours.

LAMB

Use good quality, fresh lamb. The fat should be crisp and white with the lean, fine-grained, firm and pink-brown. Freshly cut surfaces should look slightly moist and the bones pinkish white. Lamb is a particularly tender meat and all the joints can be roasted. Removing bones will save space in the freezer; butcher in suitable quantities. Joints can be roasted and frozen for serving cold, but take care not to overcook them. Reheated whole joints are not very satisfactory. Sliced and frozen cooked meat tends to be dry when reheated.

To freeze: Pack carefully in heavy-duty polythene bags. Group in similar types, then overwrap with mutton cloth, stockinette, thin polythene or newspaper, to protect against puncturing and loss of quality. If freezing a cooked joint, best results are achieved by freezing the whole joint, but small pieces can be sliced and packed in polythene if required to serve cold, or put in foil containers (or plastic if thawing in the microwave) and covered with gravy if to be served hot. Cover or seal, label and freeze.

Storage time: Raw, 6 months; cooked and sliced with gravy, 3 months; without gravy, 2 months.

To thaw/cook: Joints up to 2.7kg (6lb) can be cooked from frozen. Cooking times for frozen joints over this weight are difficult to calculate, so to prevent the outside being overcooked before the inside is thawed, it is better to thaw large joints before cooking. For joints on the bone under 1.8kg (4lb), roast at 180°C (350°F) mark 4 for 35 minutes

per 450g (1lb) plus 35 minutes, thermometer reading 82°C (180°F) for well done. For joints weighing 1.8–2.7kg (4–6lb), 40 minutes per 450g (1lb) plus 40 minutes, thermometer reading 82°C (180°F), for well done.

Rolled joints, such as breasts of lamb, whether stuffed or not, must be thawed before cooking. This is because all the surfaces of the meat have been handled and rolled up, so it is important to ensure thorough cooking to destroy any bacteria which might be present in the meat.

Chops, cubed and minced meat for stews and kebabs can be cooked from frozen. Start the cooking at a lower temperature than normal and cook for almost twice as long, increasing the temperature halfway through the cooking. It will probably be necessary to thaw meat for frying if it has become mis-shapen during frozen storage to ensure good contact with the frying pan.

If leaving to thaw, joints of less than 1.4kg (3lb) take 6–8 hours per 450g (1lb) in the refrigerator, 1–2 hours per 450g (1lb) at room temperature. Joints over 1.4kg (3lb) take 14 hours per 450g (1lb) in the refrigerator, 2–3 hours per 450g (1lb) at room temperature. Chops take 5–6 hours in the refrigerator, 2–3 hours at room temperature. Partial thawing is necessary if food is to be egg-and-breadcrumbed before cooking.

To thaw cooked meat, thaw in the wrapping and allow about 4 hours per 450g (1lb) at room temperature, or double that time in the refrigerator. Sliced meat requires less time.

To thaw in the microwave (see page 31), microwave on LOW for 5–6 minutes per 450g (1lb) for boned, rolled joints. Turn over regularly during thawing and leave to rest if the meat shows signs of cooking. Allow to stand for 30–45 minutes. For joints on the bone, microwave on LOW for 5–6 minutes per 450g (1lb). Turn over joint during thawing. The meat will still be icy in the centre but will complete thawing if left to stand for 30–45 minutes. For minced lamb, microwave on LOW for 8–10 minutes per 450g (1lb). Allow to stand for 10 minutes. For chops, microwave on LOW for 8–10 minutes per 450g (1lb). Separate during thawing. Allow to stand for 10 minutes.

LEEK

Frozen leeks are only suitable for using in casseroles or as a base for Vichyssoise.

To freeze: Cut off tops and roots, remove coarse outside leaves. Slice into 1cm (½ inch) slices and wash well. Sauté for 4 minutes in butter or oil. Cool, drain and pack in rigid containers or polythene bags. Cover or seal, label and freeze.

Storage time: 6 months.

To thaw/cook: Cook from frozen.

LEMON

Lemons can be frozen whole, in slices or as rind for decoration or grated.

To freeze: Freeze by one of the following methods. (a) Squeeze out the juice and freeze it in ice cube trays; when frozen, transfer the cubes to polythene bags. (b) Leave lemons whole, slice or segment before freezing by the dry pack method (see page 16). (c) Remove all pith from the rind, cut into julienne strips, blanch for 1 minute (see page 16), cool and pack; use for decoration. (d) Mix grated lemon rind and a little sugar; use for serving with pancakes. (e) Remove slivers of peel, free of pith, and freeze in small quantities in polythene bags for adding to drinks. Cover or seal, label and freeze.

Storage time: 12 months.

To thaw: Unwrap and leave to thaw at room temperature for 1–1½ hours.

LEMON SOLE

The flesh of lemon sole is more stringy and has less flavour than Dover sole. It is sold whole or as fillets.

To freeze: Wash, remove scales and gut (see page 15). Place whole fish unwrapped in freezer until solid. Remove and dip in cold water. This forms thin ice over the fish. Return to the freezer; repeat process until the ice glaze is 0.5cm (¼ inch) thick. Wrap in plastic wrap and support with a thin board. Separate fillets with a double layer of plastic wrap, then overwrap in foil or plastic wrap.

Storage time: 3 months.

To thaw: Allow whole fish to thaw in a cool place for 24 hours. Once thawed, use promptly. Fillets can be cooked from frozen. To thaw in the microwave, microwave on LOW for 3–4 minutes per 450g (1lb) plus 2–3 minutes. Allow to stand for 5 minutes after each 2 minutes.

LETTUCE

Lettuce does not freeze satisfactorily as it loses its crisp texture due to its high water content. However, if you have a glut of lettuces, it is worth freezing the hearts for use in soups.

To freeze: Blanch for 2 minutes (see page 16). To blanch in the microwave, put 450g (1lb) lettuce hearts in a dish with 45ml (3 tbsp) water, cover, and microwave on HIGH for 3–3½ minutes. Cool, drain and squeeze out the water. Pack in polythene bags. Seal, label and freeze.

Storage time: 6 months.

To thaw: Use from frozen.

LIME (See LEMON)

LIVER (See OFFAL)

LOBSTER

Lobster must be absolutely fresh and freshly boiled for freezing; within 12 hours of being caught.

To freeze: If a lobster has been bought alive ask the fishmonger to weigh it so that you can calculate the cooking time. Bring a large saucepan of water to the boil, then boil vigorously. Leave until completely cold, then immerse the lobster in the water and leave for 30 minutes. The lack of oxygen renders the lobster unconcious before it is put over the heat. Bring to the boil slowly, simmer gently for 8 minutes per 450g (1lb). Remove and cool.

Alternatively, bring a large saucepan of water to the boil, grasp the lobster by the back and drop it into the water, covering the pan with a lid, then weigh it down for the first 2 minutes. Simmer gently for 12 minutes for the first 450g (1lb), 10 minutes for the next 450g (1lb) and 5 minutes more for each addition 450g (1lb). Remove and cool.

Pack the lobster in a polythene bag or foil. Seal, label and freeze. Alternatively, split the lobster in half lengthways, remove tail and claw meat, cut into neat pieces and pack in rigid containers or polythene bags. Cover or seal, label and freeze.

Storage time: 1 month.

To thaw: Leave to thaw in wrapping in the refrigerator for about 6 hours.

Right: Chelsea Buns (page 212)

LYCHEE

Lychees are a stone fruit the size of plums which grow in bunches. They have hard skins, ranging from pink to brown, and sweet, juicy flesh. Avoid fruit with shrivelled dry skins.

To freeze: Remove skin. Pack in cold syrup (see page 17), made with 450g (1lb) sugar to 1 litre (2 pints) water. Pack in rigid containers, leaving headspace. Cover, label and freeze.

Storage time: 12 months.

To thaw: Leave to thaw in container in the refrigerator and use while still frosted.

MACKEREL

Mackerel is a fairly small, round, oily fish with blue-black markings on the back, cream-coloured flesh and a very distinct flavour. It is sold whole. Mackerel must be frozen very fresh, preferably within 1 hour of being caught.

To freeze: Clean, remove scales and gut (see page 15). Wash and pat dry. Pack tightly in polythene bags. Alternatively, place fish unwrapped in the freezer until solid. Remove and dip in cold water. This forms thin ice over the fish. Return to the freezer; repeat process until the ice glaze is 0.5cm (¼ inch) thick. Wrap in plastic wrap and support with a thin board. Seal, label and freeze.

Storage time: 2 months.

To thaw/cook: Cook from frozen or leave to thaw in a cool place before cooking. Once thawed, use promptly. To thaw in the microwave, microwave on LOW for 2–3 minutes per 225g (8oz) plus 3–4 minutes. Stand for 5 minutes after each 2 minutes.

MANGE TOUT

Choose tender young pods for freezing.

To freeze: Trim the ends. Blanch for 2 minutes (see page 16). To blanch in the microwave, put 450g (1lb) mange tout in a dish with 45ml (3 tbsp) water, cover and microwave on HIGH for 2–3 minutes. Cool, drain and pack in rigid containers or polythene bags. Cover or seal, label and freeze.

Storage time: 12 months.

To thaw/cook: Cook from frozen.

MANGO

Freeze fully ripe fruit.

To freeze: Peel, then stone and slice flesh. Pack in cold syrup (see page 17), made with 450g (1lb) sugar to 1 litre (2 pints) water; add 30ml (2 tbsp) lemon juice to each 1 litre (2 pints) syrup. Pack in rigid containers. Cover, label and freeze.

Storage time: 9–12 months.

To thaw: Leave to thaw in container at room temperature for 1½ hours. Serve with additional lemon juice.

MARROW

Freeze young marrows.

To freeze: Cut into 1–2.5cm (½–1 inch) slices, then blanch for 3 minutes (see page 16). To blanch in the microwave, put 450g (1lb) marrow in a dish with 45ml (3 tbsp) water, cover and microwave on HIGH for 2–3 minutes. Cool, drain and pack in rigid containers or polythene bags. Cover or seal, label and freeze.

Storage time: 6 months.

To thaw/cook: Cook from frozen.

MELON

Cantaloup and honeydew melons freeze well, though they lose their crispness when thawed. The seeds of watermelon make it more difficult to prepare.

To freeze: Cut in half and seed, then cut flesh into balls, cubes or slices. Freeze by (a) Dry pack (see page 16) with a little sugar sprinkled over. Wrap well in polythene bags. (b) Cold syrup pack (see page 17), made with 450g (1lb) sugar to 1 litre (2 pints) water. Pack in rigid containers, leaving headspace. Cover or seal, label and freeze.

Storage time: 9–12 months.

To thaw: Leave to thaw in container in the refrigerator and use while still frosted.

MERINGUE

Making meringues is a useful way of using up leftover egg whites. Meringues should be frozen plain.

To freeze: Open freeze on baking trays until solid, then carefully pack in rigid containers. If packing cream-filled meringues, separate each one with cardboard or foil. Cover, label and freeze.

Storage time: 3 months.

To thaw: Use straight from the freezer for decorative purposes. If sandwiching with cream, leave to thaw at room temperature for about 2 hours.

MILK
Ordinary pasteurised milk does not freeze well; homogenised is satsifactory.

To freeze: Do not freeze in the bottle. Pack in rigid containers, leaving 2.5cm (1 inch) headspace. Cover, label and freeze.

Storage time: 1 month.

To thaw: Leave to thaw in the refrigerator. Thawing may be accelerated by heating gently or thawing in the microwave if the milk is to be used for cooking.

MONKFISH
Monkfish is a round fish with a very large, ugly head. Only the tail is eaten and it is sold as fillets. The flesh is similar to lobster.

To freeze: Separate fillets with a double layer of plastic wrap, then overwrap in foil or plastic wrap. Seal, label and freeze.

Storage time: 3 months.

To thaw/cook: Fillets can be cooked from frozen. To thaw in the microwave, microwave on LOW for 3–4 minutes per 450g (1lb) plus 2–3 minutes. Allow to stand for 5 minutes after each 2 minutes.

MULLET, GREY
Grey mullet is a round fish which looks and tastes similar to sea bass. It is sold whole or as fillets.

To freeze: Wash, remove scales and gut (see page 15). Place whole fish unwrapped in the freezer until solid. Remove and dip in cold water. This forms thin ice over the fish. Return to the freezer; repeat process until the ice glaze is 0.5cm (¼ inch) thick. Wrap in plastic wrap and support with a thin board.

Separate fillets with a double layer of plastic wrap, then overwrap in foil or plastic wrap. Seal, label and freeze.

Storage time: 3 months.

To thaw/cook: Allow whole fish to thaw in a cool place for up to 24 hours. Once thawed, use promptly. Fillets can be cooked from frozen. To thaw fillets in the microwave, microwave on LOW for 3–4 minutes per 450g (1lb) plus 2–3 minutes. Allow to stand for 5 minutes after each 2 minutes.

MULLET, RED
Red mullet is no relation to the grey mullet. It is smaller, crimson in colour with a delicate flavour. It is sold whole. Freeze and thaw as for whole GREY MULLET.

MUSHROOM
Choose small button mushrooms and leave whole. Mushrooms larger than 2.5cm (1 inch) in diameter can be sliced for using in cooked dishes. Duxelles, a paste made of mushrooms or mushroom stalks and peelings, is used for flavouring sauces, soups, ragouts, stuffings and stews. It can be frozen in small handy quantities (use ice cube trays for freezing).

To freeze: Wipe clean but do not peel or blanch. Sauté in butter for 1 minute. Pack in rigid containers or polythene bags in 100 g (4 oz) quantities. Pack duxelles in small rigid containers. Cover or seal, label and freeze.

Storage time: 3 months.

To thaw: Heat in melted butter or under the grill. Alternatively, thaw in wrapping in the refrigerator until soft. To thaw in the microwave, put 225g (8oz) in a dish, cover and microwave on HIGH for 2–3 minutes.

MUSSEL
Mussels freeze well but they must be very fresh. They should be frozen within 12 hours of being caught. For best results, buy live mussels for freezing.

To freeze: Put the mussels in a large bowl and, under cold running water, scrape off any mud, barnacles, seaweed and 'beards' with a small sharp knife. Discard any that are open and do not close when sharply tapped with the back of a knife. Rinse again until there is no trace of sand in the bowl. Put the mussels in a frying pan, cover and cook on high heat for about 5 minutes, until the shells open. Discard any shells which do not open. Alternatively, put the mussels in a saucepan of water or wine, flavoured with onion and herbs. Cover and cook for 3–5 minutes, until the mussels open, shaking the pan frequently. Pack the mussels with or without their shells, in their juices, in rigid containers. Cover, label and freeze.

Storage time: 1 month.

To thaw: Leave to thaw in container in the refrigerator for 3 hours.

NECTARINE (See PEACH)

NUTS
Nuts will keep as well stored in the freezer as in the storecupboard, except for salted varieties which do not freeze well and soon become rancid.

To freeze: Pack whole or chopped nuts in small quantities in rigid containers or polythene bags. Cover or seal, label and freeze.

Storage time: 12 months.

To thaw: Leave to thaw in wrapping at room temperature for about 3 hours.

OCTOPUS
Small octopus may be sold whole; larger ones are ready prepared in pieces.

To freeze: Rinse the octopus, then hold the body in one hand and with the other firmly pull off the head and tentacles. The soft contents of the body will come out and can be discarded. Cut the tentacles just in front of the eyes. Rinse the body and tentacles, then beat well with a wooden mallet. Cut the flesh into rings or pieces or keep whole for stuffing. The ink sac has a musky flavour and is not usually used. Blanch for 2 minutes (see page 16). Plunge into cold water, then strip off skin. Pack in polythene bags. Seal, label and freeze.

Storage time: 3 months.

To thaw: Leave to thaw in wrapping in the refrigerator for 3 hours.

OFFAL
All offal for freezing must be very fresh.

To freeze: Prepare as for cooking. Wrap kidneys individually, then in polythene bags. Place slices of liver or heart in shallow containers. Cover, label and freeze.

Storage time: 3 months.

To thaw: Leave to thaw in wrapping in the refrigerator for about 8 hours. To thaw in the microwave, remove foil if used, then microwave liver or heart on LOW for 8–10 minutes per 450g (1lb); separate during thawing. Allow to stand for 5 minutes. To thaw kidneys, microwave on LOW for 6–9 minutes per 450g (1lb); separate during thawing. Allow to stand for 5 minutes.

OKRA
Also called lady's fingers. Okra for freezing should be only about 7.5cm (3 inches) long.

To freeze: Cut off stems without breaking into the pods. Blanch for 3 minutes (see page 16). To blanch in the microwave, put 450g (1lb) okra in a dish with 45ml (3 tbsp) water, cover and microwave on HIGH for 2–3 minutes. Cool, drain and pack. Cover or seal, label and freeze.

Storage time: 12 months.

To thaw/cook: Cook from frozen.

ONION
It is sometimes useful to have chopped or small onions in the freezer.

To freeze: Peel, finely chop and pack in rigid containers. Overwrap in plastic wrap to prevent the smell filtering out. Small onions can be blanched whole for 4 minutes (see page 16) for use in casseroles. Seal, label and freeze.

Storage time: 3 months.

To thaw: Leave chopped onions to thaw in wrapping at room temperature for 15 minutes. Add frozen whole onions to casseroles. To thaw in the microwave, microwave small, whole onions on HIGH for 2–3 minutes.

Right: Steak and Kidney Pie (page 136)

ORANGE

Oranges, particularly Sevilles, can be frozen for making marmalade. However, some pectin is destroyed by enzymes so allow for this in recipes.

To freeze: Freeze by one of the following methods. (a) Peel whole fruits, removing all pith, segment and pack in cold syrup (see page 17), made with equal quantities of sugar and water – use any juice from the fruit to make up the syrup. (b) Dry sugar pack, using 225g (8oz) sugar to 450g (1lb) fruit; when juices start to run, pack in rigid containers. (c) Squeeze out and freeze the juice; add sugar if wished. Freeze in small quantities in containers or in ice cube trays. (d) Grate rind and mix with a little sugar for serving with pancakes.

Seville oranges may be scrubbed, packed in suitable quantities and frozen whole until required for making marmalade. (Do not thaw whole frozen fruit in order to cut it up before cooking as some discoloration often occurs – use whole fruit method for marmalade. It is advisable to add one-eighth extra weight of Seville or bitter oranges or tangerines when freezing for subsequent marmalade making in order to offset pectin loss.) Cover or seal, label and freeze.

Storage time: Syrup pack or dry sugar pack, 9–12 months; packed alone, 6–8 months; juice, 4–6 months.

To thaw: Leave to thaw in wrapping at room temperature for about 2 hours. Unwrap Seville oranges and leave to thaw at room temperature.

OXTAIL

Choose oxtails with a good proportion of lean meat with a layer of firm, white fat.

To freeze: Pack raw oxtail in polythene bags. Seal, label and freeze.

Storage time: 3 months.

To thaw: Leave to thaw in wrapping in the refrigerator overnight. To thaw in the microwave, microwave on LOW for 8–10 minutes per 450g (1lb). Separate during thawing and arrange in a circle. Allow to stand for 10 minutes.

OYSTER

Oysters must be frozen within 12 hours of being caught.

To freeze: Scrub oysters with a stiff brush. Holding them over a muslin-lined sieve set over a bowl to catch the juices, prise open each shell at the hinge and loosen the oysters, leaving them in one half-shell. Wash in salted water, allowing 15ml (1 tbsp) salt to 600ml (1 pint) water. Pack in rigid containers and cover with strained juices. Cover, label and freeze.

Storage time: 1 month.

To thaw: If serving raw, leave in container in the refrigerator for 6 hours. Alternatively, add frozen oysters to soups and sauces and cook without boiling for about 4 minutes.

PANCAKE

Cooked pancakes, either filled or unfilled, make a good stand-by to have in the freezer. Add 15ml (1 tbsp) corn oil to a basic 100g (4oz) flour recipe. Make pancakes and cool quickly on a wire rack. If filling before freezing, choose fillings suitable for freezing and do not over-season.

To freeze: Interleave unfilled pancakes with lightly oiled non-stick paper or plastic wrap. Pack in foil or polythene bags. Place filled pancakes in a rigid container or foil dish, cover and overwrap in plastic wrap or a polythene bag. Seal, label and freeze.

Storage time: Unfilled, 2 months; filled 1–2 months depending on the filling.

To thaw: Unfilled pancakes: leave in wrapping at room temperature for 2–3 hours, or overnight in the refrigerator. For quick thawing, unwrap, spread out separately and leave at room temperature for about 20 minutes. To reheat, place stack of pancakes wrapped in foil in the oven at 190°C (375°F) mark 5 for 20–30 minutes. Alternatively, separate pancakes and place in a lightly greased heated frying pan, allowing 30 seconds each side. Filled pancakes: place frozen, covered, in the oven at 200°C (400°F) mark 6, for about 30 minutes. To reheat in the microwave, see page 32.

PAPAYA

Papaya resembles a melon with a yellowish colour and orange flesh.

To freeze: Wash and peel, remove the seeds and cut the flesh into slices. Pack in cold syrup (see page 17), made with 450g (1lb) sugar to 1 litre (2 pints) water; add 30ml (2 tbsp) lemon juice to each 1 litre (2 pints) syrup. Pack in rigid containers. Cover, label and freeze.

Storage time: 9–12 months.

To thaw: Leave to thaw in container at room temperature for 1½ hours. Serve with additional lemon juice.

PARSNIP
Freeze tender young parsnips.

To freeze: Trim and peel, then cut into narrow strips. Blanch for 2 minutes (see page 16). To blanch in the microwave, put 450g (1lb) parsnips in a dish with 45ml (3 tbsp) water, cover and microwave on HIGH for 2 minutes. Cool and pat dry. Pack in polythene bags. Seal, label and freeze.

Storage time: 6 months.

To thaw/cook: Cook from frozen. If roasting, thaw at room temperature first.

PASSION FRUIT
These tropical vine fruit look like large wrinkled plums. The inedible skin is deeply wrinkled when the fruit is ripe. The sweet, juicy flesh is pitted with small, edible seeds. Passion fruit should be frozen as soon as possible after picking. Freeze and thaw as for PAPAYA.

PASTA
Pasta such as spaghetti, noodles, lasagne, macaroni and ravioli will freeze successfully. Freeze in quantities suitable for future use – allow 50–75g (2–3oz) uncooked pasta per person if serving as a starter; 100–175g (4–6oz) per person for a main course.

To freeze: Cook in boiling salted water until slightly undercooked and just chewy. Drain, cool under cold running water, then drain again. Pack in polythene bags. Seal, label and freeze.

Storage time: Cooked pasta, 1 month; pasta frozen in made-up dishes such as macaroni cheese, 3 months.

To thaw/cook: Add fresh pasta to boiling salted water and cook until tender. For pasta dishes, see recipes.

PASTRY
Pastry freezes well, particularly shortcrust, flaky and puff. It can be frozen baked or unbaked, in a piece or made into pies (see PIE).

To freeze: Uncooked: Roll out to size required (or shape into vol-au-vent cases). Stack pastry shapes with a double layer of plastic wrap between the layers, so that if necessary one piece can be removed without thawing the whole batch. Place the stack on a piece of cardboard, then wrap. Prepare flaky and puff pastry up to the last rolling. Pack in polythene bags or heavy duty foil and overwrap. For pastry cases and cooked pastry, see PIE. Seal, label and freeze.

Storage time: 3 months.

To thaw: Unshaped pastry: leave to thaw at room temperature or in the refrigerator. Unshaped pastry will take 3–4 hours at room temperature before it can be rolled out; shaped, rolled-out pastry will take less time.

PEA
Freeze young, sweet garden peas, not old or starchy ones.

To freeze: Shell, then blanch for 1–2 minutes (see page 16); shake the blanching basket from time to time to distribute the heat evenly. To blanch in the microwave, put 450g (1lb) peas in a dish with 45ml (3 tbsp) water, cover and microwave on HIGH for 1½–2 minutes. Cool, drain, then open freeze on baking sheets until solid. Pack in polythene bags. Seal, label and return to freezer. Alternatively, pack directly into rigid containers or polythene bags. Cover and seal, label and freeze.

Storage time: 12 months.

To thaw/cook: Cook from frozen.

PEACH
Freeze ripe peaches which are slightly soft with a yellow to orange skin.

To freeze: Really ripe peaches are best skinned and stoned under cold running water, as scalding will soften and slightly discolour the flesh. Skin firm peaches by immersing them in boiling water for about 15 seconds, then cool in cold water. Brush with lemon juice. Put halves or slices in cold syrup (see page 17), made with 450g (1lb) sugar to 1 litre (2 pints) water, with the juice of 1 lemon added. Pack in rigid containers, leaving 1cm (½ inch) headspace. Alternatively, purée stoned peaches, then mix in 15ml (1 tbsp) lemon juice and 100g (4oz) sugar to each 450g (1lb) fruit. Pack in rigid containers. Cover, label and freeze.

Storage time: In syrup, 9–12 months; purée, 6–8 months.

To thaw: Leave to thaw in container in the refrigerator for 3 hours.

PEAR
Only freeze pears if you have a large crop from your garden, as they discolour rapidly, and the texture of thawed pears can be soft.

To freeze: Peel, quarter, core and dip pears in lemon juice immediately. Poach in syrup (see page 17), made with 450g (1lb) sugar to 1 litre (2 pints) water, for 1½ minutes. Cool and pack in the syrup in rigid containers. Cover, label and freeze.

Storage time: 9–12 months.

To thaw: Leave to thaw in container at room temperature for 3 hours.

PEPPER
Freeze red and green peppers separately.

To freeze: Wash well, remove stems and all traces of seeds and membranes. They can be frozen as halves for stuffed peppers, or in thin slices for stews and casseroles. Blanch for 3 minutes (see page 16). To blanch in the microwave, put 450g (1lb) peppers in a dish with 45ml (3 tbsp) water, cover and microwave on HIGH for 2 minutes. (For better colour, when storage is going to be less than 6 months, do not blanch.) Cook, drain and open freeze on baking sheets until solid, then pack in polythene bags. Seal, label and return to the freezer. Or, pack directly into polythene bags.

Storage time: 12 months.

To thaw: Leave to thaw in wrapping at room temperature for 1–2 hours. Alternatively, add slices direct to casseroles and stews towards the end of cooking. Microwave 225g (8oz) on HIGH for 6–8 minutes, stirring during cooking.

PERCH
This large, round freshwater fish has firm, sweet flesh. It is an angler's fish. Perch should be frozen within 12 hours of being caught.

To freeze: Wash, remove scales and gut (see page 15). Place whole fish unwrapped in the freezer until solid. Remove and dip in cold water. This forms thin ice over the fish. Return to the freezer; repeat process until the ice glaze is 0.5cm (¼ inch) thick. Wrap in plastic wrap and support with a thin board. Seal, label and freeze.

Storage time: 3 months.

To thaw: Leave to thaw in a cool place for up to 24 hours. Once thawed, use promptly.

PERSIMMON
Persimmons are fruits that look rather similar to a large tomato. They have shiny, tough yellow to red skins. The orangey-yellow flesh is soft and juicy when ripe, with a refreshing, sharp flavour.

To freeze: Persimmons should be soft and ripe for freezing. Wash and dry fruit, remove stem ends, then peel. Pack, either whole or quartered, in cold syrup (see page 17) made with 450g (1lb) sugar to 1 litre (2 pints) water, with 30ml (2 tbsp) lemon juice added. Pack in rigid containers, leaving 1cm (½ inch) headspace. Cover, label and freeze.

Storage time: 9–12 months.

To thaw: Fruit that is to be eaten without further preparation needs the gentlest possible thawing. Thaw unopened in container for 3 hours at room temperature, then use immediately. Persimmons in syrup can also be gently reheated in a saucepan.
 To thaw 450g (1lb) in the microwave, transfer to a shallow dish and microwave on HIGH for 6–8 minutes, re-arranging the fruit as it thaws.

PIE
Uncooked pastry pies freeze successfully, so prepare pastry and filling as required.

To freeze: Make large double crust pies in a foil dish or plate, or line an ordinary dish or plate with foil and use as a preformer. Make small pies in patty

Right: Carrot Cake (page 216)

tins or foil cases. Do not slit top crust of fruit pies. Freeze uncovered. When frozen, remove small or preformed pies from containers and pack all pies in foil or polythene bags. Seal, label and return to the freezer.

Prepare top crust pies in the usual way. Cut fruit into fairly small pieces and blanch if necessary; toss with sugar; or use a cold savoury filling. Cover with pastry. Do not slit crust. Use ovenproof glass or foil dishes. Wrap in foil or plastic wrap, protect the tops of pies with an inverted paper or aluminium pie plate. Overwrap, seal, label and freeze.

To freeze biscuit pie crust, shape in a sandwich tin or pie plate, lined with foil or waxed paper. Add filling if suitable. Freeze until firm, then remove from tin in foil lining and pack in a rigid container. Cover, label and return to the freezer.

Storage time: Uncooked double and top crust pies, 3 months; biscuit pie crust, 2 months.

To thaw: Unwrap unbaked fruit pies and place, still frozen, in the oven at 220°C (425°F) mark 7 for 40–60 minutes, according to type and size. Slit tops of double crust pies when beginning to thaw. (Ovenproof glass should first stand for 10 minutes at room temperature.) Add a few minutes to the cooking time. Unwrap top crust pies, place in a preheated oven and bake, allowing extra time. Cut a vent in the pastry when it begins to thaw. For filled biscuit pie crust, thaw at room temperature for 6 hours. Serve cold.

To thaw in the microwave, remove from foil wrapping or containers. Microwave savoury pies on LOW for 5–7 minutes and stand for 10–15 minutes. Microwave sweet pies on LOW for 1–2 minutes and stand for 10–15 minutes. Pies are best cooked conventionally.

PIKE
Pike is a freshwater fish that is rarely available from fishmongers – it is an angler's fish. Pike should be frozen within 12 hours of being caught.

To freeze: Wash, remove scales and gut (see page 15). Wrap small fish in polythene bags. Seal, label and freeze. For large fish, place unwrapped in the freezer until solid. Remove and dip in cold water. This forms thin ice over the fish. Return to the freezer; repeat process until the ice glaze is 0.5cm (¼ inch) thick. Wrap in plastic wrap and support with a thin board. Seal, label and return to the freezer.

Storage time: 3 months.

To thaw: Cook small fish from frozen. Allow larger fish to thaw for several hours before cooking. Once thawed, use promptly. To thaw small pike in the microwave, microwave on LOW for 4–6 minutes per 450g (1lb). Allow to stand for 15 minutes after every 5–6 minutes.

PILCHARD
These small, round, oily fish are called sardine when small and young, and pilchard when larger and mature. They must be really fresh for freezing – ideally they should be frozen within 12 hours of being caught.

To freeze: Wash, remove scales and gut (see page 15). Wrap pilchards in polythene bags. Seal, label and freeze.

Storage time: 2 months.

To thaw: Can be cooked from frozen. To thaw in the microwave, arrange in a circle with tails towards the centre and microwave on LOW for 2–3 minutes per 225g (8oz). Allow to stand for 5 minutes after every 2–3 minutes.

PINEAPPLE
Only freeze good quality ripe fruit. Look for fruits with skins that are blemish-free with stiff, green, leafy tops.

To freeze: Peel and core, then slice, dice, crush or cut into wedges. Freeze by one of the following methods. (a) Pack unsweetened in containers, separated by non-stick paper. (b) Cold syrup pack (see page 17), made with 450g (1lb) sugar to 1 litre (2 pints) water, in rigid containers; include any pineapple juice from preparation. (c) Pack the crushed pineapple in rigid containers, allowing 100g (4oz) sugar to about 350g (12oz) fruit. Cover, label and freeze.

Storage time: Unsweetened and crushed, 6–8 months; in syrup pack or sugar, 9–12 months.

To thaw: Fruit that is to be eaten without further preparation needs the gentlest possible thawing. Thaw unopened in container for 3 hours at room temperature, then use immediately. To serve hot, pineapple in syrup can be gently reheated in a saucepan.

PLAICE

These flat fish are easily recognised by their skin which is creamy in colour on the underside and grey-brown with orange or red spots on the upper side. They are sold whole or as fillets.

To freeze: Wash, remove scales and gut (see page 15). Wrap small plaice in polythene bags. Seal, label and freeze. For larger plaice, place fish unwrapped in the freezer until solid. Remove and dip in cold water. This forms thin ice over the fish. Return to the freezer; repeat process until the ice glaze is 0.5cm (¼ inch) thick. Wrap in plastic wrap and support with a thin board. Separate fillets with a double layer of plastic wrap, then overwrap in foil or plastic wrap. Seal, label and freeze.

Storage time: 3 months.

To thaw: Cook small whole fish from frozen. Allow larger fish to thaw in a cool place for several hours. Once thawed, use promptly. Fillets can be cooked from frozen. To thaw small whole plaice in the microwave, microwave on LOW for 3–4 minutes per 450g (1lb) plus 2–3 minutes. Allow to stand for 5 minutes after each 2 minutes. Finish thawing in a bowl of cold water for 30 minutes with the fish still in its wrapping.

PLUM

There are many varieties of plum to choose from for freezing – either home grown or imported. Select fresh ones which feel firm and avoid any bruised or split fruit.

To freeze: Wash, halve and discard stones. Freeze in syrup made with 450g (1lb) sugar to 1 litre (2 pints) water, with the juice of 1 lemon added. Pack in rigid containers. Do not open container until required as the fruit loses colour rapidly. Cover, label and freeze.

Storage time: 9–12 months.

To thaw: Fruit that is to be eaten without further preparation needs the gentlest possible thawing. Thaw unopened in container for 3 hours at room temperature, then use immediately. Plums in syrup can be gently reheated in a saucepan. To thaw in the microwave, put plums in syrup in a dish, cover and microwave on HIGH for 4–8 minutes per 450g (1lb), breaking up the block as it thaws and stirring once or twice.

PORK

Use good quality, fresh pork. The lean part should be pale pink, moist and slightly marbled with fat. There should be a good outer layer of firm, white fat with a thin elastic skin. Removing bones will save space in the freezer. Joints can be roasted and frozen for serving cold, but take care not to overcook them. Reheated whole joints are not very satisfactory. Sliced and frozen cooked meat tends to be dry when reheated.

To freeze: Pack carefully in heavy-duty polythene bags. Group in similar types, placing non-stick paper between individual chops. Overwrap with mutton cloth, stockinette, thin polythene or newspaper, to protect against puncturing and loss of quality. If freezing a cooked joint, best results are achieved by freezing the whole joint, but small pieces can be sliced and packed in polythene if required to serve cold, or put in foil containers (or plastic if thawing in the microwave) and covered with gravy if to be served hot. Cover or seal, label and freeze.

Storage time: Raw, 6 months; cooked and sliced with gravy, 3 months; without gravy, 2 months.

To thaw/cook: Joints up to 2.7kg (6lb) can be cooked from frozen. Cooking times for frozen joints over this weight are difficult to calculate, so to prevent the outside being overcooked before the inside is thawed, it is better to thaw large joints before cooking. For joints on the bone weighing 1.8–2.7kg (4–6lb), roast at 180°C (350°F) mark 4 for 45 minutes per 450g (1lb) plus 45 minutes, thermometer reading 88°C (190°F), for well done.

Rolled joints, whether stuffed or not, must be thawed before cooking (see page 18). Chops, cubed and minced meat for stews and kebabs can be cooked from frozen. Start the cooking at a lower temperature than normal and cook for almost twice as long, increasing the temperature halfway through the cooking.

It will probably be necessary to thaw meat for frying if it has become mis-shapen during frozen storage to ensure good contact with the frying pan.

If leaving to thaw, joints of less than 1.4kg (3lb) take 6–8 hours per 450g (1lb) in the refrigerator, 1–2 hours per 450g (1lb) at room temperature. Joints over 1.4kg (3lb) take 14 hours per 450g (1lb) in the refrigerator, 2–3 hours per 450g (1lb) at room temperature. Chops take 5–6 hours in the refrigerator, 2–3 hours at room temperature.

Partial thawing is necessary if food is to be
egg-and-breadcrumbed before cooking.

To thaw cooked meat, thaw in the wrapping and
allow about 4 hours per 450g (1lb) at room
temperature, or double that time in the
refrigerator. Sliced meat requires less time.

To thaw in the microwave (see page 31),
microwave on LOW for 7–8 minutes per 450g (1lb)
for boned, rolled joints. Turn over regularly during
thawing and leave to rest if the meat shows signs of
cooking. Allow to stand for 1 hour. For joints on
the bone, microwave as above. The meat will still
be icy in the centre but will complete thawing if left
to stand for 1 hour.

For tenderloin and chops, microwave on LOW for
8–10 minutes per 450g (1lb). Allow to stand for 10
minutes. Separate chops during thawing and
arrange 'spoke' fashion. Allow to stand for 10
minutes.

POUSSIN

A poussin is a young chicken between 4–6 weeks
old. It usually weighs up to 450g (1lb). Allow one
poussin per person.

To freeze: Use fresh poussin only. Prepare in the
usual way (see page 14). Do not stuff before
freezing. Cover protruding bones with non-stick
paper. Pack trussed bird tightly in a polythene bag.
Seal, label and freeze.

Storage time: 12 months.

To thaw: Leave to thaw overnight in wrapping in
the refrigerator. To thaw in the microwave, thaw
the bird in its freezer wrapping which should be
pierced first and any metal tag removed.
Microwave on LOW for 5–7 minutes per 450g (1lb).

POTATO

Maincrop and new potatoes are suitable for freezing
in cooked or partially-cooked form.

To freeze: Potatoes are best frozen in the cooked
form, as partially-cooked chips, croquettes or
duchesse potatoes. Prepare croquette or duchesse
potatoes in the normal way. Open freeze until solid,
then pack into polythene bags. Seal, label and
freeze. Soak chipped potatoes in cold water for
about 30 minutes. Drain and dry. Part-fry in deep
fat for 2 minutes. Cool, then open freeze until solid.
Pack in polythene bags. Seal, label and freeze.

New potatoes for freezing should be small and

even-sized. Scrape, cook fully and cool. Pack in
polythene bags or rigid containers. Cover or seal,
label and freeze.

Storage time: Croquette and duchesse potatoes,
3 months; partially-cooked chips, 6 months; new
potatoes, 3 months.

To thaw: Thaw croquette potatoes for about 1 hour
at room temperature, then deep fry or bake. Glaze
duchesse potatoes with beaten egg and reheat from
frozen. Deep fry chips from frozen. Thaw new
potatoes for 1 hour at room temperature before
reheating.

To thaw croquette potatoes in the microwave,
arrange in a single layer and microwave on LOW for
4–6 minutes per 450g (1lb), re-arranging during
cooking. New potatoes can be cooked from frozen.
Arrange in a shallow serving dish and microwave on
HIGH for 5–7 minutes per 450g (1lb), re-arranging
during cooking.

PRAWN

Only very fresh prawns are suitable for freezing –
they should be frozen within 12 hours of being
caught.

To freeze: Prawns may be frozen raw or cooked. To
freeze raw prawns, remove heads, wash well in
salted water, then drain. Pack in polythene bags.
Seal, label and freeze. To cook prawns for freezing,
wash prawns well and cook in lightly salted, boiling
water until pink; cool in the liquor. Shell, if wished.
Pack tightly in polythene bags. Seal, label and
freeze.

Storage time: 1 month.

To thaw: Cook raw prawns from frozen or thaw for
several hours in a cool place, then cook promptly.
Thaw cooked, frozen prawns in refrigerator to use
cold in salads and cocktails, or cook from frozen in
hot dishes. To thaw in the microwave, pierce the
bag and microwave on LOW for 2½ minutes per
100g (4oz). Allow to stand for 2 minutes.
Microwave 225g (8oz) for 3–4 minutes; separate
and arrange in a circle as soon as possible, then
cover with absorbent kitchen paper. Allow to stand
for 2 minutes, then plunge into cold water and
drain.

Right: Chocolate and Orange Cake (page 213)

PUMPKIN

This delicious vegetable is not always available in the shops, so it is well worth freezing some to enjoy at a later date.

To freeze: Wash, cut into manageable-sized pieces and peel. Remove seeds and stringy parts, then slice or cut into cubes. Steam or boil until tender. Drain and dry, then mash. Cool and pack in rigid containers, leaving headspace. Cover, label and freeze.

Storage time: 6–8 months.

To thaw: Cook from frozen in a double boiler or heavy saucepan. Use as a vegetable with seasonings and butter, or use to make soups or as a filling for pumpkin pies.

QUINCE

This aromatic fruit is generally used for making preserves, such as jellies and jams. It also adds flavour and interest to apple and pear pies as it turns an attractive pink colour when cooked.

To freeze: Peel, quarter and core quinces. Cut into small chunks. Blanch for 2 minutes (see page 16). To blanch in the microwave, put in a dish with 45ml (3 tbsp) water, cover and microwave on HIGH for 2–3 minutes per 450g (1lb). Drain, cool and pack in small quantities in polythene bags. Seal, label and freeze.

Storage time: 12 months.

To thaw: Cook from frozen with a little sugar and water until tender, then use as required. To thaw in the microwave, arrange quince in a shallow container, cover and microwave on HIGH for 4–8 minutes per 450g (1lb).

RABBIT (See GAME)

RED SNAPPER

This round fish has a distinctive red skin and delicious white flesh. It is usually sold whole, but steaks and fillets are also available. Check when buying from the fishmonger that it has not been frozen already, as re-freezing is not recommended.

To freeze: Wash, remove scales and gut (see page 15). Wrap small whole fish in polythene bags. Seal, label and freeze. For large whole fish, place fish unwrapped in the freezer until solid. Remove and dip in cold water. This forms thin ice over the fish. Return to the freezer; repeat process until the ice glaze is 0.5cm (¼ inch) thick. Wrap in plastic wrap and support with a thin board. Separate steaks and fillets with a double layer of plastic wrap, then overwrap in foil or plastic wrap. Seal, label and freeze.

Storage time: 3 months.

To thaw: Allow whole fish to thaw in a cool place for up to 24 hours. Once thawed, use promptly. Steaks and fillets can be cooked from frozen. To thaw steaks and fillets in the microwave, microwave on LOW for 3–4 minutes per 450g (1lb) plus 2–3 minutes. Allow to stand for 5 minutes after each 2 minutes.

RHUBARB

Forced or early rhubarb has tender pink stalks and is delicately flavoured; maincrop rhubarb is tougher with a stronger flavour. Avoid limp stalks when buying rhubarb.

To freeze: Wash, trim off leaves and stalk bases, then cut into 1–2.5cm (½–1 inch) lengths. Blanch for 1 minute and cool quickly. Freeze by (a) Dry pack to use later for pies and crumbles. (b) Cold syrup pack (see page 17), made with 450g (1lb) sugar to 1 litre (2 pints) water. Pack in rigid containers. Cover, label and freeze.

Storage time: Syrup pack, 9–12 months; dry pack, 6–8 months.

To thaw: Rhubarb in syrup can be gently reheated in a saucepan until thawed, then cooked as wished. Dry pack rhubarb can be either partially thawed at room temperature for pies and crumbles or cooked gently from frozen with sugar to taste and a little water. To thaw in the microwave, spread out fruit in a single layer in a dish, cover and microwave on HIGH for 7–8 minutes per 450g (1lb), re-arranging carefully during thawing.

ROE

Cod's roe, smoked cod's roe and herring roe should all be really fresh for freezing. Do not freeze uncooked roe from the fishmonger – these have usually already been frozen. Only freeze roe from freshly caught fish.

To freeze: Slice fresh cooked cod's roe about 1cm (½ inch) thick. Separate slices with a double layer of plastic wrap and pack in rigid containers. Seal, label and freeze. Pack smoked cod's roe whole tightly in polythene bags and exclude as much air as possible. If liked, make into taramasalata and pack in rigid containers. For soft and hard herring roe, wash well, drain and dry on absorbent kitchen paper. Pack in rigid containers. Cover or seal, label and freeze.

Storage time: Cooked cod's roe, 1 month; herring roe, 2 months; smoked cod's roe and taramasalata, 3 months.

To thaw: Leave to thaw for 2 hours at room temperature. Once thawed, cook promptly. To thaw in the microwave, microwave on LOW for 2–3 minutes per 100g (4oz), 3–4 minutes per 225g (8oz).

SALMON
This king of fish must be really fresh for freezing – ideally within 12 hours of being caught.

To freeze: Wash, remove scales and gut (see page 15). Place whole fish unwrapped in the freezer until solid. Remove and dip in cold water. This forms thin ice over the fish. Return to the freezer; repeat process until the ice glaze is 0.5cm (¼ inch) thick. Wrap in plastic wrap and support with a thin board. Separate steaks with a double layer of plastic wrap, then overwrap in foil or plastic wrap. Seal, label and freeze.

To freeze smoked salmon, check that it has not already been frozen – as re-heating is not recommended. Freeze smoked salmon slices separated with double layers of plastic wrap or non-stick paper. Overwrap in foil or plastic wrap.

Storage time: Fresh salmon, 2 months; smoked salmon, 2–3 months.

To thaw: Allow whole fish to thaw in a cool place for 24 hours. Once thawed, use promptly. Salmon steaks can be cooked from frozen. Allow smoked salmon slices to thaw at room temperature for 30–60 minutes. To thaw salmon steaks in the microwave, microwave on LOW for 3–4 minutes per 450g (1lb).

SALSIFY
This root vegetable has a delicate oyster-like flavour. Choose only young, tender roots for freezing.

To freeze: Scrub roots well, but do not peel. Blanch for 2 minutes (see page 16). To blanch in the microwave, put in a dish with 45ml (3 tbsp) water, cover and microwave on HIGH for 2–3 minutes, according to the thickness of the root. Cut into 5–7.5cm (2–3 inch) lengths and peel while still warm. Cool, then pack in polythene bags. Seal, label and freeze.

Storage time: 10–12 months.

To thaw/cook: Cook from frozen, by steaming or in boiling water, until tender. Toss in melted butter or coat in a white sauce. To thaw/cook in the microwave, put salsify into a dish with 45ml (3 tbsp) water, cover and microwave on HIGH for 9–10 minutes per 450g (1lb).

SARDINE
Sardines are small, immature pilchards. They must be really fresh for freezing – ideally within 12 hours of being caught.

To freeze: Wipe fish with a damp cloth; cut off heads just below gills and squeeze out entrails. Rinse well, drain and dry on absorbent kitchen paper. Wrap closely in polythene bags. Seal, label and freeze.

Storage time: 2 months.

To thaw: Cook from frozen. To thaw in the microwave, arrange in a circle, tails towards the centre, and microwave on LOW for 2–3 minutes per 225g (8oz). Allow to stand for 5 minutes after every 2–3 minutes.

SATSUMA
A small type of orange similar to a tangerine, but without pips.

To freeze: Peel, remove pith and separate into segments. Freeze by one of the following methods (a) Cold syrup pack (see page 17), made with 450g (1lb) sugar to 1 litre (2 pints) water; add any juice from the fruit to the syrup. (b) Dry sugar pack, using 225g (8oz) sugar to 450g (1lb) fruit. Sprinkle sugar over fruit and when juices start to run, pack in rigid containers. (c) Squeeze out and freeze the juice. Add sugar if liked. Freeze in small quantities in containers or in ice-cube trays. (d) Grate rind and mix with a little sugar. Pack in containers. Cover or seal, label and freeze.

Storage time: Syrup pack or dry sugar pack, 9–12 months; as juice or grated rind, 4–6 months.

To thaw: Fruit that is to be eaten without further preparation needs the gentlest possible thawing. Thaw unopened in containers for 3 hours at room temperature, then use immediately. Satsumas in syrup can be gently reheated in a saucepan. Thaw juice for several hours at room temperature; thaw and use satsuma rind and sugar mix as liked.

SAUCES

Sauces, such as a basic white type, bolognese, cranberry, curry, apple and bread sauce, are all useful stand-bys to have in the freezer.

To freeze: When cold, pack useful quantities of sauce into rigid containers, leaving headspace. Cover, label and freeze.

For convenience, when only a small amount of sauce is needed at any one time, make up a well flavoured curry, tomato, espagnole or other sauce. Cool and pour into ice-cube trays. Freeze unwrapped until solid, divide into cubes and freeze in polythene bags. Seal, label and freeze.

Storage time: White sauce, bolognese, curry and bread sauces, 3 months; apple and cranberry sauces, 12 months.

To thaw: Thaw larger quantities for 1–2 hours at room temperature before reheating, or heat gently from frozen until boiling point is reached. Beat sauces well during reheating, adding a little extra liquid if necessary. To thaw small cubes of sauce, select the number of cubes required and reheat slowly with a little extra liquid if necessary. To thaw in the microwave, dip base of container into hot water to loosen sauce. Turn sauce into a bowl. Cover and microwave on HIGH until sauce begins to bubble around the edges, breaking up the sauce with a fork during thawing. Stir well and continue microwaving on HIGH, stirring several times during thawing, until piping hot. Thawing times will vary.

SAUSAGEMEAT AND SAUSAGES

Only freeze fresh sausagemeat and sausages.

To freeze: Pack sausagemeat or sausages in polythene bags in useful 225g (8oz) or 450g (1lb) quantities. Seal, label and freeze.

Storage time: 3 months.

To thaw: Bake large sausages from frozen at 180°C (350°F) mark 4 for 1 hour, or grill for 20 minutes, starting at a low temperature and turning occasionally during cooking. For small chipolata sausages, bake at 180°C (350°F) mark 4 for 45 minutes, or grill for 15 minutes. Frozen sausages tend to split when fried. Thaw sausagemeat for several hours in the refrigerator and use as required. To thaw sausagemeat and sausages in the microwave, microwave on LOW for 5–6 minutes per 450g (1lb). Separate sausages during thawing; break up sausagemeat with a fork during thawing. Allow to stand for 5 minutes.

SCALLOP

Only freeze scallops if really fresh – ideally within 12 hours of being caught.

To freeze: Scallops may be frozen raw or as a cooked dish. Scrub outside of shells well. Put scallops into a hot oven for a few minutes; remove immediately shells open. Discard black fringe around scallops. Remove scallop and orange roe from shell. Rinse well, drain and pat dry. Pack in rigid containers. Cover, label and freeze.

Storage time: 1 month.

To thaw: Cook from frozen. If scallops are to be coated with egg and crumbs, allow to thaw for several hours in refrigerator before cooking. Once thawed, use promptly. To thaw in the microwave, pierce wrapping and microwave on LOW for 2–3 minutes for 100g (4oz), 3–4 minutes for 225g (8oz); stir and break apart during thawing and as soon as possible arrange in a circle and cover with absorbent kitchen paper. Allow to stand for 2 minutes, then plunge into cold water. Drain and dry.

SCAMPI

These large prawns are generally available all year. They must be really fresh for freezing.

To freeze: Best results are achieved when scampi is frozen raw and unshelled. Twist off head and carapace with legs and claws attached. Rinse tails under cold running water. Drain and dry on absorbent kitchen paper. Pack tightly in polythene bags. Seal, label and freeze.

Storage time: 1 month.

Right: Coconut Chocolate Cookies (page 215)

To thaw/cook: Cook from frozen in small quantities. Drop scampi tails (a few at a time) into a pan of boiling, salted water, then allow the water to return to the boil. Simmer for 4–6 minutes according to size. To thaw in the microwave, put scampi into a dish and pierce wrapping. Microwave on LOW for 2½ minutes per 100g (4oz). Allow to stand for 2 minutes. Microwave 225g (8oz) scampi for 3–4 minutes. Separate with a fork after 2 minutes. Allow to stand for 2 minutes, then plunge into cold water. Drain and pat dry.

SCONE
Scones are an indispensable item to have in the freezer.

To freeze: Allow freshly baked scones to cool, then freeze in polythene bags in convenient numbers for serving. Seal, label and freeze.

Storage time: 3 months.

To thaw: Cook tea scones from frozen, wrapped in foil, at 200°C (400°F) mark 6 for 10 minutes. Thaw girdle scones for 1 hour at room temperature. Thaw drop scones for 30 minutes, or cover and bake for 10 minutes. To thaw in the microwave, place scones on absorbent kitchen paper on a plate. Microwave on LOW for 15–20 seconds for 2 scones, and 25–35 seconds for 4 scones; time carefully. Allow to stand for 2–3 minutes.

SEA BASS
Sea bass is a round fish which makes an excellent dinner party dish. It can be poached or stuffed and baked whole. It is available whole or as steaks and fillets.

To freeze: Wash, remove scales and gut (see page 15). Place whole fish unwrapped in the freezer until solid. Remove and dip in cold water. This forms thin ice over the fish. Return to the freezer; repeat process until the ice glaze is 0.5cm (¼ inch) thick. Wrap in plastic wrap and support with a thin board. Separate steaks and fillets with a double layer of plastic wrap, then overwrap in foil or plastic wrap. Seal, label and freeze.

Storage time: 3 months.

To thaw: Allow whole fish to thaw in a cool place for up to 24 hours. Once thawed, use promptly. Steaks and fillets can be cooked from frozen. To thaw steaks and fillets in the microwave, microwave on LOW for 3–4 minutes per 450g (1lb) plus 2–3 minutes. Allow to stand for 5 minutes after each 2 minutes.

SHALLOT
This mild flavoured member of the onion family is a useful addition to many dishes and well worth keeping in the freezer.

To freeze: Shallots can be peeled and left whole or finely chopped as liked. Blanch chopped shallots for 2 minutes and whole shallots for 4 minutes (see page 16). To blanch in the microwave, put in a dish with 60ml (4 tbsp) water, cover and microwave on HIGH for 4–5 minutes. Cool, drain and pack in small containers. Cover and overwrap with plastic wrap to prevent the smell filtering out. Label and freeze.

Storage time: 6 months.

To thaw: Use chopped shallots from frozen in soups, sauces and casseroles. Whole shallots may be used from frozen in casseroles or as required in recipes. To thaw/cook whole shallots in the microwave, put in a dish with 90ml (4 tbsp) water. Cover and microwave on HIGH for 2–3 minutes per 100g (4oz), stirring halfway. Stand for 2–3 minutes.

SHELLFISH (See individual names)

SHRIMP (See PRAWN)

SKATE
Skate is a large, flat, kite-shaped fish. Only the wings (side parts) and nuggets of flesh known as 'nobs' are eaten. They are usually sold already cut from the body.

To freeze: Wrap individual portions in a double layer of plastic wrap, then pack in polythene bags. Seal, label and freeze.

Storage time: 3 months.

To thaw: Can be cooked from frozen. To thaw in the microwave, microwave on LOW for 3–4 minutes per 450g (1lb) plus 2–3 minutes. Allow to stand for 5 minutes after each 2 minutes.

SMOKED SALMON (See SALMON)

SOFT FRUIT (See BERRY)

SOUP

Soups freeze very successfully.

To freeze: Make soup (see pages 84–89), then cool. Pour into rigid containers, leaving headspace. Cover, label and freeze. Remember that soup in concentrated form takes up less room and can be diluted with stock, milk or cream after thawing.

Storage time: 3 months.

To thaw: Either thaw soup for 1–2 hours at room temperature or heat immediately until boiling point is reached, stirring frequently. Dilute as necessary. To thaw in the microwave, dip base of container into hot water to loosen soup. Turn soup into a bowl. Cover and microwave on HIGH for 10–12 minutes for each 300ml (½ pint) or until soup begins to bubble round edges, breaking mixture up with a fork during thawing. Stir well and continue microwaving on HIGH until piping hot; stir several times during thawing. Thawing times vary according to the density of the soup.

SORBET

Either home-made or bought sorbet can be stored in the freezer.

To freeze: See recipe for Lemon Sorbet, page 207.

Storage time: Home-made and commercially-made, 2–3 months.

To thaw: Place sorbet in the refrigerator for a short time, about 10–15 minutes, to soften a little before serving. Some 'soft' bought sorbets can be used straight from the freezer, provided they have not been kept in the coldest part.

SPINACH

As spinach wilts quickly, buy fresh young leaves.

To freeze: Wash spinach very thoroughly under cold running water, then strip leaves off stalks. Blanch for 2 minutes (see page 16). To blanch in the microwave, put 450g (1lb) in a dish with no extra water, cover and microwave on HIGH for 3–3½ minutes. Cool quickly and press out excess moisture; or purée. Pack in rigid containers or polythene bags. Cover or seal, label and freeze.

Storage time: Leaf spinach, 10–12 months; puréed, 6–8 months.

To thaw: Reheat gently from frozen in a heavy saucepan, stirring and breaking up frequently. To thaw/cook in the microwave, microwave on HIGH for 7–9 minutes per 275g (10oz) for leaf or puréed; break apart during cooking. Do not add water.

SPRING GREENS (See CABBAGE)

SQUID

Whole squid, bought from the fishmonger, must be really fresh for freezing. Check that it has not already been frozen, as re-freezing is not recommended.

To freeze: Pull head and attachments out of body sac of squid; reserve body sac. Cut across head just above eyes; discard everything below this and reserve tentacles. Wash sac and tentacles under cold running water; remove small polyp from centre of tentacles and transparent fin from sac. Squeeze out sac to clean; rinse well. Pull away skin from sac and discard. Cut sac into thin rings; leave tentacles whole or halve if large. Drain and dry on absorbent kitchen paper. Pack in rigid containers or polythene bags. Cover or seal, label and freeze.

Storage time: 3 months.

To thaw: Cook from frozen. If squid is to be coated with egg and crumbs, allow to thaw for several hours in a cool place before cooking. Once thawed, use promptly. To thaw in the microwave, microwave on LOW for 4–5 minutes per 450g (1lb). Allow to stand for 30 minutes.

STAR FRUIT

This attractive fruit, also known as carambola and star apple, is now widely available from greengrocers and supermarkets.

To freeze: Thinly trim tough ridges off fruit, if liked. Slice fruit thinly and remove the seeds. Brush slices with lemon juice to prevent discoloration. Pack slices in cold syrup (see page 17), made with 450g (1lb) sugar to 1 litre (2 pints) water, with the juice of 1 lemon added. Pack in rigid containers, leaving 1cm (½ inch) headspace. Cover, label and freeze.

Storage time: 9–12 months.

To thaw: Fruit that is to be eaten without further preparation needs the gentlest possible thawing.

Thaw unopened in container for 3 hours at room temperature, then use immediately. Star fruit in syrup can be gently reheated from frozen in a saucepan.

STOCK

Making good quality stock is a simple affair, particularly if you use a pressure cooker. It is well worth keeping a supply in the freezer. Even chicken bones, with skin, giblets, etc, are worth converting into a jellied stock. Cooked meat bones, browned carrot, onion and celery, bacon rinds and mushroom peelings make a very useful concentrated stock. Or you can start from scratch with raw beef and veal bones.

Incidentally, the freezer is the ideal place to store a few odd trimmings and bones left when you have prepared or carved a bird, to wait until you have enough accumulated, or enough time, to turn them into stock.

To freeze: Cool the prepared stock. Pour into rigid containers or ice-cube trays – useful when only a small amount is needed – or use polythene bags fitted into a regular-shaped container with straight sides. Freeze until solid. Ease the bag out of the preformer. Seal, label and freeze.

Storage time: 6 months.

To thaw: Leave to thaw for 1–2 hours at room temperature or heat immediately until boiling point is reached. Add frozen cubes of stock to soups, casseroles, etc. To thaw in the microwave, dip base of container into hot water to loosen stock. Turn stock into a bowl. Cover and microwave on HIGH until stock begins to bubble around edges; breaking up mixture with a fork during thawing. Stir well and continue microwaving on HIGH until piping hot, stirring several times during thawing.

STRAWBERRY

Frozen whole strawberries become mushy on thawing, although they do make excellent purée for serving with ice cream or pancakes, or for making mousses, sorbets and ice creams.

To freeze: Choose firm, clean, dry fruit. Remove hulls. Freeze by one of the following methods (a) Dry pack (see page 16). (b) Dry sugar pack, adding 100g (4oz) sugar to each 450g (1lb) fruit (see page 16). Pack in polythene bags. (c) Purée; add a little lemon juice and sweeten to taste – about 50g (2oz)

per 225g (8oz) purée – and freeze in small containers, leave headspace. Cover or seal, label and freeze.

Storage time: Dry sugar pack, 9–12 months; dry pack or as purée, 6–8 months.

To thaw: Fruit that is to be eaten without further preparation needs the gentlest possible thawing. Thaw unopened in container for 3 hours at room temperature, then use immediately. Puréed strawberries can be gently reheated in a saucepan to serve hot.

SWEDE

Use small, young swedes for freezing.

To freeze: Wash, peel and dice. Blanch for 2 minutes (see page 16). To blanch in the microwave, put 450g (1lb) swede in a dish with 45ml (3 tbsp) water, cover and microwave on HIGH for 3–4 minutes. Cool, pack in suitable quantities for requirements, in polythene bags or rigid containers. If liked, cook swede completely and purée. Cool and pack in rigid containers. Cover or seal, label and freeze.

Storage time: Diced, 10–12 months; puréed, 6–8 months.

To thaw: Cook diced swede from frozen in boiling water for 8–12 minutes, or until tender. Add diced frozen swede to stews and casseroles during cooking. Allow puréed swede to thaw at room temperature for 2–3 hours or reheat gently in a double boiler or heavy saucepan. Add butter and seasoning before serving. To thaw/cook in the microwave, microwave on LOW for 6–7 minutes per 225g (8oz), 8–10 minutes for 450g (1lb). Stir or shake during cooking.

SWEET POTATO

Sweet potato is best frozen par-cooked or fully cooked.

To freeze: Wash, peel and prepare in one of the following ways: (a) Cut into 1cm (½ inch) slices; par-boil, drain and cool. (b) Halve and boil until barely tender. Cool in iced water, drain and pat dry. (c) Cook fully until tender; purée. Pack in polythene bags or rigid containers. Cover or seal, label and freeze.

Right: Honey Cake (page 217)

Storage time: 6 months.

To thaw: Reheat and finish cooking from frozen. Allow puréed sweet potato to thaw for 2–3 hours at room temperature or heat gently in a double boiler or heavy saucepan. To thaw/cook in the microwave, microwave on HIGH for 4–6 minutes per 450g (1lb).

SWEETCORN

Sweetcorn kernels freeze well. Choose only fresh, young cobs with tender kernels.

To freeze: Remove husks and 'silks' from cobs. Blanch small cobs for 4 minutes, medium cobs for 6 minutes or large cobs for 8 minutes (see page 16). To blanch in the microwave, put in a dish with 45ml (3 tbsp) water, cover and microwave on HIGH for 3, 4 and 5 minutes respectively. Cool and dry on absorbent kitchen paper. Scrape off the kernels with a knife and spread on a tray. Open freeze until hard. Pack frozen kernels in polythene bags. Seal, label and freeze.

Storage time: 10–12 months.

To thaw/cook: Cook from frozen in boiling water for about 5 minutes or until tender. To thaw/cook in the microwave, put kernels into a dish with 30ml (2 tbsp) water, cover and microwave on HIGH for 7–8 minutes per 450g (1lb), stirring once halfway through cooking. Allow to stand for 2–3 minutes.

SWORDFISH

Swordfish must be really fresh for freezing. Check that it has not already been frozen, as re-freezing is not recommended.

To freeze: Wipe swordfish steaks or fillets and pat dry on absorbent kitchen paper. Separate steaks or fillets with a double layer of plastic wrap, then overwrap. Seal, label and freeze.

Storage time: 2 months.

To thaw: Cook steaks and fillets from frozen. To thaw steaks in the microwave, microwave on LOW for 3–4 minutes per 450g (1lb) plus 2–3 minutes. Allow to stand for 5 minutes after each 2 minutes.

TANGERINE

Tangerines are a small type of orange similar to a satsuma, but with pips. See SATSUMA.

TEABREAD

Useful to have in the freezer for busy weekends or during school holidays, so next time you are baking teabread, double the quantity and freeze one. Shop-bought teabreads also freeze well.

To freeze: Bake in the usual way (see recipe for Spiced Pecan and Apple Loaf, page 218). Cool, then pack in a polythene bag or wrap securely in foil. If liked, cut the teabread into slices, putting a piece of non-stick paper between the slices. Pack the sliced teabread in a polythene bag. Seal, label and freeze.

Storage time: 3 months.

To thaw: Leave to thaw in wrapping at room temperature for 2–3 hours. For sliced teabread, simply remove a slice as required and thaw for about 30 minutes. To thaw slices of teabread in the microwave, place on absorbent kitchen paper on a plate. Microwave on LOW for 15–20 seconds for 2 slices and 25–35 seconds for 4 slices. Allow to stand for 2–3 minutes.

TOMATO

Although frozen tomatoes will collapse into pulp once thawed, so are not suitable for salads, they are ideal for cooking purposes.

To freeze: Cover tomatoes with boiling water for a few seconds. Drain, then peel off skins. Cool and pack in rigid containers or polythene bags. Cover or seal, label and freeze. Tomatoes are most useful if frozen as purée. Skin (as above) and core tomatoes. Simmer in their own juice for 5 minutes until soft. Rub through a nylon sieve or purée in a blender. Cool, then pack in small containers, leaving headspace. Cover, label and freeze.

Storage time: Whole, 10–12 months; purée, 6–8 months.

To thaw: Cook whole tomatoes from frozen, adding them to soups, stews and casseroles during cooking. Thaw purée in container for 2–3 hours at room temperature. Use as required in soups, sauces and cooked dishes. To thaw in the microwave, microwave on LOW for 5–6 minutes per 450g (1lb).

TROUT

Trout must be really fresh for freezing – ideally within 12 hours of being caught.

To freeze: Wash, remove scales and gut (see page 15). Wrap small trout closely in polythene bags. Seal, label and freeze. Place large rainbow trout unwrapped in the freezer until solid. Remove and dip in cold water. This forms thin ice over the fish. Return to the freezer; repeat process until the ice glaze is 0.5cm (¼ inch) thick. Wrap in plastic wrap and support with a thin board. Seal, label and return to the freezer.

Storage time: 2 months.

To thaw: Cook small trout from frozen. Allow large rainbow trout to thaw for up to 24 hours in a cool place before cooking. Once thawed, use promptly. To thaw small trout in the microwave, microwave on LOW for 4–6 minutes per 450g (1lb). Allow to stand for 5 minutes after each 2–3 minutes.

TUNA
Fresh tuna is becoming more widely available; it is usually sold as steaks. It must be really fresh for freezing; check that it has not been frozen already, as re-freezing is not recommended.

To freeze: Wipe tuna steaks and pat dry on absorbent kitchen paper. Separate steaks with a double layer of plastic wrap, then overwrap in foil or plastic wrap. Seal, label and freeze.

Storage time: 2 months.

To thaw: Cook tuna steaks from frozen. To thaw in the microwave, microwave on LOW for 3–4 minutes per 450g (1lb) plus 2–3 minutes. Allow to stand for 5 minutes after each 2 minutes.

TURBOT
Turbot is an expensive but delicious, large flat fish with delicately flavoured flesh. It is sold whole or in fillets or steaks.

To freeze: Wash, remove scales and gut (see page 15). Place whole fish unwrapped in the freezer until solid. Remove and dip in cold water. This forms thin ice over the fish. Return to the freezer; repeat process until the ice glaze is 0.5cm (¼ inch) thick. Wrap in plastic wrap and support with a thin board. Separate fillets or steaks with a double layer of plastic wrap, then overwrap in foil or plastic wrap. Seal, label and freeze.

Storage time: 3 months.

To thaw: Allow whole fish to thaw in a cool place for up to 24 hours. Once thawed, use promptly. Fillets or steaks can be cooked from frozen. To thaw steaks or fillets in the microwave, microwave on LOW for 3–4 minutes per 450g (1lb) plus 2–3 minutes. Stand for 5 minutes after each 2 minutes.

TURKEY
Because turkeys are so bulky, they take up a lot of valuable freezer space so do not freeze for long.

To freeze: Only freeze a very fresh bird. Prepare and draw in the usual way (see Freezing poultry, page 14). Do not stuff before freezing. Cover protruding bones with non-stick paper. Pack trussed bird in a large polythene bag. Seal, label and freeze. Freeze giblets separately. Turkey can be frozen in joints, individually wrapped.

Storage time: 6 months; giblets, 3 months.

To thaw: In the light of new research, it is recommended that poultry is thawed in its wrapping at room temperature of 16–17°C (65–70°F) rather than in the refrigerator. A 6.8kg (15lb) bird takes 24 hours. To thaw a whole turkey in the microwave, thaw in the wrapping, which should be pierced first and any metal tag removed. Microwave on LOW for 10–12 minutes per 450g (1lb). Finish thawing by standing the bird, still in its bag, in cold water for 2–3 hours.

TURNIP
Use small, young turnips for freezing.

To freeze: Trim and peel. Small turnips can be left whole. Blanch for 4 minutes (see page 16). To blanch in the microwave, put in a dish with 45ml (3 tbsp) water, cover and microwave on HIGH for 3 minutes. Alternatively, cut turnips into small dice, about 1cm (½ inch), and blanch for 2½ minutes. Cool, drain and pack in rigid containers or polythene bags. Turnips may also be fully cooked and puréed. Cover or seal, label and freeze.

Storage time: Whole or diced, 10–12 months; purée, 6–8 months.

To thaw/cook: Cook blanched turnip from frozen. Gently reheat cooked purée from frozen in a heavy-based saucepan. To thaw/cook in the microwave, microwave on HIGH for 9–11 minutes per diced 450g (1lb) with 60ml (4 tbsp) water.

UGLI FRUIT (See GRAPEFRUIT)

VEAL

Use good quality, fresh veal. Use breast and shoulder for roasting; pie veal for pâtés, goulash and stews; fillet cut into escalopes for making schnitzels. Removing bones from joints will save space in the freezer; butcher in suitable quantities.

To freeze: Place non-stick paper between individual chops, steaks and escalopes. Pack in polythene bags and overwrap with mutton cloth, stockinette, thin polythene or newspaper.

Storage time: 6 months.

To thaw: Joints of less than 1.4kg (3lb) take 6–8 hours per 450g (1lb) in the refrigerator, 1–2 hours per 450g (1lb) at room temperature. Joints over 1.4kg (3lb) take 14 hours per 450g (1lb) in the refrigerator, 2–3 hours per 450g (1lb) at room temperature.

To thaw in the microwave (see page 31), microwave on LOW for 5–6 minutes per 450g (1lb) for boned, rolled joints. Turn over regularly during thawing and leave to rest if the meat shows signs of cooking. Allow to stand for 30–45 minutes. For joints on the bone, microwave as above. The meat will still be icy in the centre but will complete thawing if it is left to stand for 30–45 minutes. For minced veal and chops, microwave on LOW for 8–10 minutes per 450g (1lb). Separate chops during thawing. Allow to stand for 10 minutes.

VENISON (See GAME)

WHITEBAIT

These are the tiny, silvery fry of sprats or herring, which are eaten whole and require no gutting. They must be really fresh. If buying from the fishmonger, check that they have not already been frozen.

To freeze: Rinse in a colander under cold running water. Drain and pat dry. Open freeze. Pack in polythene bags. Seal, label and freeze.

Storage time: 2 months.

To thaw: Cook from frozen in deep fat. Alternatively, allow to thaw in a cool place for several hours. Once thawed, use promptly. To thaw in the microwave, microwave on LOW for 2–3 minutes per 100g (4oz) or 3–4 minutes per 225g (8oz).

WHITING

Whiting is a smallish fish with a pale brown to olive-green back and flaky white flesh. It is sold whole or as fillets.

To freeze: Wash, remove scales and gut (see page 15). Wrap whole fish in a polythene bag. Separate fillets with a double layer of plastic wrap, then overwrap in foil or plastic wrap. Seal, label and freeze.

Storage time: 3 months.

To thaw: Cook whole fish and fillets from frozen. To thaw fillets in the microwave, microwave on LOW for 3–4 minutes per 450g (1lb) plus 2–3 minutes. Allow to stand for 5 minutes after each 2 minutes.

WINKLE

Freezing is advisable only if winkles are frozen within 12 hours of being caught.

To freeze: Wash thoroughly. Cook in boiling water for 20 minutes, then drain. Remove winkles from shells and cool. Pack in rigid containers. Cover, label and freeze.

Storage time: 1 month.

To thaw: Leave to thaw in unopened container for 2 hours in the refrigerator. Serve cold in salads. To thaw in the microwave, microwave on LOW for 2–3 minutes per 100g (4oz), 3–4 minutes per 225g (8oz). Separate with a fork after 2 minutes.

Right: Broad Bean and Bacon Soup (page 86)

SOUPS AND STARTERS

FINNAN HADDIE SOUP

SERVES 8

700g (1½lb) finnan haddock or smoked haddock fillet

1.7 litres (3 pints) milk

1 bay leaf

50g (2oz) butter

15ml (1 tbsp) vegetable oil

100g (4oz) onion, skinned and finely chopped

50g (2oz) celery, finely chopped

450g (1lb) potatoes, peeled and finely chopped

pinch of grated nutmeg

pepper

50ml (2fl oz) single cream

chopped fresh parsley, to garnish

1 Skin and roughly chop the haddock fillet. Place in a large saucepan with the milk and bay leaf. Bring to the boil, cover and simmer gently for 15 minutes.
2 Strain the milk and reserve. Flake the fish and reserve.
3 Heat the butter and oil in a large saucepan and fry the onion, celery and potatoes until golden brown and beginning to soften.
4 Add the reserved milk, nutmeg and pepper. Bring to the boil, cover and simmer for 20–25 minutes or until the potatoes are very soft.
5 Cool slightly, then purée in a blender or food processor until smooth. Press through a fine-mesh sieve. Return the soup to the rinsed-out pan with the single cream and most of the fish. Adjust seasoning, and reheat gently. Garnish with a little of the reserved flaked fish (freeze the remainder for fishcakes) and parsley.

To Microwave
Arrange the fish in a single layer in a large shallow dish. Pour over enough of the milk to cover and add the bay leaf. Cover and microwave on HIGH for about 8 minutes or until the fish flakes easily. Complete step 2. Put the butter and oil in a large bowl with the finely chopped vegetables. Cover and microwave on HIGH for 10–15 minutes or until softened. Add all of the milk, the nutmeg and

pepper. Cover and microwave on HIGH for about 8 minutes or until boiling. Complete step 5. Transfer the soup to a serving bowl and microwave on HIGH for 5 minutes or until piping hot. Garnish.

To Freeze
Cool, pack without the fish in usable quantities in rigid containers, leaving headspace. For reheating in the microwave, pour the soup into single portion containers. Freeze for up to 3 months.

To Thaw
Leave overnight at cool room temperature.

To Serve
Reheat in a heavy-based saucepan, stirring, until boiling. Stir in the fish and heat through. Alternatively, microwave each portion on HIGH for about 10–12 minutes or until piping hot. Stir in the fish and microwave on HIGH for further 2 minutes. Garnish.

CREAM OF WATERCRESS AND CHEESE SOUP

SERVES 4

1.1 litres (2 pints) milk

slices of carrot and onion, bay leaf, blade of mace and whole black peppercorns, for flavouring

50g (2oz) butter

1 large onion, skinned and chopped

1 bunch watercress, chopped

40g (1½oz) plain flour

salt and pepper

75–100g (3–4oz) white Cheshire or Caerphilly cheese, finely grated

1 Place the milk and flavouring ingredients in a saucepan. Bring to scalding point, then cover and leave to infuse for about 20 minutes.
2 Meanwhile, melt the butter in a medium saucepan and add the onion and watercress. Cover and cook gently for about 10 minutes until soft but not coloured.

3 Mix in the flour and cook for 1 minute. Gradually add the strained milk and seasoning. Bring to the boil, stirring, and simmer gently for 10 minutes.
4 Cool slightly, then lightly purée in a blender or food processor; leave the soup speckled.
5 Return to the rinsed-out pan and add the cheese. Reheat gently and adjust seasoning.

To Microwave
Put the milk and flavouring ingredients in a large bowl and microwave on HIGH for 5 minutes or until very hot. Leave to infuse. Put the butter, onion and watercress in a large bowl and microwave on HIGH for 3–5 minutes or until softened, stirring. Sprinkle in the flour and microwave on HIGH for 1 minute, stirring once. Gradually add half of the strained milk and seasoning. Cover and microwave on HIGH for 5 minutes or until boiling and thickened, stirring frequently. Complete step 4. Add the remaining milk. Transfer the soup to a serving bowl and microwave on HIGH for 2–3 minutes or until hot. Add the cheese and microwave on HIGH for 5 minutes or until piping hot.

To Freeze
Cool, pack at the end of step 4 in usable quantities in rigid containers, leaving headspace. For reheating in the microwave, freeze the soup in single portions. Freeze for up to 3 months.

To Thaw and Serve
Reheat from frozen in a heavy-based saucepan, adding the cheese as above. Alternatively, microwave each portion on LOW for about 8–10 minutes, breaking up the block as it thaws. Once thawed, microwave on HIGH for 3–4 minutes or until piping hot. Stir in the cheese and heat.

PUMPKIN SOUP

SERVES 6

15ml (1 tbsp) vegetable oil
25g (1oz) butter
1 small leek, trimmed, washed and chopped
1 large carrot, peeled and thinly sliced
900g (2lb) pumpkin
2 large eating apples, peeled, cubed and chopped
about 450ml (¾ pint) light stock
salt and pepper
450–568ml (¾–1 pint) milk
pinch of grated nutmeg
squeeze of lemon juice
chopped fresh basil, to garnish (optional)

1 Heat the oil and butter in a large pan and add the leek and carrot. Cover tightly and cook gently or about 10 minutes or until the vegetables are soft but not coloured.
2 Prepare the pumpkin, removing the skin and seeds as necessary. Cut the flesh into small chunks.
3 Add the pumpkin and apple to the pan with the stock and seasoning. Bring to the boil, cover and simmer for about 20 minutes or until the vegetables are tender.
4 Cool slightly, then purée in a blender or food processor until smooth.
5 Return the soup to the rinsed-out pan. Add the milk and nutmeg and warm gently, adding more stock if necessary. Stir in a squeeze of lemon juice, adjusting seasoning as necessary. Sprinkle the top liberally with chopped fresh basil, if using. Serve the soup hot or chilled.

To Microwave
Put the oil, butter, leek and carrot in a large bowl. Cover and microwave on HIGH for 5–7 minutes or until softened. Complete step 2, cutting the pumpkin and apple very small. Add to the leek and carrot with 300ml (½ pint) stock. Cover and microwave on HIGH for 15 minutes or until the vegetables are tender. Complete step 4. Transfer the soup to a serving bowl and add the milk, seasoning and lemon juice. Chill if serving cold. Microwave on HIGH for 5 minutes or until piping hot, if serving hot. Garnish.

To Freeze
Cool, pack without the lemon juice and basil in usable quantities in rigid containers, leaving headspace. For reheating in the microwave, pour the soup into single portion containers. Freeze for up to 3 months.

To Thaw and Serve
Reheat from frozen in a heavy-based saucepan, stirring, until boiling. Alternatively, microwave each portion on LOW for about 8–10 minutes, breaking up the block as it thaws. Once thawed, microwave on HIGH for 3–4 minutes or until piping hot, stirring occasionally. Add the lemon juice and garnish.

If serving cold, thaw overnight at cool room temperature. Alternatively, microwave on LOW for about 8–10 minutes, then chill. Add the lemon juice and garnish.

CURRIED PARSNIP AND APPLE SOUP

SERVES 4

40g (1½oz) butter

15ml (1 tbsp) vegetable oil

15ml (1 tbsp) mild curry powder

350g (12oz) leeks, trimmed, washed and sliced

550g (1¼lb) parsnips, peeled and sliced

350g (12oz) cooking apples, peeled, cored and sliced

1.1 litres (2 pints) chicken stock (see page 186)

300ml (½ pint) milk

150ml (¼ pint) dry white wine

salt and pepper

green apple slices, to garnish

1 Heat the butter and oil in a large saucepan. Add the curry powder, leeks, parsnips and cooking apples, stirring well to mix. Cover and cook gently for 10–15 minutes or until the vegetables are soft but not coloured.
2 Pour in the stock, milk and wine. Bring to the boil, cover and simmer gently for 25–30 minutes.
3 Cool slightly, then purée in a food processor or blender until quite smooth. Return to the rinsed-out pan and reheat, adjusting seasoning. Garnish.

To Microwave
Finely chop the vegetables and apple, then put in a large bowl with the butter, oil and curry powder. Cover and microwave on HIGH for 10 minutes, stirring occasionally. Add half of the stock and the wine, cover and microwave on HIGH for 10–15 minutes or until the vegetables are tender, stirring occasionally. Add the remaining stock and the milk. Microwave on HIGH for 5 minutes. Complete step 3. Transfer the soup to a serving bowl and microwave on HIGH for 5 minutes or until hot.

To Freeze
Cool, pack without the garnish in usable quantities in rigid containers, leaving headspace. For reheating in the microwave, pour the soup into single portion containers. Freeze for up to 3 months.

To Thaw and Serve
Reheat from frozen in a heavy-based saucepan, stirring, until boiling. Alternatively, microwave each portion on LOW for about 10–12 minutes, breaking up the block as it thaws. Once thawed, microwave on HIGH for 3–4 minutes or until piping hot, stirring occasionally. Garnish.

BROAD BEAN AND BACON SOUP

SERVES 4

225g (8oz) shelled broad beans

225g (8oz) shelled peas

1 large onion, skinned and chopped

450ml (¾ pint) fresh milk

300ml (½ pint) vegetable stock

salt and pepper

2 rashers back bacon, rinded, grilled and chopped, to garnish

1 In a large saucepan, simmer the broad beans, peas and onion in the milk and stock for 20 minutes, until the beans are tender.
2 Purée one-third of the soup in a blender or food processor and add to the remaining soup, then season to taste. Reheat gently. Serve hot, garnished with chopped bacon.

To Microwave
Cook the vegetables, milk and stock in a large bowl on HIGH for 20–25 minutes, stirring occasionally. Complete step 2, reheating on HIGH for 2–3 minutes.

To Freeze
Cool quickly. Pack, cover, label and freeze without the garnish. For reheating in the microwave, pour the soup into single portion containers, label and freeze.

To Thaw and Serve
Reheat from frozen in a heavy-based saucepan, stirring until boiling. Alternatively, microwave each portion on LOW for 10–12 minutes, breaking up the block as it thaws. Once thawed, microwave on HIGH for 3–4 minutes or until boiling, stirring occasionally. Garnish as above.

Right: Vegetable Borsch (page 89)

ASPARAGUS SOUP

SERVES 4

100g (4oz) blanched almonds
1.1 litres (2 pints) light stock or water
15ml (1 tbsp) vegetable oil
4 celery sticks, diced
450g (1lb) asparagus, trimmed and chopped
15ml (1 tbsp) chopped fresh tarragon or 5ml (1 tsp) dried
30ml (2 tbsp) chopped fresh parsley or 10ml (2 tsp) dried
45ml (3 tbsp) single cream
salt and pepper
cream, toasted flaked almonds and parsley, to garnish

1 Place the almonds and stock in a food processor or blender and grind until very smooth. Sieve the mixture, reserving the liquid, and discard the grains.
2 Heat the oil in a large pan and gently fry the celery for 5–6 minutes. Add the asparagus and cook for 5 minutes. Pour over the stock and add the herbs. Cover and simmer for 15 minutes.
3 Cool slightly, then purée in a blender or food processor until smooth. Return to the pan and stir in the cream. Heat gently. Season and garnish.

To Microwave
Complete step 1. Place the oil and celery in a large bowl. Cover and microwave on HIGH for 2½–3 minutes or until softened. Add the asparagus, almond stock and herbs, stirring well. Cover and microwave on HIGH for 8–10 minutes or until the asparagus has softened. Complete step 3. Transfer the soup to a serving bowl and microwave on HIGH for 2–2½ minutes or until piping hot. Garnish.

To Freeze
Cool, pack without the cream and seasoning in usable quantities in rigid containers, leaving headspace. For reheating in microwave, freeze soup in single portions. Freeze for up to 3 months.

To Thaw
Leave overnight in the refrigerator. Alternatively, microwave each portion on LOW for about 10–12 minutes, breaking up the block as it thaws. Stand for 30–35 minutes.

To Serve
Reheat in a heavy-based saucepan, stirring, until boiling. Stir in the cream and season to taste. Do not boil. Garnish. Alternatively, microwave each portion on HIGH for about 10–12 minutes or until piping hot. Stir in the cream and season to taste. Microwave on HIGH for a further 1½–2 minutes.

RED PEPPER AND TOMATO SOUP

SERVES 3–4

30ml (2 tbsp) vegetable oil
100g (4oz) onion, skinned and chopped
2 red peppers, cored, seeded and sliced
450g (1lb) tomatoes, skinned, seeded and roughly chopped
600ml (1 pint) vegetable stock
1 bay leaf
2.5ml (½ tsp) dried basil
10ml (2 tsp) granulated sugar
20ml (4 tsp) tomato purée
15ml (1 tbsp) lemon juice
salt and pepper
natural yogurt, to serve

1 Heat the oil in a saucepan and fry the onion and peppers for about 8 minutes. Add the tomatoes.
2 Pour in the stock, then add remaining ingredients, except the yogurt. Bring to the boil, cover and simmer for about 35 minutes.
3 Cool slightly, then discard the bay leaf. Remove a few slices of red pepper for garnish. Purée in a blender or food processor until smooth.
4 Return the soup to the rinsed-out pan, adjust seasoning and reheat. Garnish each serving with a small spoonful of yogurt and reserved red pepper.

To Microwave
Place the onion, pepper and oil in a large bowl. Cover and microwave on HIGH for 5–7 minutes or until softened, stirring occasionally. Add the tomatoes to the pepper mixture with all the remaining ingredients, except the yogurt. Cover and microwave on HIGH for 15 minutes, stirring occasionally. Complete step 3. Transfer the soup to a serving bowl and microwave on HIGH for 2–3 minutes or until piping hot. Garnish.

To Freeze
Cool, pack at the end of step 3 in usable quantities in rigid containers, leaving headspace. For reheating in the microwave, pour the soup into single portion containers. Freeze for up to 3 months.

To Thaw and Serve
Reheat from frozen in a heavy-based saucepan, stirring, until boiling. Alternatively, microwave each portion on LOW for about 10–12 minutes, breaking up the block as it thaws. Once thawed, microwave on HIGH for 3–4 minutes or until piping hot, stirring.

SUMMER GARDEN SOUP

SERVES 4

50g (2oz) butter

50g (2oz) onion, skinned and finely chopped

1 bunch watercress, roughly chopped

½ round lettuce, roughly chopped

½ cucumber, about 175g (6oz), peeled and chopped

100g (4oz) potato, peeled and chopped

1 litre (1¾ pints) jellied chicken stock (see page 186)

150ml (¼ pint) single cream

salt and pepper

fresh mint ice cubes, crushed (see Note)

watercress sprigs and cucumber slices, to garnish

1 Melt the butter in a large saucepan and gently fry the onion for 2–3 minutes until soft and golden. Stir in the watercress, lettuce, cucumber and potato. Gently fry for 2 minutes, add the stock.
2 Bring to the boil, cover and simmer for 15–20 minutes or until the potato is cooked and very soft.
3 Cool slightly, then purée in a blender or food processor. Press through a sieve into a bowl.
4 Stir in the cream and seasoning. Cover and chill for at least 2 hours. Garnish with crushed ice cubes, watercress sprigs and cucumber slices.
Note: To make clear mint ice cubes, simply stir 30ml (2 tbsp) chopped fresh mint into 300ml (½ pint) distilled water. Pour into ice-cube trays and freeze until solid. Place in a clean tea towel and crush lightly with a rolling pin.

To Microwave

Put the butter and onion in a large bowl. Cover and microwave on HIGH for 2 minutes or until softened. Add the remaining vegetables and half of the stock. Cover and microwave on HIGH for 8 minutes or until boiling, stirring occasionally. Continue to microwave on HIGH for 5 minutes or until the potato is very soft. Add the remaining stock and complete steps 3 and 4.

To Freeze

Pack at the end of step 3 in usable quantities in rigid containers, leaving headspace. For reheating in the microwave, pour the soup into single portion containers. Freeze for up to 3 months.

To Thaw and Serve

Leave at cool room temperature. Alternatively, microwave on LOW for 10–12 minutes, stirring occasionally and breaking up the block as it thaws. Stir in the cream and seasoning. Chill and garnish.

VEGETABLE BORSCH

SERVES 8

450g (1lb) raw beetroot, peeled

225g (8oz) onion, skinned

100g (4oz) carrot, peeled

100g (4oz) parsnips, peeled

3 celery sticks

2.3 litres (4 pints) light stock

350g (12oz) ripe tomatoes

1 garlic clove, skinned and crushed

15ml (1 tbsp) tomato purée

10ml (2 tsp) red wine vinegar

salt and pepper

sugar

90ml (6 tbsp) chopped fresh parsley

150ml (¼ pint) soured cream

1 Cut the beetroot, onion, carrot, parsnips and celery into matchsticks. Place in a large pan with the stock. Cover and simmer gently for 1 hour.
2 Meanwhile, scald and skin the tomatoes. Seed, reserving the juices, and cut the flesh into strips. Add to the pan with the garlic, tomato purée, vinegar and plenty of seasoning. Simmer for a further 30 minutes or until the vegetables are tender. Adjust seasoning, adding sugar to taste.
3 Sprinkle with parsley and serve with cream.

To Microwave

Halve the ingredients. Complete step 1, putting the vegetables and half of the stock in a large bowl. Cover and microwave on HIGH for 25 minutes or until the vegetables are tender, stirring occasionally. Complete step 2, adding the tomatoes, garlic, tomato purée, vinegar, seasoning and the remaining stock. Cover and microwave on HIGH for 10 minutes or until boiling. Adjust seasoning. Complete step 3. Serves 4.

To Freeze

Cool, pack at the end of step 2 in usable quantities in rigid containers, leaving headspace. For reheating in microwave, freeze soup in single portions. Freeze for up to 3 months.

To Thaw and Serve

Reheat from frozen in a heavy-based saucepan, stirring, until boiling. Alternatively, microwave each portion on LOW for about 10–12 minutes, breaking up the block as it thaws. Once thawed, microwave on HIGH for 3–4 minutes or until piping hot, stirring occasionally. Complete step 3.

ROUGH GAME PÂTÉ

SERVES 10–12

450g (1lb) streaky bacon

225g (8oz) pig's liver

225g (8oz) onion, skinned

700g (1½lb) hare joints or venison

225g (8oz) pork sausagemeat

grated rind and juice of 1 small orange

45ml (3 tbsp) brandy

45ml (3 tbsp) chopped fresh coriander or parsley

1 egg

salt and pepper

orange slices and fresh coriander, to garnish

1 Cut the rind off the bacon. Stretch half the rashers with the back of a blunt-edged knife. Coarsely mince the remaining bacon with the liver and onion, then place the mixture in a large bowl.
2 Cut all the hare meat off the bone and divide into small pieces (not larger than 0.5cm (¼ inch) cubes). Add to the bowl with the sausagemeat, grated rind of half the orange and 45ml (3 tbsp) orange juice, the brandy, coriander, egg and plenty of seasoning. Stir well until evenly mixed. Cover tightly and chill for about 8 hours or overnight.
3 Line a 1.4–1.7 litre (2½–3 pint) terrine dish with the prepared bacon rashers. Stir the pâté mixture, then spoon into the lined terrine. Cover tightly with foil and stand the dish in a roasting tin half filled with water.
4 Bake in the oven at 170°C (325°F) mark 3 for 2½–3 hours or until the juices run clear when the pâté is tested with a fine skewer. Remove from the oven; cool slightly.
5 Place a few heavy weights on top of the pâté and complete cooling. Cover and chill overnight.
6 Turn out the pâté, reserving any juices to add to gravies or stocks. Slice for serving, garnished with orange slices and fresh coriander.

To Microwave

Complete steps 1 and 2. Line a 1.4–1.7 litre (2½–3 pint) non-metallic terrine dish or ring mould with the prepared bacon rashers. Spoon the pâté mixture into the lined dish. Cover and microwave on HIGH for 4–5 minutes, then on MEDIUM for 45 minutes or until the juices run clear when the pâté is tested with a fine skewer. Cool slightly, then complete steps 5 and 6.

To Freeze

Pack in individual portions or as a whole. Freeze for up to 1 month.

To Thaw and Serve

Leave overnight in the refrigerator. The pâté will be slightly crumbly after freezing.

CHICKEN LIVER PÂTÉ

SERVES 6–8

175g (6oz) butter

100g (4oz) onion, skinned and chopped

6 chicken livers, trimmed

30–45ml (2–3 tbsp) brandy

45ml (3 tbsp) chicken stock (see page 186)

225g (8oz) pork sausagemeat

2.5ml (½ tsp) dried thyme

salt and pepper

1 lemon

1 Melt 50g (2oz) of the butter in a frying pan and gently fry the onion and chicken livers for 5 minutes. Purée in a blender with the brandy and stock until smooth.
2 Gently fry the sausagemeat for a few minutes until broken down. Add the puréed liver, thyme and seasoning to taste. Stir over a moderate heat for 10 minutes.
3 Pack into individual pots, level the surface, place a slice of lemon on each and seal with melted butter. Chill.

To Microwave

Finely chop the chicken livers. Place in a bowl with the onion and 50g (2oz) of the butter. Cover and microwave on HIGH for about 3 minutes. Purée in a blender with the brandy and stock until smooth. Place the sausagemeat in a shallow bowl and microwave on HIGH for 3 minutes or until broken down, stirring occasionally. Mix together with the puréed liver, thyme and seasoning to taste, stirring well. Place in a shallow dish and microwave on HIGH for about 5 minutes. Complete step 3.

To Freeze

Pack in the pots and freeze for up to 3 months.

To Thaw and Serve

Leave overnight in the refrigerator.

Right: Asparagus Soup (page 88)

FISH MOUSSES WITH CORIANDER AND TOMATO SAUCE

SERVES 4

225g (8oz) haddock or cod fillets, skinned

100g (4oz) peeled prawns

salt and pepper

pinch of cayenne

1 egg

150ml (¼ pint) double cream

150ml (¼ pint) low fat natural yogurt

30ml (2 tbsp) chopped fresh coriander or 10ml (2 tsp) ground coriander

10ml (2 tsp) lemon juice

SAUCE

25g (1oz) butter

3 spring onions, trimmed and chopped

400g (14oz) can chopped tomatoes

15ml (1 tbsp) tomato purée

5ml (1 tsp) sugar

15ml (1 tbsp) chopped fresh coriander or 5ml (1 tsp) ground coriander

coriander sprigs, to garnish

1 Blend the fish and prawns in a blender or food processor. Blend in the seasonings, egg, cream, yogurt, coriander and lemon juice or foil.

2 Butter four 175ml (6fl oz) ramekins and divide the fish mixture between them. Cover loosely with foil and place in a roasting tin with hot water coming halfway up to sides. Cook in the oven at 180°C (350°F) mark 4 for 20–30 minutes or until firm.

3 For the sauce, melt the butter in a small pan and cook the spring onions for 3 minutes. Purée the tomatoes in a food processor or blender until smooth. Add the tomatoes to the onions and stir in the tomato purée and sugar. Cook for 5–6 minutes. Sieve the sauce, discarding the contents remaining in the sieve. Stir in the chopped coriander. Unmould the mousses and serve with the sauce. Garnish with coriander sprigs.

To Microwave

Complete step 1. Divide the mixture between four buttered ramekins and cover with a circle of greaseproof paper. Microwave on HIGH for 10–12 minutes, re-arranging once during cooking. Stand for 2 minutes. Lift off the paper and carefully pour off any liquid. For the sauce, place the butter in a medium bowl and microwave on HIGH for 30 seconds. Add the spring onions and microwave on HIGH for a further 1½–2 minutes. Blend the tomatoes in a food processor or blender and add to the onions with the tomato purée and sugar. Microwave on HIGH for about 2½–3 minutes. Sieve the sauce and stir in the chopped coriander. Unmould the fish mousses and serve with the sauce. Garnish.

To Freeze

Cool, pack in the ramekins. Pack the chilled sauce in a small rigid container. Freeze for up to 3 months.

To Thaw and Serve

Place the frozen ramekins in a roasting tin with hot water coming half way up the sides. Cook in the oven at 180°C (350°F) mark 4 for 1½–2 hours. Alternatively, microwave on HIGH for about 12–15 minutes, re-arranging twice during cooking, or until cooked through.

Gently heat the sauce in a small pan, stirring occasionally, until heated through. Alternatively, microwave on HIGH for about 7–8 minutes, stirring occasionally, until piping hot. Serve.

TARAMASALATA MOUSSES

SERVES 6

10ml (2 tsp) powdered gelatine

225g (8oz) ready-made taramasalata

150g (5oz) low fat soft cheese

45ml (3 tbsp) single cream

salt and pepper

1 egg white, whisked

175g (6oz) thinly sliced smoked salmon

225g (8oz) thin asparagus spears

endive or lettuce leaves, to garnish

1 Sprinkle the gelatine over 30ml (2 tbsp) water in a small bowl. Leave to stand for about 5 minutes or until spongy. Meanwhile, beat the taramasalata, cheese, cream and seasoning together.

2 To dissolve the gelatine, stand the bowl in a pan of simmering water. When liquid and clear, stir into the mousse mixture. Fold in the egg white.

3 Lightly oil six 150ml (¼ pint) ramekin dishes and line with smoked salmon. Spoon in the mousse mixture and chill until set. When firm, cover and return to the refrigerator until required.

4 Cut the asparagus heads off the stalks and simmer gently until tender; drain. (Reserve stalks for soup recipes.)

5 To serve, turn out the mousses on to a bed of leaves and garnish with the asparagus.

To Microwave

Sprinkle the gelatine over 30ml (2 tbsp) water, leave for about 5 minutes or until spongy. Microwave on HIGH for 30–35 seconds or until dissolved, stirring occasionally. Do not boil. Complete steps 1–3. Cut asparagus heads off the stalks and arrange in a shallow dish with 60ml (4 tbsp) water. Microwave on HIGH for 5–6 minutes, rearranging during cooking, until tender. Complete steps 4 and 5.

To Freeze

Pack in the ramekins at the end of step 3 and freeze for up to 1 month.

To Thaw and Serve

Leave at cool room temperature for 4–6 hours. Alternatively, microwave on LOW for about 10–15 minutes. Stand for 30 minutes. Complete steps 4 and 5.

SMOKED MACKEREL MOUSSE

SERVES 6

300ml (½ pint) milk
a few slices of onion and carrot, for flavouring
1 bay leaf
25g (1oz) butter
30ml (2 tbsp) plain flour
10ml (2 tsp) powdered gelatine
275g (10oz) smoked mackerel fillet
50g (2oz) onion, skinned and chopped
15ml (1 tbsp) creamed horseradish
150ml (¼ pint) natural yogurt
15ml (1 tbsp) lemon juice
salt and pepper
2 egg whites
lamb's lettuce or watercress sprigs and lemon twists, to garnish

1 Pour the milk into a saucepan, add the flavourings and bay leaf, then bring slowly to the boil. Remove from the heat, cover and leave to infuse for 30 minutes.

2 Strain the infused milk into a jug. Discard the flavourings. Melt the butter in the rinsed-out pan, add the flour and cook gently, stirring, for 1–2 minutes. Remove from the heat and gradually blend in the infused milk. Bring to the boil, stirring constantly, then simmer for 3 minutes until thick and smooth.

3 Remove the pan from the heat and sprinkle in

the gelatine. Stir briskly until dissolved. Pour into a bowl and leave to cool for 20 minutes.

4 Meanwhile, flake the smoked mackerel fillet, discarding the skin and bones.

5 Purée the cooled sauce, mackerel, onion and horseradish in a blender or food processor until smooth. Pour into a bowl and stir in the yogurt, lemon juice and seasoning to taste.

6 Whisk the egg whites until they stand in soft peaks, then fold gently through the fish mixture.

7 Spoon the mousse into six individual ramekins or soufflé dishes. Chill for at least 2 hours until set. Serve chilled, garnished with lamb's lettuce or watercress sprigs and lemon twists.

To Microwave

Pour the milk into a measuring jug and add the flavourings. Microwave on HIGH for 1–2 minutes or until boiling. Cover and leave to infuse for 30 minutes. Strain, discarding the flavourings. Put the butter, flour and flavoured milk into a medium bowl and whisk together. Microwave on HIGH for 4–5 minutes or until the sauce has boiled and thickened, whisking frequently. Sprinkle in the gelatine and whisk until dissolved. Cool for 20 minutes. Complete steps 4–7.

To Freeze

Pack in the ramekins and freeze for up to 3 months.

To Thaw and Serve

Leave overnight in the refrigerator. Alternatively, arrange the ramekins in a circle on the turntable and microwave on LOW for about 10–15 minutes, re-arranging during cooking. Stand for 10–15 minutes. Garnish.

GARLIC MUSHROOM PARCELS

SERVES 4–6

15ml (1 tbsp) olive oil

1 onion, skinned and finely chopped

1–2 garlic cloves, skinned and crushed

225g (8oz) button mushrooms, chopped

15ml (1 tbsp) chopped fresh thyme or 5ml (1 tsp) dried

pepper

50g (2oz) full fat soft cheese

6 sheets of frozen filo pastry, thawed

25g (1oz) butter, melted

1 Heat the oil in a medium saucepan and gently cook the onion and garlic for 3–5 minutes until the onion has softened. Add the mushrooms, thyme and pepper. Cook for 5–6 minutes, stirring.

2 Drain off any excess juices and add the cheese, stirring continuously until the cheese has melted. Cook for a further 2 minutes. Cool.

3 To make the parcels, lay the first sheet of filo pastry lengthways on a surface. Brush with butter, then lay a second sheet on top. Brush with butter, then cut into eight equal strips.

4 Place 5ml (1 tsp) of the cooked filling in one corner of a strip of pastry. Fold this corner over to make a triangle, encasing the filling. Continue to fold in the shape of a triangle, brushing with a little extra melted butter just before the final fold. Make 24 parcels. Place on a greased baking sheet.

5 Bake in the oven at 200°C (400°F) mark 6 for 10–15 minutes or until golden brown and crisp, turning the parcels over halfway during cooking. Serve hot or cold, with a few salad leaves.

To Microwave

Place the oil, onion and garlic in a medium bowl. Cover and microwave on HIGH for 2½–3 minutes or until the onion has softened. Add the mushrooms, thyme and pepper to taste. Microwave on HIGH for 2½–3½ minutes, stirring once. Drain. Stir in the cheese and microwave on HIGH for 1–1½ minutes. Cool. Complete steps 3–5.

To Freeze

Open freeze the uncooked parcels and pack in a rigid container. Freeze for up to 1 month.

To Thaw and Serve

Unwrap and place the parcels on a baking sheet. Lightly brush with melted butter. Bake in the oven at 200°C (400°F) mark 6 for 20–25 minutes or until golden brown and crisp, turning them over halfway.

SPANAKOPITTES

MAKES 60

30ml (2 tbsp) olive oil

1 small onion, skinned and chopped

227g (8oz) packet frozen chopped spinach, thawed and squeezed dry

75g (3oz) Feta cheese, crumbled

1 egg, beaten

pepper

175g (6oz) bought filo pastry

100g (4oz) butter, melted

1 Heat the oil in a saucepan and gently fry the onion for 5 minutes until soft. Remove the pan from the heat and stir in the spinach, cheese, egg and pepper to taste.

2 Cut the filo pastry sheets widthways into 5cm (2 inch) strips. Place the strips on waxed paper and cover with a slightly damp tea towel.

3 Brush one strip of the pastry with melted butter and place 5ml (1 tsp) of the spinach mixture at the end of the strip.

4 Fold one corner of the strip diagonally over the filling, so the short edge lies on top of the long edge and forms a right angle.

5 Continue folding the pastry at right angles until you reach the end of the strip, forming a neat triangular package. Repeat with remaining strips and filling to make 60 triangles.

6 Place the packages seam side down in a large roasting tin, then brush with melted brush. Bake in the oven at 220°C (425°F) mark 7 for 15 minutes until golden brown. Serve hot.

To Microwave

Place the oil and onion in a small bowl and microwave on HIGH for 3 minutes or until soft, stirring occasionally. Stir in the spinach, cheese, egg and pepper to taste. Complete steps 2–6.

To Freeze

Pack in a rigid container at the end of step 5 and freeze for up to 3 months.

To Thaw and Serve

Cook straight from frozen in the oven at 220°C (425°F) mark 7 for 15–20 minutes or until golden brown. Serve hot.

Right: Garlic Mushroom Parcels

HOT MUSHROOM TERRINE

SERVES 4

20g (¾oz) butter

20g (¾oz) plain flour

300ml (½ pint) milk

salt and pepper

75g (3oz) button mushrooms, finely chopped

75g (3oz) fresh breadcrumbs

2 eggs, separated

30ml (2 tbsp) chopped fresh parsley

30ml (2 tbsp) grated Parmesan cheese

12 small button mushrooms

CHIVE SAUCE

45ml (3 tbsp) natural yogurt

45ml (3 tbsp) mayonnaise

1.25ml (¼ tsp) lemon juice

15ml (1 tbsp) snipped chives

1 Lightly grease and line a 450g (1lb) loaf tin or 15cm (6 inch) soufflé dish with greaseproof paper.
2 Melt the butter in a saucepan, stir in the flour and cook for 1 minute. Stir in the milk and bring to the boil. Add the seasoning and chopped mushrooms. Simmer for 5 minutes.
3 Beat the breadcrumbs, egg yolks, parsley and cheese into the sauce. Whisk the egg whites until stiff, then fold into the mixture.
4 Spoon the mixture into the prepared loaf tin, adding the whole mushrooms at random. Level the surface and cover with a piece of lightly greased foil. Stand the tin in a roasting tin and add hot water to come halfway up the sides of the loaf tin.
5 Bake in the oven at 170°C (325°F) mark 3 for 45 minutes until the terrine is set.
6 Meanwhile, for the sauce, mix the yogurt, mayonnaise, lemon juice and chives together in a bowl. Cover and chill until ready to serve.
7 Turn out the loaf on to a warmed serving dish. Serve, cut into slices, accompanied by the sauce.

To Microwave
Follow step 1, using a soufflé or loaf dish. Put the butter, flour and milk in a medium bowl and whisk together. Microwave on HIGH for 4–5 minutes or until the sauce has boiled and thickened, whisking frequently. Add seasoning and chopped mushrooms and microwave for 1–2 minutes. Complete steps 3 and 4, but do not cover. Stand the terrine in a large dish and add hot water. Microwave on MEDIUM for 13–15 minutes or until the terrine is just set in the centre, turning the dish two or three times. Complete steps 6 and 7.

To Freeze
Cool, pack in individual portions or as a whole at the end of step 5. Freeze for up to 3 months.

To Thaw and Serve
Leave overnight in the refrigerator. Alternatively, microwave on LOW for about 5 minutes. Stand for 10–15 minutes. Complete steps 6 and 7.

SOLE AND MUSHROOM PROFITEROLES

SERVES 6

2 egg quantity choux pastry (see page 205)

225g (8oz) fillet of sole, skinned

225g (8oz) button mushrooms, thinly sliced

150ml (¼ pint) milk

50g (2oz) butter

25g (1oz) plain flour

1.25ml (¼ tsp) ground coriander

60ml (4 tbsp) dry white wine

salt and pepper

chopped fresh tarragon, to garnish

1 Spoon or pipe six balls of choux pastry on to a wetted baking sheet. Bake in the oven at 200°C (400°F) mark 6 for about 25 minutes or until well risen and crisp.
2 With a sharp, pointed knife, make a slit in the side of each profiterole. Return to the oven for a further 5 minutes. Cool for 20 minutes on a rack.
3 Meanwhile, slice the fish into thin strips. Put the mushrooms in a saucepan with the milk and fish. Poach gently for 10–12 minutes. Strain, reserving the milk.
4 Melt 25g (1oz) of the butter in a small pan, add the flour and coriander and cook gently, stirring, for 1–2 minutes. Remove from the heat and gradually blend in the reserved milk. Bring to the boil, stirring constantly. Add the wine, then simmer for 3 minutes until thick and smooth. Fold in the fish, mushrooms and seasoning. Cool for at least 1 hour.
5 To serve, fill the cold profiteroles with the cold sauce. Cover loosely with foil and reheat in the oven at 190°C (375°F) mark 5 for about 15 minutes. Serve profiteroles hot, garnished with tarragon.

To Microwave
Complete steps 1 and 2. Slice the fish into thin strips. Put the mushrooms, milk and fish in a shallow dish and microwave on HIGH for about 2 minutes. Strain, reserving the milk. Put the milk,

flour, coriander and half the butter into a medium bowl and whisk together. Microwave on HIGH for 2–3 minutes or until the sauce has boiled and thickened, whisking frequently. Stir in the wine, fish, mushrooms and season well to taste. Cool for 1 hour. Complete step 5.

To Freeze

Open freeze the unfilled choux buns on baking sheets. Remove carefully and pack in polythene bags. Freeze for up to 6 months. Pack the filling in a rigid container. Freeze for up to 1 month.

To Thaw and Serve

Place the frozen buns on a greased baking sheet and bake in the oven at 170°C (325°F) mark 3 for 10 minutes. Cool. Thaw the filling at room temperature for 4–6 hours or until thawed, stirring occasionally. Alternatively, microwave on LOW for 10–12 minutes, breaking up the block as it thaws. Stand for 30 minutes. Complete step 5.

LAYERED FISH TERRINE

SERVES 6–8

700g (1½lb) whiting, sole, plaice or hake, skinned and chilled

3 egg whites, chilled

salt and white pepper

15ml (1 tbsp) lemon juice

30ml (2 tbsp) chopped fresh tarragon or 10ml (2 tsp) dried

30ml (2 tbsp) chopped fresh dill or 10ml (2 tsp) dried

300ml (½ pint) double cream, chilled

25g (1oz) butter, for greasing

450g (1lb) piece of fresh salmon tail, filleted and skinned

15ml (1 tbsp) green peppercorns, drained

300ml (½ pint) smetana or soured cream

a little milk

30ml (2 tbsp) snipped chives (optional)

dill sprigs, to garnish

1 Trim the fish, remove any bones and cut into small pieces. Work in a blender or food processor until finely minced. Alternatively, put the fish through a mincer and mince finely.

2 Add the egg whites and pepper to the fish and process or beat until completely incorporated. Turn into a bowl, cover and chill for at least 30 minutes.

3 Stir in the lemon juice, tarragon and dill and process or beat again, gradually adding the double cream. Add salt to taste, cover and chill again for at least 30 minutes.

4 Meanwhile, grease a 1.1 litre (2 pint) terrine or loaf tin with the butter and line the bottom with greaseproof paper.

5 Cut the salmon into chunky strips, about 1cm (½ inch) square and the length of the loaf tin or terrine. Cover and chill until required.

6 Carefully stir the green peppercorns into the fish mixture. Spoon a third of the fish mixture into the terrine and spread out evenly to cover the bottom. Lay half of the salmon strips on top, leaving a 1cm (½ inch) border all the way round. Cover this with half of the remaining fish mixture, levelling it carefully.

7 Repeat the salmon layer, using the remaining salmon strips. Finally cover with the remaining fish mixture and smooth the top.

8 Cover the terrine with buttered foil and place in a roasting tin with water coming halfway up the sides. Bake in the oven at 180°C (350°F) mark 4 for 45 minutes or until a skewer inserted into the centre comes out clean.

9 Transfer the terrine to a wire rack and leave to cool for 2 hours at room temperature. Remove from the rack, cover with cling film and chill for at least 4 hours.

10 When ready to serve the terrine, mix the smetana or soured cream with a little milk to make a thin sauce. Add the chives, if using, and seasoning to taste.

11 Turn the terrine out on to a plate and wipe with absorbent kitchen paper to remove any butter or liquid. Slice thickly. Flood individual serving plates with the sauce, then place a slice of terrine in the centre. Garnish with dill.

To Microwave

Complete steps 1, 2 and 3. Grease a 1.1 litre (2 pint) non-metallic terrine or loaf dish with butter and line with greaseproof paper. Complete steps 5–7. Cover the terrine with buttered greaseproof paper and stand in a shallow dish of hot water. Microwave on HIGH for 15–20 minutes or until a skewer inserted into the centre comes out clean, turning occasionally. Complete steps 9–11.

To Freeze

Pack the cold, cooked terrine at the end of step 9 and freeze for up to 1 month.

To Thaw and Serve

Leave overnight in the refrigerator. Complete steps 10 and 11.

LIGHT MEALS AND SNACKS

GLAMORGAN SAUSAGES

MAKES 8

175g (6oz) fresh breadcrumbs

100g (4oz) Caerphilly cheese, grated

1 small leek, trimmed, washed and very finely chopped

15ml (1 tbsp) chopped fresh parsley

large pinch of mustard powder

salt and pepper

2 eggs, separated

about 60ml (4 tbsp) milk, to mix

plain flour, for coating

15ml (1 tbsp) vegetable oil

15g (1/2oz) butter

1 Mix the breadcrumbs, cheese, leek, parsley and mustard together in a bowl. Season to taste. Add 1 whole egg and 1 egg yolk and mix thoroughly. Add enough milk to bind the mixture together.

2 Divide into eight and shape into sausages.

3 Beat the remaining egg white on a plate with a fork until frothy. Dip the sausages into the egg white, then roll in the flour to coat.

4 Heat the oil and butter in a pan and fry the sausages for 5–10 minutes until golden. Serve hot or cold.

To Microwave

Complete steps 1–3. Heat a large browning dish on HIGH for 5–8 minutes according to the manufacturers' instructions. When the browning dish is hot, add 15ml (1 tbsp) oil and quickly put the sausages on to the dish. Microwave on HIGH for 1½ minutes. Turn the sausages over and microwave on HIGH for a further 1 minute.

To Freeze

Open freeze the uncooked sausages on a baking sheet. Pack in a polythene bag and freeze for up to 3 months.

To Thaw and Serve

Leave at cool room temperature for 2–4 hours or overnight. Alternatively, microwave on LOW for 3–5 minutes. Stand for 10 minutes. Complete step 4. Or microwave as above.

PANZEROTTI

MAKES 16

1 quantity of basic pizza dough (see page 101)

300ml (1/2 pint) tomato sauce (see page 193)

100g (4oz) Mozzarella cheese

25g (1oz) grated Parmesan cheese

50g (2oz) boiled ham, finely diced

salt and pepper

vegetable oil, for deep frying

1 Make the basic pizza dough according to the instructions on page 101 and leave to rise.

2 Cook the tomato sauce over high heat, stirring constantly, until reduced to a thick pulp. Leave to cool for about 30 minutes.

3 Meanwhile, turn out the risen dough on to a floured surface. Roll out and cut into sixteen 10cm (4 inch) rounds. Use a plain pastry cutter or the rim of a wine glass or cup as a guide.

4 Spread the cold tomato sauce over the rounds of dough, leaving a border at the edge.

5 Roughly chop the Mozzarella. Mix with Parmesan, ham and seasoning. Sprinkle over one half of the dough.

6 Brush the edge of the dough with water, then fold the plain half over the filled half. Press the edges of the panzerotti together well to seal in the filling, then crimp to make a decorative edge.

7 Heat the oil in a deep-fat fryer to 180°C (350°F). Deep fry the pizzas in batches for 2–3 minutes on both sides until golden. Drain and serve immediately.

To Freeze

Open freeze on baking sheets at the end of step 6. Overwrap and freeze for up to 3 months.

To Thaw and Serve

Fry the frozen panzerotti, adding an extra few minutes to the cooking time.

Right: Glamorgan Sausages and Breakfast Pancakes

SPRING ROLLS

MAKES 8

225g (8oz) pork fillet or tenderloin

30ml (2 tbsp) sesame or vegetable oil

2.5cm (1 inch) piece of fresh root ginger, peeled and crushed

1 clove garlic, skinned and crushed

4 spring onions, trimmed and thinly sliced

100g (4oz) button mushrooms, roughly chopped

30ml (2 tbsp) soy sauce

15ml (1 tbsp) dark soft brown sugar

5ml (1 tsp) five-spice powder

salt and pepper

100g (4oz) beansprouts

beaten egg, for sealing

8 squares of spring roll pastry, thawed if frozen

vegetable oil, for deep frying

spring onion tassels, to garnish

1 With a very sharp knife, cut the pork fillet into wafer thin, even-sized strips, discarding any fat and sinews.

2 Heat the oil in a wok or heavy-based frying pan and stir-fry the pork for about 10 minutes until just tender. Add the ginger and garlic and stir-fry over gentle heat for 2–3 minutes until lightly coloured.

3 Add the spring onions and mushrooms to the pan, increase the heat and stir-fry for a further 2–3 minutes, tossing the ingredients and shaking the pan constantly so that they colour evenly.

4 Mix the soy sauce, sugar and five-spice powder together. Add seasoning to taste, then stir into the pan. Add the beansprouts and toss to combine with the other ingredients for 1–2 minutes. Remove from the heat and leave to cool completely for about 1 hour.

5 Brush beaten egg all over one square of pastry. Put one eighth of the filling in the corner nearest to you, then fold the corner over to cover the filling. Fold in the corner at right angles to the first corner, then fold in the opposite corner.

6 Roll up the filling in the pastry until the last corner is reached so that the filling is completely enclosed. Seal with a little beaten egg. Repeat with the remaining filling and seven sheets of pastry.

7 Heat the oil in a deep-fat fryer to 180°C (350°F). Add the spring rolls and deep fry in batches for 5 minutes until crisp and golden. Remove with a slotted spoon and drain on absorbent kitchen paper. Serve hot, garnished with spring onion tassels.

To Microwave

Complete step 1. Place oil in a large bowl and microwave on HIGH for 1 minute. Add the pork and stir well. Microwave on HIGH for 4–5 minutes or until just tender. Add the ginger and garlic, stir well and microwave on HIGH for 1 minute. Add the spring onions and mushrooms. Microwave on HIGH for 1 minute, stirring well. Mix soy sauce, sugar and five-spice powder together, then add seasoning to taste. Stir into the pork mixture with the beansprouts. Microwave on HIGH for 1 minute. Stir well, then leave to cool. Complete steps 5–7.

To Freeze

Open freeze the rolls and pack in a rigid container at the end of step 6. Freeze for up to 3 months.

To Thaw and Serve

Deep fry the frozen spring rolls, adding a few minutes to the cooking time. Garnish.

MACARONI AND BROCCOLI CHEESE

SERVES 2

75g (3oz) wholewheat macaroni

salt and pepper

25g (1oz) butter

25g (1oz) plain flour

300ml (½ pint) milk

75g (3oz) Red Leicester cheese, grated

100g (4oz) broccoli florets

15ml (1 tbsp) fresh wholemeal breadcrumbs

1 Cook the macaroni in boiling salted water for 15 minutes. Drain.

2 Put the butter, flour and milk in a saucepan. Heat whisking continuously, until the sauce boils and thickens and is smooth. Simmer for 1–2 minutes.

3 Remove pan from the heat, add most of the cheese and stir until melted. Season to taste.

4 Blanch the broccoli in boiling water for 7 minutes or until tender. Drain well.

5 Put the broccoli in the base of a 900ml (1½ pint) flameproof serving dish. Cover with the macaroni and cheese sauce.

6 Sprinkle with remaining cheese and bread-crumbs. Brown under a hot grill.

To Microwave

Put the macaroni in a large bowl. Pour over boiling water to cover the pasta by about 2.5cm (1 inch). Cover and microwave on HIGH for 4 minutes. Stand for 3 minutes. Put the butter, flour and milk in a medium bowl and microwave on HIGH for about 4 minutes, until boiling and thickened, whisking frequently. Complete step 3. Microwave the broccoli in a large bowl with 45ml (3 tbsp) water on HIGH for 3½ minutes. Drain well. Complete step 5 and 6.

To Freeze
Pack in a rigid container at the end of step 5 and freeze for upto 3 months.

To Thaw and Serve
Cook from frozen in the oven at 180°C (350°F) mark 4 for 30–40 minutes or until piping hot, adding the remaining cheese and the breadcrumbs after 15 minutes.
Alternatively, microwave on LOW for 15 minutes. Sprinkle with the remaining cheese and the breadcrumbs and microwave on HIGH for 10 minutes or until piping hot. Brown under a hot grill, if liked.

PIZZA NAPOLETANA

SERVES 4

BASIC PIZZA DOUGH

45ml (3 tbsp) lukewarm milk

20g (¾oz) fresh yeast

3.75ml (¾ tsp) sugar

300g (11oz) strong white bread flour

7.5ml (1½ tsp) salt

30ml (2 tbsp) olive oil

TOPPING

60ml (4 tbsp) olive oil

450g (1lb) ripe tomatoes, skinned and chopped, or 397g (14oz) can tomatoes, drained

pinch of sugar, or to taste

salt and pepper

225g (8oz) Mozzarella cheese, thinly sliced

50g (2oz) can anchovy fillets, drained and cut in half lengthways

20ml (4 tsp) chopped fresh oregano or 10ml (2 tsp) dried

1 For the dough, put the milk in a warmed jug and crumble in the yeast with your fingers. Add the sugar and stir to dissolve, then stir in 60ml (4 tbsp) of the flour.
2 Cover the jug with a clean tea towel and leave in a warm place for about 30 minutes or until frothy.
3 Sift the remaining flour and the salt into a warmed large bowl. Mix in the yeast with a fork, then add the oil and enough lukewarm water, about 90ml (6 tbsp), to draw the mixture together.

4 Turn the dough out on to a floured surface and knead for 10 minutes until it is smooth and elastic.
5 Put the ball of dough in a large floured bowl, cover with a clean tea towel and leave in a warm place for 1½–2 hours until doubled in size.
6 For the topping, put 30ml (2 tbsp) of the oil in a pan with the tomatoes, sugar and seasoning to taste. Simmer for about 10 minutes, stirring from time to time.
7 Meanwhile, turn out the risen dough on to a floured surface. Roll out and cut into two 27.5cm (11 inch) rounds. (Use a large plate, flan dish or ring as a guide.) Make the edges slightly thicker than the centres.
8 Put the rounds of dough on oiled baking sheets and spread the tomato mixture evenly over them, right to the edges. Arrange the slices of Mozzarella over the tomatoes.
9 Arrange the anchovies in a lattice pattern over the top of the tomatoes.
10 Sprinkle over the remaining oil, with the oregano and seasoning to taste. Leave to prove in a warm place for about 30 minutes.
11 Bake in the oven at 220°C (425°F) mark 7 for 25 minutes or until the topping is melted and the dough well risen. Swap the baking sheets over halfway through the cooking time. Serve hot or cold.

To Freeze
Open freeze on baking sheets at the end of step 9. Overwrap and freeze for up to 3 months.

To Thaw and Serve
Complete steps 10 and 11, adding an extra 30 minutes to the proving time.

TAGLIATELLE WITH CURD CHEESE AND HERBS

SERVES 1–2

15g (½oz) butter

1 garlic clove, skinned and crushed

50g (2oz) mushrooms, sliced

5ml (1 tsp) chopped fresh sage or 2.5ml (½ tsp) dried

45ml (3 tbsp) dry white wine

50g (2oz) cooked ham, diced

salt and pepper

100g (4oz) tagliatelle

50g (2oz) medium fat curd cheese

1 Melt the butter in a frying pan and fry the garlic, mushrooms and sage for 2 minutes, then sitr in the ham, wine and bring to the boil. Stir in the ham.
2 Bring 900ml (1½ pints) salted water to the boil and cook the pasta for 10 minutes or according to packet instructions. Drain well and keep warm.
3 Heat the cheese with the mushroom mixture until melted, then stir in the pasta. Season to taste. Serve immediately.

To Microwave

Melt the butter in a medium bowl on HIGH for 30 seconds. Microwave the mushrooms, garlic and sage on HIGH for 1 minute, then stir in the wine and microwave on HIGH for 1 minute. Stir in the ham. Put the noodles in a large bowl. Pour over boiling water to cover the pasta by about 2.5cm (1 inch). Cover and microwave on HIGH for 5 minutes. Stand for 3 minutes. Drain. Microwave the cheese with the mushroom mixture on HIGH for 1 minute. Stir in pasta. Season to taste. Serve immediately.

To Freeze

Complete steps 1, 2 and 3 slightly undercooking the pasta. Pack in a rigid container and freeze for up to 3 months.

To Thaw

Leave overnight at cool room temperature.

To Serve

Add 45ml (3 tbsp) water then reheat in a heavy-based saucepan, stirring to prevent sticking. Alternatively add 30ml (2 tbsp) water, cover microwave on HIGH for 5–7 minutes, stirring occasionally.

CHINESE PORK BROTH

SERVES 4–6

450g (1lb) lean belly of pork

30ml (2 tbsp) vegetable oil

225g (8oz) carrots, peeled and sliced into thin strips

4 spring onions, trimmed and cut into 1cm (½ inch) lengths

2.5cm (1 inch) fresh root ginger, peeled and cut into slivers

2.3 litres (4 pints) chicken stock

15ml (1 tbsp) medium dry sherry

1 large garlic clove, skinned and crushed

100g (4oz) chick peas, soaked overnight then drained

salt and pepper

450g (1lb) Chinese leaves, finely shredded

1 Cut the belly pork into fine strips, discarding the skin and bone.
2 Heat the oil in a wok or large saucepan and fry the pork, carrots, onions and ginger for about 6 minutes or until all the ingredients are browned.
3 Add the stock, sherry, garlic and chick peas with pepper to taste. Bring to the boil, cover and simmer for about 1¼ hours or until the pork and chick peas are just tender. Skim if necessary.
4 Stir the Chinese leaves into the soup with salt to taste. Simmer for a further 5 minutes. Taste and adjust seasoning. Serve hot.

To Microwave

Place the oil in a large bowl and microwave on HIGH for 1 minute or until hot. Add the pork, carrots, onions and ginger and microwave on HIGH for 4–6 minutes until softened. Add the stock, sherry, garlic and chick peas with pepper to taste. Cover and microwave on HIGH for 35–40 minutes or until tender. Stir the Chinese leaves into the soup with salt to taste. Microwave on HIGH for 3 minutes. Serve hot.

To Freeze

Cook, pack in a rigid container at the end of step 3 and freeze for up to 3 months.

To Thaw

Leave overnight in the refrigerator. Alternatively, microwave on LOW for about 10–15 minutes, breaking up the block as it thaws.

To Serve

Complete step 4.

Right: Macaroni and Broccoli Cheese (page 100)

AUBERGINE AND MINCE PASTRIES

MAKES ABOUT 30

15ml (1 tbsp) vegetable oil

50g (2oz) onion, skinned and finely chopped

225g (8oz) lean minced beef or lamb

1.25ml (¼ tsp) ground cumin

large pinch of medium-hot curry powder

2 large tomatoes, about 225g (8oz), skinned and chopped

1 medium aubergine, about 350g (12oz), cut into 1cm (½ inch) cubes

salt and pepper

5 large sheets filo pastry

100g (4oz) butter

1 Heat the oil in a medium saucepan and cook the onion until beginning to soften. Stir in the minced beef, cumin and curry powder. Cook over a high heat, stirring continuously, for 3–4 minutes. Add the tomatoes, aubergine and seasoning. Partially cover and simmer for about 20 minutes. Cool.
2 Cut the filo pastry into thin strips about 7.5 × 30.5cm (3 × 12 inches). Work with one strip at a time, keeping the remainder covered with a clean tea towel to prevent them from drying out.
3 Brush one strip with melted butter. Place about 15ml (1 tbsp) of the meat mixture into the bottom left-hand corner. Fold over diagonally to form a triangle. Continue to fold diagonally, keeping the triangle shape and brushing occasionally with butter until you reach the end of the strip. Trim away any excess. Place on a baking sheet and brush with butter. Repeat until all the meat mixture is used.
4 Bake in the oven at 190°C (375°F) mark 5 for about 20–25 minutes or until golden.

To Microwave
Place the oil in a medium bowl and add the onion. Microwave on HIGH for 5 minutes or until soft. Add the mince, cumin and curry powder, stirring well to mix. Microwave on HIGH for 2 minutes, stirring occasionally. Add the tomatoes, aubergine and seasoning. Cover and microwave on HIGH for about 10 minutes. Leave to cool. Complete steps 2–4.

To Freeze
Cool, pack in a rigid container at the end of step 3 and freeze for up to 3 months.

To Thaw and Serve
Place the pastries on baking sheets. Bake at 190°C (375°F) mark 5 for 25–30 minutes until golden.

CREAMY HAM PUFFS

SERVES 4–6

40g (1½oz) butter

75g (3oz) button mushrooms, very finely chopped

1 small onion, skinned and very finely chopped

30ml (2 tbsp) plain flour

100ml (3½fl oz) milk

100ml (3½fl oz) double cream

75g (3oz) boiled ham, finely diced

10ml (2 tsp) chopped fresh tarragon or 5ml (1 tsp) dried

salt and pepper

350g (12oz) packet frozen puff pastry, thawed

1 egg, beaten, to glaze

1 Melt 20g (¾oz) of the butter in a pan and fry the mushrooms and onion for 2–3 minutes. Drain.
2 Melt the remaining butter in the pan, add the flour and cook gently, stirring, for 1–2 minutes. Remove from the heat and gradually blend in the milk. Bring to the boil, stirring constantly. Add the cream and simmer for 3 minutes until thick. Off the heat, fold in the mushroom mixture, ham, tarragon and seasoning. Cool.
3 Roll out the pastry and cut out 12 rounds using a 10cm (4 inch) plain round cutter.
4 Put spoonfuls of the ham and mushroom filling on one half of each pastry round.
5 Brush the edges of the pastry rounds with beaten egg, then fold the plain half of the pastry over the filling. Seal the edges and crimp.
6 Place the turnovers on a dampened baking sheet. Brush with beaten egg to glaze. Bake in the oven at 220°C (425°F) mark 7 for 15–20 minutes until puffed up and golden. Serve hot.

To Microwave
Place 20g (¾oz) of the butter with the mushrooms and onion in a bowl and microwave on HIGH for 1–2 minutes, drain. Put the remaining butter, flour and milk in a bowl and whisk well. Microwave on HIGH for 1–2 minutes or until boiling and thickened, whisking frequently. Add the cream and stir well. Fold in the mushroom mixture, ham, tarragon and seasoning. Cool. Complete steps 3–6.

To Freeze
Open freeze the pastries on baking sheets at the end of step 5 and pack in rigid containers. Freeze for up to 1 month.

To Thaw and Serve
Bake the frozen pastries in the oven at 220°C (425°F) mark 7 for 15–20 minutes or until puffed up.

SAUSAGE AND SPINACH FLAN

SERVES 4

15g (½oz) butter

225g (8oz) chipolata sausages, halved

1 large onion, skinned and chopped

25g (1oz) plain wholemeal flour

300ml (½ pint) milk

salt and pepper

50g (2oz) spinach, washed, blanched and chopped

1 egg, beaten

18–20cm (7–8 inch) uncooked wholemeal pastry case (see page 110)

1 Melt the butter in a large frying pan and lightly fry the sausages and onion for 8 minutes, stirring occasionally. Stir in the flour and cook for 1 minute. Gradually add the milk, stirring continuously, until the sauce thickens and is smooth. Simmer for 1–2 minutes. Season to taste.
2 Stir in the spinach and cook for 1 minute. Beat in the egg.
3 Pour the mixture into the pastry case. Bake in the oven at 190°C (375°F) mark 5 for 45 minutes. Serve hot or cold.

To Microwave
Place the butter in a large bowl and microwave on HIGH for 30 seconds. Add the sausages and onion, cover and microwave on HIGH for 7 minutes. Stir in the flour and microwave on HIGH for 1 minute. Add the milk and microwave on HIGH for 4–5 minutes or until boiling and thickened, whisking frequently. Add the spinach and egg and microwave on HIGH for 1 minute. Complete step 3.

To Freeze
Cool, open freeze, overwrap and freeze for up to 3 months.

To Thaw
Leave for 4–6 hours at cool room temperature. Alternatively, microwave on LOW for about 2–5 minutes. Stand for 15–20 minutes.

To Serve
Serve cold with salad. Or reheat in the oven at 190°C (375°F) mark 5 for 10–15 minutes or until crisp and hot.

MUSHROOM RISOTTO

SERVES 4

25g (1oz) butter

1 onion, skinned and chopped

225g (8oz) brown rice

450ml (¾ pint) hot chicken or vegetable stock (see page 186)

150ml (¼ pint) dry white wine

1 red pepper, cored, seeded and diced

50g (2oz) frozen sweetcorn kernels

salt and pepper

1 bunch spring onions, trimmed and cut in half crossways

225g (8oz) button mushrooms, quartered

15g (½oz) grated Parmesan cheese

1 Melt the butter in a large saucepan and cook the onion and rice for 3–5 minutes until the rice is opaque. Add the stock and wine, cover and cook over low heat for 25 minutes.
2 Add the pepper and sweetcorn, then simmer for a further 10 minutes until the liquid is absorbed.
3 Season to taste, stir in the spring onions and mushrooms and cook for 5 minutes more. Serve hot with a little Parmesan cheese sprinkled over.

To Microwave
Place the butter in a large bowl and microwave on HIGH for 1 minute or until melted. Add the onion and rice and microwave on HIGH for 2–3 minutes or until the rice is opaque, stirring frequently. Add the stock and wine, cover and microwave on HIGH for 2 minutes, then MEDIUM for 10 minutes. Add the pepper and sweetcorn to the rice mixture. Cover and microwave on HIGH for 15 minutes or until the rice is tender. Season and stir in the onions and mushrooms. Cover and microwave on HIGH for 3 minutes, stirring occasionally. Add the cheese.

To Freeze
Cool, pack in a rigid container at the end of step 2 and freeze for up to 6 months.

To Thaw
Leave overnight in the refrigerator. Alternatively, microwave on LOW for about 5 minutes. Stand for 10 minutes.

To Serve
Reheat in a heavy-based saucepan, stirring to prevent sticking. Alternatively, microwave on HIGH for 2–4 minutes or until piping hot, stirring once. Complete step 3.

HADDOCK AND CORN CHOWDER

SERVES 4–6

25–50g (1–2oz) butter
450g (1lb) old potatoes, peeled and thinly sliced
225g (8oz) onion, skinned and thinly sliced
2.5ml (½ tsp) chilli powder
600ml (1 pint) light stock
568ml (1 pint) milk
298g (10½oz) can cream-style sweetcorn
salt and pepper
225g (8oz) fresh haddock fillet
225g (8oz) smoked haddock fillet
100g (4oz) peeled prawns
chopped fresh parsley

1 Heat the butter in a large saucepan and stir the potatoes, onion and chilli powder over moderate heat for 2–3 minutes.
2 Pour in the stock and milk with the corn and a little seasoning. Bring to the boil, cover and simmer for 10 minutes.
3 Meanwhile, skin the fresh and smoked haddock fillets, then divide the flesh into fork-sized pieces, discarding all the bones.
4 Add the haddock to the pan. Bring back to the boil, cover and simmer until the potatoes are tender and the fish begins to flake. Skim.
5 Stir in the prawns with plenty of parsley. Adjust seasoning.

To Microwave

Place the butter, onion, potatoes and chilli powder in a large bowl. Cover and microwave on HIGH for 5–6 minutes or until softened, stirring occasionally. Pour in the stock and milk with the corn and a little seasoning. Microwave uncovered on HIGH for 8 minutes. Complete step 3. Add the haddock and microwave on HIGH for 12–15 minutes or until the potatoes are tender. Skim. Complete step 5.

To Freeze

Cool, pack in a rigid container at the end of step 4 and freeze for up to 3 months.

To Thaw and Serve

Leave overnight at cool room temperature. Reheat in a heavy-based saucepan for 10–15 minutes until piping hot. Alternatively, microwave on HIGH for about 10–12 minutes, breaking up the block as it thaws, until piping hot. Add the prawns and parsley.

CASHEW STUFFED MUSHROOMS

SERVES 4

8 medium flat mushrooms
15ml (1 tbsp) olive oil
2 small onions, skinned and finely chopped
2 garlic cloves, skinned and crushed
50g (2oz) unsalted cashew nuts, chopped
15ml (1 tbsp) chopped fresh oregano or 2.5ml (½ tsp) dried
10ml (2 tsp) tomato purée
30–45ml (2–3 tbsp) grated Parmesan cheese

1 Remove the stalks from the mushrooms, chop and set aside. Bring a large pan of salted water to the boil and cook the mushroom caps for 30–60 seconds. Drain, set aside and keep warm.
2 Heat the oil in a medium saucepan and gently fry the onion and garlic for 3–5 minutes or until the onion has softened. Stir in the mushroom stalks, cashew nuts and oregano. Cook for 3–5 minutes until nuts begin to brown. Stir in the tomato purée.
3 Arrange the mushroom caps on a lightly oiled baking sheet. Divide the topping mixture between them and sprinkle over the Parmesan cheese.
4 Bake in the oven at 190°C (375°F) mark 5 for 10–15 minutes until golden.

To Microwave

Complete step 1. Place the oil, onion and garlic in a bowl, cover and microwave on HIGH for 2½–3 minutes. Add the chopped mushroom stalks, cashew nuts and oregano. Cover and microwave on HIGH for 2–3 minutes. Stir in the tomato purée. Arrange four mushrooms in a circle on a plate and microwave on HIGH for about 3–4 minutes, re-arranging occasionally. Repeat with the remaining four mushrooms. Grill, if liked.

To Freeze

Open freeze at the end of step 3 and pack in a rigid container. Freeze for up to 3 months.

To Thaw and Serve

Place the frozen mushrooms on a lightly greased baking sheet. Bake in the oven at 200°C (400°F) mark 6 for 20–25 minutes. Alternatively, arrange four mushrooms in a circle on a plate and microwave on HIGH for about 4–6 minutes, re-arranging occasionally. Repeat with the remaining four mushrooms. Grill, if liked.

Right: Tagliatelle with Curd Cheese and Herbs (page 102)

SESAME CHICKEN PITTAS

SERVES 4

30ml (2 tbsp) sesame oil
1 onion, skinned and sliced
100g (4oz) broccoli, cut into tiny florets
1 red pepper, cored, seeded and diced
225g (8oz) cooked chicken breast, sliced into thin strips
100g (4oz) beansprouts
15ml (1 tbsp) dark soy sauce
30ml (2 tbsp) toasted sesame seeds
4 large pitta breads

1 Heat the oil in a large frying pan and stir-fry the onion for 2 minutes. Add the broccoli and pepper and cook for 3–4 minutes, stirring frequently
2 Add the chicken strips to the pan, stir well, then add the beansprouts and soy sauce. Continue to cook for 2–3 minutes. Sprinkle over the sesame seeds and stir to combine. Remove from the heat, keeping the pan covered to keep warm.
3 Cut through a long side of each pitta bread and open the cavity to form a pocket. Place the pitta breads on a baking sheet. Bake in the oven at 200°C (400°F) mark 6 for 5–10 minutes to heat.
4 Using a slotted spoon, fill each pitta pocket with the chicken mixture.

To Microwave
Place the oil and onion in a medium bowl. Cover and microwave on HIGH for 2–2½ minutes. Add the broccoli and pepper, cover and microwave on HIGH for 2–2½ minutes. Add the chicken, beansprouts and soy sauce, stir and microwave on HIGH for 2–2½ minutes. Stir in the sesame seeds. To warm the pitta breads, place on a double thickness of absorbent kitchen paper and microwave on HIGH for 1–1½ minutes or until warm. Complete step 4.

To Freeze
Cool the chicken mixture, pack in a rigid container. Open freeze the pitta breads and pack in a polythene bag. Freeze for up to 6 months.

To Thaw
Leave the chicken mixture overnight in the refrigerator. Alternatively, cover and microwave on LOW for about 18–20 minutes, stirring frequently. Stand for 30–40 minutes.

Leave the pitta breads at room temperature for 2–3 hours. Alternatively, unwrap and place on a double thickness of kitchen paper. Microwave on LOW for 3–4 minutes, re-arranging once.

To Serve
Gently heat the chicken mixture in a heavy-based saucepan, stirring frequently, for 10–15 minutes. Alternatively, microwave on HIGH for 3½–4½ minutes or until piping hot. Complete steps 3 and 4.

Alternatively, place the pitta breads on absorbent kitchen paper and microwave on HIGH for 1–1½ minutes. Complete step 4.

TORTILLA

SERVES 4

30ml (2 tbsp) olive oil
225g (8oz) potatoes, peeled and thinly sliced
1 Spanish onion, skinned and thinly sliced
1 red pepper, cored, seeded and chopped
5 eggs, beaten
salt and pepper
15ml (1 tbsp) chopped fresh parsley or 10ml (2 tsp) dried

1 Heat the oil in a deep frying pan and gently fry the potatoes, onion and pepper for 20–25 minutes or until the potatoes are golden and cooked.
2 Pour the beaten egg into the pan, season and sprinkle over the parsley.
3 Cook the tortilla over a gentle heat for 7–10 minutes or until golden. Carefully invert the tortilla on to a plate, then slide it back into the frying pan to cook the other side for a further 3–5 minutes.
4 Turn the tortilla on to a warmed serving plate.

To Microwave
Place the oil, potatoes, onion and pepper in a shallow 20.5cm (8 inch) dish. Cover and microwave on HIGH for 7–10 minutes or until tender, re-arranging occasionally. Pour in the beaten eggs, season and sprinkle over the parsley. Cover and microwave on HIGH for 3–4 minutes or until almost set. Carefully invert the tortilla on to a plate, then slide back into the dish and microwave on HIGH for a further 2–3 minutes or until almost set. Complete step 4.

To Freeze
Cool, wrap in plastic wrap and overwrap with foil at the end of step 3. Freeze for up to 3 months.

To Thaw and Serve
Place the frozen tortilla on an ovenproof plate and cover with foil. Cook in the oven at 200°C (400°F) mark 6 for 30–40 minutes until heated through. Alternatively, cover and microwave on HIGH for about 10–12 minutes or until piping hot. Garnish.

CHEESY FISH CAKES

SERVES 4

450g (1lb) potatoes, peeled and diced

275g (10oz) cod or haddock fillets, skinned

150ml (¼ pint) milk

100g (4oz) mature Cheddar cheese, grated

1 egg, beaten

salt and pepper

30ml (2 tbsp) chopped fresh parsley or 10ml (2 tsp) dried

75g (3oz) fresh breadcrumbs

25g (1oz) ground almonds

1 egg, beaten

lemon wedges, to serve

1 Place the potatoes in a saucepan of salted water, bring to the boil and simmer for 10–15 minutes or until tender. Drain.

2 Place the fish fillets in a frying pan and pour over the milk. Gently poach the fillets for 5–8 minutes or until the fish is firm and flakes easily. Drain.

3 Mash the potatoes well until smooth. Add the cheese, egg, seasoning and parsley. Flake the fish and stir into the potato mixture. Cool completely.

4 With lightly floured hands, shape the mixture into eight cakes. Mix the breadcrumbs and almonds together in a small bowl. Coat each fish cake in the egg, then in the crumb mixture and repeat. Place on a lightly greased baking sheet. Cover and chill for 15–20 minutes.

5 Bake in the oven at 190°C (375°F) mark 5 for 20–25 minutes, turning over once or until golden brown. Serve with lemon wedges.

To Microwave

Complete step 1. Arrange the fish fillets in a shallow dish and pour over the milk. Cover and microwave on HIGH for 3½–4 minutes or until the fish is firm and flakes easily. Stand for 1 minute. Drain. Complete steps 3–5.

To Freeze

Open freeze the fish cakes at the end of step 4 and pack in a rigid container. Freeze for up to 3 months.

To Thaw and Serve

Place the frozen fish cakes on a lightly greased baking sheet. Bake in the oven at 200°C (400°F) mark 6 for 45–50 minutes or until golden brown, turning over once.

CRISPY STUFFED POTATO SKINS

SERVES 4–6

4 medium baking potatoes, scrubbed and pricked

175g (6oz) mature Cheddar cheese, grated

45ml (3 tbsp) snipped chives or 15ml (1 tbsp) dried

25g (1oz) fresh breadcrumbs

vegetable oil, for deep frying

DIPPING SAUCE

30ml (2 tbsp) snipped chives or 10ml (2 tsp) dried

300ml (½ pint) soured cream

1 Place potatoes on a baking sheet. Bake at 220°C (425°F) mark 7 for 1–1½ hours until cooked.

2 Cut each potato in half and scoop out the flesh. Chop the flesh into chunks and place in a medium bowl. Add 100g (4oz) of the cheese and 30ml (2 tbsp) of the snipped chives or 10ml (2 tsp) dried. Season. Cover with foil to keep warm.

3 Heat the oil to 190°C (375°F) in a deep fat fryer and deep fry the potato skins in batches for 3–4 minutes until crisp. Drain. Arrange the skins, hollow side up, on a baking sheet.

4 Spoon the potato mixture into the skins. Mix the remaining cheese, chives and breadcrumbs together and sprinkle over each stuffed potato skin. Grill until golden. For the dipping sauce, stir the chives into the soured cream.

To Microwave

Prick the potatoes all over with a fork and place on a double thickness of kitchen paper. Microwave on HIGH for 10–15 minutes, re-arranging. Stand for 5 minutes. Complete steps 2–4.

To Freeze

Complete steps 1 and 2. Cool the filling, pack in a rigid container and freeze for up to 3 months. Open freeze the potato skins, pack in a rigid container and freeze for up to 3 months. Mix the remaining cheese, chives and breadcrumbs together, pack in a polythene bag and freeze for up to 3 months.

To Thaw and Serve

Leave the breadcrumb mixture at room temperature for 1–2 hours. Place the frozen potato mixture in an ovenproof dish and cover with foil. Bake in the oven at 200°C (400°F) mark 6 for 40–50 minutes or until heated through. Alternatively, cover and microwave on HIGH for about 12–14 minutes or until piping hot. Complete steps 3 and 4, frying the potato skins from frozen.

BREAKFAST PANCAKES

MAKES 4

25g (1oz) plain wholemeal flour

25g (1oz) medium oatmeal

salt and pepper

4 eggs, beaten

250ml (9fl oz) milk

100g (4oz) back bacon, grilled and chopped

2 tomatoes, sliced and grilled

butter for frying

1 Put the flour, oatmeal, salt and 15ml (1 tbsp) egg into a bowl. Gradually add 150ml (¼ pint) milk to form a smooth batter

2 Heat a little butter in a 20.5cm (8 inch) frying pan. When hot, pour in 45ml (3 tbsp) of the batter, tilting the pan to cover the base. Cook until the pancake moves freely, turn over and cook until golden. Makes 4 pancakes.

3 Beat together the remaining eggs, milk, salt and pepper. Scramble in a small saucepan over a gentle heat, stirring until the egg starts to set.

4 Place spoonfuls of the egg into the pancakes, add the bacon and tomato slices. Fold the pancakes over. Serve immediately as a snack or for breakfast.

To Microwave

Complete steps 1 and 2. To scramble the eggs, microwave in a medium bowl on HIGH for 3–4 minutes, stirring frequently. Complete step 4.

To Freeze

Freeze and pancakes at the end of step 2. Interleave with greaseproof paper and wrap in foil. Store for up to 2 months.

To Thaw and Serve

Reheat the foil wrapped pancakes in the oven at 190°C (375°F) mark 5 for 20–30 minutes. Alternatively, cover the pancakes with greaseproof paper and microwave on HIGH for 1½-2 minutes or until piping hot. Complete steps 3 and 4.

JANSSON'S TEMPTATION

SERVES 6

4 medium baking potatoes

two 50g (2oz) cans anchovy fillets, soaked in milk for 20 minutes and drained

1 large onion, skinned and finely chopped

25g (1oz) butter

salt and pepper

450ml (¾ pint) single cream

30ml (2 tbsp) chopped fresh parsley, to garnish

1 Peel the potatoes and cut into very thin matchstick strips. Cut the anchovies into thin strips.

2 Arrange half of the potato strips in a layer in the base of a well buttered ovenproof dish. Sprinkle with a little salt and plenty of pepper.

3 Arrange the strips of anchovy and chopped onion over the potato layer, then top with the remaining potato. Sprinkle with seasoning as before. Pour half the cream slowly into the dish, then dot with the remaining butter.

4 Bake in the oven at 180°C (350°F) mark 4 for 30 minutes. Add the remaining cream and bake for a further 1 hour or until the potatoes feel tender when pierced with a skewer. Cover the dish with foil if the potatoes show signs of over-browning during cooking. Serve hot, sprinkled with parsley.

To Microwave

Complete steps 1–3. Microwave on HIGH for 15–17 minutes or until the potatoes are tender, turning the dish during cooking. Grill, if liked.

To Freeze

Cool, pack in a rigid container and freeze for up to 1 month.

To Thaw and Serve

Leave at cool room temperature for 5–6 hours. Bake in the oven at 180°C (350°F) mark 4 for 15–20 minutes, covering if the top becomes too brown. Alternatively, microwave on HIGH for 5–6 minutes or until piping hot, turning the dish.

Right: Stoved Chicken (page 116)

POULTRY AND GAME MAIN COURSES

CHICKEN AND CRANBERRY PIE

SERVES 8

1.6kg (3½lb) oven-ready chicken

sliced carrot, onion and celery, for flavouring

75g (3oz) onion, skinned and thinly sliced

100g (4oz) cranberries

grated rind of 1 orange

10ml (2 tsp) roughly chopped fresh sage

25g (1oz) butter

salt and pepper

150g (5oz) plain wholemeal flour

150g (5oz) plain flour

65g (2½oz) lard

beaten egg, to glaze

5ml (1 tsp) powdered gelatine

1 Remove the flesh from the chicken, discard the skin and place the carcass and all the other bones into a large saucepan. Add the flavouring ingredients and cover with cold water. Bring to the boil, cover and simmer for about 1 hour.

2 Meanwhile, cut the chicken flesh into bite-sized pieces and place in a bowl. Add the onion and cranberries. Beat in the orange rind, sage and butter. Season.

3 Place the flours in a bowl and make a well in the centre. Heat the lard and 200ml (7fl oz) water together, bring to the boil, then pour into the well. Beat the ingredients together, then knead against the side of the bowl until smooth. Use the pastry immediately and keep the trimmings covered.

4 Place a 20.5cm (8 inch) flan ring on to a baking sheet. On a lightly floured surface, roll out two-thirds of the pastry and use to line the flan ring. Ease the pastry into the base of the ring and fold the excess outwards.

5 Spoon the chicken mixture into the pastry case, pressing down gently. Roll out the remaining pastry and use to cover the pie. Seal the edges, trim and flute. Reserve the trimmings. Make a hole in the centre of pie and three around outer edge. Decorate with the pastry trimmings. Glaze with the beaten egg.

6 Bake in the oven at 220°C (425°F) mark 7 for about 20 minutes. Reduce the oven temperature to 180°C (350°F) mark 4 and bake for a further 1 hour. Cool.

7 Strain the stock. Return the liquor to the saucepan and boil to reduce until 300ml (½ pint) remains. Cool.

8 In a small bowl, sprinkle the gelatine over 15ml (1 tbsp) water. Leave until spongy. To dissolve the gelatine, stand the bowl over pan of simmering water. Stir into the skimmed stock. Chill until beginning to set.

9 Ease the pie from the flan ring and place on a plate. Place a small icing nozzle in the holes in the pie and pour through as much stock as the pie will take. Chill to set.

To Microwave

Complete step 1, placing the ingredients and 600ml (1 pint) water in a large bowl. Cover and microwave on HIGH for 20 minutes. Stand for 20 minutes. Complete steps 2 and 3. Put the lard and 200ml (7fl oz) water in a heatproof jug and microwave on HIGH for 2 minutes or until boiling. Complete steps 4–6. Sprinkle the gelatine over 15ml (1 tbsp) water in a small bowl and microwave on HIGH for 30 seconds or until hot but not boiling. Stir until dissolved, then add to 300ml (½ pint) of the stock. Chill until beginning to set. Complete step 9.

To Freeze

Pack without the jelly in a rigid container and freeze for up to 4 months. Pack the stock separately in a rigid container and freeze for up to 6 months.

To Thaw and Serve

Leave overnight in the refrigerator. Alternatively, microwave on LOW on a serving dish for about 10–15 minutes, turning occasionally. Stand for 10 minutes. Refrigerate until required. Microwave the frozen stock on LOW for 4–6 minutes. Stand for 3–5 minutes. Complete steps 8–9.

Note: The pie will be much softer after freezing.

CHICKEN PAPRIKASH

SERVES 4

1.4kg (3lb) chicken, jointed into 8 pieces
50g (2oz) plain flour
salt and pepper
50g (2oz) butter or chicken fat
450g (1lb) onions, skinned and sliced
1 red pepper, cored, seeded and sliced
15ml (1 tbsp) paprika
1 garlic clove, skinned and crushed
397g (14oz) can tomatoes
300ml (½ pint) chicken stock
1 bay leaf
150ml (¼ pint) soured cream

1 Toss the chicken joints in the flour, liberally seasoned with salt and pepper, to coat.

2 Melt the butter in a frying pan and fry the chicken joints until golden brown. Transfer the joints to a casserole large enough to take them in a single layer.

3 Add the onions and red pepper to the frying pan and fry gently for 5 minutes until soft. Stir in the paprika, garlic and any remaining flour. Cook gently, stirring, for a few minutes.

4 Add the tomatoes with their juice, the stock and bay leaf. Season and bring to the boil. Pour over the chicken and cover tightly.

5 Cook in the oven at 170°C (325°F) mark 3 for about 1 hour or until tender. Discard the bay leaf.

6 Stir half the soured cream into the casserole. Spoon the remaining soured cream over the top.

To Microwave
Complete steps 1 and 2. Pour any excess fat into a large bowl. Add the onions, red pepper, paprika, garlic and any remaining flour. Cover and microwave on HIGH for 5–7 minutes or until the onion is softened. Add the chicken, tomatoes, stock, bay leaf and seasoning. Cover and microwave on HIGH for 25–30 minutes or until tender, stirring occasionally. Complete step 6.

To Freeze
Cool quickly, pack in a rigid container and freeze for up to 3 months.

To Thaw
Leave overnight in the refrigerator. Alternatively, microwave on LOW in a covered serving dish for about 20–25 minutes, stirring occasionally. Stand for 15 minutes.

To Serve
Cook in a covered casserole in the oven at 180°C (350°F) mark 4 for 35–40 minutes. Alternatively, cover and microwave on HIGH for 15 minutes or until piping hot, stirring frequently.

CHICKEN KIEV

SERVES 4

4 large boneless chicken breasts, skinned
100g (4oz) butter
finely grated rind of ½ lemon
15ml (1 tbsp) lemon juice
15ml (1 tbsp) chopped fresh parsley
1 garlic clove, skinned and crushed
salt and pepper
25g (1oz) plain flour
1 egg, beaten
100g (4oz) fresh white breadcrumbs
vegetable oil, for deep frying

1 Place the chicken breasts on a wooden board and pound them to an even thickness with a meat mallet or rolling pin.

2 Work the butter with the lemon rind and juice, the parsley, garlic and seasoning to taste.

3 Place the butter on a sheet of non-stick or waxed paper and form into a roll. Refrigerate until the butter is firm.

4 Cut the butter into four pieces and place one piece on each of the flattened chicken breasts.

5 Roll up the chicken, folding the ends in to enclose the butter completely. Secure with wooden cocktail sticks.

6 Coat the chicken breasts in the flour seasoned with salt and pepper, then in beaten egg and breadcrumbs. Pat the crumbs firmly so that the chicken is well coated. Chill for at least 1 hour or until required.

7 Heat the oil to 170°C (325°F). Deep fry two chicken portions at a time for about 15 minutes. Drain on absorbent kitchen paper.

To Freeze
Only use chicken that has not been previously frozen. Pack in a rigid container at the end of step 6 and freeze for up to 6 months.

To Thaw and Serve
Leave overnight in the refrigerator. Alternatively, microwave on LOW on a plate for 3–4 minutes. Stand for 5–10 minutes. Complete step 7.

SPICED CHICKEN

SERVES 4

350g (12oz) boneless chicken, skinned and diced

40g (1½ oz) plain wholemeal flour

5ml (1 tsp) curry powder

2.5ml (½ tsp) cayenne pepper

40g (1½ oz) butter

1 medium onion, skinned and chopped

450ml (¾ pint) milk

60ml (4 tbsp) apple chutney

100g (4oz) sultanas

150ml (5fl oz) soured cream

2.5ml (½ tsp) paprika

1 Toss the chicken in the flour, curry powder and cayenne pepper, shaking off the excess.
2 Melt the butter and lightly fry the chicken and onion for 5–6 minutes, until the chicken is brown.
3 Stir in remaining flour. Blend in the milk, stirring, until the sauce thickens, boils and is smooth.
4 Add the chutney and sultanas and simmer gently for 30–35 minutes, until the chicken is tender.
5 Drizzle with cream. Sprinkle with paprika.

To Microwave
Complete step 1. Cube the butter and microwave in a large bowl on HIGH for 1 minute. Microwave the onion on HIGH for 5 minutes. Add the chicken and microwave on HIGH for 3–4 minutes, stirring occasionally. Stir in the flour. Gradually blend in the milk and microwave on HIGH for 7–8 minutes, stirring occasionally, until boiling and thickened. Add the chutney and sultanas and microwave on MEDIUM for 12–15 minutes, until tender.

To Freeze
Cool, pack in a rigid container without the cream and paprika and freeze for up to 3 months.

To Thaw
Leave overnight in the refrigerator. Alternatively microwave on LOW for about 15–20 minutes, breaking up the block as it thaws.

To Serve
Cover and heat gently in a heavy-based saucepan for 15–20 minutes, stirring occasionally. Add a little milk or water to prevent sticking, if necessary. Stir in the cream and paprika. Alternatively add 30ml (2 tbsp) milk or water then microwave covered on HIGH for 7–10 minutes or until piping hot, stirring occasionally. Stir in the cream and paprika and cook for a further 2 minutes on HIGH.

CHICKEN AND CHERVIL PANCAKES

SERVES 4

BATTER

100g (4oz) plain flour

1 egg

about 250ml (9fl oz) milk

salt and pepper

vegetable oil, for frying

FILLING

25g (1oz) butter

8 spring onions, trimmed and roughly chopped

30ml (2 tbsp) plain flour

400ml (14fl oz) milk

200g (7oz) Cheddar cheese, grated

60ml (4 tbsp) chopped fresh chervil or parsley

225g (8oz) cooked chicken, chopped

75g (3oz) fresh breadcrumbs

1 For the pancake batter, beat the flour, egg, milk and seasoning together in a bowl. Make 8–10 pancakes (see page 156). Cover and set aside.
2 For the filling, melt the butter in a pan and stir-fry the spring onions for 1 minute. Stir in the flour and cook gently for 30 seconds. Gradually add the milk, then bring to the boil, stirring.
3 Season and pour half the sauce into a bowl. Add half the cheese, the chervil and chicken.
4 Divide the filling between the pancakes and roll up or fold into triangles. Arrange in a shallow greased ovenproof dish. Pour the remaining sauce on top.
5 Mix remaining cheese and the breadcrumbs together and sprinkle over the top of the pancakes.
6 Bake in the oven at 200°C (400°F) mark 6 for 20–25 minutes or until crisp and golden.

To Microwave
Complete step 1. Place the butter, flour, milk and spring onions in a medium bowl. Microwave on HIGH for about 4 minutes or until boiling and thickened, whisking. Complete steps 3–6.

To Freeze
Pack in a rigid container at the end of step 5 and freeze for up to 2 months.

To Thaw and Serve
Leave overnight in the refrigerator. Alternatively, microwave on LOW for about 10–12 minutes, turning occasionally. Stand for 15 minutes. Complete step 6.

Right: Spiced Chicken

CHICKEN WITH MUSHROOMS AND BACON

SERVES 4

30ml (2 tbsp) vegetable oil

100g (4oz) streaky bacon, rinded and chopped

1 medium onion, skinned and chopped

1 garlic clove, skinned and crushed

175g (6oz) button mushrooms, sliced

4 chicken quarters, skinned

300ml (½ pint) chicken stock

400g (14oz) can chopped tomatoes

1 bay leaf

salt and pepper

30ml (2 tbsp) chopped fresh parsley, to garnish

1 Heat the oil in a large saucepan and fry the bacon for 5 minutes until crisp.

2 Add the onion, garlic and mushrooms to the pan and fry gently for 3–5 minutes or until the onion has softened. Add the chicken and fry for 8–10 minutes or until evenly browned, turning once.

3 Pour over the stock. Add the tomatoes with their juice and the bay leaf. Season to taste. Gradually bring to the boil, stirring occasionally. Simmer for 35–40 minutes or until tender.

4 Remove the bay leaf, transfer to a warmed serving dish and sprinkle with the chopped parsley. Serve with boiled rice to soak up the juices.

To Microwave

Place the oil, bacon, onion and garlic in a large bowl, cover and microwave on HIGH for 5 minutes or until softened, stirring occasionally. Add the mushrooms, chicken, tomatoes, bay leaf and 300ml (½ pint) boiling stock. Cover and microwave on HIGH for 20–25 minutes or until the chicken is tender and the juices run clear. Turn and re-arrange the chicken portions twice during cooking. Complete step 4.

To Freeze

Cool, pack in a rigid container and freeze for up to 2 months.

To Thaw

Leave overnight in the refrigerator. Alternatively, cover and microwave on LOW for about 25–30 minutes, breaking up the block as it thaws. Stand for 30–35 minutes until completely thawed.

To Serve

Cover and heat gently in a large saucepan for 20–30 minutes or until the chicken is heated through. Alternatively, cover and microwave on HIGH for 15–20 minutes or until piping hot, stirring frequently. Garnish.

STOVED CHICKEN

SERVES 4

25g (1oz) butter

15ml (1 tbsp) vegetable oil

4 chicken quarters, halved

100g (4oz) lean back bacon, rinded and chopped

1.1kg (2½lb) floury potatoes, such as King Edwards, peeled and cut into 0.5cm (¼ inch) slices

2 large onions, skinned and sliced

salt and pepper

10ml (2 tsp) chopped fresh thyme or 2.5ml (½ tsp) dried

600ml (1 pint) chicken stock (see page 186)

snipped chives, to garnish

1 Heat 15g (½oz) of the butter and the oil in a large frying pan and fry the chicken and bacon for 5 minutes until lightly browned.

2 Place a thick layer of potato slices, then onion slices, in the base of a large casserole. Season well, add the thyme and dot with half the remaining butter.

3 Add the chicken and bacon, season to taste and dot with the remaining butter. Cover with the remaining onions and finally a layer of potatoes. Season and dot with butter. Pour over the stock.

4 Cover and bake in the oven at 150°C (300°F) mark 2 for about 2 hours or until the chicken is tender and the potatoes are cooked, adding a little more hot stock if necessary. Just before serving, sprinkle with snipped chives.

To Freeze

Cool quickly, pack in a rigid container and freeze for up to 4 months.

To Thaw

Leave overnight in the refrigerator. Alternatively, microwave on LOW in a covered serving dish for about 20–25 minutes, stirring occasionally. Stand for 15 minutes.

To Serve

Cook in a covered casserole in the oven at 180°C (350°F) mark 4 for about 35–40 minutes. Alternatively, cover and microwave on HIGH for about 15 minutes or until piping hot, stirring.

CHICKEN THIGHS WITH SPICY TOMATO SAUCE

SERVES 4

15g (½oz) butter
15ml (1 tbsp) vegetable oil
1 medium onion, skinned and chopped
1 garlic clove, skinned and crushed
5ml (1 tsp) ground cumin
5ml (1 tsp) ground coriander
large pinch of chilli powder
8 chicken thighs
397g (14oz) can tomatoes
15ml (1 tbsp) tomato purée
salt and pepper
30ml (2 tbsp) chopped fresh parsley

1 Heat the butter and oil in a large frying pan, add the onion and garlic, cover and cook for 4–5 minutes until the onion is softened. Add the cumin, coriander and chilli powder and cook for 1 minute, stirring continuously.
2 Push the onions to one side of the pan, then add the chicken and brown on both sides. Stir in the tomatoes and tomato purée. Season to taste.
3 Bring to the boil, stirring. Cover and simmer gently for 30 minutes until tender. Stir in the parsley.

To Microwave
Place all the ingredients, except the butter, oil, chicken and parsley, in a large bowl. Cover and microwave on HIGH for 10 minutes. Meanwhile, melt the butter and oil in a frying pan and brown the chicken on both sides. Add the chicken to the sauce, cover and microwave on HIGH for 15 minutes or until the chicken is tender, stirring occasionally. Stir in the parsley.

To Freeze
Cool quickly, then pack in a rigid container and freeze for up to 4 months.

To Thaw
Leave overnight in the refrigerator. Alternatively, microwave on LOW in a covered serving dish for about 15–20 minutes, stirring occasionally. Stand for 15 minutes.

To Serve
Cover and heat in a heavy-based saucepan for 30–40 minutes, stirring frequently. Alternatively, cover and microwave on HIGH for about 15 minutes or until piping hot, stirring frequently.

CHICKEN STRUDELS

SERVES 6

225g (8oz) broccoli florets
salt and pepper
225g (8oz) frozen leaf spinach
150ml (¼ pint) soured cream
30ml (2 tbsp) chopped walnuts
30ml (2 tbsp) grated Parmesan cheese
1 egg, beaten
200g (7oz) cooked chicken, finely diced
6 sheets filo pastry, measuring about 28 × 45cm (11 × 18in), about 225g (8oz)
60ml (4 tbsp) vegetable oil
25g (1oz) butter
15ml (1 tbsp) sesame seeds
tomato salad and natural yogurt with cucumber, to serve

1 Break the broccoli into small florets and cook in a saucepan of boiling salted water for 2–3 minutes until just tender. Drain well. Cook the frozen spinach in 15ml (1 tbsp) water until thawed, drain.
2 Stir the broccoli, spinach, seasoning, cream, walnuts, cheese and egg together. Add the chicken.
3 Brush each sheet of pastry with oil, arranging the sheets one on top of the other. Cut in half lengthways and widthways and stack the piles.
4 Spoon a little of the filling along the longer edge of each piece, then roll one at a time into a long thin sausage. Roll each end towards the centre, then place on a greased baking sheet.
5 Brush the strudels with melted butter and sprinkle with sesame seeds. Bake in the oven at 190°C (375°F) mark 5 for 20–25 minutes.

To Microwave
Place the broccoli in a large bowl with 45ml (3 tbsp) water. Cover and microwave on HIGH for 2–3 minutes or until just tender. Place the spinach in shallow dish and microwave on HIGH for 5–6 minutes or until thawed, stirring occasionally. Complete steps 2–4. Microwave the butter on HIGH for 45 seconds. Complete step 5.

To Freeze
Cool, pack in a rigid container and freeze for up to 3 months.

To Thaw and Serve
Leave overnight at cool room temperature. Alternatively, microwave on LOW for 10–12 minutes, re-arranging halfway. Stand for 4–5 minutes. Place on a baking sheet and cover lightly. Reheat at 180°C (350°F) mark 4 for 25 minutes.

TURKEY ESCALOPES WITH DAMSONS

SERVES 2–3

2 turkey breast fillets, each weighing about 225g (8oz), skinned and cut widthways into 5cm (2 inch) slices

75ml (3fl oz) unsweetened apple juice

45ml (3 tbsp) soy sauce

45ml (3 tbsp) dry sherry

1 small clove garlic, skinned and crushed

5ml (1 tsp) chopped fresh thyme or 1.25ml (¼ tsp) dried thyme

15g (½oz) butter

15ml (1 tbsp) vegetable oil

225g (8oz) damsons or plums, halved and stoned

pepper

1 Bat out the turkey slices with a rolling pin or meat mallet until about 2.5cm (1 inch) thick.
2 Place in a large shallow dish and pour over the apple juice, soy sauce, sherry, garlic and thyme. Cover and leave in the refrigerator to marinate for 3–4 hours or overnight.
3 Remove the turkey from the marinade, reserving the marinade. Heat butter and oil and quickly fry the turkey until browned on both sides. Add the damsons, reserved marinade and pepper.
4 Cover and simmer gently for 10–15 minutes, until tender, stirring occasionally.

To Microwave
Complete steps 1 and 2. Remove the turkey from the marinade, reserving the marinade. Microwave a large browning dish on HIGH for 5–8 minutes or according to the manufacturer's instructions. Add 15ml (1 tbsp) vegetable oil (omit butter) then quickly add the turkey and microwave on HIGH for 2 minutes, stirring once. Add the damsons and pepper to taste. Cover and microwave on HIGH for 5 minutes or until tender, stirring once. Serve hot.

To Freeze
Cool quickly, pack in a rigid container and freeze for up to 3 months.

To Thaw
Leave overnight in the refrigerator.

To Serve
Cook in a heavy-based saucepan for about 15 minutes until piping hot, stirring occasionally. Add a little water to prevent sticking if necessary. Alternatively, microwave, covered on HIGH for 5–8 minutes or until piping hot, stirring occasionally.

TURKEY FRICASSÉE

SERVES 4

65g (2½oz) butter

175g (6oz) button mushrooms, thinly sliced

50g (2oz) plain flour

600ml (1 pint) chicken or turkey stock (see page 186)

15ml (1 tbsp) lemon juice

700g (1½lb) cooked turkey, cut into bite-size pieces

salt and pepper

45ml (3 tbsp) double cream

lemon slices dipped in chopped fresh parsley, to garnish

1 Melt 15g (½oz) of the butter in a frying pan and fry the mushrooms for 5 minutes until soft.
2 Melt the remaining butter in a saucepan, add the flour and cook, stirring, for 2 minutes. Remove from the heat and gradually stir in the stock. Bring to the boil and cook for about 5 minutes, stirring until the sauce thickens.
3 Add the lemon juice to the sauce with the turkey, mushrooms and seasoning. Heat gently, then stir in the cream. Serve hot, garnished with the lemon slices.

To Microwave
Place the mushrooms in a large bowl with 15g (½oz) of the butter. Microwave on HIGH for 2–3 minutes or until soft. Add the remaining butter and flour and gradually stir in the stock. Microwave on HIGH for 5–6 minutes or until the sauce has boiled and thickened, whisking frequently. Add the lemon juice and turkey to the sauce and season well. Microwave on HIGH for 2–3 minutes until hot, then stir in the cream. Garnish with the lemon slices.

To Freeze
Cool, pack in a rigid container without the cream and freeze for up to 4 months.

To Thaw
Leave overnight in the refrigerator. Alternatively, microwave on LOW for about 15–20 minutes, stirring occasionally. Stand for 10 minutes.

To Serve
Cover and heat gently in a heavy-based saucepan for 15–20 minutes or until piping hot, stirring frequently. Alternatively, microwave on HIGH for 8–10 minutes, or until piping hot. Add the cream and garnish.

Right: Turkey Escalopes with Damsons

TURKEY MEDALLIONS WITH BASIL AND MOZZARELLA

SERVES 4

4 turkey breast slices, about 400g (14oz)
salt and pepper
1 garlic clove, skinned and crushed
45ml (3 tbsp) pesto sauce
50g (2oz) Mozzarella cheese
1 egg, beaten
100g (4oz) fine dry white breadcrumbs
vegetable oil, for frying
450g (1lb) courgettes, coarsely grated or shredded
15g (½oz) butter
fresh basil, to garnish

1 Place the turkey slices between two sheets of greaseproof paper or cling film, then pound with a wooden rolling pin until thin and evenly flat. Season generously.
2 Spread the garlic and pesto sauce over the turkey. Cut the cheese into eight sticks, about 6cm (2½ inches) long, and place one in the centre of each slice. Fold over the edges and roll up the turkey, enclosing the cheese completely.
3 Dip each roll into the beaten egg, then into the breadcrumbs. Cover and chill for at least 4 hours.
4 Deep fry the rolls or fry in medium hot oil, 1cm (½ inch) deep, for about 4–5 minutes on each side. When crisp and golden, drain well. Keep hot.
5 Meanwhile, heat 15–30ml (1–2 tbsp) oil and stir-fry the courgettes until just tender. Season and stir in the butter.
6 Spoon a bed or ring of courgettes on four warmed dinner plates. Cut each roll of turkey across into three neat medallions and arrange on the courgettes. Garnish with basil.

To Microwave
Complete steps 1–4. Place the courgettes and oil in a large bowl. Microwave on HIGH for 2–3 minutes or until softened, stirring occasionally. Season and stir in the butter. Complete step 6.

To Freeze
Only use turkey that has not been previously frozen. Pack in a rigid container at the end of step 3 and freeze for up to 6 months.

To Thaw and Serve
Leave overnight in the refrigerator. Complete steps 4–6.

RABBIT CASSEROLE

SERVES 4

100g (4oz) streaky bacon rashers, rinded and chopped
4 rabbit portions
4 celery sticks, chopped
2 leeks, trimmed, washed and sliced
1 bay leaf
225g (8oz) carrots, peeled and sliced
30ml (2 tbsp) plain wholemeal flour
600ml (1 pint) chicken stock (see page 186)
salt and pepper
DUMPLINGS
75g (3oz) self raising flour
40g (1½oz) shredded beef suet
15ml (1 tbsp) snipped chives

1 Fry the bacon in a flameproof casserole until the fat runs. Add the rabbit and fry gently until browned. Stir in the celery, leeks, bay leaf and carrots, mixing well. Sprinkle in the wholemeal flour and stir well. Cook for 1 minute, then remove from the heat and gradually add the stock. Bring to the boil, stirring continuously. Season to taste.
2 Cover and bake in the oven at 170°C (325°F) mark 3 for about 1½ hours or until tender.
3 To make the dumplings, mix the self raising flour, suet, chives and seasoning together. Add enough cold water to make a soft dough.
4 Twenty to twenty-five minutes before the end of the cooking time, shape the dough into 12 balls and place on top of the casserole. Cover again and bake until the dumplings are well risen and cooked.

To Microwave
Complete step 1. Transfer the casserole to a large bowl. Cover and microwave on HIGH for 15 minutes, then on MEDIUM for 45 minutes or until the rabbit is tender. Add the dumplings 2–5 minutes before the end of the cooking time.

To Freeze
Cool quickly, pack in a rigid container at the end of step 2. Freeze for up to 2 months.

To Thaw
Leave overnight in the refrigerator. Alternatively, cover and microwave on LOW for 20–25 minutes, stirring occasionally. Stand for 15 minutes.

To Serve
Cook in a covered casserole in the oven at 180°C (350°F) mark 4 for 35–40 minutes or until piping hot, stirring frequently. Complete steps 3 and 4.

RICH VENISON CASSEROLE

SERVES 4

900g (2lb) stewing venison

150ml (¼ pint) red wine

100ml (4fl oz) vegetable oil

12 juniper berries, lightly crushed

4 cloves

8 black peppercorns

1 garlic clove, skinned and crushed

100g (4oz) streaky bacon rashers, rinded

225g (8oz) onions, skinned and sliced

30ml (2 tbsp) plain flour

150ml (¼ pint) beef stock

30ml (2 tbsp) redcurrant jelly

salt and pepper

chopped fresh parsley, to garnish

1 Cut the meat into cubes, discarding any fat or gristle. Place in a bowl and add the wine, 50ml (2fl oz) of the oil, juniper berries, cloves, peppercorns and garlic. Stir well and leave to marinate for at least 24 hours, stirring occasionally.
2 Stretch each bacon rasher using a knife, cut in half and roll up. Heat the remaining oil in a flameproof casserole and fry the bacon for about 3 minutes until coloured. Remove from the casserole. Strain the venison, reserving the marinade, and quickly fry in several batches until coloured. Remove from the casserole. Add the onions and cook for 3 minutes.
3 Stir in the flour and cook for 2 minutes, stirring. Add the stock, redcurrant jelly and the marinade, then replace the meat. Season. Place the bacon rolls on the top of the casserole and bring to the boil.
4 Cover and cook in the oven at 170°C (325°F) mark 3 for 3 hours or until tender. Garnish.

To Freeze
Cool quickly, pack in a rigid container and freeze for up to 3 months.

To Thaw
Leave overnight in the refrigerator. Alternatively, microwave on LOW for about 15–20 minutes. Stand for 15 minutes.

To Serve
Cook in a covered casserole in the oven at 170°C (325°F) mark 3 for 35–40 minutes. Alternatively, microwave on HIGH for 15–20 minutes or until piping hot, stirring frequently. Garnish.

GROUSE WITH APPLE AND BRANDY

SERVES 4

2 old grouse

100g (4oz) rindless streaky bacon, in one thick rasher

30ml (2 tbsp) vegetable oil

60ml (4 tbsp) brandy

225g (8oz) cooking apples, peeled, cored and chopped

450ml (¾ pint) boiling chicken stock

salt and pepper

15ml (1 tbsp) cornflour

chopped fresh parsley, to garnish

1 Halve the grouse and cut away the backbone, then wash and dry them. Cut the bacon into small pieces. Heat the oil in a flameproof casserole and lightly brown the grouse and bacon.
2 Add the brandy, heat gently, ignite and leave until the flames subside. Add the apples to the grouse with the stock and seasoning.
3 Cover tightly and cook in the oven at 170°C (325°F) mark 3 for about 2½ hours or until the birds are tender. Lift the grouse on to a warm serving dish.
4 Boil up the juices. Blend the cornflour with a little water until smooth. Stir into the juices and cook until thickened. Spoon over the grouse and garnish with parsley.

To Freeze
Cool quickly, pack in a rigid container at the end of step 3 and freeze for up to 2 months.

To Thaw
Leave overnight in the refrigerator. Alternatively, microwave on LOW for about 10–15 minutes. Stand for 10–15 minutes, stirring occasionally.

To Serve
Cook in a covered casserole in the oven at 180°C (350°F) mark 4 for 30–35 minutes. Alternatively, microwave on HIGH for 10–12 minutes or until piping hot, stirring frequently. Complete step 4.

PIGEON WITH PRUNES

SERVES 4

4 young pigeons
15ml (1 tbsp) plain flour
50g (2oz) lard or dripping
1 rasher fat bacon
1 medium onion, skinned and chopped
2 carrots, peeled and chopped
225g (8oz) tomatoes, chopped
50g (2oz) mushrooms
600ml (1 pint) beef stock
1 bay leaf
1 bouquet garni
225ml (8fl oz) red wine
pinch of sugar
salt and pepper
100g (4oz) no-soak prunes, stoned
chopped fresh parsley, to garnish

1 Lightly dust the whole pigeons in the flour. Heat the lard in a large frying pan and cook the pigeons until lightly browned. Remove and place in a deep flameproof casserole.

2 Add the bacon and vegetables to the fat and fry for 2 minutes to soften. Add the stock and herbs, then simmer for 10–15 minutes or until the vegetables are soft and mushy.

3 Push through a sieve, add 100ml (4fl oz) of the wine, the sugar and seasoning. Pour over the birds, cover and simmer for 1½–2 hours. Add the prunes to the casserole 30 minutes before the end of cooking. Garnish with parsley.

To Freeze

Cool quickly, pack in a rigid container and freeze for up to 2 months.

To Thaw

Leave overnight in the refrigerator. Alternatively, microwave on LOW for about 8–10 minutes. Stand for 10–15 minutes.

To Serve

Cook in a covered casserole in the oven at 180°C (350°F) mark 4 for 25–30 minutes or until piping hot. Alternatively, microwave on HIGH for 12–15 minutes or until piping hot, stirring frequently. Garnish.

WOOD PIGEONS IN BEER

SERVES 4

4 small wood pigeons
30ml (2 tbsp) vegetable oil
25g (1oz) butter
450g (1lb) onions, skinned and sliced
45ml (3 tbsp) plain flour
20ml (4 tsp) French mustard
600ml (1 pint) light ale
20ml (4 tsp) soft brown sugar
30ml (2 tbsp) vinegar
salt and pepper
150ml (¼ pint) soured cream
200g (7oz) can pimientos, drained and thinly sliced

1 Cut the backbone from each pigeon, leaving the rest of the bird whole. Heat the oil in a large flameproof casserole. Add the butter and, when frothing, brown the birds lightly on all sides. Remove the birds.

2 Add the onions and fry until golden. Stir in the flour, mustard, ale, sugar, vinegar and seasoning. Bring to the boil, stirring. Return the birds to the casserole.

3 Cover tightly and cook in the oven at 170°C (325°F) mark 3 for about 2½ hours or until tender.

4 Serve the pigeons on a warmed dish. Heat the juices gently with the cream and pimiento. Spoon over the pigeons.

To Freeze

Cool quickly, pack in a rigid container at the end of step 3 and freeze for up to 4 months.

To Thaw

Leave overnight in the refrigerator. Alternatively, microwave on LOW for about 10–15 minutes, re-arranging occasionally. Stand for 10–15 minutes.

To Serve

Cook in a covered casserole in the oven at 170°C (325°F) mark 3 for 35–40 minutes. Alternatively, microwave on HIGH for 12–15 minutes or until piping hot, stirring frequently. Complete step 4.

Right: Rabbit Casserole (page 120)

DUCKLING ROULADES WITH PEACHES

SERVES 6

6 duckling wing portions, about 350g (12oz) each

slices of onion and carrot, for flavouring

1 bay leaf

salt and pepper

65g (2½oz) butter

1 small onion, skinned and finely chopped

25g (1oz) hazelnuts, roughly chopped

2 firm, ripe peaches, skinned and chopped

30ml (2 tbsp) brandy

50g (2oz) fresh brown breadcrumbs

30ml (2 tbsp) plain flour

bay leaves and peach slices, to garnish

1 Using a small sharp knife, carefully ease the skin and fat together off each of the duckling portions.

2 Carefully fillet the duckling flesh in one piece away from the breastbone. Place the breast meat between sheets of cling film and beat out thinly with a meat mallet or rolling pin. Cover and refrigerate until required. Cut any remaining duckling flesh off the wing bones. Chop finely and set aside until required.

3 To make the stock, place the wing bones in a saucepan together with the slices of onion and carrot, bay leaf and seasoning. Just cover with water and bring to the boil.

4 Simmer, uncovered, for 30–40 minutes or until about 300ml (½ pint) stock remains. Strain off the stock and reserve.

5 Meanwhile, make the stuffing. Melt 25g (1oz) of the butter and fry the onion, chopped duckling flesh and hazelnuts for 3–4 minutes, turning frequently.

6 Stir in the peaches and fry for a few minutes longer or until the peaches are beginning to soften. Remove from the heat, stir in the brandy, breadcrumbs and seasoning. Cool.

7 Divide the cold stuffing between the duckling fillets and roll them up tightly. Secure each one with two wooden cocktail sticks. Sprinkle the flour over the rolls.

8 Melt the remaining butter in a large shallow flameproof casserole. Add the duckling rolls and brown lightly all over. Sprinkle in any remaining flour, then pour in 300ml (½ pint) duckling stock. Season. Bring to the boil.

9 Cover and cook in the oven at 180°C (350°F) mark 4 for about 40 minutes. Adjust seasoning and skim the juices before serving, garnished with peach slices and bay leaves.

To Microwave

Complete steps 1 and 2. Place the wing bones, onion, carrot, bay leaf and seasoning in a large bowl. Pour over 600ml (1 pint) boiling water, cover and microwave on HIGH for 20 minutes. Strain off the stock and reserve 300ml (½ pint). Place the onion, chopped duckling flesh, hazelnuts and 25g (1oz) butter in a medium bowl. Microwave on HIGH for 2 minutes, stirring occasionally. Add the peaches and microwave on HIGH for 2 minutes. Complete steps 6–9.

To Freeze

Cool, pack in a rigid container at the end of step 9 and freeze for up to 4 months.

To Thaw

Leave overnight in the refrigerator. Alternatively, microwave on LOW on a serving dish for about 5 minutes, turning occasionally. Stand for 10 minutes.

To Serve

Cook in a covered casserole in the oven at 180°C (350°F) mark 4 for 30–35 minutes. Alternatively, microwave on HIGH for 12–15 minutes or until piping hot, stirring frequently. Garnish.

DUCK JULIENNE EN CROÛTE

SERVES 4

25g (1oz) butter

2 garlic cloves, skinned and crushed

30ml (2 tbsp) chopped fresh parsley or 10ml (2 tsp) dried

4 duck breasts, about 200g (7oz) each, boned and skinned

175g (6oz) carrots, peeled

2 courgettes

450g (1lb) ready-made puff pastry

salt and pepper

1 egg, beaten

1 Melt the butter in a large frying pan and fry the garlic and parsley for 2 minutes. Add the duck breasts and fry until browned. Drain and cool.

2 Cut the carrots and courgettes into thin 5cm (2 inch) strips. Blanch in boiling water for 1–2 minutes, then drain under cold running water.

3 Roll out one third of the pastry to a 40.5 × 15cm (16 × 6 inch) rectangle. Divide into four 10 × 15cm (4 × 6 inch) bases and place on a lightly greased baking sheet. Roll the remaining two thirds to a 51 × 15cm (20 × 6 inch) rectangle. Divide into four 12.5 × 15cm (5 × 6 inch) lids.

4 Divide the vegetables between the bases, leaving 0.5cm (¼ inch) border. Place the duck breasts on the vegetables and season well. Brush the border with egg. Add the lids and seal.
5 Glaze with beaten egg. Bake in the oven at 200°C (400°F) mark 6 for 45–55 minutes.

To Microwave
Complete step 1. Cut the carrots and courgettes into thin 5cm (2 inch) strips. Place in a medium bowl and cover with boiling water. Microwave on HIGH for 1–1½ minutes. Drain under cold running water. Complete steps 3–5.

To Freeze
Open freeze at the end of step 4, then pack in a rigid container. Freeze for up to 3 months.

To Thaw and Serve
Place the duck en croûte on a lightly greased baking sheet. Leave, covered, at room temperature for 4–6 hours or until thawed. Complete step 5.

PHEASANT WITH PORT

SERVES 6

30ml (2 tbsp) vegetable oil
3 young pheasants
300ml (½ pint) chicken stock
120ml (8 tbsp) port
finely grated rind and juice of 2 oranges
50g (2oz) sultanas
salt and pepper
20ml (4 tsp) cornflour
25g (1oz) flaked almonds, toasted, to garnish

1 Heat the oil in a large flameproof casserole and brown the pheasants all over. Pour the stock and port over the birds. Add the orange rind and juice, sultanas and season well. Bring to the boil.
2 Cover tightly and cook in the oven at 170°C (325°F) mark 3 for 1–1½ hours.
3 Remove the birds from the casserole. Joint each pheasant into two or three pieces, depending on size. Arrange on a serving dish and keep warm.
4 Boil up the juices. Blend the cornflour with a little water until smooth. Stir into the juices and cook until thickened. Adjust seasoning and spoon over the pheasant. Garnish with the almonds.

To Freeze
Cool, pack in a rigid container at the end of step 2 and freeze for up to 3 months.

To Thaw
Leave overnight in the refrigerator. Alternatively, microwave on LOW for about 7–8 minutes. Stand for 10–15 minutes, stirring occasionally.

To Serve
Cook in a covered casserole in the oven at 180°C (350°F) mark 4 for 30–35 minutes. Alternatively, microwave on HIGH for 12–15 minutes or until piping hot, stirring frequently. Complete steps 3 and 4.

PARTRIDGE WITH GRAPES

SERVES 2

2 young partridges
30ml (2 tbsp) vegetable oil
175ml (6fl oz) chicken stock
90ml (6 tbsp) dry white wine
salt and white pepper
15ml (1 tbsp) cornflour
1 egg yolk
30ml (2 tbsp) double cream
100g (4oz) white grapes, skinned, halved and pipped
chopped fresh parsley, to garnish

1 Halve the partridges and remove the backbones. Carefully pull off the skin. Heat the oil in a large flameproof casserole and lightly brown the birds.
2 Pour over the stock and wine, season and bring to the boil. Cover tightly and cook gently for about 25 minutes or until the meat is tender.
3 Drain the partridges and keep warm on a serving dish. Blend the cornflour, egg yolk and cream together. Add to the pan juices with the grapes and cook gently, without boiling, until the sauce thickens. Adjust seasoning. Spoon the sauce over.

To Freeze
Cool quickly, pack in a rigid container at the end of step 2 and freeze for up to 4 months.

To Thaw
Leave overnight in the refrigerator. Alternatively, microwave on LOW for about 5–7 minutes. Stand for 10–15 minutes.

To Serve
Cover and heat in a heavy-based saucepan for 20 minutes, stirring occasionally. Alternatively, microwave on HIGH for 12–15 minutes or until piping hot, stirring frequently. Complete step 3.

MEAT MAIN COURSES

LAMB IN RED WINE

SERVES 6–8

175g (6oz) dried black beans
450ml (¾ pint) red wine
3 allspice berries
2 bay leaves
pared rind of 1 lemon
1.6kg (3½lb) shoulder lamb
350g (12oz) turnips
350g (12oz) carrots
100g (4oz) onion
4 celery sticks
vegetable oil
salt and pepper
15ml (1 tbsp) cornflour
chopped fresh parsley, to garnish

1 Two days ahead, soak the beans in plenty of cold water overnight. Drain. Place the beans in a saucepan with fresh water, partly cover and simmer for about 1½ hours until tender. Drain.
2 Place the wine, 300ml (½ pint) water, allspice berries, bay leaves and lemon rind in a large bowl. Stir in the warm drained beans. Cool.
3 Remove the lamb from the bone and cut into bite sized pieces, discard any excess fat and bones. Stir the lamb into the wine marinade. Cover and refrigerate overnight.
4 Peel the turnips and cut into bite sized pieces. Peel the carrots and cut into similar sized pieces. Skin and roughly chop the onion. Slice the celery.
5 Drain the meat, reserving the marinade. Heat a little oil in a large flameproof casserole dish and brown the meat, a few pieces at a time. Remove the meat and set aside.
6 Brown the vegetables, adding a little more oil if necessary. Return the meat to the casserole, stir in the beans and reserved marinade. Season to taste.
7 Cover tightly and cook in the oven at 180°C (350°F) mark 4 for about 1¼ hours or until the lamb is quite tender.
8 Mix the cornflour to a smooth paste with a little cold water, then stir into the casserole. Bring to

the boil and cook, stirring, until the juices have thickened. Adjust seasoning and garnish with parsley.

To Microwave
Complete steps 1–4. Place a little oil in a large bowl and microwave on HIGH for 1 minute. Add half the drained lamb and microwave on HIGH for 6 minutes, stirring occasionally. Remove with a slotted spoon. Seal the remaining lamb in the same way. Add the vegetables to the meat juices, cover and microwave on HIGH for 3–4 minutes, stirring occasionally. Stir in the meat, the cooked beans and reserved marinade. Cover with a plate and microwave on HIGH for 20 minutes or until the lamb is tender. Mix the cornflour to a smooth paste with a little cold water, then stir into the casserole. Microwave on HIGH for 2–3 minutes, stirring once. Season to taste. Stand, covered, for 10 minutes before serving. Garnish.

To Freeze
Cool, pack in a rigid container, or lined container, at the end of step 7. Freeze for up to 6 months.

To Thaw
Leave overnight in the refrigerator. Alternatively, microwave on LOW for about 10–15 minutes. Stand for 15–20 minutes, breaking up the block as it thaws.

To Serve
Add 150ml (¼ pint) stock or water. Cover and reheat in the oven at 200°C (400°F) mark 6 for about 40 minutes. Alternatively, microwave on HIGH for 8–10 minutes or until piping hot. Complete step 8.

Right: Lamb and Watercress Bake (page 128)

126

LAMB AND APRICOT PILAFF

SERVES 4

100g (4oz) burghul wheat
15ml (1 tbsp) olive oil
450g (1lb) lean boneless lamb, such as leg or fillet, trimmed and cut into bite-sized cubes
1 onion, skinned and finely chopped
1 garlic clove, skinned and crushed
10ml (2 tsp) tomato purée
5ml (1 tsp) ground cinnamon
2.5ml (½ tsp) powdered saffron or turmeric
salt and pepper
175g (6oz) brown rice
juice of 1 orange
75g (3oz) ready-to-eat dried apricots, roughly chopped
50g (2oz) seedless raisins
25g (1oz) pine nuts or blanched almonds, toasted, and fresh coriander leaves, to garnish

1 Put the burghul in a large bowl, pour over enough warm water to cover, then leave to soak.
2 Meanwhile, heat the oil in a heavy flameproof casserole or saucepan and cook the lamb over high heat until browned on all sides. Remove with a slotted spoon and drain on absorbent kitchen paper.
3 Lower the heat, add the onion to the pan and cook gently, stirring frequently, until soft and lightly coloured. Add the garlic, tomato purée, cinnamon, saffron and seasoning. Cook for a further 2–3 minutes, stirring, until the mixture gives off a spicy aroma.
4 Pour in 600ml (1 pint) water and bring to the boil, stirring. Lower the heat, return the lamb to the pan, cover and simmer for 30 minutes.
5 Add the rice and orange juice to the pan, stir once, then cover again and simmer for a further 20 minutes.
6 Stir in the apricots, raisins and 300ml (½ pint) boiling water. Cover and simmer for a further 20 minutes or until the rice is tender and has absorbed most of the liquid.
7 Drain the burghul, then wring out in a clean cloth to extract as much moisture as possible. Fold gently into the pilaff and heat through.
8 Turn the pilaff into a warmed serving dish. Garnish with the pine nuts and coriander leaves.

To Microwave

Complete step 1. Place the oil in a large bowl and microwave on HIGH for 1 minute. Add the lamb and microwave on HIGH for 4–5 minutes, stirring occasionally. Remove with a slotted spoon. Add the onion, stir and microwave on HIGH for 3–4 minutes until soft. Add the garlic, tomato purée, cinnamon and saffron. Microwave on HIGH for 1–2 minutes, stirring once. Pour over 600ml (1 pint) boiling water, then add the rice, lamb and orange juice. Cover and microwave on HIGH for 10–15 minutes. Add the apricots and raisins. Cover and microwave on HIGH for 10–15 minutes or until the rice is tender and most of the liquid has been absorbed. Add the drained burghul, season well and microwave on HIGH for 2–3 minutes, stirring twice. Complete step 8.

To Freeze

Cool, pack in a rigid container after adding the burghul and freeze for up to 3 months.

To Thaw

Leave overnight in the refrigerator. Alternatively, microwave on LOW for about 15–20 minutes. Stand for 10–15 minutes, gently breaking up the block as it thaws.

To Serve

Gently reheat in a heavy based saucepan, adding a little hot water as necessary. Alternatively, microwave on HIGH for about 8–10 minutes or until piping hot. Complete step 8.

LAMB AND WATERCRESS BAKE

SERVES 4–6

450g (1lb) minced lamb
2 large onions, skinned and finely chopped
2 bunches watercress, trimmed and finely chopped
10ml (2 tsp) dried oregano
105ml (7 tbsp) plain flour
450ml (¾ pint) lamb or chicken stock
50ml (2fl oz) dry white wine
25g (1oz) butter
salt and pepper
568ml (1 pint) milk
175g (6oz) Lancashire cheese, crumbled
about 225g (8oz) oven-ready lasagne verdi

1 Brown the lamb well in its own fat in a large saucepan. Pour off excess fat. Add the onion and cook for 5 minutes, stirring occasionally. Add the watercress, oregano and 30ml (2 tbsp) of the flour. Cook for 1–2 minutes, then gradually stir in the stock and wine and season with salt and pepper. Bring to the boil, then simmer gently, covered, for 45 minutes, stirring occasionally.

2 Put the butter, remaining flour and milk in a saucepan. Heat, whisking continuously, until the sauce thickens, boils and is smooth. Simmer for 1–2 minutes. Remove the pan from the heat and stir in 100g (4oz) of the cheese, stir until melted and season with salt and pepper.

3 Layer the mince mixture and half of the sauce with the uncooked lasagne in a deep ovenproof serving dish. Spoon over the cheese sauce. Sprinkle over remaining cheese.

4 Bake at 190°C (375°F) mark 5 for about 40 minutes, until browned. Serve hot straight from the dish.

To Microwave

The cheese sauce can be prepared in the microwave. Put the butter, remaining flour and milk in a medium bowl and stir together. Microwave on HIGH for 5–6 minutes, until the sauce has boiled and thickened, whisking frequently. Complete the sauce as in step 2.

To Freeze

Cool, pack in a rigid container at the end of step 4 and freeze for up to 3 months.

To Thaw and Serve

Cook from frozen in the oven at 180°C (350°C) mark 4 for 50–60 minutes or until piping hot. Cover with foil if the top becomes too brown. Alternatively, microwave on LOW for 10–15 minutes, stand for 10 minutes. Microwave on HIGH for 25–35 minutes (depending on the size and depth of the dish) or until piping hot. Brown under a hot grill if liked.

EASTERN LAMB KEBABS

SERVES 4–6

450g (1lb) lean minced lamb
1 large onion, skinned and grated
15ml (1 tbsp) chopped fresh dill or 5ml (1 tsp) dried
30ml (2 tbsp) chopped fresh coriander or 10ml (2 tsp) ground
5ml (1 tsp) ground fenugreek
10ml (2 tsp) ground turmeric
salt and pepper
30ml (2 tbsp) sultanas
1 egg, beaten
coriander sprigs, to garnish

1 Place the minced lamb and onion in a medium bowl. Add the remaining ingredients and mix well, using your fingers.

2 Divide the mixture into 30 walnut sized pieces. Using dampened hands, form into even round shapes.

3 Thread about five balls on to six metal skewers, leaving about 2.5cm (1 inch) of each skewer exposed at both ends. Place the kebabs on a grill rack as you prepare them.

4 Cook the kebabs under a grill for 5–8 minutes. Turn them over and continue to cook for a further 5–8 minutes or until the meat is cooked. Garnish.

To Microwave

Complete steps 1 and 2. Thread the balls on to wooden skewers and arrange on a microwave roasting rack. Microwave on HIGH for 12–15 minutes, re-arranging occasionally. Stand for 2 minutes. Garnish.

To Freeze

Thread the balls on to the skewers and open freeze on a baking sheet lined with greaseproof paper. Pack in a rigid container for up to 3 months.

To Thaw

Leave overnight in the refrigerator. Alternatively, if you have used wooden skewers, arrange on a microwave roasting rack. Microwave on LOW for about 18–20 minutes, re-arranging occasionally. Stand for 30–40 minutes until completely thawed.

To Serve

Complete step 4. Alternatively, place the kebabs on a microwave roasting rack and microwave on HIGH for 12–15 minutes, re-arranging occasionally. Stand for 2 minutes. Garnish.

ROLLED STUFFED BREASTS OF LAMB

SERVES 4

25g (1oz) butter
1 medium onion, skinned and chopped
25g (1oz) streaky bacon, rinded and chopped
226g (8oz) packet frozen leaf spinach, thawed
75g (3oz) fresh breadcrumbs
45ml (3 tbsp) chopped fresh parsley
finely grated rind of ½ lemon
15ml (1 tbsp) lemon juice
pinch of grated nutmeg
1 egg, beaten
salt and pepper
2 large breasts of lamb, boned and trimmed, total weight about 1.1kg (2½lb)
45ml (3 tbsp) vegetable oil
watercress, to garnish

1 Melt the butter in a saucepan and fry the onion and bacon for about 5 minutes until lightly browned.
2 Drain the spinach and chop roughly. Place in a bowl with the onion and bacon, breadcrumbs, parsley, lemon rind and juice, nutmeg and egg. Mix together well, adding seasoning to taste.
3 Lay the breasts of lamb, fat side down, on a work surface and spread the stuffing evenly over them with a palette knife.
4 Roll up the lamb breasts loosely and tie in several places with string to hold their shape.
5 Weigh each joint and calculate the cooking time, allowing 25 minutes per 450g (1lb) plus 25 minutes for each joint. Heat the oil in a roasting tin and place the joints in the tin. Roast in the oven at 180°C (350°F) mark 4 for the calculated time, basting occasionally. Garnish with watercress.

To Microwave
Place the butter in a medium bowl and add the onion and bacon. Microwave on HIGH for 3–4 minutes. Complete steps 2–5.

To Freeze
Only use previously unfrozen lamb. Pack in a rigid container at the end of step 4 and freeze for up to 3 months.

To Thaw and Serve
Leave covered overnight at cool room temperature. Alternatively, microwave on LOW for about 15–18 minutes. Stand for 30–45 minutes. Complete step 5.

LAMBS' LIVER AND MUSHROOMS

SERVES 3–4

15g (½oz) butter
1 medium onion, skinned and sliced
450g (1lb) lamb's liver, cut into strips
15ml (1 tbsp) plain flour
100g (4oz) button mushrooms
150ml (¼ pint) beef stock
4 tomatoes, skinned and roughly chopped
30ml (2 tbsp) Worcestershire sauce
salt and pepper
150ml (5fl oz) soured cream

1 Melt the butter in a large frying pan and gently fry the onion for 5 minutes, until softened.
2 Coat the liver strips with the flour and add to the pan with the mushrooms. Fry for 5 minutes, stirring well, then add the stock and bring to the boil.
3 Stir in the tomatoes and Worcestershire sauce. Season to taste, then simmer for 3–4 minutes. Stir in the soured cream, and reheat without boiling. Serve hot with tagliatelle.

To Microwave
Cut the butter into small pieces and microwave in a large bowl on HIGH for 30 seconds. Add the onion, cover and microwave on HIGH for 5–7 minutes, until softened. Coat the liver in the flour and add to the bowl with the mushrooms. Cover and microwave on HIGH for 2–3 minutes or until the liver just changes colour, stirring once. Add the stock, tomatoes, Worcestershire sauce and salt and pepper, re-cover and microwave on HIGH for 2–3 minutes or until boiling, stirring once. Stir in the soured cream and serve immediately.

To Freeze
Omit the cream. Cool, pack in a rigid container and freeze for up to 3 months.

To Thaw
Leave overnight in the refrigerator

To Serve
Cover and reheat in the oven at 180°C (350°F) mark 4 for 15–20 minutes until piping hot. Stir in the cream. Alternatively, microwave, covered, on MEDIUM for 15–18 minutes, stirring occasionally. Stir in the cream.

Right: Lambs' Liver and Mushrooms

SPICED LAMB WITH BEANS

SERVES 4

15ml (1 tbsp) vegetable oil
1 large onion, skinned and chopped
1 red pepper, cored, seeded and chopped
450g (1lb) minced lamb
400g (14oz) can chopped tomatoes
30ml (2 tbsp) tomato purée
grated rind and juice of ½ lemon
2.5ml (½ tsp) sugar
5ml (1 tsp) chilli powder
15ml (1 tbsp) ground coriander
397g (15½oz) can red kidney beans, drained
salt and pepper

1 Heat the oil in a pan and gently fry the onion and pepper until soft. Add the minced lamb and fry until browned, stirring and pressing with a wooden spoon to remove any lumps.
2 Stir in the tomatoes with their juice, the tomato purée, lemon rind and 15ml (1 tbsp) lemon juice, sugar and spices. Stir well to mix. Simmer for 30 minutes or until reduced and thick, stirring occasionally.
3 Add the beans and simmer for a further 10–15 minutes, stirring frequently. Season to taste.

To Microwave

Place the onion, pepper and oil in a large bowl. Cover and microwave on HIGH for 5 minutes, stirring occasionally. Stir in the lamb, cover and microwave on HIGH for 6 minutes, stirring once. Blend in the tomatoes, tomato purée, lemon rind and juice, sugar and spices. Cover and microwave on HIGH for 10 minutes, stirring once. Add the beans, cover and microwave on HIGH for about 5 minutes. Season to taste.

To Freeze

Cool, pack in a rigid container, or lined container, and freeze for up to 6 months.

To Thaw

Leave overnight in the refrigerator. Alternatively, microwave on LOW for about 8–10 minutes. Stand for 10–15 minutes, breaking up the block as it thaws.

To Serve

Reheat in a heavy-based saucepan, stirring frequently. Alternatively, cover and microwave on HIGH for 10 minutes or until piping hot.

MULLED BEEF AND KIDNEY CASSEROLE

SERVES 4

300ml (½ pint) red wine
2 cinnamon sticks
6 juniper berries
450g (1lb) stewing steak, in one piece
100g (4oz) onion, skinned and thinly sliced
vegetable oil
225g (8oz) carrots, peeled and cut into large chunks
225g (8oz) parsnips, peeled and cut into large chunks
300ml (½ pint) stock
salt and pepper
4 lamb's kidneys, halved and cored
100g (4oz) small button mushrooms, halved
5ml (1 tsp) arrowroot

1 Pour the wine into a saucepan and add the cinnamon sticks and juniper berries. Bring to the boil, remove from the heat and cool.
2 Meanwhile, cut the meat into bite-sized pieces, discarding excess fat. Place the meat and onion into a bowl and pour over the cold wine. Cover and refrigerate overnight.
3 Drain the meat, reserving the marinade. Heat 30ml (2 tbsp) oil in a large flameproof casserole and brown the meat, a few pieces at a time, adding a little more oil if necessary. Stir in the carrots and parsnips and brown well. Return the meat to the casserole, add the onion, stock and reserved marinade. Season to taste. Bring to the boil and cover.
4 Cook in the oven at 180°C (350°F) mark 4 for about 1½ hours or until the meat is almost tender.
5 Meanwhile, cut the kidneys into bite-sized pieces. Stir the kidneys and mushrooms into the casserole. Cover, return to the oven and cook for a further 20 minutes or until all the ingredients are tender.
6 Mix the arrowroot to a smooth paste with a little water. Stir into the casserole, bring to the boil, then cook, stirring, until the juices have thickened.

To Microwave

Pour the wine into a jug and add the cinnamon sticks and juniper berries. Microwave on HIGH for 2–3 minutes or until boiling. Cool. Complete step 2. Place the oil in a large bowl or dish and microwave on HIGH for 30 seconds. Add half the drained meat and microwave on HIGH for 3–4 minutes, stirring occasionally. Remove with a slotted spoon. Repeat with the remaining meat. Put the carrots and parsnips in the bowl, cover and microwave on HIGH for 4–5 minutes. Return the meat to the dish, with the onion, stock and reserved marinade. Cover and microwave on HIGH for 10–12 minutes. Prepare the kidneys. Stir the kidneys and mushrooms into the casserole. Cover and microwave on HIGH for 5–7 minutes or until tender. Mix the arrowroot to a smooth paste, stir into the casserole and microwave on HIGH for 2–3 minutes, stirring occasionally, until thickened. Stand, covered, for 10 minutes before serving.

To Freeze

Cool, pack in a rigid container, or lined container, at the end of step 4. Freeze for up to 6 months.

To Thaw

Thaw overnight in the refrigerator. Alternatively, microwave on LOW for about 6–10 minutes. Stand for 10–15 minutes, breaking up the block as it thaws.

To Serve

Reheat in a covered casserole in the oven at 180°C (350°F) mark 4 for 30–35 minutes, adding a little water if necessary. Complete steps 5 and 6. Alternatively, cover and microwave on HIGH for 6–8 minutes. Complete as above from preparing the kidneys.

BEEF AND DUMPLING RAGOUT

SERVES 6

45ml (3 tbsp) vegetable oil
50g (2oz) butter
900g (2lb) lean stewing beef, cubed
450g (1lb) onions, skinned and quartered
450g (1lb) parsnips, peeled and cut into chunks
60ml (4 tbsp) plain flour
30ml (2 tbsp) tomato purée
1 litre (1¾ pints) hot beef stock (see page 186)
salt and pepper
100g (4oz) streaky bacon rashers, rinded
175g (6oz) self raising flour
75g (3oz) shredded suet
45ml (3 tbsp) chopped fresh parsley

1 Heat the oil and butter in a heavy flameproof casserole and cook the cubes of beef over high heat until browned on all sides. Remove with a slotted spoon and drain on absorbent kitchen paper.

2 Lower the heat, add the onions and parsnips to the pan and cook gently, stirring frequently, until soft and lightly coloured. Add the flour and cook for 1 minute, stirring well to absorb all the juices. Stir in the tomato purée, stock and seasoning.

3 Bring to the boil, stirring. Lower the heat, return the beef to the pan and cover tightly. Cook in the oven at 170°C (325°F) mark 3 for about 1¼ hours.

4 Meanwhile, grill the bacon until crispy and snip into small pieces. Mix with the self raising flour, suet, parsley and seasoning. Bind together with about 90ml (6 tbsp) cold water to form a soft dough.

5 Shape the dough into 12 small balls, then drop them on to the stew. Cover with a tight fitting lid and return to the oven for 30–40 minutes or until the dumplings are light and fluffy.

To Microwave

Place the oil and butter in a large bowl and microwave on HIGH for 1 minute. Add the beef and microwave on HIGH for 5–7 minutes. Remove with a slotted spoon and drain on absorbent kitchen paper. Add the onions and parsnips to the bowl, stir well. Cover and microwave on HIGH for 3–5 minutes, stirring once. Add the flour, tomato purée and hot beef stock, stir well to blend. Microwave on HIGH for 2–3 minutes or until boiling. Return the meat and season to taste. Cover and microwave on HIGH for 12–16 minutes or until the beef is tender, stirring occasionally. Complete step 4. Shape the dough into small balls and arrange around the edge of the stew. Cover and microwave on HIGH for a further 5 minutes or until the dumplings are light and fluffy. Stand, covered, for 10 minutes before serving.

To Freeze

Cool, pack in a rigid container, or lined container, without the dumplings. Freeze for up to 2 months.

To Thaw

Leave overnight in the refrigerator. Alternatively, microwave on LOW for about 12–18 minutes. Stand for 10 minutes, breaking up the block as it thaws.

To Serve

Heat in a covered casserole in the oven at 180°C (350°F) mark 4 for 30–35 minutes, adding a little water if necessary. Alternatively, cover and microwave on HIGH for 6–8 minutes or until piping hot, stirring occasionally. Complete steps 4 and 5.

BEEFBURGERS

SERVES 4

450g (1lb) lean beef, such as chuck, shoulder or rump steak, minced

½ small onion, skinned and grated (optional)

salt and pepper

melted butter or vegetable oil, for grilling, or vegetable oil, for shallow frying

4 large soft buns

butter, for spreading

lettuce and onion rings, to serve (optional)

1 Mix the minced beef well with the onion (if using) and plenty of seasoning.

2 Shape the mixture lightly into four round, flat patties. Brush sparingly with melted butter or vegetable oil.

3 Grill the burgers for 8–10 minutes or until cooked according to taste, turning once. Alternatively, fry in a little oil in a frying pan, turning them once and allowing the same amount of time.

4 Meanwhile, split the buns in half and spread with a little butter. Put one beefburger inside each bun. Add a lettuce leaf and some onion rings, if liked.

Variations

CHEESEBURGERS

Top the cooked beefburgers with a slice of Cheddar or Gruyère cheese. Cook under the grill for a further minute or until the cheese has melted.

CHILLIBURGERS

Add 15ml (1 tbsp) chilli seasoning when mixing the beefburgers.

To Microwave

Complete steps 1–3. If liked, cook the burgers on a browning dish, preheated following the manufacturer's instructions. Complete step 4.

To Freeze

Open freeze on baking sheets before greasing in step 2, then pack in a rigid container. Freeze for up to 3 months.

To Thaw and Serve

Leave overnight in the refrigerator. Alternatively, arrange the four beefburgers around the edge of a plate. Microwave on LOW for 5–6 minutes, re-arranging halfway through cooking. Stand for 10 minutes. Complete steps 3 and 4.

KEEMA CURRY WITH PEAS

SERVES 4

45ml (3 tbsp) ghee or butter

1 medium onion, skinned and finely chopped

1–2 garlic cloves, skinned and crushed

700g (1½lb) minced beef

4 medium tomatoes, skinned and roughly chopped

15ml (1 tbsp) tomato purée

20ml (4 tsp) ground coriander

10ml (2 tsp) ground cumin

7.5 ml (1½ tsp) ground fenugreek

2.5ml (½ tsp) chilli powder

5ml (1 tsp) salt

350g (12oz) frozen peas

juice of ½ lemon

45ml (3 tbsp) chopped fresh coriander

10ml (2 tsp) garam masala

150ml (¼ pint) natural yogurt

1 Heat the ghee in a heavy pan and fry the onion and garlic for 5 minutes until soft.

2 Add and fry the minced beef in batches.

3 Add the tomatoes, tomato purée, coriander, cumin, fenugreek, chilli powder and salt, stir well. Pour in 300ml (½ pint) water. Cover and simmer for 30 minutes.

4 Pour 150ml (¼ pint) water into the pan and bring to the boil. Cook the peas for 10 minutes.

5 Remove the curry mixture from the heat and stir in the lemon juice, fresh coriander and garam masala. Stand for 5 minutes. Add the yogurt.

To Microwave

Place the ghee in a large bowl and microwave on HIGH for 1 minute until hot. Add the onion and garlic and microwave on HIGH for 3–5 minutes until soft. Stir in the beef. Add the tomatoes, purée, coriander, cumin, fenugreek, chilli, salt and 300ml (½ pint) boiling water, stir well. Cover and microwave on HIGH for 10 minutes. Add peas and microwave for 2–5 minutes. Complete step 5.

To Freeze

Cool, pack in a rigid container, or lined container, at the end of step 3. Freeze for up to 3 months.

To Thaw and Serve

Leave overnight in the refrigerator. Alternatively, microwave on LOW for about 10–12 minutes. Stand for 10 minutes. Complete steps 4 and 5.

Right: Pork in Plum Sauce (page 140)

STEAK AND KIDNEY PIE

SERVES 4

200g (7oz) plain flour
salt and pepper
700g (1½lb) braising steak, trimmed and cubed
175g (6oz) ox kidney, cored and chopped
100g (4oz) butter
1–2 garlic cloves, skinned and crushed
1 large onion, skinned and chopped
100g (4oz) mushrooms
150ml (¼ pint) beef stock
150ml (¼ pint) brown ale
1 bay leaf
thyme sprig or 2.5ml (½ tsp) dried
15ml (1 tbsp) Worcestershire sauce
15ml (1 tbsp) tomato purée
milk, to glaze

1 Season 25g (1oz) of the flour, then toss the steak and kidney in the flour, shaking off any excess.
2 Melt 25g (1oz) of the butter in a large saucepan and lightly fry the garlic, onion and mushrooms for 3 minutes. Add the steak, kidney and remaining coating flour and cook for 5 minutes until lightly browned.
3 Gradually stir in the stock, ale, bay leaf, thyme, Worcestershire sauce and tomato purée. Cover and simmer gently for about 1¼ hours. Spoon the mixture into a 1.7 litre (3 pint) pie dish.
4 Put the remaining flour and a pinch of salt into a bowl. Rub in the remaining butter until the mixture resembles fine breadcrumbs. Add 60ml (4 tbsp) cold water and mix to form a dough.
5 Roll out on a lightly floured work surface to 5cm (2 inches) wider than the pie dish. Cut a 2.5cm (1 inch) wide strip from the outer edge and place on the dampened rim of the dish. Brush the strip with water. Cover with the pastry lid, press lightly to seal the edges. Trim off the excess pastry, seal and crimp. Decorate with pastry leaves and brush with milk.
6 Bake in the oven at 200°C (400°F) mark 6 for 30–45 minutes.

To Microwave
Complete step 1. Dice the butter into a large bowl and microwave on HIGH for 45 seconds. Add the garlic, onion and mushrooms and microwave on HIGH for 5–7 minutes. Add the meats and flour, microwave on HIGH for 4 minutes. Gradually stir in the stock, 50ml (2fl oz) of the ale, bay leaf, thyme, Worcestershire sauce and tomato purée.

Microwave on HIGH for 10 minutes, stirring occasionally. Stand, covered, for 5 minutes. Complete steps 4–6.

To Freeze
Pack the uncooked pie after decorating in a polythene bag and freeze for up to 3 months.

To Thaw and Serve
Leave overnight in the refrigerator. Alternatively, microwave on LOW for about 5–10 minutes. Stand for 10 minutes. Complete step 6.

HUNGARIAN GOULASH

SERVES 6

45ml (3 tbsp) beef dripping or vegetable oil
3 medium onions, skinned and chopped
2 garlic cloves, skinned and crushed
1.1kg (2½lb) chuck steak or shin of beef, trimmed and cut into 4cm (1½ inch) pieces
15ml (1 tbsp) paprika
1.25ml (¼ tsp) caraway seeds
397g (14oz) can tomatoes
salt and pepper
1 green or red pepper, cored, seeded and chopped
550g (1¼lb) potatoes, peeled and cut into 2.5cm (1 inch) chunks
2 green chillies (optional)

1 Melt the dripping in a flameproof casserole and cook the onions and garlic over moderate heat for 10 minutes, stirring occasionally, until the onions are soft and golden brown.
2 Add the meat and cook over high heat, stirring constantly, until browned slightly. Add the paprika, caraway seeds, tomatoes with their juice, 300ml (½ pint) water and seasoning to taste. Stir well to break up the tomatoes.
3 Bring to the boil and cover. Cook in the oven at 170°C (325°F) mark 3 for 1½ hours.
4 Remove the casserole from the oven and stir in the chopped pepper and potatoes, adding the whole chillies, if using. Cover and return to the oven for a further 45 minutes or until the potatoes are tender. The goulash should be of a fairly thin consistency.
5 Remove the chillies before serving, then adjust seasoning.

To Microwave
Place the dripping in a large bowl or dish and microwave on HIGH for 1 minute. Add the onions

and garlic and microwave on HIGH for 4–5 minutes or until soft, stirring occasionally. Add the meat and microwave on HIGH for 6–8 minutes until sealed, stirring occasionally. Add the paprika, caraway seeds, tomatoes with their juice and 300ml (½ pint) boiling water, stir well to break up the tomatoes. Cover with a plate and microwave on HIGH for 10–15 minutes. Stir in the pepper, potatoes and whole chillies, if using. Cover and microwave on HIGH for 8–10 minutes or until the potatoes are tender. Remove the chillies before serving, then adjust seasoning. Stand, covered, for 10 minutes before serving.

To Freeze
Cool, pack in a rigid container, or lined container, at the end of step 3. Freeze for up to 6 months.

To Thaw
Leave overnight in the refrigerator. Alternatively, microwave on LOW for about 12–16 minutes. Stand for 10 minutes, breaking up the block as it thaws.

To Serve
Add 150ml (¼ pint) water and stir well. Cook in the oven at 170°C (325°F) mark 3 for 30 minutes or until hot. Alternatively, microwave on HIGH for 6–8 minutes or until piping hot. Complete steps 4 and 5.

GOURMET PORK ROLLS

SERVES 4

350g (12oz) pork fillet
4 thin slices of lean cooked ham
1 garlic clove, skinned and crushed
30ml (2 tbsp) pine nuts
100g (4oz) fresh wholemeal breadcrumbs
50g (2oz) no-soak apricots, chopped
45ml (3 tbsp) chopped fresh parsley or 15ml (1 tbsp) dried
4 slices of Gruyère cheese
30ml (2 tbsp) seasoned flour
15ml (1 tbsp) vegetable oil
200ml (7fl oz) dry white wine
200ml (7fl oz) unsweetened apple juice
15g (½oz) butter
15g (½oz) plain flour
sliced apple and parsley sprigs, to garnish

1 Cut the pork into four equal pieces. Place one piece of pork fillet between sheets of cling film and beat with a rolling pin to flatten to about 0.5cm (¼

inch) thick. Repeat with the remaining pork. Lay a slice of ham on each pork escalope.

2 Mix the garlic, pine nuts, breadcrumbs, apricots and 30ml (2 tbsp) of the chopped fresh parsley or 10ml (2 tsp) dried together in a bowl. Spread the mixture evenly over each escalope and lay a slice of Gruyère cheese on top.

3 Roll up each escalope, securing with a wooden cocktail stick. Dust with seasoned flour. Heat the oil in a frying pan and cook the rolls for 5–7 minutes, turning them frequently to brown on all sides.

4 Pour over the wine and apple juice. Bring to the boil and simmer gently for 20–25 minutes or until the meat is cooked and tender.

5 Using a slotted spoon, transfer the rolls to a warmed serving dish. Remove the cocktail sticks and keep warm.

6 Increase the heat and reduce the liquor in the pan to about 150ml (¼ pint). Mix the butter with the flour and gradually whisk into the sauce until thickened. Stir in the remaining parsley and pour the sauce over the rolls. Garnish.

To Microwave
Complete steps 1–3. Transfer the browned rolls to a shallow dish and pour over the wine and apple juice. Cover and microwave on HIGH for 10–13 minutes or until the rolls are cooked through, re-arranging occasionally. Transfer to a warmed serving dish. Remove the cocktail sticks and cover to keep warm. Return the liquor to the microwave and microwave on HIGH, uncovered, for 5–7 minutes until reduced. Whisk in the butter and flour and microwave on HIGH for 3–4 minutes until thick, whisking occasionally. Stir in the remaining parsley and serve poured over the rolls.

To Freeze
Cool, pack in a rigid container and freeze for up to 3 months.

To Thaw
Leave overnight in the refrigerator. Alternatively, microwave on LOW for about 15–20 minutes, re-arranging frequently. Stand for 30–35 minutes until completely thawed.

To Serve
Place in an ovenproof dish, cover with foil and reheat in the oven at 200°C (400°F) mark 6 for 35–40 minutes. Alternatively, cover and microwave on HIGH for about 7–10 minutes or until piping hot.

ROAST PORK TENDERLOIN

SERVES 6

50g (2oz) butter

175g (6oz) button mushrooms, roughly chopped

1 onion, skinned and finely chopped

100g (4oz) fresh brown breadcrumbs

5ml (1 tsp) dried rubbed sage

salt and pepper

1 egg, beaten

3 pork tenderloins, about 900g (2lb) total weight

100g (4oz) thin rashers streaky bacon, rinded

150ml (¼ pint) dry white wine

300ml (½ pint) chicken stock

10ml (2 tsp) arrowroot

1 Melt 25g (1oz) of the butter in a pan and fry the mushrooms and onion until golden. Mix in the crumbs and sage with seasoning and egg to bind. Cool.

2 Carefully trim the pork tenderloins and slit lengthwise, three-quarters of the way through each tenderloin. Open the meat out flat.

3 Spread one piece of meat with half of the mushroom mix. Top with one of the tenderloins. Add the remaining stuffing and tenderloin.

4 Stretch out each rasher thinly. Wrap up the meat in the rashers and tie with string to form a joint.

5 Put the pork parcel in a small roasting tin and spread the remaining butter over the top. Season well. Pour the wine around.

6 Roast in the oven at 180°C (350°F) mark 4 for about 1¾ hours, basting. Lift on to a platter, remove string. Keep warm.

7 Add the stock to the tin and boil well. Blend the arrowroot with a little water to a smooth paste and add to the tin, stirring. Boil for 1 minute.

To Microwave

Dice the butter into a medium bowl and microwave on HIGH for 1 minute. Add the mushrooms and onion and microwave on HIGH for 5–6 minutes or until soft. Mix in the crumbs and sage with seasoning and egg to bind. Cool. Complete steps 2–7.

To Freeze

Use only previously unfrozen pork and bacon. Pack in a rigid container at the end of step 4 and freeze for up to 2 months.

To Thaw and Serve

Leave overnight at cool room temperature. Alternatively, microwave on LOW for 14–16 minutes. Stand for 1 hour, turning halfway through thawing. Complete steps 5–7.

PORK AND CORIANDER

SERVES 4

700g (1½lb) pork fillet, cut into 1cm (½inch) slices

15g (½oz) butter

15ml (1 tbsp) vegetable oil

1 small green pepper, cored, seeded and sliced into rings

1 medium onion, skinned and chopped

15g (½oz) plain flour

15ml (1 tbsp) coriander seeds, ground

150ml (¼ pint) chicken stock

150ml (¼ pint) dry white wine

salt and pepper

1 Place the pork between two sheets of greaseproof paper and flatten with a mallet.

2 Melt the butter and oil in a large saucepan, and brown the pork on both sides. Add the pepper and onion and cook for 8–10 minutes until softened.

3 Stir in the flour and coriander and cook for 1 minute. Gradually add the stock and wine, stirring until the sauce thickens, boils and is smooth. Season. Simmer for 5–10 minutes until tender.

To Microwave

Complete step 1. Put the butter and oil in a shallow dish and microwave on HIGH for 30 seconds. Stir in the pepper and onion and microwave on HIGH for 5 minutes. Stir in the flour and coriander and microwave on HIGH for 1 minute. Gradually add the stock and wine. Microwave on HIGH for 4–5 minutes, stirring frequently, until boiling and thickened. Add the pork and microwave on HIGH for 5 minutes until boiling, stirring occasionally. Microwave on LOW for 4 minutes until tender. Stand, covered, for 5 minutes.

To Freeze

Cool, pack in a rigid container and freeze for up to 3 months.

To Thaw

Leave overnight at cool room temperature. Alternatively, microwave on LOW for about 7–8 minutes. Stand for 10 minutes, breaking up the block as it thaws.

To Serve

Gently reheat in a heavy-based pan for 5–10 minutes or until piping hot, stirring frequently. Alternatively, cover and microwave on HIGH for about 5–6 minutes or until piping hot.

Right: Pork and Coriander

PORK IN PLUM SAUCE

SERVES 4

450g (1lb) plums
300ml (½ pint) rosé wine
salt and pepper
25g (1oz) plain wholemeal flour
700g (1½lb) pork fillet or tenderloin, trimmed and cubed
25g (1oz) butter
1 large onion, skinned and chopped
175g (6oz) white cabbage, shredded
30ml (2 tbsp) natural yogurt

1 Simmer the plums in the wine for 5 minutes, until tender. Strain, reserving the juice. Remove the stones from the plums and purée half in a blender or food processor.
2 Season the flour, then coat the pork cubes.
3 Melt the butter in a large saucepan or flameproof casserole and lightly fry the onion and cabbage for 3–4 minutes. Add the meat and fry until brown on all sides.
4 Pour in the reserved plum juice and puréed plums, then simmer, covered, for 10–15 minutes, until tender. Just before serving add the remaining plums and yogurt and reheat gently.

To Microwave

Put the plums and wine in a large bowl and microwave on HIGH for 3–4 minutes. Complete the remainder of step 1 and step 2. Microwave the butter in a large bowl on HIGH for 45 seconds until melted. Add the onion and cabbage and microwave on HIGH for 7 minutes, stirring occasionally. Add the pork and microwave on HIGH for 3 minutes. Pour in 200ml (7fl oz) plum juice and puréed plums and microwave on HIGH for 3–4 minutes, until boiling, stirring occasionally. Microwave on LOW for 7–8 minutes, until the pork is tender. Stir in the remaining plums and yogurt. Stand covered, for 5 minutes.

To Freeze

Omit the yogurt. Cool, pack in rigid containers, packing the reserved plums separately, and freeze for up to 3 months.

To Thaw

Leave overnight at cool room temperature.

To Serve

Gently reheat in a heavy-based saucepan for 10 minutes or until piping hot, stirring frequently. Stir in the reserved plums and heat for a further 2 minutes. Alternatively, cover and microwave on HIGH for 12–14 minutes or until piping hot, stirring occasionally. Stir in the yogurt and the reserved plums and cook on HIGH for a further minute.

CREAMY HAM AND LEEK PIES

SERVES 4

50g (2oz) butter
450g (1lb) leeks, trimmed, washed and thickly sliced
225g (8oz) carrots, peeled and sliced
50g (2oz) plain flour
300ml (½ pint) vegetable stock
300ml (½ pint) milk
225g (8oz) cooked ham, diced
30ml (2 tbsp) chopped fresh parsley or 10ml (2 tsp) dried
5ml (1 tsp) grated nutmeg
salt and pepper
350g (12oz) packet puff pastry
beaten egg, to glaze

1 Melt the butter in a large saucepan and fry the leeks and carrots for 5 minutes. Stir in the flour and cook, stirring continuously, for 1 minute.
2 Gradually stir in the stock, then add the milk. Cook over medium heat, stirring until the mixture comes to the boil and thickens. Stir in the ham, parsley, nutmeg and seasoning. Leave to cool.
3 Roll out the pastry on a lightly floured surface to 0.5cm (¼ inch) thick. Use a 350ml (12fl oz) individual pie dish as a template to cut out four lids for the pies.
4 Divide the ham and leek filling between four 350ml (12fl oz) individual pie dishes. Dampen the edges of the dishes with water. Cut the remaining trimmings of pastry into thin strips and place around the rim of each dish. Moisten the strips and lay a lid over each pie. Seal the edges, trim and flute.
5 Make a small cut in the top of each pie and brush with beaten egg to glaze. Bake in the oven at 220°C (425°F) mark 7 for 25–30 minutes or until golden brown.

To Microwave

Dice the butter into a large bowl and microwave on HIGH for 1–1½ minutes until melted. Add the leeks and carrots and microwave on HIGH for a further 2½–3½ minutes. Stir in the flour, then gradually add the stock. Stir in the milk. Cover and microwave on HIGH for 4–6 minutes, stirring twice during cooking, until thickened. Stir in the ham, parsley, nutmeg and seasoning. Leave to cool. Complete steps 3–5.

To Freeze
Wrap the uncooked pies individually in plastic wrap, then overwrap in foil at the end of step 4. Freeze for up to 3 months.

To Thaw and Serve
Unwrap and brush the frozen pies with beaten egg. Bake in the oven at 200°C (400°F) mark 6 for about 55–65 minutes or until golden and piping hot.

STUFFED CABBAGE PARCELS

SERVES 4

350g (12oz) lean minced pork
1 medium onion, skinned and finely chopped
227g (8oz) can tomatoes
salt and pepper
283g (10oz) can red kidney beans, drained and rinsed
16 large Savoy cabbage leaves
40g (1½oz) butter
40g (1½oz) plain flour
450ml (¾ pint) milk
50g (2oz) mature Cheddar cheese, grated
pinch of cayenne pepper

1 Put the minced pork in a large saucepan, preferably non-stick, over medium heat and cook in its own fat until beginning to brown, stirring from time to time to ensure that it does not stick.
2 Add the onion and fry until softened and lightly coloured. Add the tomatoes with their juice and bring to the boil, stirring. Season to taste, then simmer over a moderate heat for 20 minutes, stirring occasionally, until the pork is cooked and the sauce is thick and well reduced. Stir in the kidney beans and remove the pan from the heat. Set aside, covered, while preparing the cabbage leaves for stuffing.
3 Blanch the cabbage for 3 minutes, in batches of 4 leaves at a time, in a large pan of boiling salted water. Drain the cabbage leaves, rinse them under cold running water and pat them dry with absorbent kitchen paper.
4 Lay the cabbage leaves flat on a chopping board. Using a sharp knife, cut out and discard the thick central stalks.
5 Put 15–25ml (1–1½ tbsp) filling mixture at the stalk end of each cabbage leaf. Fold the 2 sides inwards to cover the filling mixture, then roll up to make a neat, compact parcel.

6 Arrange the cabbage parcels, seam side down, close together in a single layer in a well-buttered flameproof serving dish.
7 Put the butter, flour and milk in a saucepan. Heat, whisking continuously, until the sauce thickens, boils and is smooth. Simmer for 1–2 minutes. Season to taste. Pour the sauce evenly over the cabbage parcels in the dish. Sprinkle with the cheese and cayenne pepper.
8 Bake in the oven at 180°C (350°F) mark 4 for 20 minutes or until golden brown and bubbling. Serve the cabbage parcels hot, straight from the dish. Accompany them with boiled rice.

To Microwave
Put the onion in a large bowl with a little juice from the tomatoes, cover and microwave on HIGH for 5 minutes or until softened. Add the pork and microwave on HIGH for a further 5 minutes, stirring to break up any lumps. Add the remaining tomatoes with their juice and microwave on HIGH, uncovered for a further 8 minutes or until the meat is cooked and the sauce is reduced, stirring. Stir in the kidney beans. Complete steps 3, 4, 5 and 6. Put the butter, flour and milk in a medium bowl and microwave on HIGH for 5 minutes, until boiling and thickened, whisking frequently. Season to taste. Pour evenly over the cabbage parcels. Microwave on HIGH for 5 minutes to heat through then sprinkle with the cheese and cayenne pepper and brown under a hot grill.

To Freeze
Cool and pack the parcels and sauce separately in rigid containers. Freeze for up to 6 months.

To Thaw
Leave overnight at cool room temperature. Alternatively arrange the parcels evenly on a plate and microwave on LOW for about 15–20 minutes. Test and reposition the parcels after 5 minutes. Stand for 15–20 minutes. Microwave the sauce on HIGH for 3–4 minutes. Stand for 15 minutes, breaking up the block as it thaws.

To Serve
Arrange the parcels in a shallow dish and pour over the sauce. Sprinkle with the cheese and cayenne pepper. Cover and bake in the oven at 180°C (350°F) mark 4 for 20–25 minutes or until piping hot. Alternatively, microwave on HIGH for 20–25 minutes or until piping hot then sprinkle with the cheese and cayenne pepper and brown under a hot grill.

CANNELLONI

SERVES 4

30ml (2 tbsp) olive oil
1 small onion, skinned and very finely chopped
1 garlic clove, skinned and crushed
225g (8oz) minced veal
100g (4oz) chicken livers, roughly chopped
225g (8oz) frozen chopped spinach, thawed
5ml (1 tsp) chopped fresh basil or 2.5ml (½ tsp) dried
2.5ml (½ tsp) dried oregano
1.25ml (¼ tsp) grated nutmeg
salt and pepper
2 eggs, beaten
50g (2oz) Parmesan cheese, freshly grated
600ml (1 pint) tomato sauce (see page 193)
16 sheets of fresh lasagne
600ml (1 pint) Coating white sauce (see page 188)

1 Heat the oil in a heavy-based frying pan and gently fry the onion and garlic for about 5 minutes until soft and lightly coloured.

2 Add the minced veal and chicken livers and fry until brown, pressing the veal with the back of a wooden spoon to break up any lumps.

3 Add the spinach, basil, oregano, nutmeg and seasoning to taste. Cook, stirring, until all the liquid has evaporated. Transfer to a bowl and leave to cool slightly. Add the eggs and half of the Parmesan. Stir well to mix.

4 Coat the bottom of a large ovenproof dish with a thin layer of tomato sauce. Spoon a little of the veal and spinach filling on one of the sheets of lasagne. Roll up the lasagne around the filling, then place seam side down in the dish.

5 Repeat with the remaining filling and lasagne until used up, arranging the cannelloni side by side in a single layer.

6 Pour the remaining tomato sauce over the cannelloni. Cover with the white sauce and sprinkle with the remaining Parmesan.

7 Bake in the oven at 190°C (375°F) mark 5 for 30 minutes or until golden brown and bubbling.

To Microwave

Place the oil in a medium bowl and microwave on HIGH for 30 seconds. Add the onion and garlic, cover and microwave on HIGH for 2 minutes. Add the minced veal and chicken livers and microwave on HIGH for 4–5 minutes or until browned, stirring occasionally to break up any lumps. Add the spinach, basil, oregano and nutmeg. Microwave on HIGH for 2–3 minutes or until the liquid has evaporated. Transfer to a bowl and cool slightly. Add the eggs and half the Parmesan. Stir well to mix, then season to taste. Complete steps 4–6. Microwave on HIGH for 10 minutes or until piping hot. If liked, place under a hot grill until golden and bubbling.

To Freeze

Cool, pack in a rigid container at the end of step 6 and freeze for up to 3 months.

To Thaw and Serve

Microwave on LOW for 20–25 minutes, then leave to stand for 30 minutes. Cook in the oven at 180°C (350°F) mark 4 for 40–50 minutes or until piping hot. Cover with foil if the top becomes too brown.

OSSO BUCO WITH TOMATO

SERVES 4–6

1.6kg (3½lb) veal knuckle (veal shin, hind cut), sawn into 5cm (2 inch) lengths
30ml (2 tbsp) plain flour
salt and pepper
400ml (¾ pint) dry white wine
30ml (2 tbsp) vegetable oil
25g (1oz) butter
225g (8oz) onions, skinned and sliced
450g (1lb) tomatoes, skinned and roughly chopped
30ml (2 tbsp) tomato purée
1 garlic clove, skinned and crushed
2.5ml (½ tsp) dried basil
chopped fresh parsley, to garnish

1 Trim the veal to remove any excess fat. Season the flour well and use to lightly coat the meat. In a small pan, boil down the wine to reduce by half.

2 Heat the oil and butter in a large shallow flameproof dish and brown the meat well on both sides. Remove the meat from the pan. Lightly brown the onions in the remaining fat. Add the tomatoes, wine, tomato purée, garlic, basil and seasoning.

3 Bring to the boil, replace the meat and cover the dish tightly. Cook in the oven at 170°C (325°F) mark 3 for 1¾–2 hours or until the meat is tender.

4 Lift the meat out of the cooking juices and keep warm. Reduce the cooking juices for 2–3 minutes to thicken slightly. Adjust seasoning, then spoon

Right: Stuffed Cabbage Parcels (page 141)

the sauce over the veal. Garnish with chopped parsley.

To Microwave

Complete step 1, pouring the wine into a large bowl. Microwave on HIGH for 5–7 minutes or until reduced by half. Put the oil and butter in a large shallow dish and microwave on HIGH for 45 seconds. Add the veal in a single layer and microwave on HIGH for 3–4 minutes, re-arranging halfway through cooking. Remove from the dish and set aside. Place the onions in the remaining fat and microwave on HIGH for 5 minutes or until soft. Add the tomatoes, wine, tomato purée, garlic, basil and seasoning. Microwave on HIGH for 3–4 minutes or until boiling, stirring occasionally. Add the meat, cover and microwave on HIGH for 10–15 minutes or until tender, stirring occasionally. Remove the veal and stand, covered, for 15 minutes. Meanwhile, microwave the sauce on HIGH for 4 minutes or until thick. Adjust seasoning, then spoon over the veal. Garnish.

To Freeze

Cool, pack in a rigid container at the end of step 3 and freeze for up to 4 months.

To Thaw

Leave overnight at cool room temperature.

To Serve

Place in a covered casserole dish and reheat in the oven at 200°C (400°F) mark 6 for about 40 minutes. Alternatively, cover and microwave on HIGH for about 8–10 minutes or until piping hot, stirring occasionally. Complete step 4.

OXTAIL AND ORANGE CASSEROLE

SERVES 6

2 whole oxtails, cut up, about 2.3kg (5lb) total weight
175g (6oz) onions, skinned and sliced
300ml (½ pint) red wine
700ml (1¼ pints) stock
2 oranges
3 garlic cloves, skinned and crushed
100g (4oz) parsnips, peeled and sliced
2 bay leaves
salt and pepper
about 60ml (4 tbsp) vegetable oil
45ml (3 tbsp) plain flour

1 Trim the oxtails of excess fat and place in a large bowl with the sliced onions. Mix the wine and stock together with the pared rind of 1 orange and strained juice of 2 oranges – about 90ml (6 tbsp) juice. Add the garlic, parsnips, bay leaves and seasoning. Pour over the oxtail. Cover and marinate in a cool place for 12 hours, turning occasionally.

2 Drain the meat, reserving the marinade, and pat dry with absorbent kitchen paper. Heat oil in a large flameproof casserole and brown the oxtail, a few pieces at a time. Remove from the pan. Stir the flour into the pan and cook for 1 minute. Pour in the marinade and vegetables and bring to the boil. Replace the oxtail and cover.

3 Cook in the oven at 170°C (325°F) mark 3 for about 3 hours or until the oxtail is nearly tender. Cool for about 1 hour. Lift out the pieces of oxtail, allow to cool, cover and refrigerate overnight. Discard the bay leaves then cool, cover and refrigerate the pan juices and vegetables separately overnight.

4 The next day, skim off all the fat from the juices. Purée the vegetables and juices in a blender or food processor until smooth. Reheat until boiling. Place in a casserole and pour over the sauce. Cover and reheat in the oven at 200°C (400°F) mark 6 for about 45 minutes.

To Microwave

Complete step 1. Drain the meat, reserving the marinade, and pat dry with absorbent kitchen paper. Place the oil in a large shallow dish and microwave on HIGH for 1 minute. Arrange the oxtail in a single layer in the dish and microwave on HIGH for 4–5 minutes, re-arranging halfway through the cooking time. Remove the meat. Stir in the flour, then pour in the marinade and vegetables. Microwave on HIGH for 5–6 minutes or until boiling. Add the oxtail and microwave on MEDIUM for 1 hour or until the oxtail is nearly tender, stirring occasionally. Cool for about 1 hour. Finish step 3. The next day, skim off all the fat from the juices. Purée the vegetables and juices in a blender or food processor. Place in a bowl and microwave on HIGH for 8–10 minutes. Place the oxtail in a large shallow dish and pour over the sauce. Microwave on MEDIUM for 20–25 minutes until the oxtail is really tender, stirring occasionally.

To Freeze

Cool and pack the meat in a rigid container at the end of step 3. Purée the juices as directed in step

4. Cool and pack the juices separately in a rigid container. Freeze for up to 2 months.

To Thaw and Serve
Leave overnight at cool room temperature. Complete step 4.

SWEDISH VEAL MEATBALLS

SERVES 4

450g (1lb) lean veal, pork or beef (or a mixture of these)

100g (4oz) smoked streaky bacon, rinded

½ small onion, skinned

50g (2oz) stale brown bread

2.5ml (½ tsp) ground allspice

salt and pepper

75g (3oz) unsalted butter

300ml (½ pint) chicken stock (see page 186)

juice of ½ lemon

10ml (2 tsp) chopped fresh dill or 5ml (1 tsp) dried

15ml (1 tbsp) cornflour

150ml (¼ pint) soured cream

dill sprigs, to garnish (optional)

1 Put the meat, bacon, onion and bread through the blades of a mincer twice so that they are minced very fine. Or work them in a food processor.

2 Add the allspice to the mixture with seasoning to taste, then mix in with the fingertips to bind the mixture. (Pick up a handful and press firmly in the hand – it should cling together, but not be too wet.) Chill for 1 hour.

3 Gently melt the butter in a large flameproof casserole. Dip a tablespoon in the butter, then use to shape a spoonful of the minced mixture.

4 Add the meatball to the casserole, then continue dipping the spoon in the butter and shaping meatballs until there are 12–14 altogether.

5 Fry the meatballs, half at a time if necessary, over moderate heat until browned on all sides. Return all the meatballs to the casserole, pour in the stock and lemon juice and bring slowly to boiling point. Lower the heat, add the dill and seasoning to taste. Cover and simmer gently for 30 minutes.

6 Remove the meatballs with a slotted spoon and keep warm. Blend the cornflour with 30ml (2 tbsp) water until smooth, then stir into the sauce. Bring to the boil and simmer for 1–2 minutes until thickened.

7 Stir the soured cream into the sauce and mix gently to combine evenly with the cooking liquid.

Taste and adjust the seasoning of the sauce and pour over the meatballs. Garnish with dill sprigs, if liked.

To Microwave
Complete steps 1 and 2. Dice the butter into a large shallow dish and microwave on HIGH for 1½ –2 minutes. Arrange the meatballs in a single layer in the dish. Microwave on HIGH for 5 minutes. Carefully reposition the meatballs, then microwave on HIGH for 5 minutes. Pour in the stock, lemon juice, dill and seasoning. Microwave on HIGH for 10–15 minutes or until the sauce is boiling and the meatballs are cooked. Stand, covered, for 5 minutes. Complete step 6, microwaving the sauce on HIGH for 1–1½ minutes or until thickened. Complete step 7.

To Freeze
Cool, pack the meatballs and sauce separately in rigid containers at the end of step 6. Freeze for up to 3 months.

To Thaw
Leave overnight in the refrigerator. Alternatively, microwave the meatballs on low for about 10–12 minutes, re-arranging halfway through. Stand for 10 minutes. Meanwhile, microwave the sauce on LOW for about 10–12 minutes, breaking up the block as it thaws.

To Serve
Put the meatballs in a heavy-based saucepan, pour over the sauce and gently reheat for 10–15 minutes or until piping hot, stirring frequently. Alternatively, microwave on HIGH for about 5–6 minutes or until piping hot, stirring frequently. Stand, covered, for 5 minutes. Complete step 7.

FISH MAIN COURSES

SMOKED HADDOCK GOUGÈRE

SERVES 4

100g (4oz) plain or strong plain flour
75g (3oz) butter
200ml (7fl oz) water
3 eggs, lightly beaten
FILLING
450g (1lb) smoked haddock fillets
25g (1oz) butter
1 medium onion, skinned and chopped
25g (1oz) plain flour
300ml (½ pint) milk
10ml (2 tsp) capers
2 eggs, hard-boiled and chopped
2 tomatoes, skinned, seeded and cut into thin strips
salt and pepper
about 30ml (2 tbsp) lemon juice
15ml (1 tbsp) fresh breadcrumbs
15ml (1 tbsp) grated hard cheese
chopped fresh parsley, to garnish

1 For the choux pastry, sift the flour on to a plate or piece of paper. Put the butter and water in a saucepan and heat gently until the butter has melted. Bring to the boil, then remove from the heat. Tip all the flour at once into the hot liquid. Beat thoroughly with a wooden spoon, then return the pan to the heat.

2 Continue beating the mixture until it is smooth and forms a ball in the centre of the pan (take care not to over-beat or the mixture will become fatty). Leave the mixture to cool for 1–2 minutes.

3 Beat in the egg, a little at a time, adding just enough to give a piping consistency.

4 Using a 1cm (½ inch) plain nozzle, pipe the mixture in two circles (one on top of the other) round the bottom of four 12.5cm (5 inch) ovenproof dishes. Bake in the oven at 220°C (425°F) mark 7 for about 25 minutes.

5 Meanwhile for the filling, put the haddock in a large frying pan with just enough water to cover. Simmer for 10–15 minutes or until tender. Drain, skin and flake the fish, discarding the bones.

6 Melt the butter in a saucepan and gently fry the onion until golden brown. Stir in the flour and cook for 1 minute, stirring. Remove the pan from the heat and gradually stir in the milk. Bring to the boil slowly and continue to cook, stirring, until the sauce is thick and smooth.

7 Stir in the capers, eggs, fish and tomatoes. Season well; add the lemon juice to taste.

8 Spoon the mixture equally into the centre of each gougère. Combine the breadcrumbs and cheese and sprinkle over each gougère. Bake in the oven for a further 10 minutes. Garnish with parsley.

To Microwave
Complete steps 1–4. Place the haddock in a dish with the thicker parts towards the outside of the dish, then pour over 30ml (2 tbsp) water. Cover and microwave on HIGH for 4 minutes or until tender. Remove skin and any bones and flake the fish. Put the butter, flour and milk in a medium bowl and whisk together. Microwave on HIGH for 4–5 minutes or until the sauce has boiled and thickened, whisking frequently. Stir in the capers, eggs, fish and tomatoes. Season well; add lemon juice to taste. Complete step 8.

To Freeze
Cool and pack the sauce and cooked gougère separately at the end of step 7 in a rigid container. Freeze the sauce for up to 2 months, choux pastry for up to 6 months.

To Thaw and Serve
Unwrap the gougère and leave at room temperature for 1 hour. Alternatively, microwave on LOW for about 1–1½ minutes. Stand for 10–15 minutes. Refresh in the oven at 180°C (350°F) mark 4 for 5 minutes.

Meanwhile, gently reheat the sauce in a pan for 5 minutes, stirring frequently. Alternatively, microwave on HIGH for 4–5 minutes or until piping hot, stirring frequently. Complete step 8.

Right: Scallop and Mushroom Pie (page 149)

CREAMED FISH PIE

SERVES 4

450g (1lb) cod fillets, skinned
100g (4oz) button mushrooms
1 bay leaf
300ml (½ pint) milk, plus 60ml (4 tbsp)
25g (1oz) butter
25g (1oz) plain flour
2.5ml (½ tsp) caraway seeds
salt and pepper
700g (1½lb) potatoes, peeled and diced
1 egg

1 Place the cod, mushrooms and bay leaf in a saucepan. Pour over the 300ml (½ pint) milk and bring to the boil. Cover lightly and simmer for 15–20 minutes or until the fish is just cooked. Drain, reserving the cooking liquor. Discard the bay leaf. Flake the fish, discarding any bones. Set the fish aside while making the sauce.
2 Melt the butter in a saucepan, add the flour and cook gently, stirring, for 1–2 minutes. Remove from the heat and gradually stir in the reserved milk. Bring to the boil, stirring continuously, until the sauce is smooth and thickened. Stir in the caraway seeds. Simmer for 1–2 minutes.
3 Add the flaked fish and mushrooms to the sauce. Season to taste. Spoon into a shallow 1.4 litre (2½ pint) ovenproof serving dish. Set aside.
4 Cook the potatoes in a saucepan of boiling salted water for 20–30 minutes or until very tender. Drain the potatoes thoroughly.
5 Mash the potatoes and remaining milk with a potato masher. Beat in the egg and season the taste. Spoon evenly over the fish mixture.
6 Bake in the oven at 200°C (400°F) mark 6 for about 35 minutes or until golden brown.

To Microwave

Put the cod, mushrooms and bay leaf in a shallow dish. Pour over the milk, cover and microwave on HIGH for 3–4 minutes or until the fish is cooked. Complete step 1. Put the butter, flour, reserved milk and caraway seeds in a medium bowl and microwave on HIGH for 3–4 minutes or until the sauce has boiled and thickened, whisking frequently. Complete step 3. Put the potatoes in a medium bowl with 30ml (2 tbsp) water. Cover and microwave on HIGH for 10–12 minutes or until very tender. Drain well. Complete step 5. Microwave on HIGH for 4–5 minutes to heat through, then brown under a hot grill.

To Freeze

Cool, pack in a polythene bag at the end of step 5 and freeze for up to 2 months.

To Thaw and Serve

Leave at cool room temperature for 6–8 hours. Bake in the oven at 200°C (400°F) mark 6 for about 35 minutes or until golden brown. Alternatively, microwave on LOW for about 4–5 minutes. Stand for 5–10 minutes. Microwave on HIGH for 4–5 minutes or until piping hot, then brown under a hot grill.

CHEESY SMOKED SALMON ROULADE

SERVES 4–6

ROULADE
100g (4oz) butter
100g (4oz) plain flour
300ml (½ pint) milk
100g (4oz) Gruyère cheese, grated
4 eggs, separated
30ml (2 tbsp) grated fresh Parmesan cheese
FILLING
225g (8oz) smoked salmon, finely shredded
75ml (5 tbsp) double cream
5ml (1 tsp) lemon juice
15ml (1 tbsp) chopped fresh dill or 5ml (1 tsp) dried
dill sprigs and lemon slices, to garnish

1 Grease and line a 23 × 33cm (9 × 13 inch) Swiss roll tin. Grease the paper.
2 For the roulade, melt the butter in a saucepan, stir in the flour and cook for 1 minute. Remove from the heat and gradually stir in the milk. Gently bring to the boil, stirring continuously. Beat in the Gruyère cheese and egg yolks.
3 Whisk the egg whites until stiff. Fold into the cheese mixture and pour into the prepared tin. Bake in the oven at 190°C (375°F) mark 5 for 25–30 minutes or until firm to the touch and golden.
4 Lay a sheet of greaseproof paper on the work surface and sprinkle with the Parmesan cheese. Turn the roulade on to the paper and remove the lining paper. Cover with a damp cloth.
5 For the filling, place the smoked salmon in a small saucepan and stir in the cream, lemon juice and chopped dill. Heat very gently for 1–2 minutes. Spread the filling over the roulade and roll up, using the greaseproof paper to assist. Serve immediately,

cut into slices and garnish with dill sprigs and lemon slices.

To Microwave

Complete step 1. Dice the butter and place in a medium bowl. Cover and microwave on HIGH for 1½–2 minutes. Stir in the flour and gradually add the milk. Cover and microwave on HIGH for 3½–4½ minutes or until thickened, stirring once. Beat in the Gruyère cheese and egg yolks. Complete steps 3–5.

To Freeze

Cool, wrap in plastic wrap, then overwrap in foil. Freeze for up to 2 months.

To Thaw

Leave overnight in the refrigerator. Alternatively, unwrap and microwave on LOW for about 3–5 minutes. Stand for 1–2 hours until completely thawed.

To Serve

Serve cold. Alternatively, place on a lightly greased baking sheet and cover with foil. Bake in the oven at 200°C (400°F) mark 6 for 35–40 minutes or until heated through. Garnish.

SCALLOP AND MUSHROOM PIE

SERVES 4

4 scallops
450g (1lb) haddock fillet, skinned, boned and cut into chunks
1 bay leaf
6 black peppercorns
1 small onion, skinned and finely chopped
450ml (¾ pint) milk
700g (1½lb) potatoes, cooked
65g (2½oz) butter
salt and pepper
100g (4oz) mushrooms, sliced
25g (1oz) plain flour
60ml (4 tbsp) dry sherry
30ml (2 tbsp) single cream
chopped fresh parsley, to garnish

1 If necessary, remove and discard the tough white 'muscle' from each scallop. Separate the red corals from the scallops, then cut the white part into fairly thick slices.

2 Put the sliced scallops and the haddock in a medium saucepan with the bay leaf, peppercorns, onion and 300ml (½ pint) of the milk. Simmer gently for 10–15 minutes or until tender. Five minutes before the end of the cooking time, add the corals.

3 Meanwhile, mash the potatoes with the rest of the milk and 25g (1oz) of the butter. Season to taste. Drain the haddock and scallops, reserving the milk.

4 Melt 25g (1oz) of the butter in another medium saucepan and fry the mushrooms for 2 minutes. Stir in the flour and cook for 1 minute. Remove from the heat and gradually stir in the reserved milk. Bring to the boil, stirring constantly, then simmer for 2–3 minutes until thick and smooth. Add the sherry, cream, haddock and scallops and mix well. Season to taste.

5 Turn the fish mixture into an ovenproof serving dish, cover with the mashed potatoes and dot with the remaining butter.

6 Bake in the oven at 180°C (350°F) mark 4 for 20 minutes or until the top is brown. Garnish with parsley.

To Microwave

Complete step 1. Put the scallops, without the corals, haddock, bay leaf, peppercorns, onion and 300ml (½ pint) of the milk in a large shallow dish. Cover and microwave on HIGH for 4 minutes. Add the corals, cover and microwave on HIGH for 2 minutes or until all of the fish is tender. Complete steps 3 and 4. Turn into a flameproof serving dish, cover with the mashed potatoes and dot with the remaining butter. Microwave on HIGH for 3–4 minutes to reheat, then brown under a hot grill. Garnish.

To Freeze

Cool at the end of step 5 and freeze for up to 1 month.

To Thaw and Serve

Dot the top of the pie with butter and bake from frozen at 150°C (300°F) mark 2 for 50–60 minutes or until piping hot. Alternatively, microwave on MEDIUM for about 10–15 minutes, then on HIGH for about 3–4 minutes or until piping hot. Grill as above if liked. Garnish.

HALIBUT CREOLE

SERVES 4

30ml (2 tbsp) vegetable oil
1 onion, skinned and chopped
2 garlic cloves, skinned and crushed
1 celery stick, chopped
1 green pepper, cored, seeded and chopped
397g (14oz) can chopped tomatoes
5ml (1 tsp) brown sugar
1.25ml (¼ tsp) Tabasco sauce
30ml (2 tbsp) chopped fresh parsley or 10ml (2 tsp) dried
salt and pepper
butter, for greasing
four 275–350g (10–12oz) halibut or cod steaks

1 Heat the oil in a medium saucepan and fry the onion and garlic for 3 minutes. Add the celery and pepper and cook for 5 minutes until softened.

2 Add the tomatoes, sugar, Tabasco, parsley and seasoning. Cook for 15–20 minutes or until the vegetables have softened and the sauce has thickened.

3 Butter a large shallow dish and lay the halibut steaks in it. Pour the creole sauce over the fish and cover with foil. Bake in the oven at 200°C (400°F) mark 6 for 25–30 minutes or until the fish is firm and flakes easily.

4 Transfer the fish to a warmed serving platter and spoon the remaining sauce over the top.

To Microwave

Place the oil, onion and garlic in a medium bowl. Cover and microwave on HIGH for 3 minutes. Add the celery, green pepper, tomatoes, sugar, Tabasco, parsley and seasoning. Microwave, uncovered, on HIGH for 9–10 minutes. Arrange the fish in a buttered shallow dish and pour over the sauce. Cover and microwave on HIGH for 12–14 minutes or until the fish is firm and flakes easily. Complete step 4.

To Freeze

Cool the sauce at the end of step 2. Pack the fish in a rigid container and pour over the sauce. Freeze for up to 2 months.

To Thaw and Serve

Place in an ovenproof dish and cover with foil. Bake in the oven at 190°C (375°F) mark 5 for 1–1¼ hours or until the fish is firm and flakes easily. Alternatively, microwave on HIGH for 30–40 minutes or until the fish is firm and flakes easily, re-arranging frequently. Complete step 4.

TANDOORI COD

SERVES 4

four 200g (7oz) cod or haddock fillets
60ml (4 tbsp) natural yogurt
30ml (2 tbsp) lemon juice
15ml (1 tbsp) tandoori paste
15ml (1 tbsp) chopped fresh coriander or 5ml (1 tsp) ground coriander
15ml (1 tbsp) vegetable oil
coriander sprigs, to garnish

1 Place the fish fillets in a shallow dish. In a small bowl, mix the yogurt, lemon juice, tandoori paste, coriander and vegetable oil together.

2 Spread the yogurt mixture evenly over the fish, turning the fillets over to ensure they are evenly coated. Cover and refrigerate for 8 hours or overnight.

3 Cover the grill pan with foil and add the fillets, leaving any excess marinade in the dish.

4 Grill the fillets for 5–7 minutes, basting them with the remaining marinade. Turn over and grill for a further 5 minutes, continuing to baste, until the fish is firm and flakes easily. Transfer the fillets to a warmed serving dish and garnish with coriander sprigs.

To Microwave

Complete steps 1 and 2. Cover and microwave on HIGH for 13–15 minutes or until the fish is firm and flakes easily, re-arranging occasionally. Stand for 2 minutes. Garnish.

To Freeze

Complete steps 1 and 2, marinating the fish for 3 hours. Cover with plastic wrap and overwrap with foil. Freeze for up to 3 months.

To Thaw

Leave overnight in the refrigerator. Alternatively, microwave on LOW for about 20–25 minutes, re-arranging occasionally. Stand for 50–60 minutes until completely thawed.

To Serve

Complete steps 3 and 4. Alternatively, place the fish and marinade in a shallow dish. Cover and microwave on HIGH for 13–15 minutes, re-arranging occasionally, until the fish is firm and flakes easily. Stand for 2 minutes. Garnish.

Right: Fish Mousse with Coriander and Tomato Sauce (page 92)

FISH MEDALLIONS WITH DILL SAUCE

SERVES 4

225g (8oz) salmon fillets, skinned

350g (12oz) plaice fillets, skinned

150ml (¼ pint) dry white wine

30ml (2 tbsp) lemon juice

pepper

few dill sprigs

25g (1oz) butter

1 small onion, skinned and very finely chopped

15ml (1 tbsp) plain flour

salt and pepper

300ml (½ pint) single cream

1 bay leaf

30ml (2 tbsp) chopped fresh dill or 10ml (2 tsp) dried

dill sprigs and lemon or lime wedges, to garnish

1 Cut the fish fillets lengthways into 0.5cm (¼ inch) thick strips. Using two of one colour and one of another colour, lay alternate colours alongside each other and coil round to form a spiral, securing with a wooden cocktail stick. Continue to make eight medallions.

2 Place the wine and lemon juice in a frying pan. Add the medallions, season with pepper and scatter over the dill sprigs. Poach gently for 5–7 minutes or until the fish is firm and moist. Remove the dill sprigs and cocktail sticks. Transfer the medallions to a warmed serving dish and cover with foil to keep warm.

3 For the sauce, melt the butter in a saucepan and cook the onion for 2–3 minutes until softened. Stir in the flour and cook, stirring continuously, for a further minute. Remove from the heat and gradually stir in the cream. Add the bay leaf. Cook gently, stirring continuously, for 3–5 minutes until the sauce has thickened, but do not boil. Remove the bay leaf and stir in the dill.

4 Serve the fish medallions with the dill sauce, garnished with dill sprigs and lemon wedges.

To Microwave

Complete step 1. Place the medallions in a shallow dish with the wine, lemon juice, pepper and dill sprigs. Cover and microwave on HIGH for about 4–5 minutes, re-arranging once during cooking. Transfer to a warmed serving dish and remove the dill sprigs and cocktail sticks. Cover with foil to keep warm. Complete steps 3 and 4.

To Freeze

Wrap the medallions in plastic wrap, then in foil at the end of step 1. Freeze for up to 2 months.

To Thaw and Serve

Unwrap the medallions and continue with step 2, increasing the cooking time to 15–20 minutes, adding a little extra water to the pan if necessary during cooking. Alternatively, unwrap the medallions and place in a shallow dish with the wine, lemon juice, pepper and dill sprigs. Cover and microwave on HIGH for 7–9 minutes or until the fish is firm but still moist, re-arranging twice during cooking. Remove the dill sprigs and cocktail sticks. Complete steps 3 and 4.

SALMON AND PRAWN LASAGNE

SERVES 4

450ml (¾ pint) milk

1 small onion, skinned and studded with 4 cloves

2 blades mace

4 black peppercorns

7.5cm (3 inch) piece carrot, peeled

7.5cm (3 inch) piece celery

1 bay leaf

10ml (2 tsp) vegetable oil

150g (5oz) wholemeal lasagne

50g (2oz) butter

25g (1oz) plain wholemeal flour

25g (1oz) plain flour

15ml (1 tbsp) chopped fresh dill or 10ml (2 tsp) dried

220g (7½oz) can red or pink salmon, drained and roughly flaked

100g (4oz) white crab meat, flaked

100g (4oz) peeled cooked prawns

30ml (2 tbsp) grated Parmesan cheese

unpeeled prawns and dill, to garnish

1 Put the milk into a saucepan with the onion, mace, peppercorns, carrot, celery and bay leaf. Bring to simmering point, then remove from the heat, cover and set aside while cooking pasta.

2 Add 5ml (1 tsp) of the oil to a large saucepan of boiling water. Add the lasagne strips and cook for 8–10 minutes or until just tender. Drain.

3 Strain the milk. Melt the butter in a saucepan, stir in the flours and cook for 2 minutes. Remove from the heat and gradually stir in the milk. Return the pan to the heat, bring to the boil, stirring constantly, and cook until the sauce is thick and smooth. Remove from the heat and mix in the dill, salmon, crab meat and prawns.

4 Grease a 1.7 litre (3 pint) square or rectangular ovenproof dish with the remaining oil. Put one third of the fish sauce in the base of the dish and cover with half the lasagne. Top with a further third of the sauce, cover with the remaining lasagne, then finish with sauce. Sprinkle with the Parmesan cheese.

5 Cook in the oven at 180°C (350°F) mark 4 for 35–40 minutes or until golden brown. Garnish with prawns and dill.

To Microwave

Put the milk, onion, mace, peppercorns, carrot, celery and bay leaf in a large jug. Microwave on HIGH for 3–4 minutes or until just boiling. Set aside. Complete step 2. Put the butter, flour and strained milk in a medium bowl and whisk together. Microwave on HIGH for 4–5 minutes or until the sauce has boiled and thickened, whisking frequently. Complete steps 3 and 4. Microwave on HIGH for 5–8 minutes or until hot and bubbling, turning twice during cooking. Brown the top under a hot grill. Garnish.

To Freeze

Cool at the end of step 4 and freeze for up to 1 month.

To Thaw and Serve

Leave at cool room temperature overnight. Alternatively, stand on a rack and microwave on LOW for about 6–8 minutes, turning after 6 minutes. Stand for 10 minutes. Complete step 5.

TROUT STUFFED WITH SPINACH AND WALNUTS

SERVES 4

4 small trout, cleaned, boned and heads removed
75g (3oz) butter
1 onion, skinned and finely chopped
350g (12oz) frozen chopped spinach, thawed
50g (2oz) fresh breadcrumbs
50g (2oz) walnuts, chopped
juice of 1 lemon
30ml (2 tbsp) chopped fresh parsley or 10ml (2 tsp) dried
5ml (1 tsp) grated nutmeg
salt and pepper
parsley sprigs, lemon and lime slices, to garnish

1 Butter a large, shallow ovenproof dish and lay the trout in it.

2 Melt 50g (2oz) of the butter in a deep frying pan

and cook the onion for 4–5 minutes to soften. Stir in the spinach and cook for 5 minutes, stirring frequently.

3 Add the breadcrumbs, walnuts, lemon juice, parsley, nutmeg and seasoning. Stir well to combine and continue to cook over gentle heat for 10 minutes, stirring frequently. Cool.

4 Spoon the stuffing into the cavity of each fish. Lay the fish on their sides and dot with the remaining butter. Season, cover with buttered foil.

5 Bake in the oven at 180°C (350°F) mark 4 for 40–60 minutes or until the fish is firm and flakes easily. Remove the skin. Transfer to a warmed serving dish. Garnish.

To Microwave

Butter a large shallow dish and lay the trout in it, slashing the skin slightly to prevent bursting. Dice 50g (2oz) of the butter and place in a large bowl. Cover and microwave on HIGH for 1 minute. Add the onion and microwave on HIGH for a further 3 minutes or until softened. Add the spinach, breadcrumbs, walnuts, lemon juice, parsley, nutmeg and seasoning. Stir well to combine. Microwave on HIGH for 5–6 minutes, stirring once. Cool. Spoon the stuffing into the cavity of each fish. Dot with the remaining butter and season. Cover and microwave on HIGH for 15–20 minutes until the fish is firm and flakes easily, re-arranging occasionally. Stand for 3 minutes. Remove the skin. Transfer to a warmed serving dish. Garnish.

To Freeze

Omit step 1. Complete steps 2 and 3, cooling the stuffing. Lay each fish on a piece of plastic wrap. Spoon the stuffing into the cavity of each fish, then wrap the plastic wrap around the fish to seal completely. Overwrap and freeze for up to 2 months.

To Thaw

Leave overnight in the refrigerator. Alternatively, unwrap the fish and lay in a large, shallow dish. Microwave on LOW for about 25–30 minutes, re-arranging occasionally. Stand for 1½–2½ hours.

To Serve

Complete steps 1, 4 and 5. Alternatively, butter a large shallow dish and lay the fish in it. Dot with butter and season. Cover and microwave on HIGH for 15–20 minutes, re-arranging occasionally, until the fish is firm and flakes easily. Remove the skin. Transfer to a warmed serving dish. Garnish.

FISH KOULIBIAC

SERVES 6–8

350g (12oz) whiting fillets
150ml (¼ pint) dry white wine
salt and pepper
75g (3oz) butter
100g (4oz) spring onions, trimmed and chopped
75g (3oz) long grain white rice
1.25ml (¼ tsp) dried dill weed
100g (4oz) small button mushrooms, quartered
213g (7½oz) can red salmon, drained
3 eggs, hard-boiled and chopped
30ml (2 tbsp) lemon juice
225g (8oz) puff pastry or 368g (13oz) packet frozen puff pastry, thawed
1 egg, lightly beaten
lime wedges and parsley sprigs, to garnish

1 Place the whiting in a shallow saucepan. Pour over the wine with 150ml (¼ pint) water, season and bring to the boil. Cover and poach gently for 5–8 minutes or until tender. Strain and reserve the juices. Flake the fish and place in a large bowl, discarding skin and any bones.

2 Melt the butter in a saucepan and fry the onions until lightly browned. Stir in the rice with the reserved fish juices, dill weed and seasoning. Bring to the boil, cover and simmer for 10 minutes. Stir in the mushrooms and cook until the rice is tender and the liquid absorbed.

3 Flake the salmon, discarding any skin and bone. Combine the salmon, eggs, whiting and rice mixture. Stir in lemon juice and season. Cool.

4 Roll one third of the pastry to an oblong about 35.5 × 15cm (14 × 6 inch) and place on a large baking sheet. Spoon the filling down the centre of the pastry, leaving a 2.5cm (1 inch) border around the edge. Mould the filling up well – the finished koulibiac should look high and narrow.

5 Brush the rim of pastry with beaten egg. Roll out the remaining pastry to a rectangle 43 × 23cm (17 × 9 inch) and wind loosely round a floured rolling pin. Unroll over the filling and press the edges well together. Neaten them with a sharp knife, leaving a 2.5cm (1 inch) pastry rim all round.

6 Roll the cut edges inwards and press firmly. Mark the new edge at regular intervals with the back of a knife. Chill for at least 30 minutes.

7 Add a pinch of salt to the beaten egg and use to glaze the pastry. Bake in the oven at 220°C (425°F) mark 7 for 35 minutes or until well browned. Serve hot, garnished with lime wedges and parsley sprigs.

To Microwave

Place the whiting in a shallow dish, and pour over the wine. Cover and microwave on HIGH for 2–3 minutes, turning dish halfway through cooking. Strain and reserve the juices. Remove any skin or bones and flake the flesh. Dice the butter into a bowl and add the onions. Microwave on LOW for 5–7 minutes, stirring occasionally. Add the rice, reserved fish juices, dill weed and season to taste. Cover and microwave on HIGH for 5 minutes. Stir in the mushrooms and cook for a further 2–3 minutes or until the rice is tender and the liquid absorbed. Complete steps 3–7.

To Freeze

Pack in a polythene bag at the end of step 6 and freeze for up to 2 months.

To Thaw

Leave at cool room temperature overnight. Alternatively, microwave on LOW for about 5–8 minutes. Test and turn after 6 minutes. Stand for 15–20 minutes.

To Serve

Bake in the oven at 220°C (425°F) mark 7 for 40–45 minutes or until browned and heated through, covering with foil if it becomes too brown. Garnish.

Right: Turkey Medallions with Basil and Mozzarella (page 120)

PRAWNS WITH SPINACH

SERVES 4

60ml (4 tbsp) ghee or vegetable oil
1 small onion, skinned and finely chopped
10ml (2 tsp) ground ginger
10ml (2 tsp) garam masala
5ml (1 tsp) mustard seeds
2.5ml (½ tsp) chilli powder
2.5ml (½ tsp) ground turmeric
450g (1lb) peeled prawns, thawed and thoroughly dried if frozen
450g (1lb) frozen leaf spinach
60ml (4 tbsp) desiccated coconut
5ml (1 tsp) salt

1 Heat 30ml (2 tbsp) of the ghee in a heavy-based saucepan or flameproof casserole and gently fry the onion for about 5 minutes until soft.

2 Add the spices and fry, stirring, for a further 2 minutes. Add the prawns, increase the heat and toss to coat in the spiced onion mixture. Remove with a slotted spoon and set aside.

3 Heat the remaining ghee in the pan, add the spinach and heat gently until thawed. Stir frequently and cook for 8–10 minutes, or according to packet instructions.

4 Return the prawns to the pan, add half of the coconut and the salt and fold gently to mix. Cook for 5 minutes to allow the flavours to mingle, then turn into a warmed serving dish. Sprinkle with the remaining coconut.

To Microwave

Dice half the ghee into a shallow dish and add the onion. Cover and microwave on HIGH for 5–7 minutes or until soft. Add the spices and microwave on HIGH for 1–2 minutes, stir once. Add the prawns and stir well to coat in the spiced onion mixture. Remove with a slotted spoon and set aside. Add remaining ghee to the dish and stir in the frozen spinach. Microwave on HIGH for 5–6 minutes, stirring occasionally. Return the prawns to the dish with half the coconut and salt, mixing well. Microwave on HIGH for 3–4 minutes, stirring occasionally. Turn into a warmed serving dish and sprinkle over the remaining coconut.

To Freeze

Cool, pack in a rigid container and freeze for up to 1 month.

To Thaw

Leave overnight in the refrigerator. Alternatively, microwave on LOW for about 2–3 minutes. Stand for 10–15 minutes, breaking up the block as it thaws.

To Serve

Gently reheat in a heavy-based saucepan for 5–10 minutes, stirring. Alternatively, microwave on HIGH for 5–6 minutes or until piping hot, stirring occasionally.

CURRIED PRAWN CRÊPES

SERVES 4

CRÊPES
100g (4oz) plain flour
salt
1 egg, beaten
300ml (½ pint) milk
vegetable oil, for frying
FILLING
25g (1oz) butter
15ml (1 tbsp) curry powder
25g (1oz) plain flour
300ml (½ pint) milk
225g (8oz) fresh prawns, shelled
30ml (2 tbsp) chopped fresh parsley or 10ml (2 tsp) dried
salt and pepper
100g (4oz) mature Cheddar cheese, grated
parsley sprigs and lemon wedges, to garnish

1 For the crêpes, sift the flour and salt into a bowl. Add the egg and 150ml (¼ pint) of the milk and beat well. Gradually beat in the remaining milk.

2. Heat a small frying or crêpe pan and brush with oil. Add about 45ml (3 tbsp) of the batter and swirl to coat the pan. Cook for 1–2 minutes, then flip over and cook the other side until golden. Turn on to a plate and repeat the process, making eight to ten crêpes.

3 For the filling, melt the butter in a saucepan, stir in the curry powder and flour and cook for 1 minute. Remove from the heat and gradually stir in the milk. Return to the heat and slowly bring to the boil, stirring continuously. Add the prawns, parsley and seasoning.

4 Divide the filling between the crêpes, placing it towards one edge. Roll up and arrange side by side in an ovenproof dish. Sprinkle over the cheese.

5 Bake in the oven at 180°C (350°F) mark 4 for 15–20 minutes. Garnish.

To Microwave

Complete steps 1 and 2. To make the filling, place the milk, curry powder, flour and butter in a jug, then whisk together to combine. Microwave on HIGH for 3–4 minutes, stirring occasionally, until thick and smooth. Add the prawns, parsley and seasoning. Microwave on HIGH for a further 1½ minutes. Complete steps 4 and 5.

To Freeze

Cool, wrap in plastic wrap and overwrap in foil at the end of step 4. Freeze for up to 2 months.

To Thaw and Serve

Unwrap and cover with foil. Bake at 180°C (350°F) mark 4 for 1¼–1½ hours until piping hot.

SPICED BARBECUED MACKEREL

SERVES 12

12 mackerel, about 175g (6oz) each, cleaned with heads removed
90ml (6 tbsp) vegetable oil
5ml (1 tsp) chilli powder
5ml (1 tsp) paprika
1 garlic clove, skinned and crushed
grated rind and juice of 2 large oranges
wedges of orange, to serve

1 Make three deep slashes along one side of each mackerel. Place in a shallow dish.

2 Mix the oil, chilli powder, paprika, garlic, orange rind and 120ml (8 tbsp) orange juice together. Spoon the spice mixture over the mackerel. Cover lightly and marinate in the refrigerator for 2–3 hours. Turn once during this time.

3 Grill or barbecue the mackerel for about 7 minutes on each side, spooning any excess marinade over the fish as they cook.

To Freeze

Only use previously unfrozen fish. Pack in a rigid container at the end of step 2 and freeze for up to 2 months.

To Thaw and Serve

Leave overnight in the refrigerator. Alternatively, arrange 4–6 fish at a time, in a circle on a plate, with their tails towards the centre. Microwave on LOW for about 8–12 minutes. Stand for 5 minutes, every 2–3 minutes. Complete step 3.

ROAST SALMON WITH SPINACH CREAM

SERVES 4

700g (1½lb) middle-cut salmon
100g (4oz) spinach, washed
50g (2oz) low fat soft cheese
1 garlic clove, skinned and crushed
pinch of grated nutmeg
finely grated rind of 1 lemon
salt and pepper
50g (2oz) butter, melted
25g (1oz) dried white breadcrumbs

1 With a sharp, long-bladed knife, remove the central and side bones and the skin of the salmon. Cut in half.

2 Place the spinach in a saucepan with no added water. Cover and cook over a low heat for about 5 minutes or until wilted. Drain well. Finely chop and squeeze out any moisture.

3 Beat the spinach into the soft cheese with the garlic, nutmeg, lemon rind and seasoning. Spread half of the spinach mixture over the inside of each piece of salmon.

4 Shape the salmon pieces into a small joint by sandwiching the two plumper ends of salmon together, then fold round the thinner ends. Secure fairly tightly with three or four pieces of string.

5 Place the salmon in a small ovenproof dish. Brush all over with melted butter and sprinkle over the breadcrumbs.

6 Bake uncovered in the oven at 200°C (400°F) mark 6 for about 30–35 minutes or until golden brown and firm to the touch. Baste occasionally with the cooking liquid.

7 Remove the string and serve the salmon joint thickly sliced.

To Microwave

Complete step 1. Place the spinach in bowl with no added water. Cover and microwave on HIGH for 2–3 minutes or until wilted. Drain well. Finely chop and squeeze out any moisture. Complete steps 3–7.

To Freeze

Pack in a rigid container at the end of step 4 and freeze for up to 2 months.

To Thaw and Serve

Leave wrapped overnight on a plate in the refrigerator. Complete steps 5–7.

SEAFOOD SAFFRON RISOTTO

SERVES 4–6

good pinch of saffron strands

45ml (3 tbsp) olive oil

30ml (2 tbsp) butter

1 onion, skinned and chopped

2 garlic cloves, skinned and crushed

½ green pepper, cored, seeded and finely chopped

½ red pepper, cored, seeded and finely chopped

400g (14oz) Italian risotto rice

about 600ml (1 pint) hot fish stock (see page 186)

120ml (8 tbsp) dry white wine

1 bay leaf

salt and pepper

350–450g (12oz–1lb) peeled scampi or jumbo prawns

24 cooked mussels, shelled

a few mussels in shells, to garnish

freshly grated Parmesan cheese, to serve

1 Soak the saffron strands in 150ml (¼ pint) boiling water for at least 30 minutes.

2 Meanwhile, heat the oil and 15ml (1 tbsp) of the butter in a heavy-based saucepan. Gently fry the onion, garlic and peppers for 5 minutes until soft.

3 Add the rice and stir until well coated. Pour in a few spoonfuls of the stock and the wine, then add the saffron liquid.

4 Add the bay leaf and seasoning to taste and simmer gently, stirring frequently, until all the liquid is absorbed by the rice.

5 Add a few more spoonfuls of stock and simmer again until absorbed. Continue adding stock in this way for about 15 minutes or until the rice is *al dente*, stirring frequently.

6 Melt the remaining butter in a separate pan, add the scampi and toss gently for about 5 minutes until the change colour.

7 Remove the bay leaf from the risotto, then stir in the scampi and juices and the mussels. Warm through, taste and adjust seasoning. Turn into a warmed serving dish. Top with whole mussels and serve at once with grated Parmesan cheese handed separately.

To Microwave

Complete step 1. Place the oil and half the butter in a bowl and add the onion, garlic and peppers. Microwave on HIGH for 5–7 minutes or until soft, stirring once. Complete step 3. Add the bay leaf and season to taste. Microwave, uncovered, on HIGH for 13–15 minutes or until all the liquid is absorbed and the rice is tender, stirring frequently.

Place the remaining butter in a separate bowl and microwave on HIGH for 30 seconds. Add the scampi and microwave on HIGH for 2–4 minutes or until they change colour, stirring occasionally. Remove the bay leaf, stir in the scampi and juices and the mussels. Microwave on HIGH for 3–4 minutes or until heated through, stirring occasionally. Complete step 7.

To Freeze

Cool, pack in a rigid container before reheating in step 7 and freeze for up to 2 months.

To Thaw

Leave overnight in the refrigerator. Alternatively, microwave on LOW for about 3–4 minutes. Stand for 10–15 minutes, breaking up the block as it thaws.

To Serve

Gently reheat in a heavy-based saucepan for 5–10 minutes, stirring frequently to prevent sticking. Alternatively, microwave on HIGH for 3–5 minutes or until piping hot.

MONKFISH AND PRAWN TERRINE

SERVES 4

450g (1lb) monkfish fillet, skinned

60ml (4 tbsp) chopped fresh dill or 30ml (2 tbsp) dried

50ml (2fl oz) dry white wine

1 egg white

salt and pepper

100g (4oz) peeled prawns, thawed if frozen and chopped

small bunch of watercress, trimmed and finely chopped

4 tomatoes, skinned, seeded and finely chopped

1 garlic clove, skinned and crushed

150ml (¼ pint) low fat natural yogurt

unpeeled cooked prawns, to garnish

1 Purée the monkfish, dill, wine, egg white and seasoning in a blender or food processor until smooth. In another bowl, mix the prawns and watercress together.

2 Spread half the monkfish purée in the base of a lightly oiled 450g (1lb) loaf tin. Sprinkle over the prawns and watercress, then spread the remaining purée over the top. Smooth with a knife, then cover with foil.

Right: Smoked Haddock and Watercress Soufflé (page 160)

3 Put the dish in a roasting tin with enough boiling water to come half way up the sides. Cook in the oven at 200°C (400°F) mark 6 for 45 minutes or until firm. Drain off any liquid, then leave to cool for 1 hour.

4 Meanwhile, make the tomato sauce. Put the tomatoes and garlic in a small saucepan and simmer for 10 minutes, stirring occasionally. Mix in the yogurt and seasoning, then leave to cool.

5 Turn out the terrine on to a serving dish and garnish with the prawns. Cut into slices and serve with the tomato sauce.

To Microwave

Complete steps 1 and 2, using a microwaveproof 450g (1lb) loaf dish. Lift the loaf dish into a larger dish with enough boiling water to come half way up the sides. Cover with greased greaseproof paper and microwave on MEDIUM for 10 minutes, turning the dish twice. Complete step 3. Put the tomatoes and garlic into a bowl and microwave, uncovered, on HIGH for 2–3 minutes, stirring occasionally. Complete steps 4 and 5.

To Freeze

Cool, pack the cooked terrine and sauce separately at the end of step 4. Freeze for up to 2 months.

To Thaw and Serve

Leave the terrine and sauce overnight in the refrigerator. Alternatively, microwave the sauce on LOW for about 5–10 minutes, breaking up the block as it thaws. Microwave the terrine on LOW for about 10–15 minutes. Stand for 5–10 minutes. Complete step 5.

SMOKED HADDOCK AND WATERCRESS SOUFFLÉ

SERVES 00

400g (14oz) smoked haddock fillets
milk
bay leaves and peppercorns, for flavouring
50g (2oz) butter
30ml (2 tbsp) Parmesan cheese
45ml (3 tbsp) plain flour
1 bunch watercress, trimmed and roughly chopped
3 eggs, separated
1.25ml (¼ tsp) grated nutmeg
30ml (2 tbsp) lemon juice
pepper

1 Place the fish in a large sauté pan, add 300ml (½ pint) milk and the flavouring ingredients. Cover and poach for about 12 minutes or until the fish is just cooked.

2 Meanwhile, lightly grease a 1.4 litre (2½ pint) soufflé dish, then dust out with 15ml (1 tbsp) of the Parmesan cheese.

3 Using a fish slice, remove the fish from the pan and flake, discarding any skin and bones. Strain the milk into a jug and make up to 300ml (½ pint) again.

4 Melt the butter in a saucepan, add the flour and cook for 1–2 minutes. Stir in the milk, bring to the boil and simmer for 2–3 minutes or until thickened, stirring. Take off the heat, cool slightly then stir in the fish, watercress, egg yolks, nutmeg, lemon juice and plenty of pepper.

5 Whisk the egg whites until stiff but not dry, then fold into the fish mixture. Pour into the prepared soufflé dish and sprinkle over the remaining cheese.

6 Bake in the oven at 180°C (350°F) mark 4 for 40–45 minutes or until well risen and golden brown in colour and just firm to the touch. Serve immediately.

To Microwave

Place the fish in a dish with 150ml (¼ pint) milk and flavouring ingredients. Cover and microwave on HIGH for 3–4 minutes or until the fish is just cooked. Complete steps 2–3. Put the butter, flour and milk in a medium bowl and whisk together. Microwave on HIGH for 4–5 minutes or until the sauce has boiled and thickened, whisking frequently. Stir in the fish, watercress, egg yolks, nutmeg, lemon juice and plenty of pepper. Complete steps 5 and 6.

To Freeze

Cool, pack in a rigid container at the end of step 4. Freeze the unwhisked egg whites separately in a rigid container. Freeze the smoked haddock mixture for up to 2 months, egg whites for up to 6 months.

To Thaw and Serve

Leave overnight in the refrigerator. Complete steps 5 and 6, adding an extra 5 minutes to the cooking time.

VEGETARIAN MAIN COURSES

MIXED VEGETABLE CURRY

SERVES 4–6

60ml (4 tbsp) ghee or vegetable oil
2 onions, skinned and thinly sliced
1 garlic clove, skinned and crushed
1 cooking apple, peeled, cored and roughly chopped
2.5cm (1 inch) piece of fresh root ginger, peeled and roughly chopped
15ml (1 tbsp) mustard seeds
10ml (2 tsp) coriander seeds
10ml (2 tsp) cumin seeds
5ml (1 tsp) ground turmeric
2.5–5ml (½–1 tsp) chilli powder
225g (8oz) tomatoes, skinned and roughly chopped
salt and pepper
350g (12oz) potatoes, peeled and diced
225g (8oz) carrots, peeled and diced
225g (8oz) cauliflower florets
50g (2oz) flaked almonds
150g (5 oz) natural yogurt

1 Heat 30ml (2 tbsp) of the ghee in a heavy-based large saucepan or flameproof casserole. Gently fry the onions, garlic, apple and ginger for about 10 minutes, stirring occasionally, until soft and lightly coloured.

2 Meanwhile, put the mustard, coriander and cumin seeds in a small, heavy-based frying pan and dry fry for 2–3 minutes, shaking the pan and stirring the spices frequently.

3 Turn the spices into a mortar and crush finely with a pestle (or work in a nut mill). Add the crushed spices to the onion mixture, with the turmeric and chilli powder. Fry gently, stirring, for 2–3 minutes, then add the tomatoes. Stir well to mix, breaking up the tomatoes with a wooden spoon. Add seasoning.

4 Add the potatoes and carrots to the pan, then pour in 600ml (1 pint) water. Bring to the boil, stirring, then lower the heat, cover and simmer for 15 minutes.

5 Separate the cauliflower florets into small sprigs. Add to the pan and cook until tender.

6 Before serving, heat the remaining ghee in the frying pan. Add the nuts and fry over moderate heat, shaking the pan constantly.

7 Taste and adjust seasoning, then stir in the yogurt. Turn into a warmed serving dish. Sprinkle with the nuts and serve.

To Microwave

Put the ghee, onions, garlic, apple and ginger in a bowl. Cover and microwave on HIGH for 5–7 minutes, stirring occasionally. Put the mustard, coriander and cumin seeds in a small bowl. Cover and microwave on HIGH for 1 minute, shaking the bowl occasionally. Crush the spice mixture as step 3, then stir into the onion mixture with the turmeric and chilli powder. Microwave on HIGH for 1–2 minutes. Add the tomatoes, stirring well to mix and break up a little. Season. Add the potatoes and carrots and 450ml (¾ pint) boiling water. Part cover and microwave on HIGH for 10 minutes. Break up the cauliflower florets into smaller sprigs and add to the bowl. Cover and microwave on HIGH for 5–6 minutes or until tender. Meanwhile, complete steps 6 and 7.

To Freeze

Cool, pack in a rigid container at the end of step 5 and freeze for up to 3 months.

To Thaw

Leave at cool room temperature for 5–6 hours. Alternatively, microwave on HIGH for about 4–5 minutes. Test and turn after 4 minutes. Stand for 10 minutes, breaking up the block as it thaws.

To Serve

Gently reheat in a heavy-based saucepan, stirring frequently. Alternatively, microwave on HIGH for 4–5 minutes or until piping hot, stirring frequently. Complete steps 6 and 7.

SPRING GREEN PARCELS

SERVES 4

50g (2oz) brown rice
8 large spring green leaves
2.5ml (½ tsp) olive oil
1 onion, skinned and chopped
75g (3oz) blanched almonds, chopped and toasted
15ml (1 tbsp) chopped fresh parsley
5ml (1 tsp) grated lemon rind
25g (1oz) raisins
2.5ml (½ tsp) paprika
salt and pepper
225g (8oz) button mushrooms, sliced
150ml (¼ pint) vegetable stock
50ml (2fl oz) dry white wine
15g (½oz) butter
15g (½oz) plain flour
75ml (3fl oz) low fat natural yogurt

1 Put the rice in a saucepan with 300ml (½ pint) boiling water. Cover and simmer for 30 minutes or until tender and all the water has been absorbed.

2 Meanwhile, blanch the spring green leaves in boiling water for 2 minutes. Drain and rinse under cold water. Leave to drain well. Cut off any tough stalks.

3 Heat the oil in a frying pan and cook the onion over gentle heat for 5 minutes. Drain on absorbent kitchen paper to remove excess oil. Place in a bowl and add the rice, nuts, parsley, lemon rind, raisins, paprika and seasoning. Mix well.

4 Lay out the spring green leaves on a work surface and arrange the remaining leaves on top, to provide a casing for the stuffing. Divide the stuffing between the leaves, placing it in mounds in the centre. Fold the sides of the leaves over and roll up to form small neat parcels.

5 Put the mushrooms in the base of a shallow ovenproof dish just large enough to hold the parcels. Arrange the parcels on top and pour in the stock and wine. Cover. Cook in the oven at 190°C (375°F) mark 5 for 40 minutes.

6 Remove the vegetable parcels to a serving plate and keep warm. Strain the stock into a pan, reserving the mushrooms. Blend the butter and flour together and add to the stock in small pieces. Simmer, stirring, for 1 minute or until thickened. Add the mushrooms and reheat for 1 minute.

7 Remove from the heat and stir in the yogurt. Pour over the spring green parcels and serve.

To Microwave

Put the rice in a medium bowl and pour over 300ml (½ pint) boiling water. Microwave on HIGH for 10–12 minutes or until tender, then drain off any water. Put the spring green leaves in a bowl and pour over boiling water to cover. Microwave on HIGH for 1 minute. Drain and rinse under cold water, leave to drain. Put the oil and onion in a medium bowl and microwave on HIGH for 4–5 minutes or until softened, stirring occasionally. Complete steps 3 and 4. Put the mushrooms in the base of a shallow dish, arrange the parcels on top, then pour over vegetable stock and wine. Microwave on HIGH for 10–12 minutes. Remove the parcels and keep warm. Strain the stock into a jug and reserve the mushrooms. Add the butter and flour, then whisk together. Microwave on HIGH for 1–2 minutes or until boiling and thickened. Add the mushrooms. Complete step 7.

To Freeze

Cool, pack the parcels and sauce separately in rigid containers. Freeze for up to 6 months.

To Thaw

Leave overnight at cool room temperature. Alternatively, arrange the parcels evenly on a plate and microwave on LOW for about 10–20 minutes. Test and reposition after 5 minutes. Stand for 15–20 minutes. Microwave the sauce on HIGH for 2–3 minutes. Stand for 15 minutes, breaking up the block as it thaws.

To Serve

Arrange the parcels in a shallow dish and pour over 30ml (2 tbsp) stock or water. Cover and bake in the oven at 180°C (350°F) mark 4 for 15–20 minutes. Pour over the sauce and cook for a further 5–10 minutes or until piping hot. Alternatively, microwave on HIGH for 15–20 minutes or until piping hot. Microwave the sauce on HIGH for 2–3 minutes or until piping hot. Stir in the yogurt then pour over the panels.

Right: Mixed Vegetable Curry (page 161)

RATATOUILLE PANCAKES

SERVES 6

175g (6oz) plain flour
medium oatmeal
salt and pepper
2 eggs
568ml (1 pint) milk
550g (1¼lb) aubergines
450g (1lb) courgettes
45ml (3 tbsp) vegetable oil
225g (8oz) green pepper, cored, seeded and thinly sliced
225g (8oz) red pepper, cored, seeded and thinly sliced
350g (12oz) onion, skinned and sliced
2 garlic cloves, skinned and crushed
30ml (2 tbsp) tomato purée
400g (14oz) can tomatoes
10ml (2 tsp) cornflour
75g (3oz) Gruyère cheese, grated

1 Place the flour, 50g (2oz) oatmeal and a pinch of salt in a blender or food processor. Add the eggs and milk and work for about 1 minute until smooth. Use the batter to make twelve 20.5cm (8 inch) pancakes.

2 Cut the aubergines into 0.5cm (¼ inch) slices, place in a colander and sprinkle well with salt. Leave to stand for about 30 minutes. Meanwhile, cut the courgettes into similar sized slices.

3 Heat the oil in a large saucepan and cook the courgettes, pepper and onion for about 1 minute, stirring. Rinse the aubergine, drain well then add to the pan. Stir in the garlic, tomato purée and canned tomatoes. Season. Cover and simmer for about 30 minutes.

4 Mix the cornflour to a smooth paste with a little water, then add to the pan. Bring the contents to the boil, then boil for 2–3 minutes or until the juices have thickened slightly.

5 Spoon the ratatouille mixture over each pancake. Fold the pancake in half, then half again to form fan shapes. Place in a greased shallow ovenproof dish in overlapping layers. Sprinkle with the cheese and 30ml (2 tbsp) oatmeal.

6 Bake in the oven at 190°C (375°F) mark 5 for about 40 minutes or until thoroughly hot, covering lightly with foil if necessary.

To Microwave

Complete step 1 and 2. Place the oil in a large bowl and add the courgette, pepper and onion. Microwave on HIGH for 2–3 minutes, stirring once. Rinse the aubergine, drain well, then add to the bowl. Stir in the garlic, tomato purée, canned tomatoes and season to taste. Cover and microwave on HIGH for 25–30 minutes. The vegetables should be soft and well mixed, most of the liquid should have evaporated. Mix the cornflour to a smooth paste with a little water, stir into the bowl and microwave on HIGH for 1–2 minutes, stirring frequently. Complete steps 5 and 6.

To Freeze

Cool, pack the cooked pancakes interleaved with non-stick paper and overwrap with foil. Store for up to 4 months. Cool, pack the ratatouille separately in a rigid container. Freeze for up to 2 months.

To Thaw and Serve

Leave the pancakes and ratatouille overnight at cool room temperature. Alternatively, place the pancakes on a plate still interleaved with paper and microwave on LOW for about 1–2 minutes. Stand for 5 minutes. Thaw the ratatouille in the microwave on LOW for about 3–4 minutes. Stand for 10 minutes, breaking up the block as it thaws. Complete steps 5 and 6.

MIXED NUT AND CHEESE LOAF

SERVES 4–6

175g (6oz) mixed nuts, such as almonds, Brazil nuts, hazelnuts, unsalted peanuts
10ml (2 tsp) bottled green peppercorns
175g (6oz) butter
50g (2oz) onion, skinned and roughly chopped
cayenne
100g (4oz) wholemeal breadcrumbs
100g (4oz) Cheddar cheese, grated
1 egg, beaten
salt and pepper
275g (10oz) plain flour
150ml (¼ pint) natural yogurt
grated rind of 1 lemon
shredded radicchio and endive, to garnish

1 Roughly chop 100g (4oz) of the nuts, finely chop the remainder. Drain and finely chop the peppercorns. Melt 25g (1oz) of the butter in a frying pan and cook the onion, peppercorns and 1.25ml (¼ tsp) cayenne for 2–3 minutes, stirring.

2 Remove from the heat, stir in the roughly chopped nuts, breadcrumbs and cheese with sufficient egg just to bind the ingredients together (reserve the remaining egg for glazing). Season, then cool completely.

3 Meanwhile, place the flour and all but 15ml (1 tbsp) of the finely chopped nuts into a bowl with a pinch of cayenne. Using a fork, cut in the remaining butter until the mixture resembles breadcrumbs. Stir in about 60ml (4 tbsp) water and gradually bring the mixture together to form a dough.

4 Roll out the pastry to a 25.5 × 33cm (10 × 13 inch) rectangle. Using the rolling pin as support, carefully life the pastry on to a baking sheet. Make 7.5cm (3 inch) deep slits at 2cm (¾ inch) intervals along both long edges of the rectangle.

5 Spoon the filling down the centre of the pastry, leaving a 4cm (1½ inch) border at the top and bottom. Brush the strips with beaten egg, then fold the top and bottom border over. Work down the 'loaf', alternating the strips of pastry form a plaited effect. Chill for 10 minutes.

6 Brush the loaf with egg and sprinkle over the reserved nuts. Bake in the oven at 200°C (400°F) mark 6 for about 35 minutes or until well browned.

7 Meanwhile, mix the yogurt with the grated lemon rind and a little cayenne. Serve the loaf, warm and thickly sliced, accompanied by the yogurt dressing. Garnish.

To Microwave

Roughly chop 100g (4oz) nuts, finely chop the remainder. Drain and finely chop the peppercorns. Place the butter, onion, peppercorns and cayenne in a shallow dish. Microwave on HIGH for 2–3 minutes, stirring occasionally. Complete steps 2–7.

To Freeze

Cool, pack at the end of step 6 and freeze for up to 4 months.

To Thaw

Leave overnight at cool room temperature. Alternatively, microwave on LOW for about 5–6 minutes. Stand for 10–15 minutes.

To Serve

Reheat, lightly covered, in the oven at 180°C (350°F) mark 4 for about 30 minutes. Complete step 7.

GNOCCHI VERDI

SERVES 4

900g (2lb) washed fresh spinach or 450g (1lb) frozen spinach

225g (8oz) ricotta or curd cheese

2 eggs, beaten

225g (8oz) plain flour

1.25ml (¼ tsp) freshly grated nutmeg

100g (4oz) grated Parmesan cheese

salt and pepper

100g (4oz) butter

1 Place the spinach in a saucepan without any water and cook gently for 5–10 minutes (or until thawed if using frozen spinach). Drain very well and finely chop the spinach.

2 Mix together the ricotta cheese, eggs, flour, spinach, nutmeg, half the Parmesan and seasoning.

3 With floured hands, form the mixture into cork-sized croquettes, or balls the size of large marbles. Chill for at least 1 hour.

4 Bring a large pan of salted water to the boil and reduce to barely simmering. Drop in 10–12 gnocchi at a time and cook for 8–10 minutes or until they float to the surface.

5 With a slotted spoon, remove the gnocchi from the pan, then place them in a buttered serving dish. Cover and keep warm while cooking the remainder.

6 Melt the butter in a small saucepan and pour it over the gnocchi. Sprinkle with the remaining Parmesan cheese. Serve immediately.

To Microwave

Place the spinach in a shallow dish and microwave on HIGH for 4–5 minutes. Drain very well and finely chop the spinach. Complete steps 2–5. Place the butter in a bowl and microwave on HIGH for 1½–2 minutes, then pour over the gnocchi. Sprinkle with the remaining cheese.

To Freeze

Open freeze the uncooked gnocchi at the end of step 3, then pack in a rigid container. Freeze for up to 6 months.

To Thaw and Serve

Spread the gnocchi out on a plate and leave at cool room temperature for 4–6 hours. Alternatively, arrange about eight gnocchi at a time, in a circle around the edge of a plate, and microwave on LOW for about 1–2 minutes. Stand for 5–10 minutes. Complete steps 4–6.

VEGETABLE CHILLI

SERVES 4

30ml (2 tbsp) olive oil

1 large onion, skinned and chopped

2 garlic cloves, skinned and crushed

5–10ml (1–2 tsp) chilli powder

225g (8oz) courgettes, diced

100g (4oz) carrots, peeled and sliced

1 red pepper, cored, seeded and diced

397g (14oz) can chopped tomatoes

150ml (¼ pint) dry red wine

30ml (2 tbsp) chopped fresh oregano or 5ml (1 tsp) dried

397g (14oz) can red kidney beans, drained

15ml (1 tbsp) cornflour

150ml (¼ pint) Greek strained yogurt and chopped parsley, to serve

1 Heat the oil in a large saucepan and cook the onion, garlic and chilli powder for 2–3 minutes until softened. Add the courgettes and carrots and cook for a further 3–4 minutes.

2 Add the red pepper and chopped tomatoes. Cook for 5 minutes. Stir in the wine, oregano and kidney beans. Cover and cook for 25–30 minutes.

3 Mix 45ml (3 tbsp) water with the cornflour to give a smooth paste. Stir the paste into the chilli and bring to the boil. Simmer for 2–3 minutes, stirring. Serve with yogurt and parsley.

To Microwave

Place the oil, onion, garlic and chilli powder in a large bowl. Cover and microwave on HIGH for 3 minutes. Add the courgettes and carrots, cover and microwave on HIGH for a further 2–3 minutes. Add the remaining ingredients, except the cornflour, and microwave, uncovered, for 12–15 minutes, stirring occasionally. Mix 45ml (3 tbsp) water with the cornflour to give a smooth paste. Stir the paste into the chilli. Microwave on HIGH for 2–3 minutes or until thickened. Serve with yogurt and parsley.

To Freeze

Cool, pack in a rigid container, omitting the yogurt, and freeze for up to 6 months.

To Thaw and Serve

Turn the frozen chilli into a large saucepan and heat gently for 30–40 minutes or until heated through, stirring frequently. Alternatively, cover and microwave on HIGH for about 15–20 minutes or until piping hot, stirring occasionally. Serve with the Greek strained yogurt and parsley.

SPICED POTATO AND CAULIFLOWER PASTRIES

SERVES 4

30ml (2 tbsp) vegetable oil

1 onion, skinned and finely chopped

2 garlic cloves, skinned and crushed

5ml (1 tsp) ground turmeric

15ml (1 tbsp) ground coriander

10ml (2 tsp) ground cumin

15ml (1 tbsp) mango chutney

175g (6oz) tiny cauliflower florets

100g (4oz) potatoes, peeled and diced

75ml (3fl oz) vegetable stock

350g (12oz) ready-made wholemeal puff pastry

beaten egg, to glaze

1 Heat the oil in a large saucepan and cook the onion and garlic for 2–3 minutes. Stir in the spices and cook for 4–5 minutes, stirring.

2 Add the mango chutney, cauliflower florets and potatoes. Stir in the stock and cook for 15–20 minutes or until the liquid has evaporated. Cool.

3 Roll out the pastry on a lightly floured work surface. Cut out four 18cm (7 inch) rounds. Divide the filling between the rounds, placing it towards one half of the round. Brush beaten egg around the edge of the rounds and fold the pastry over the filling to encase. Seal the edges, then flute.

4 Place on a greased baking sheet and brush with egg. Bake in the oven at 200°C (400°F) mark 6 for 20–25 minutes until golden. Serve hot or cold.

To Microwave

Place the oil, onion and garlic in a medium bowl. Cover and microwave on HIGH for 3 minutes. Stir in the spices, re-cover and microwave on HIGH for a further minute. Add the mango chutney, cauliflower and potatoes with 60ml (4 tbsp) of the stock. Microwave on HIGH for 10–12 minutes until tender. Cool. Complete steps 3 and 4.

To Freeze

Complete steps 1 and 2, cool completely. Complete step 3. Open freeze the pasties, then pack in a rigid container. Freeze for up to 3 months.

To Thaw and Serve

Arrange the frozen pasties on a lightly greased baking sheet. Brush with egg. Bake at 190°C (375°F) mark 5 for 40–50 minutes until hot.

Right: Vegetable Chilli

PARSNIP AND LENTIL POTS

SERVES 4

900g (2lb) parsnips, peeled and thinly sliced

75g (3oz) green lentils

75g (3oz) brown rice

salt and pepper

butter

50g (2oz) onion, skinned and finely chopped

30ml (2 tbsp) plain flour

568ml (1 pint) milk

pinch of grated nutmeg

1 Place the parsnips in a saucepan, cover with cold water and bring to the boil. Boil for 2 minutes, then drain immediately.

2 Place the lentils and rice together in a large saucepan and cover with cold water. Bring to the boil and simmer for 35–40 minutes or until just cooked. Drain well and season.

3 Melt 25g (1oz) butter in a medium saucepan and fry the onion for 2–3 minutes until beginning to soften. Stir in the flour and cook, stirring, for 1–2 minutes. Add the milk. Bring to the boil and simmer until thickened, stirring. Add nutmeg and seasoning.

4 Lightly grease four 450ml (¾ pint) deep ovenproof dishes or one 1.7 litre (3 pint) dish. Reserve some parsnip slices for garnish. Spoon alternate layers of parsnips, lentils and brown rice, and onion sauce into each dish. Finish with a layer of onion sauce and the reserved parsnip slices. Brush lightly with melted butter. Place the dishes on a baking sheet.

5 Bake in the oven at 190°C (375°F) mark 5 for about 1–1¼ hours or until golden and thoroughly hot. Serve immediately.

To Microwave

Complete step 1. Put the lentils and rice in a large bowl and pour over enough boiling water to cover. Microwave on HIGH for 25–30 minutes. Stand for 5 minutes. Drain and season well. Put 25g (1oz) butter and the onion in a medium bowl and microwave on HIGH for 5–6 minutes or until softened, stirring occasionally. Stir in the flour and microwave on HIGH for 30 seconds. Gradually add the milk and microwave on HIGH for 5–6 minutes or until the sauce has boiled and thickened, whisking frequently. Add nutmeg and seasoning. Complete steps 4 and 5.

To Freeze

Cool, pack in the dishes, overwrapped, at the end of step 4. Freeze for 6 months.

To Thaw and Serve

Leave overnight at cool room temperature. Alternatively, microwave on LOW for about 4–5 minutes for individual pots or 6–7 minutes for the one dish. Test and turn halfway through time. Stand for 10–15 minutes. Complete step 5.

CURRIED BEANS

SERVES 4

100g (4oz) dried chick-peas, soaked at least 8 hours

100g (4oz) dried red kidney beans, soaked at least 8 hours

30ml (2 tbsp) vegetable oil

1 onion, skinned and chopped

1 garlic clove, skinned and crushed

175g (6oz) aubergine, diced

1 green pepper, cored, seeded and sliced

10ml (2 tsp) grated fresh root ginger

10ml (2 tsp) ground coriander

10ml (2 tsp) ground cumin

2.5–5ml (½–1 tsp) ground turmeric

pepper

225g (8oz) can pineapple chunks in natural juice, drained, with juice reserved

300ml (½ pint) vegetable stock

1 banana, peeled and sliced

1 Put the chick-peas and beans with their soaking water in a large saucepan. Boil for 10 minutes, drain, then cover again with fresh water. Bring to the boil again, lower the heat, cover and simmer for 35–45 minutes or until tender. Drain.

2 Heat the oil in the rinsed-out pan and cook the onion, garlic, aubergine and green pepper for 5 minutes. Add the spices and pepper and cook for a further 2 minutes. Add the pineapple juice to the pan with the stock and the reserved chick-peas and red kidney beans.

3 Stir well, cover and simmer gently for 30 minutes, stirring occasionally. Add the pineapple and banana and cook for 5–10 minutes longer or until the fruit has been thoroughly heated. Transfer to a warmed serving bowl and serve hot.

To Microwave

Complete step 1. Place the oil, onion, garlic, aubergine and green pepper in a large bowl. Cover and microwave on HIGH for 4 minutes. Add the spices and pepper, stir and microwave on HIGH for 1 minute. Add the pineapple juice, stock, chick-peas and kidney beans, stirring well. Microwave on HIGH for 15 minutes, stirring occasionally. Add the pineapple and banana and microwave on HIGH for 5 minutes. Transfer to a warmed serving bowl and serve hot.

To Freeze
Cool, pack in a rigid container and freeze for up to 3 months.

To Thaw
Leave overnight at cool room temperature. Alternatively, microwave on LOW for about 4–5 minutes. Stand for 10–15 minutes, breaking up the block as it thaws.

To Serve
Gently reheat in a heavy-based saucepan for 5–10 minutes, stirring frequently to prevent sticking. Alternatively, microwave on HIGH for 4–5 minutes or until piping hot, stirring frequently.

SHEPHERDESS PIE

SERVES 4

75g (3oz) green lentils
75g (3oz) red lentils
1 large onion, skinned and chopped
1 bay leaf
5ml (1 tsp) ground cumin
salt and pepper
550g (1¼lb) potatoes, scrubbed
40g (1½oz) butter
150ml (¼ pint) milk, plus 60ml (4 tbsp)
2.5ml (½ tsp) grated nutmeg
100g (4oz) parsnips, scrubbed and cut into 1cm (½ inch) cubes
100g (4oz) cauliflower florets
100g (4oz) leeks, trimmed, washed and thickly sliced
50g (2oz) canned or frozen sweetcorn kernels
30ml (2 tbsp) plain wholemeal flour
15ml (1 tbsp) chopped fresh parsley
chopped fresh parsley, to garnish

1 Pick over the lentils, removing any stones, and wash thoroughly. Put into a saucepan with the onion, bay leaf, cumin and pepper. Cover with 900ml (1½ pints) water, bring to the boil, cover and simmer for about 40 minutes or until the lentils are tender.

2 Meanwhile, cook the potatoes in a saucepan of boiling water for about 15 minutes until soft. Drain and peel. Mash the potatoes with 15g (½oz) of the butter, 30ml (2 tbsp) of the milk, the nutmeg and seasoning. Set aside.

3 Cook the parsnips in a saucepan of boiling water for 8 minutes; add the cauliflower and leeks for the last 4 minutes. Drain well.

4 Drain off all but 30ml (2 tbsp) cooking liquid from the lentils, discarding the bay leaf. Mash the lentils and add the cauliflower, parsnips, leeks and sweetcorn kernels.

5 Melt 15g (½oz) of the butter in a small saucepan, stir in the flour and cook for 1 minute. Remove from the heat and gradually stir in remaining milk. Return the pan to the heat and cook, stirring, for 2 minutes or until the sauce thickens. Remove from the heat, season with pepper and stir in the parsley. Add the sauce to the lentil mixture and stir well.

6 Put the mixture into a 1.1 litre (2 pint) ovenproof pie dish. Pile the mashed potato on top of the lentil mixture, mark the top with a fork and dot with the remaining butter.

7 Cook in the oven at 190°C (375°F) mark 5 for 30–40 minutes.

To Microwave
Put lentils in a bowl with 600ml (1 pint) boiling water. Microwave on HIGH for 8–10 minutes, stirring once. Add all the vegetables (except the potatoes) and seasoning, and microwave on HIGH for 5 minutes. Cover and set aside to stand. Cut the potatoes into small pieces and put in medium bowl with 30ml (2 tbsp) water. Cover and microwave on HIGH for 8–12 minutes or until just tender, stirring twice. Mash and set aside. Put the butter, flour and milk in a bowl and whisk together. Microwave on HIGH for 3–4 minutes or until the sauce has boiled and thickened, whisking frequently. Add pepper and parsley. Stir into the lentil mixture. Complete steps 6 and 7.

To Freeze
Cool, overwrap the uncooked pie and freeze for up to 3 months.

To Thaw and Serve
Leave overnight at cool room temperature. Alternatively, microwave on LOW for about 5–6 minutes. Test and turn after 5 minutes. Stand for 15–20 minutes. Complete step 7.

BAKED AUBERGINES AND MOZZARELLA

SERVES 4

700g (1½lb) aubergines

salt and pepper

about 150ml (¼ pint) vegetable oil

100g (4oz) onion, roughly chopped

450g (1lb) tomatoes, skinned and roughly chopped

1 large garlic clove, skinned and crushed

30ml (2 tbsp) tomato purée

15ml (1 tbsp) chopped fresh marjoram or 5ml (1 tsp) dried

two 175g (6oz) packets Mozzarella, thinly sliced

1 Slice the aubergines into 0.5cm (¼ inch) thick pieces, then score the slices. Sprinkle with salt and leave for at least 20 minutes.

2 Heat 30ml (2 tbsp) of the oil in a pan and fry the onion until beginning to brown. Stir in the tomatoes, garlic, tomato purée and seasoning. Simmer for about 5 minutes or until the tomatoes have broken down. Stir in the marjoram and remove from the heat.

3 Pat the aubergines dry with absorbent kitchen paper. Fry half at a time in the remaining oil until well browned. Add a little more oil if necessary. Drain the slices on absorbent kitchen paper.

4 Layer the aubergines, tomato sauce and Mozzarella slices in a shallow ovenproof dish, topping with cheese.

5 Bake in the oven at 180°C (350°F) mark 4 for about 40 minutes or until brown and bubbling.

To Microwave

Complete step 1. Place the onion and 30ml (2 tbsp) of the oil in a large bowl and microwave on HIGH for 5–7 minutes or until softened. Stir in the tomatoes, garlic, tomato purée and seasoning. Microwave on HIGH for 3–4 minutes or until the tomatoes have broken down. Stir in the marjoram. Complete steps 3 and 4. Microwave on HIGH for 15–20 minutes. Place under a grill until golden.

To Freeze

Cool, pack in a rigid container at the end of step 4 and freeze for up to 3 months.

To Thaw and Serve

Leave overnight at cool room temperature. Complete step 5. Alternatively, microwave on LOW for about 3–5 minutes. Test and turn after 3 minutes. Stand for 15–20 minutes. Cook as above.

SAVOURY NUT BURGERS

SERVES 4

25g (1oz) butter

1 large onion, skinned and chopped

15ml (1 tbsp) chopped fresh parsley

15g (½oz) plain wholemeal flour

150ml (¼ pint) milk

225g (8oz) chopped mixed nuts

15ml (1 tbsp) soy sauce

15ml (1 tbsp) tomato purée

175g (6oz) fresh wholemeal breadcrumbs

1 egg, beaten

pepper

1 Melt the butter in a medium saucepan and lightly fry the onion and parsley until soft. Stir in the flour and cook for 2 minutes.

2 Remove from heat and gradually add the milk. Bring back to boil, stirring until the sauce is smooth and thickened. Simmer for 1–2 minutes.

3 Add the nuts, soy sauce, tomato purée, breadcrumbs, egg and pepper to taste. Mix well. Divide mixture into eight and shape into rounds.

4 Cook under a grill for 4 minutes, then turn and grill for 4 minutes more.

To Microwave

Place the butter in a large bowl and microwave on HIGH for 45 seconds. Add the onion and parsley and microwave on HIGH for 5 minutes. Add the flour and milk, whisking together. Microwave on HIGH for 3 minutes or until boiling and thickened, whisking frequently. Complete steps 3 and 4.

To Freeze

Open freeze the uncooked burgers, then pack in a rigid container interleaved with greaseproof paper. Freeze for up to 4 months.

To Thaw and Serve

Leave at cool room temperature for 4–6 hours. Alternatively, arrange the burgers in a circle on a plate and microwave on LOW for about 2–3 minutes. Test and turn after 2 minutes. Complete step 4.

Right: Savoury Nut Burgers

WHOLEMEAL VEGETABLE PIE

SERVES 4

3 medium leeks, trimmed and washed
275g (10oz) swede, peeled
225g (8oz) turnip, peeled
4 medium carrots, peeled
100g (4oz) butter
225g (8oz) large flat mushrooms, sliced
25g (1oz) plain flour
300ml (½ pint) vegetable stock
175g (6oz) Cheddar cheese, grated
30ml (2 tbsp) chopped fresh herbs, such as parsley, chives, thyme, marjoram or 10ml (2 tsp) dried
salt and pepper
175g (6oz) wholemeal shortcrust pastry (see page 110)
beaten egg, to glaze

1 Cut the leeks into 2.5cm (1 inch) lengths. Cut the swede, turnip and carrots into small bite-sized chunks.

2 Melt the butter in a large saucepan and fry the prepared vegetables over moderate heat for about 10 minutes or until turning golden brown. Add the mushrooms and cook for a further 2–3 minutes.

3 Sprinkle in the flour and cook gently, stirring, for 1–2 minutes. Gradually blend in the vegetable stock. Bring to the boil, stirring constantly, then simmer for 5–10 minutes or until the vegetables are just tender.

4 Remove the pan from the heat and stir in the cheese, herbs and seasoning to taste. Pour into a 1.1 litre (2 pint) pie dish and allow to cool for about 1 hour.

5 Roll out the pastry on a floured surface. Cut out a thin strip long enough to go around the rim of the pie dish. Moisten the rim with water and place the strip of pastry on the rim, then moisten.

6 Roll out the remaining pastry to cover the pie. Place the lid on top, trim off any excess pastry and press to seal.

7 Knock up and flute or crimp the edge. Decorate the top with any pastry trimmings and brush with beaten egg. Chill for 15 minutes.

8 Bake in the oven at 190°C (375°F) mark 5 for 15–20 minutes or until lightly browned. Serve hot.

To Microwave

Complete step 1. Dice the butter into a large bowl and microwave on LOW for 1½–2 minutes. Add the prepared vegetables and microwave on HIGH for 8–10 minutes, stirring occasionally. Add the mushrooms and microwave on HIGH for a further 2–3 minutes. Add the flour and stock, stirring well. Microwave on HIGH for 4–5 minutes or until the sauce has boiled and thickened, stirring frequently. Remove from the heat and stir in the cheese, herbs and seasoning to taste. Pour into a 1.1 litre (2 pint) pie dish and cool for 1 hour. Complete steps 5–8.

To Freeze

Pack in foil at step 7 before brushing with beaten egg. Freeze for up to 3 months.

To Thaw and Serve

Leave overnight at cool room temperature. Alternatively, microwave on LOW for about 4–5 minutes. Test and turn after 4 minutes. Complete step 8.

CABBAGE AND HAZELNUT ROLLS

MAKES 16

450g (1lb) potatoes
salt and pepper
900g (2lb) green cabbage, roughly chopped
45ml (3 tbsp) milk, if necessary
50g (2oz) butter
50g (2oz) plain flour
50g (2oz) hazelnuts, chopped and toasted
2 eggs, beaten
100g (4oz) dry breadcrumbs
vegetable oil, for deep frying
lemon twists, to garnish

1 Cook the potatoes in a saucepan of boiling salted water for 20 minutes or until tender. Drain and mash without adding liquid.

2 Cook the cabbage in boiling salted water for 5–10 minutes or until just tender. Drain well. Purée in a blender or food processor, adding the milk if necessary – there should be 450ml (¾ pint) purée.

3 Melt the butter in a saucepan, add the flour and cook gently, stirring, for 1–2 minutes. Gradually blend in the cabbage purée and milk, if necessary. Bring to the boil, then simmer for 5 minutes.

4 Stir the mashed potatoes and hazelnuts into the sauce, season to taste and mix well. Transfer to a bowl, cool, cover and chill for at least 1½ hours or until firm.

5 With dampened hands, shape the mixture into 16 rolls. Place on a greased baking sheet and chill again for at least 20 minutes.

6 Coat the croquettes in the beaten egg, then the breadcrumbs. Heat the oil to 180°C (350°F) in a deep-fat fryer. Deep-fry the rolls in batches for about 4 minutes or until crisp and golden. Remove with a slotted spoon and drain on absorbent kitchen paper while frying the remainder. Serve hot, garnished with lemon twists.

To Microwave
Cut the potatoes into small pieces and place in a medium bowl with 30ml (2 tbsp) water. Cover and microwave on HIGH for 7–10 minutes or until tender. Complete step 1. Put the cabbage in a large bowl with 30ml (2 tbsp) water. Cover and microwave on HIGH for 7–10 minutes or until just tender, stirring once. Complete steps 2–6.

To Freeze
Cool, pack in a rigid container interleaved with greaseproof paper at the end of step 6. Freeze for up to 4 months.

To Thaw and Serve
Leave at cool room temperature for 4–6 hours. Alternatively, arrange a few on a plate, in a 'cartwheel', and microwave on LOW for about 2–4 minutes. Stand for 5 minutes. Turn on to a baking sheet. Bake in the oven at 180°C (350°F) mark 4 for 15–20 minutes or until hot and crispy.

FRESH TAGLIATELLE WITH LEEK AND ROQUEFORT SAUCE

SERVES 4–6

75g (3oz) butter
1 garlic clove, skinned and crushed
450g (1lb) leeks, trimmed, washed and sliced
150g (5oz) Roquefort cheese, roughly chopped
30ml (2 tbsp) chopped fresh chervil or 10ml (2 tsp) dried
5ml (1 tsp) olive oil
700g (1½lb) fresh tagliatelle
pepper
150ml (¼ pint) whipping cream
15–30ml (1–2 tbsp) grated Parmesan cheese
chervil sprigs, to garnish

1 Melt 50g (2oz) of the butter in a medium saucepan and fry the garlic and leeks for 2–3 minutes until softened.
2 Stir in the Roquefort cheese and chervil. Cook for 2–3 minutes until the cheese has melted, stirring continuously.

3 Meanwhile, bring a large saucepan of water to the boil with the olive oil. Add the tagliatelle and cook for 3–4 minutes. Drain and return to the clean pan. Toss in the remaining butter and season with pepper.
4 Pour the cream into the sauce, whisking vigorously. Cook, stirring, for a few minutes until the sauce thickens.
5 Serve the tagliatelle on warmed individual serving plates with the sauce poured over. Sprinkle with Parmesan cheese and garnish with chervil sprigs.

To Microwave
Dice the butter into a medium bowl. Cover and microwave on HIGH for 1 minute. Add the garlic and leeks. Cover and microwave on HIGH for 2–3 minutes. Add the Roquefort and chervil and microwave for 1–1½ minutes. Whisk in the cream and microwave on HIGH for 1–1½ minutes. Complete steps 3 and 5.

To Freeze
Cool, pack the sauce in a rigid container without the cream. Freeze the pasta separately in a polythene bag. Freeze the sauce for up to 3 months, pasta for up to 1 month.

To Thaw and Serve
Place the frozen sauce in a small saucepan and heat gently for 15–20 minutes. Stir in the cream. Alternatively, place the sauce in a medium bowl, cover and microwave on HIGH for about 8–10 minutes. Stir in the cream.

Plunge the frozen tagliatelle into boiling water with 5ml (1 tsp) olive oil. Cook for 4–5 minutes. Drain and toss in the remaining butter and pepper. Complete step 5.

ITALIAN STUFFED TOMATOES

SERVES 4–6

15ml (1 tbsp) olive oil

4 spring onions, trimmed and finely chopped

2 garlic cloves, skinned and crushed

15ml (1 tbsp) tomato purée

12 pimento stuffed green olives, sliced

30ml (2 tbsp) chopped fresh basil or 15ml (1 tbsp) dried

45ml (3 tbsp) pine nuts

397g (14oz) can flageolet beans, drained

salt and pepper

4 large beefsteak tomatoes or 6 medium

basil sprigs, to garnish

1 Heat the oil in a large saucepan and cook the spring onions and garlic for 2–3 minutes to soften.
2 Add the tomato purée, olives, basil and nuts and cook for 2 minutes. Stir in the beans. Season.
3 Slice the tops off the tomatoes, reserving them for the lids, and scoop out the seeds and flesh to make them hollow. Chop the flesh and add to the filling mixture. Arrange the tomato shells in a buttered ovenproof dish and divide the filling between them. Add the lids and cover with foil.
4 Bake in the oven at 180°C (350°F) mark 4 for 15–20 minutes. Garnish and serve with Neapolitan tomato sauce (see page 193).

To Microwave

Place the oil, spring onions and garlic in a medium bowl. Cover and microwave on HIGH for 2 minutes. Add the tomato purée, olives, basil, nuts and beans. Cover and microwave on HIGH for 1–2 minutes, stirring once. Season to taste. Complete step 3. Prick the skins all over with a fork. Microwave on HIGH for 5–6 minutes, re-arranging occasionally. Serve with Neapolitan tomato sauce.

To Freeze

Cool, pack in a rigid container at the end of step 2 and freeze for up to 6 months.

To Thaw

Leave overnight in the refrigerator. Alternatively, microwave on LOW for about 25–30 minutes, stirring occasionally. Stand for 15–20 minutes.

To Serve

Complete step 3. Cover with foil and cook in the oven at 180°C (350°F) mark 4 for 15–20 minutes. Alternatively, complete step 3. Cover and microwave on HIGH for 5–6 minutes, re-arranging.

RATATOUILLE PASTA BAKE

SERVES 4–6

30ml (2 tbsp) olive oil

1 large onion, skinned and thinly sliced

1 red pepper, seeded and cut into 5cm (2 inch) strips

1 yellow pepper, seeded and cut into 5cm (2 inch) strips

225g (8oz) courgettes, cut into 5cm (2 inch) strips

450g (1lb) ripe tomatoes, skinned and chopped

2 garlic cloves, skinned and crushed

30ml (2 tbsp) tomato purée

30ml (2 tbsp) chopped fresh basil or 5ml (1 tsp) dried

pinch of sugar

salt and pepper

450ml (¾ pint) vegetable stock

350g (12oz) mixed coloured pasta twists

50g (2oz) butter

175g (6oz) mature Cheddar cheese, grated

1 Heat the oil in a large pan and cook the onion and pepper for 5 minutes until softened, stirring. Add the courgette and cook for 5 minutes.
2 Stir in the tomatoes, garlic, tomato purée, basil, sugar and seasoning. Simmer for 25–30 minutes, stirring occasionally, adding the stock gradually.
3 Meanwhile, bring a large saucepan of salted water to the boil and add the pasta twists. Cook for 15–20 minutes, stirring occasionally. Drain, then return to the pan and toss in the butter. Season. Transfer to a deep flameproof dish.
4 Pour the ratatouille sauce over the pasta and sprinkle over the cheese. Grill until golden.

To Microwave

Place the oil, onion and pepper in a large bowl. Cover and microwave on HIGH for 4 minutes. Add the courgettes, tomatoes, garlic, tomato purée, basil, sugar and seasoning. Add half the amount of stock and microwave on HIGH for 12–15 minutes, stirring occasionally. Complete steps 3 and 4.

To Freeze

Cool the sauce, pack in a rigid container at the end of step 2 and freeze for up to 3 months.

To Thaw and Serve

Place the sauce in a pan. Cover and heat gently for 20–30 minutes, stirring occasionally. Alternatively, cover and microwave the sauce on HIGH for about 10–15 minutes or until piping hot, stirring occasionally. Complete steps 3 and 4.

Right: Ratatouille Pancakes (page 164)

ACCOMPANIMENTS

SWEET POTATO AND APPLE PURÉE

SERVES 4

1.8kg (4lb) sweet potatoes, preferably white-fleshed

lemon juice

700g (1½lb) cooking apples

25g (1oz) butter

salt and pepper

1 Peel the potatoes, cut into large chunks and immediately place in water with lemon juice added to prevent discoloration. Cook in a saucepan of boiling water for about 15 minutes or until almost tender.

2 Meanwhile peel, quarter, core and thinly slice the apples. Place in water with lemon juice added to prevent discoloration.

3 Drain the apple slices and add to the sweet potatoes. Cook for a further minute. Drain well, then mash until smooth. Beat in the butter and season to taste.

4 Reheat gently to serve, stirring all the time, to evaporate any excess moisture.

To Microwave

Complete steps 1–3. Mash until smooth. Beat in the butter and season to taste. To reheat, microwave on HIGH for 2–3 minutes.

To Freeze

Cool, pack in a rigid container at the end of step 3 and freeze for up to 6 months.

To Thaw

Leave overnight in the refrigerator.

To Serve

Reheat in a heavy-based saucepan for 3–4 minutes or until piping hot, stirring frequently. Alternatively, microwave on HIGH for about 3–4 minutes or until piping hot, stirring frequently.

GLAZED CARROTS WITH CUMIN

SERVES 4–6

700g (1½lb) baby carrots, scrubbed and trimmed

15g (½oz) butter

10ml (2 tsp) demerara sugar

5ml (1 tsp) cumin seeds

salt and pepper

young carrot tops or parsley sprigs, to garnish

1 Place the carrots in a large saucepan of boiling water. Simmer for about 10 minutes or until just tender. Drain.

2 Melt the butter in the saucepan with the sugar. Add the cumin seeds and cook, stirring continuously, for 1 minute.

3 Toss the carrots into the pan and stir until coated. Add 30ml (2 tbsp) water and cook for 4–5 minutes, or until the liquid has evaporated to leave a buttery glaze, stirring frequently. Season to taste. Garnish.

To Microwave

Place the carrots in a large bowl and pour over 600ml (1 pint) boiling water. Microwave on HIGH for 10–15 minutes or until tender. Place the butter and sugar in a large bowl. Cover and microwave on HIGH for 30–60 seconds. Stir and microwave for a further 30 seconds. Add the cumin seeds and microwave on HIGH for 30 seconds. Add the carrots and stir until coated. Season to taste.

To Freeze

Cool, pack in a rigid container and freeze for up to 6 months.

To Thaw and Serve

Place in an ovenproof dish. Cover with foil and bake in the oven at 180°C (350°F) mark 4 for 30–40 minutes. Alternatively, cover and microwave on HIGH for 8–10 minutes, stirring occasionally, until piping hot.

CURRIED LENTILS

SERVES 4

15ml (1 tbsp) vegetable oil
1 small onion, skinned and finely chopped
1 garlic clove, skinned and thinly sliced
10ml (2 tsp) ground cumin
5ml (1 tsp) ground turmeric
10ml (2 tsp) ground coriander
1 small dried red chilli, crushed (optional)
2 cardamom pods, bruised
175g (6oz) red lentils
25g (1oz) desiccated coconut
salt, to taste
tomato wedges, to garnish

1 Heat the oil in a saucepan and cook the onion and garlic for about 3 minutes until softened. Add the spices and cook for 2–3 minutes, stirring constantly.
2 Add the lentils and 450ml (¾ pint) water. Cover and simmer gently for about 1 hour or until the lentils are soft but not completely mushy.
3 Stir in the coconut and seasoning. Garnish with tomato wedges and serve hot.

To Microwave
Place the oil, onion, spices and garlic in a large bowl and stir well. Cover and microwave on HIGH for 5–6 minutes. Add the lentils and 450ml (¾ pint) boiling water. Cover and microwave on HIGH for 10–12 minutes or until the lentils are soft, stirring occasionally. Complete step 3.

To Freeze
Cool quickly, wrap loosely in a polythene bag and freeze for up to 3 months.

To Thaw
Leave overnight in the refrigerator. Alternatively, microwave on LOW for about 10–12 minutes. Stand for 10–15 minutes.

To Serve
Reheat gently in a heavy-based saucepan, adding a little water if necessary, stirring frequently. Alternatively, cover and microwave on HIGH for 5–6 minutes or until piping hot, stirring occasionally.

GINGERED BEETROOT

SERVES 4

450g (1lb) beetroot
25g (1oz) butter
25g (1oz) crystallised ginger, finely chopped
2 pineapple slices, chopped
45ml (3 tbsp) white wine vinegar
30ml (2 tbsp) sugar
salt and pepper

1 Trim the stalks to within 2.5cm (1 inch) of the beetroot and leave whole. Cook in a saucepan of boiling salted water for 1–3 hours, according to size. The skin will rub off easily when cooked. Drain well, peel and cut into 0.5cm (¼ inch) cubes.
2 Melt the butter in a large saucepan, add the beetroot, ginger, pineapple, vinegar, sugar and seasoning. Heat through, stirring. Serve hot or cold.

To Microwave
Trim the stalks to within 2.5cm (1 inch) of the beetroot and leave whole. Prick the skins all over with a fork. Arrange in a circle in a shallow dish and pour over 45ml (3 tbsp) water. Cover and microwave on HIGH for 14–16 minutes or until tender. Drain, peel and cut into 0.5cm (¼ inch) cubes. Put the butter in a bowl, stir in the beetroot, ginger, pineapple, vinegar, sugar and seasoning. Cover and microwave on HIGH for 3–4 minutes or until hot, stirring occasionally.

To Freeze
Cool, pack in a rigid container and freeze for up to 6 months.

To Thaw
Leave overnight in the refrigerator. Alternatively, microwave on LOW for about 12–14 minutes. Stand for 10 minutes, turning occasionally.

To Serve
If serving hot, reheat in a heavy-based saucepan for 3–4 minutes or until hot. Alternatively, microwave on HIGH for 3–4 minutes or until piping hot.

CURRIED POTATO WITH CHICK PEAS

SERVES 3–4

700g (1½lb) potatoes

225g (8oz) cauliflower

100g (4oz) frozen green beans

15ml (1 tbsp) oil

10ml (2 tsp) ground coriander

5ml (1 tsp) ground turmeric

400g (14oz) can chopped tomatoes

396g (14oz) can chick peas

30ml (2 tbsp) chopped fresh coriander

salt and pepper

1 Peel the potatoes; cut into 2.5cm (1 inch) pieces. Put in a pan of salted water, simmer for about 5 minutes until almost tender, drain.

2 Cut the cauliflower into florets and place in a pan with the green beans, pour over boiling water and simmer for 3 minutes, drain.

3 Heat the oil and spices in a large frying pan, add the cooked vegetables, tomatoes, drained chick peas and half the fresh coriander. Simmer for about 5 minutes, until reduced a little. Season and garnish with the remaining coriander.

To Microwave

Place the peeled potatoes in a large bowl with 60ml (4 tbsp) water. Cover and microwave on HIGH for about 10 minutes or until almost tender, stirring halfway through cooking. Stir in the cauliflower and green beans. Cover and cook on HIGH for 3 minutes. Drain. Place the oil and spices into a large shallow dish and microwave on HIGH for 1 minute. Stir in the cooked vegetables and the remaining ingredients. Cover and microwave on HIGH for 3 minutes.

To Freeze

Cool quickly, pack in a rigid container and freeze for up to 2 months.

To Thaw

Leave at cool room temperature for 4–6 hours. Alternatively microwave on HIGH for about 8–10 minutes, breaking up the block as it thaws.

To Serve

Place in a shallow dish, cover and bake in the oven at 180°C (350°F) mark 4 for 15–25 minutes or until piping hot, stirring occasionally. Alternatively, microwave on HIGH for about 6–7 minutes or until piping hot, stirring occasionally.

PEPERONATA

SERVES 6

75ml (5 tbsp) olive oil

1 large onion, skinned and finely sliced

6 red peppers, cored, seeded and sliced into strips

2 garlic cloves, skinned and crushed

700g (1½lb) ripe tomatoes, skinned and roughly chopped

15ml (1 tbsp) chopped fresh parsley

salt and pepper

1 Heat the oil in a frying pan and gently fry the onion for 5 minutes until soft but not coloured.

2 Add the peppers and garlic and cook gently for 2–3 minutes. Stir in the tomatoes, parsley and seasoning to taste.

3 Cover and cook gently for 30 minutes until the mixture is quite dry: if necessary, remove the lid 10 minutes before the end of cooking and allow the liquid to evaporate. Taste and adjust seasoning before serving hot or cold.

To Microwave

Place the oil and onion in a large bowl, cover and microwave on HIGH for 5–6 minutes. Add the peppers and garlic, cover and microwave on HIGH for 2 minutes. Stir in the tomatoes, parsley and seasoning to taste. Microwave, uncovered, on HIGH for 10–15 minutes or until most of the liquid has evaporated. Adjust seasoning before serving hot or cold.

To Freeze

Cool quickly, pack in a rigid container and freeze for up to 6 months.

To Thaw

Leave overnight in the refrigerator. Alternatively, microwave on LOW for about 10–15 minutes, breaking up the block as it thaws. Stand for 10 minutes

To Serve

Reheat gently in a heavy-based saucepan for 5–10 minutes, stirring frequently. Alternatively, microwave on HIGH for 6–8 minutes or until piping hot, stirring frequently.

Right: Glazed Carrots with Cumin (page 176)

CELERIAC WITH TOMATO SAUCE

SERVES 4

60ml (4 tbsp) olive oil

1 large onion, skinned and finely chopped

3 garlic cloves, skinned and crushed

350g (12oz) ripe tomatoes, skinned and finely chopped

15ml (1 tbsp) tomato purée

30ml (2 tbsp) red wine or red wine vinegar

60ml (4 tbsp) chopped fresh parsley

5ml (1 tsp) ground cinnamon

1 bay leaf

salt and pepper

2 heads of celeriac, total weight about 900g (2lb)

5ml (1 tsp) lemon juice

50g (2oz) dried brown or white breadcrumbs

50g (2oz) Parmesan cheese, grated

1 For the tomato sauce, heat the oil in a heavy-based saucepan and gently fry the onion and garlic for about 10 minutes or until very soft and lightly coloured.

2 Add the tomatoes, tomato purée, wine, parsley, cinnamon, bay leaf and seasoning to taste. Add 450ml (¾ pint) hot water and bring to the boil, stirring with a wooden spoon to break up the tomatoes. Lower the heat, cover and simmer the tomato sauce for 30 minutes, stirring occasionally.

3 Meanwhile, peel the celeriac, then cut into chunky pieces. While preparing, place the pieces in a bowl of water with lemon juice added to prevent discoloration.

4 Drain the celeriac, then plunge quickly into a large saucepan of boiling salted water. Return to the boil and blanch for 10 minutes.

5 Drain the celeriac well, then put in an ovenproof dish. Pour over the tomato sauce, discarding the bay leaf. Sprinkle the breadcrumbs and cheese evenly over the top.

6 Bake in the oven at 190°C (375°F) mark 5 for 30 minutes or until the celeriac is tender when pierced with a skewer and the topping is golden brown.

To Microwave

For the tomato sauce, put the oil, onion and garlic in a large bowl. Cover and microwave on HIGH for 5–6 minutes or until softened, stirring occasionally. Add the tomatoes, tomato purée, wine, parsley, cinnamon, bay leaf and seasoning to taste. Pour in 300ml (½ pint) hot water. Microwave on HIGH for 15 minutes or until slightly reduced and thickened, stirring occasionally. Complete steps 3 and 4. Drain the celeriac and put into a large flameproof dish. Pour over the tomato sauce. Cover and microwave on HIGH for 8–10 minutes or until tender, stirring occasionally. Sprinkle with the breadcrumbs and cheese, then brown under a hot grill.

To Freeze

Cool, pack and freeze the sauce and celeriac separately in rigid containers at the end of step 4. Freeze for up to 3 months.

To Thaw and Serve

Thaw overnight in the refrigerator. Complete steps 5 and 6. Alternatively, cover and microwave in a serving dish on LOW for about 9–10 minutes or until piping hot, stirring occasionally. Complete as above.

GRATIN DAUPHINOISE

SERVES 4–6

700g (1½lb) large waxy potatoes, peeled

1 garlic clove

10ml (2 tsp) butter

150ml (¼ pint) double cream

75g (3oz) Gruyère cheese, grated

60ml (4 tbsp) grated Parmesan cheese

salt and pepper

5ml (1 tsp) grated nutmeg

1 Cut the potatoes into wafer-thin slices and rinse thoroughly under cold running water. Drain and pat dry with absorbent kitchen paper.

2 Cut the garlic clove in half. Rub the cut surface over the base and sides of a 25.5 × 18cm (10 × 7 inch) shallow dish. Using a piece of greaseproof paper, rub the butter generously over the dish.

3 Layer the potatoes, cream, Gruyère cheese, Parmesan cheese, seasoning and nutmeg in the dish, finishing with a layer of Gruyère, then Parmesan cheese.

4 Cover the dish with foil. Bake in the oven at 190°C (375°F) mark 5 for 1–1½ hours or until a knife can be easily inserted through the centre. Remove the foil for the final 20 minutes of cooking time.

To Microwave

Complete steps 1–3. Cover and microwave on HIGH for 12–15 minutes or until cooked through, rotating the dish occasionally. Place under a grill until golden brown, if liked.

To Freeze
Cover the dish with plastic wrap, then overwrap with foil at the end of step 3. Freeze for up to 3 months.

To Thaw and Serve
Unwrap the dish and cover with foil. Bake in the oven at 190°C (375°F) mark 5 for 1¾–2 hours or until cooked through. Alternatively, cover and microwave on HIGH for about 20–30 minutes or until piping hot, rotating the dish occasionally. Place under a grill until golden brown, if liked.

WINTER SWEDE

SERVES 4–6

700g (1½lb) swede, peeled and cut into 1cm (½ inch) cubes

75g (3oz) streaky bacon, rinded

25g (1oz) butter

45ml (3 tbsp) snipped chives or 15ml (1 tbsp) dried

salt and pepper

1 Place the swede in a large saucepan and cover with boiling water. Bring to the boil and simmer for 10–15 minutes or until just tender. Drain.
2 Meanwhile, grill the bacon until crisp. Cut into 1cm (½ inch) pieces.
3 Melt the butter in a saucepan and add the bacon and chives. Toss in the swede and stir to coat. Season to taste. Cook for 2–3 minutes, then serve.

To Microwave
Place the swede in a large bowl and pour over 600ml (1 pint) boiling water. Microwave on HIGH for about 15 minutes or until just tender. Lay the bacon on a microwave roasting rack and cover with a double thickness of absorbent kitchen paper. Microwave on HIGH for 4½–5 minutes or until crisp. Cut into 1cm (½ inch) pieces. Microwave the butter on HIGH for 45 seconds. Add the bacon, chives, swede and seasoning. Microwave on HIGH for 1–1½ minutes.

To Freeze
Cool, pack in a rigid container and freeze for up to 12 months.

To Thaw and Serve
Place the frozen swede in an ovenproof dish and cover with foil. Bake in the oven at 180°C (350°F) mark 4 for 30–40 minutes. Alternatively, cover and microwave on HIGH for about 15 minutes or until piping hot, stirring occasionally.

MUSHROOM KIEVS

SERVES 4–6

75g (3oz) butter, softened

3 garlic cloves, skinned and crushed

15ml (1 tbsp) chopped fresh parsley or 5ml (1 tsp) dried

450g (1lb) cup mushrooms, stalks removed

50g (2oz) seasoned cornflour

2 eggs, beaten

225g (8oz) fresh breadcrumbs

vegetable oil, for deep frying

1 Place the butter in a bowl and beat in the garlic and parsley.
2 Fill the hollow cavity of half the mushrooms with the garlic butter, then sandwich together with the unfilled mushrooms.
3 Coat each mushroom kiev in cornflour, egg, then in breadcrumbs. Give each kiev a second coating in egg, then breadcrumbs. Arrange on a baking sheet. Chill for 30 minutes.
4 Heat the oil in a deep fat fryer to 130–140°C (250–275°F). Deep fry the mushroom kievs in batches for 2½–3½ minutes. Drain on absorbent kitchen paper and serve immediately.

To Microwave
Place the butter in a small bowl and microwave on MEDIUM for 20–30 seconds. Beat in the garlic and parsley. Complete steps 2–4. (Do not attempt to deep fry in the microwave.)

To Freeze
Open freeze at the end of step 3, then pack in a rigid container. Freeze for up to 1 month.

To Thaw and Serve
Complete step 4, deep frying for 5–6 minutes from frozen.

BROCCOLI WITH BRIE AND SPRING ONION SAUCE

SERVES 4–6

350g (12oz) broccoli florets

15g (½oz) butter

8 spring onions, trimmed and chopped

15ml (1 tbsp) plain flour

175ml (6fl oz) milk

175g (6oz) Brie cheese, rind removed and diced

salt and pepper

1 Place the broccoli florets in a saucepan and half cover with boiling water. Boil for 5–8 minutes or until just tender.
2 Meanwhile, melt the butter in a small saucepan. Add the chopped spring onion to the pan and fry for 1 minute, stirring frequently.
3 Stir in the flour and cook for 30–60 seconds. Remove from the heat and gradually stir in the milk. Bring to the boil, stirring, until thickened.
4 Add the Brie and cook over gentle heat until melted. Season to taste.
5 Drain the broccoli well and transfer to a warmed serving dish and pour over the sauce.

To Microwave
Arrange the florets in a shallow dish, with 60ml (4 tbsp) water, with the stalks facing towards the outside of the dish. Microwave on HIGH for 6–7 minutes or just tender. Place the butter in a medium bowl. Cover and microwave on HIGH for 30 seconds until melted. Add the spring onions and microwave on HIGH for 30–60 seconds. Add the milk and flour and whisk well to combine. Microwave on HIGH for 2½–3½ minutes, until smooth and thickened, whisking occasionally. Beat in the cheese and season to taste. Microwave for 1½–2 minutes to melt the cheese. Complete step 5.

To Freeze
Blanch the broccoli for 1–2 minutes. Drain and place in a rigid container. Complete steps 2 to 4 and pour the sauce over the broccoli. Cool and freeze for up to 6 months.

To Thaw and Serve
Place in an ovenproof dish and cover with foil. Bake in the oven at 180°C (350°F) mark 4 from frozen for 30–40 minutes or until heated through. Alternatively, cover and microwave on HIGH for about 10–12 minutes or until piping hot, re-arranging occasionally.

CREAMED BROCCOLI RING

SERVES 4

450g (1lb) broccoli

100g (4oz) onion, skinned and sliced

1 garlic clove, skinned and thinly sliced

300ml (½ pint) light stock

salt and pepper

75g (3oz) low fat soft cheese

3 eggs

fresh brown breadcrumbs

butter, for greasing

1 Thinly slice the broccoli stalks and divide the heads into small florets.
2 Place the broccoli, onion and garlic in a saucepan with the stock and seasoning. Bring to the boil, cover and simmer gently for about 20–30 minutes or until the vegetables are tender; drain any remaining liquid.
3 Cool slightly, then purée with the cheese in a blender or food processor until almost smooth. Turn out into a bowl, then whisk in the eggs and 50g (2oz) breadcrumbs. Adjust seasoning.
4 Lightly grease a 1.1 litre (2 pint) ring mould and sprinkle well with breadcrumbs. Spoon in the broccoli mixture, then cover with greased foil. Stand the tin in a roasting tin half filled with water.
5 Bake in the oven at 180°C (350°F) mark 4 for about 1–1¼ hours or until just firm to the touch. Leave to firm up for about 10 minutes, then loosen from the edges of the tin. Invert on to a warmed serving plate.

To Microwave
Complete step 1. Place the broccoli, onion and garlic in a large bowl with the boiling hot stock. Cover and microwave on HIGH for 10–12 minutes or until tender. Season to taste. Complete steps 3–5.

To Freeze
Cool quickly in the ring mould, overwrap and freeze for up to 6 months.

To Thaw
Leave overnight in the refrigerator.

To Serve
Reheat in the ring mould in the oven at 180°C (350°F) mark 4 for 20–25 minutes or until piping hot. Invert on to a warmed serving plate.

Right: Cabbage and Hazelnut Rolls (page 172)

TIAN À LA PROVENÇALE

SERVES 4

450g (1lb) aubergines

salt and pepper

25g (1oz) butter

25g (1oz) plain flour

300ml (½ pint) milk

60ml (4 tbsp) Parmesan cheese, grated

1.25ml (¼ tsp) grated nutmeg

about 150ml (¼ pint) olive or vegetable oil

350g (12oz) tomatoes, skinned and sliced

2 garlic cloves, skinned and roughly chopped

2 eggs, beaten

1 Thinly slice the aubergines, then place in a colander, sprinkling each layer with salt. Cover with a plate, place heavy weights on top and leave for 30 minutes.

2 Meanwhile, melt the butter in a saucepan, add the flour and cook gently, stirring, for 1–2 minutes. Remove from the heat and gradually blend in the milk. Bring to the boil, stirring constantly, then simmer for 3 minutes until thick and smooth. Add half of the cheese, the nutmeg and seasoning to taste. Stir well to mix, then remove from the heat.

3 Rinse the aubergine slices under cold running water, then pat dry with absorbent kitchen paper.

4 Pour enough oil into a heavy-based frying pan to cover the base. Heat until very hot, then add a layer of aubergine slices. Fry over moderate heat until golden brown on both sides, turning once. Remove with a slotted spoon and drain on absorbent kitchen paper. Repeat with more oil and aubergines.

5 Arrange alternate layers of aubergines and tomatoes in an oiled gratin or baking dish. Sprinkle each layer with garlic, a little salt and plenty of pepper.

6 Beat the eggs into the sauce, then pour slowly into the dish. Sprinkle the remaining cheese evenly over the top.

7 Bake in the oven at 200°C (400°F) mark 6 for 20 minutes or until golden brown and bubbling. Serve hot.

To Microwave

Complete step 1. Place the butter, flour and milk in a medium bowl and whisk together. Microwave on HIGH 4–5 minutes or until the sauce has boiled and thickened, whisking frequently. Stir in half the cheese, the nutmeg and seasoning to taste. Complete steps 3–7.

To Freeze

Pack the sauce and aubergines separately in rigid containers at the end of step 5. Freeze for up to 3 months.

To Thaw and Serve

Leave overnight in the refrigerator. Alternatively, microwave on LOW in a covered serving dish for about 15–20 minutes, turning occasionally. Stand for 15 minutes. Complete steps 6 and 7.

HERBY BROWN RICE

SERVES 4

225g (8oz) brown rice

1.7 litres (3 pints) water

5ml (1 tsp) salt

pinch of dried sage

15g (½oz) butter

30ml (2 tbsp) chopped fresh parsley

1 Place rice, water, salt and sage in a large pan, bring quickly to the boil, stir well and cover with a tightly fitting lid.

2 Reduce the heat and simmer gently for about 30–35 minutes, until tender.

3 Remove from the heat, rinse with boiling water. Stir in the butter and parsley and separate the grains with a fork before serving.

To Microwave

Place the rice, salt, and sage in a large bowl, pour over enough boiling water to cover by 2.5cm (1 inch), then stir and cover. Microwave on HIGH for 30–35 minutes or until tender, stirring occasionally. Complete step 3.

To Freeze

Cool quickly, pack loosely in a polythene bag and freeze for up to 3 months.

To Thaw and Serve

Place the frozen rice in an ovenproof container. Cover and cook in the oven at 180°C (350°F) mark 4 for 15–20 minutes or until steaming hot, stirring once. Alternatively, place the frozen rice in a shallow dish, cover and microwave on HIGH for about 4–6 minutes or until piping hot, stirring occasionally.

FENNEL RATATOUILLE

SERVES 4–6

450g (1lb) fennel bulb (1 large or 2 small)
60ml (4 tbsp) olive oil
1 large onion, skinned and sliced
1 garlic clove, skinned and crushed
450g (1lb) tomatoes, skinned and quartered
1 red pepper, cored, seeded and thickly sliced
1 yellow or green pepper, cored, seeded and thickly sliced
450g (1lb) courgettes, thickly sliced
30ml (2 tbsp) lemon juice
salt and pepper
8 large green or black olives, halved and stoned
15ml (1 tbsp) chopped fresh basil

1 Cut the fennel in half lengthwise, then slice across the bulb.
2 Heat the oil in a large sauté pan and cook the fennel, onion and garlic, covered, until soft but not coloured. Stir occasionally.
3 Add the tomatoes, peppers and courgettes, with the lemon juice and seasoning. Stir to mix. Cover and simmer gently for 15–20 minutes or until the vegetables are just tender: they should still retain some bite. Stir occasionally but take care not to break up the vegetables.
4 Add the olives to the fennel mixture. Adjust seasoning to taste and mix in the basil.

To Microwave
Complete step 1. Place the oil in a large bowl and stir in the fennel, onion and garlic. Cover and microwave on HIGH for 7–9 minutes or until soft, stirring occasionally. Add the tomatoes, peppers and courgettes with the lemon juice and seasoning. Cover and microwave on HIGH for 6–8 minutes or until just tender. Stirring occasionally. Complete step 4.

To Freeze
Cook, pack in a rigid container at the end of step 3 and freeze for up to 3 months.

To Thaw
Leave overnight in the refrigerator.

To Serve
Gently reheat in a heavy-based saucepan until piping hot, stirring frequently. Alternatively, place in a medium bowl, cover and microwave on HIGH for 5–6 minutes or until piping hot, stirring occasionally. Complete step 4.

ONIONS À LA GRECQUE

SERVES 8

900g (2lb) small pickling onions
75ml (5 tbsp) olive oil
5ml (1 tsp) sugar
150ml (¼ pint) dry white wine
10ml (2 tsp) tomato purée
salt and pepper
30ml (2 tbsp) chopped fresh parsley

1 Blanch the onions in boiling water for 1 minute, then drain and rinse under cold running water. Remove the onion skins.
2 Put the onions in a large, heavy-based saucepan with 300ml (½ pint) water and the remaining ingredients, except the parsley. Add seasoning to taste. Bring to the boil, then lower the heat, cover and simmer gently for 30 minutes.
3 Uncover and cook for a further 15 minutes or until the onions are tender. Taste and adjust the seasoning, then stir in the chopped parsley. Turn into a warmed serving dish and serve hot.

To Microwave
Complete step 1. Place the onions in a large bowl, add 100ml (4fl oz) water and the remaining ingredients, except the parsley. Add seasoning to taste. Cover and microwave on HIGH for 15–20 minutes or until tender, re-arranging halfway through cooking. Adjust the seasoning, then stir in the chopped parsley. Turn into a warmed serving dish and serve hot.

To Freeze
Cool, pack in a rigid container without the parsley and freeze for up to 3 months.

To Thaw
Leave overnight in the refrigerator. Alternatively microwave on LOW for about 15–20 minutes, stirring occasionally. Stand for 10–15 minutes.

To Serve
Reheat gently in a heavy-based saucepan until hot, stirring frequently. Alternatively, microwave on HIGH for 6–10 minutes or until piping hot, stirring occasionally.

STOCKS AND SAUCES

CHICKEN STOCK

MAKES 1.7 LITRES (3 PINTS)

1 chicken carcass plus bones, scraps of flesh and giblets (excluding liver), or about 700g (1½lb) veal bones plus scraps of flesh

2 carrots, peeled and quartered

2 onions, skinned and quartered

2 celery sticks, sliced

bay leaf, parsley stalks, thyme sprigs, for flavouring

6–8 black peppercorns

salt

1 Place the chicken bones, flesh and giblets in a large saucepan. Cover with cold water, about 2.8 litres (5 pints), and bring to the boil. Skim any scum.
2 Add the vegetables and all the remaining ingredients, except the salt, to the pan. Bring to the boil again, skim and reduce heat.
3 Partially cover the pan and simmer very gently for about 2–3 hours, skimming as necessary at frequent intervals. The liquid should reduce by about one third of the original quantity.
4 Strain the stock, adjust seasoning, then cool. Remove fat before use.

BEEF STOCK

MAKES 1.4 LITRES (2½ PINTS)

1.4–1.8kg (3–4lb) beef and veal bones

2 onions, skinned and quartered

2 carrots, peeled and quartered

2 celery sticks, sliced

bay leaf, parsley stalks, thyme, for flavouring

6–8 black peppercorns

salt

1 Place the bones in a roasting tin with the vegetables. Brown in the oven at 220°C (425°F) mark 7 for about 30–40 minutes. Turn the bones and vegetables occasionally.
2 Transfer the ingredients to a large saucepan. Add enough cold water to cover. Bring to the boil and skim. Add flavouring ingredients, except salt.

3 Partially cover the pan and simmer very gently, skimming occasionally, for about 2–3 hours or until the liquid has reduced by one third.
4 Strain the stock, adjust seasoning, then cool. Skim off the fat before use.

FISH STOCK

MAKES ABOUT 1.1 LITRES (2 PINTS)

about 225g (8oz) clean fish bones (3–4 backbones)

1 onion, skinned and quartered

1 carrot, peeled and quartered

1 celery stick, sliced

bay leaf, parsley stalks, thyme sprigs, for flavouring

4–6 black peppercorns

salt

1 Rinse the bones and discard any heads and dark skin. Place all the ingredients, except the salt in the saucepan. Add cold water to cover.
2 Bring to the boil and skim any scum from the surface. Simmer very gently for 20–30 minutes.
3 Strain the stock, then cool. Adjust seasoning.
Note: Do not simmer the stock for more than 30 minutes – the bones will begin to give the stock a bitter flavour. However, once the stock has been strained, it can be boiled down again to reduce.

To Freeze
Cool, pack in usable quantities in polythene bag lined containers. Freeze until solid, then lift out of the containers. Freeze for up to 6 months.

To Thaw and Serve
Leave overnight in the refrigerator and reheat in a saucepan. Or gently reheat from frozen in a bowl over a pan of boiling water, stirring as the block thaws. Alternatively, transfer the solid block to a medium bowl. Microwave on HIGH for about 3–4 minutes for 300ml (½ pint), breaking up the block.

Right: Mixed Nut and Cheese Loaf (page 164)

WHITE SAUCE-ROUX METHOD

MAKES 300ML (½ PINT)

15g (½oz) butter
15g (½oz) plain flour
300ml (½ pint) milk
salt and pepper

POURING SAUCE

1 Melt the butter in a saucepan, stir in the flour and cook gently for 1 minute, stirring.
2 Remove the pan from the heat and gradually stir in the milk. Bring to the boil slowly and continue cooking, stirring all the time, until the sauce boils, thickens and is smooth.
3 Simmer very gently for a further 2–3 minutes. Season to taste.

COATING SAUCE

Follow the recipe for Pouring sauce, increasing the butter and flour to 25g (1oz) each.

BINDING SAUCE

Follow the recipe for Pouring sauce, increasing the butter and flour to 50g (2oz) each.

ONE-STAGE METHOD

Use the ingredients in the same quantities as for Pouring or Coating sauce. Place the butter, flour, milk and seasoning in a saucepan. Heat, whisking continuously, until the sauce boils, thickens and is smooth.

BLENDER OR FOOD PROCESSOR METHOD

Use the ingredients in the same quantities as for Pouring or Coating sauce. Place the butter, flour, milk and seasoning in the machine and blend until smooth. Pour into a saucepan and bring to the boil, stirring, until the sauce thickens.

Variations

Add any of these before or after freezing.

PARSLEY SAUCE

A traditional sauce for bacon, ham or fish.
Follow the recipe for the Pouring or Coating sauce. After seasoning, stir in 15–30ml (1–2 tbsp) finely chopped fresh parsley.

ONION SAUCE

For grilled and roast lamb, tripe or freshly hard-boiled eggs.
Follow the recipe for Pouring or Coating sauce.
Soften 1 large onion, skinned and finely chopped, in the butter before adding the flour.

ANCHOVY SAUCE

Serve with fish.
Follow the recipe for Pouring or Coating sauce, using half milk and half fish stock. Before seasoning, stir in 5–10ml (1–2 tsp) anchovy essence to taste, a squeeze of lemon juice and a few drops of red food colouring to tint a pale pink, if liked.

MUSHROOM SAUCE

Serve with fish, meat or eggs.
Follow the recipe for Pouring or Coating sauce. Fry 50–75g (2–3oz) sliced button mushrooms in the butter before adding the flour.

CAPER SAUCE

For lamb dishes.
Follow the recipe for Pouring or Coating sauce, using all milk or half milk and half stock, to give a better flavour. Before seasoning, stir in 15ml (1 tbsp) capers and 5–10ml (1–2 tsp) vinegar from the capers, or lemon juice. Reheat gently before serving.

EGG SAUCE

Serve with poached or steamed fish or kedgeree.
Follow the recipe for Pouring or Coating sauce, using all milk or half milk and half fish stock. Before seasoning, add 1 hard-boiled egg, shelled and chopped, and 5–10ml (1–2 tsp) snipped chives. Reheat gently before serving. Freeze without the egg.

CHEESE SAUCE

Delicious with fish, poultry, ham, bacon, egg or vegetable dishes.
Follow the recipe for Pouring or Coating sauce. Before seasoning, stir in 50g (2oz) finely grated Cheddar cheese or 50g (2oz) crumbled Lancashire cheese, 2.5–5ml (½–1 tsp) prepared mustard and a pinch of cayenne.

To Microwave

Place the butter, flour, milk and seasoning in a medium bowl and whisk together. Microwave on HIGH for 4–5 minutes for 300ml (½ pint), 5–6 minutes for 600ml (1 pint), until the sauce has boiled and thickened, whisking frequently.

ONION SAUCE
Place the butter and onion in a bowl and microwave on HIGH for 5–7 minutes. Add the flour and continue as before.

MUSHROOM SAUCE
Place the butter and 50–75g (2–3oz) sliced button mushrooms in a bowl and microwave on HIGH for 1–2 minutes. Add the flour and continue as before.

To Freeze
Cool, pack in usable quantities in polythene bag lined containers. Freeze until solid, then lift out of the containers. Freeze for up to 6 months.

To Thaw and Serve
Leave overnight in the refrigerator and reheat in a saucepan. Or gently reheat from frozen in a bowl over a pan of boiling water, stirring as the block thaws. Alternatively, transfer the solid block to a medium bowl. Microwave on HIGH for about 3–4 minutes for 300ml (½ pint), about 6–8 minutes for 600ml (1 pint), breaking up the block as it thaws. Use as required.

VELOUTÉ SAUCE

MAKES 450ML (¾ PINT)

knob of butter

30ml (2 tbsp) plain flour

450ml (¾ pint) chicken or other white stock (see page 186)

30–45ml (2–3 tbsp) single cream

few drops of lemon juice

salt and pepper

1 Melt the butter in a saucepan, stir in the flour and cook gently for 1 minute, stirring well, until the mixture is a light golden colour.
2 Remove the pan from the heat and gradually stir in the stock. Bring to the boil and continue to cook, stirring, until the sauce thickens. Simmer until slightly reduced and velvety.
3 Remove from the heat and add the cream, a few drops of lemon juice and seasoning. Serve with poultry, fish or veal.

Variations
SUPRÊME SAUCE
Makes 300ml (½ pint)
Using 300ml (½ pint) Velouté sauce, remove from the heat and stir in 1 egg yolk and 30–45ml (2–3 tbsp) single or double cream. Add a knob of butter,

a little at a time. Reheat if necessary, but do not allow to boil, or the sauce will curdle. Serve with poultry or fish. Suprême sauce is sometimes used in meat and vegetable dishes.

AURORE SAUCE
Makes 300ml (½ pint)
Using 300ml (½ pint) Velouté sauce, blend in 15–30ml (1–2 tbsp) tomato purée and 25g (1oz) butter, a little at a time. Season. Serve with eggs, chicken or fish.

NORMANDY SAUCE
Makes 300ml (½ pint)
Using 300ml (½ pint) Velouté sauce made with Fish stock (see page 186), beat in 1 egg yolk. Gradually add 25g (1oz) unsalted butter, a small piece at a time, rotating the pan in a circular fashion gently until the butter melts. Do not stir or reheat after adding the butter. Serve with poached, grilled or steamed white fish dishes, or hot crab and lobster dishes.

To Microwave
Put the butter, flour and stock in a medium bowl and whisk together. Microwave on HIGH for 4–5 minutes for 300ml (½ pint), 5–6 minutes for 600ml (1 pint), until the sauce has boiled and thickened, whisking frequently. Complete step 3.

SUPRÊME SAUCE
Reheat if necessary on HIGH for about 30–45 seconds or until hot. Do not allow to boil.

To Freeze
Cool, pack in usable quantities in polythene bag lined containers before adding the cream or egg yolks or butter. Freeze until solid, then lift out of the containers. Freeze for up to 6 months.

To Thaw and Serve
Leave overnight in the refrigerator and reheat in a saucepan. Or gently reheat from frozen in a bowl over a pan of boiling water, stirring as the block thaws. Alternatively, transfer the solid block to a medium bowl. Microwave on HIGH for about 3–4 minutes for 300ml (½ pint), about 6–8 minutes for 600ml (1 pint), breaking up the block as it thaws. Add the cream. Use as required.

BÉCHAMEL SAUCE

MAKES 300ML (½ PINT)

300ml (½ pint) milk
1 shallot, skinned and sliced, or a small piece of onion, skinned
1 small carrot, peeled and sliced
½ celery stick, chopped
1 bay leaf
3 black peppercorns
25g (1oz) butter
25g (1oz) plain flour
salt and white pepper
30ml (2tbsp) single cream (optional)

1 Put the milk, vegetables, bay leaf and peppercorns in a saucepan and slowly bring to the boil. Remove from the heat, cover and set aside to infuse for 30 minutes. Strain, reserving the flavoured milk.

2 Melt the butter in a saucepan, stir in the flour and cook gently for 1 minute, stirring.

3 Remove the pan from the heat and gradually stir in the flavoured milk. Bring to the boil slowly and continue cooking, stirring all the time, until the sauce boils, thickens and is smooth.

4 Simmer very gently for 3 minutes. Remove from the heat and season. Stir in the cream, if using. Use for fish, poultry, egg or vegetable dishes.

Variations

MORNAY SAUCE

Serve with eggs, chicken or fish.

Before seasoning, stir in 50g (2oz) finely grated mature Cheddar cheese or 25g (1oz) grated Parmesan or 50g (2oz) grated Gruyère. Do not reheat or the cheese will become overcooked and stringy.

SOUBISE SAUCE

MAKES ABOUT 300ML (½ PINT)

25g (1oz) butter
2 medium onions, skinned and chopped
300ml (½ pint) Béchamel sauce
15–30ml (1–2 tbsp) chicken stock (see page 186) or water
salt and pepper

1 Melt the butter in a saucepan and gently cook the onions for 10–15 minutes or until soft.

2 Sieve or purée with the Béchamel sauce and the stock in a blender or food processor until smooth.

3 Season and reheat gently for 1–2 minutes before serving. Use for fish, egg or meat dishes.

To Microwave

Put the milk, vegetables, bay leaf and peppercorns in a bowl and microwave on HIGH for 2–3 minutes or until boiling. Cover and set aside to infuse for 30 minutes. Strain, reserving the flavoured milk. Put the butter, flour and milk in a medium bowl and whisk together. Microwave on HIGH for 4–5 minutes or until the sauce has boiled and thickened, whisking frequently. Season and stir in the cream, if using.

SOUBISE SAUCE

Dice the butter into a bowl and microwave on HIGH for 45 seconds. Add the onions and microwave on HIGH for 10–12 minutes or until soft. Complete step 2. Season and microwave on HIGH for 1–2 minutes.

To Freeze

Cool, pack in usable quantities in polythene bag lined containers. Freeze until solid, then lift out of the containers. Freeze for up to 6 months.

To Thaw and Serve

Leave overnight in the refrigerator and reheat in a saucepan. Or gently reheat from frozen in a bowl over a pan of boiling water, stirring as the block thaws. Alternatively, transfer the solid block to a medium bowl. Microwave on HIGH for about 3–4 minutes for 300ml (½ pint), about 6–8 minutes for 600ml (1 pint), breaking up the block as it thaws. Use as required.

Right: Tipsy Coffee and Praline Ring (page 198)

BOLOGNESE SAUCE

SERVES 4

30ml (2 tbsp) olive oil
25g (1oz) butter
2 rashers of pancetta or smoked streaky bacon, rinded and finely chopped
1 small onion, skinned and finely chopped
225g (8oz) minced beef
1 garlic clove, skinned and finely chopped
1 small celery stick, finely chopped
1 small carrot, peeled and finely chopped
1 bay leaf
30ml (2 tbsp) tomato purée
150ml (¼ pint) dry white wine
150ml (¼ pint) beef stock
salt and pepper

1 Heat the oil and butter in a saucepan and fry the pancetta and onion for 2–3 minutes until soft.
2 Add the minced beef and cook for a further 5 minutes, stirring constantly, until lightly browned.
3 Add the garlic, celery, carrot and bay leaf and cook, stirring, for a further 2 minutes.
4 Stir in the tomato purée, wine, stock and seasoning. Bring to the boil, cover and simmer for 1–1½ hours, stirring occasionally. Discard the bay leaf. Adjust seasoning. Serve with pasta.

To Microwave

Place the oil, butter, onion, bacon, garlic and minced beef in a medium bowl. Microwave on HIGH for 5–7 minutes or until the onion is softened and the meat has browned, stirring occasionally. Add the remaining ingredients, except the seasoning, stirring well to mix. Microwave on HIGH for 15–20 minutes or until the mince is tender and the sauce is slightly reduced. Discard the bay leaf. Season to taste before serving.

To Freeze

Cool, pack in usable quantities in polythene bag lined containers. Freeze until solid, then lift out of the containers. Freeze for up to 3 months.

To Thaw

Leave overnight at cool room temperature.

To Serve

Gently reheat in a heavy-based saucepan for 5–10 minutes or until piping hot, stirring frequently. Alternatively, microwave on HIGH for about 4–5 minutes or until piping hot, stirring frequently.

ESPAGNOLE SAUCE

MAKES ABOUT 300ML (½ PINT)

25g (1oz) butter
1 rasher streaky bacon, rinded and chopped
1 shallot, skinned and chopped, or a small piece of onion, skinned and chopped
60ml (4 tbsp) mushroom stalks, chopped
1 small carrot, peeled and chopped
30–45ml (2–3 tbsp) plain flour
450ml (¾ pint) beef stock (see page 186), or beef stock from a cube
bouquet garni
30ml (2 tbsp) tomato purée
salt and pepper
15ml (1 tbsp) sherry (optional)

1 Melt the butter in a saucepan and fry the bacon for 2–3 minutes. Add the vegetables and fry for a further 3–5 minutes or until lightly browned. Stir in the flour, mix well and continue cooking until it turns brown.
2 Remove from the heat and gradually add the stock, stirring after each addition. Bring to the boil slowly and continue to cook, stirring, until the sauce thickens. Add the bouquet garni, tomato purée and seasoning.
3 Reduce the heat and simmer very gently for 1 hour, stirring from time to time to prevent sticking.
4 Strain the sauce, reheat and skim off any fat, using a metal spoon. Adjust seasoning and add the sherry, if using, just before serving. Serve with red meats or game.

ROBERT SAUCE

MAKES ABOUT 450ML (¾ PINT)

25g (1oz) butter
1 small onion, skinned and finely chopped
150ml (¼ pint) dry white wine
15ml (1 tbsp) wine vinegar
300ml (½ pint) Espagnole sauce
5–10ml (1–2 tsp) mild prepared mustard
pinch of sugar
salt and pepper

1 Melt the butter in a saucepan and gently fry the onion for about 10 minutes, without browning.
2 Add wine and vinegar and boil to reduce by half. Stir in the sauce and simmer for 10 minutes.
3 Add the mustard, sugar and extra seasoning, if necessary. Serve with pork.

REFORM SAUCE

MAKES ABOUT 300ML (½ PINT)

45–60ml (3–4 tbsp) vinegar

few parsley stalks

1 bay leaf

thyme sprig

6 black peppercorns

300ml (½ pint) Espagnole sauce

1 gherkin, finely sliced

15g (½oz) tongue, finely sliced

1 hard-boiled egg white, finely chopped

1 Place the vinegar, parsley stalks, bay leaf, thyme and peppercorns into a saucepan and boil, uncovered, until reduced by half.

2 Stir in the sauce and simmer for 10–15 minutes, then strain.

3 Add the gherkin, tongue and egg white. Do not reheat. Serve with lamb or beef.

To Microwave

ESPAGNOLE SAUCE

Dice the butter into a bowl, add the bacon and cover with absorbent kitchen paper. Microwave on HIGH for 1–2 minutes. Add the vegetables and microwave on HIGH for 2–3 minutes. Blend in the flour and stock, whisking well. Microwave on HIGH for 4–5 minutes or until the sauce has boiled and thickened, whisking frequently. Add the bouquet garni, tomato purée and seasoning. Microwave, uncovered, on HIGH for 20 minutes, stirring occasionally. Complete step 4.

ROBERT SAUCE

Dice the butter into a bowl and add the onion. Microwave on HIGH for 5–7 minutes or until soft, stirring occasionally. Add the wine and vinegar. Microwave, uncovered, on HIGH for 5 minutes. Complete step 3.

REFORM SAUCE

Put the vinegar, parsley stalks, bay leaf, thyme and peppercorns into a bowl. Microwave, uncovered, for 5 minutes. Stir in the sauce and microwave on HIGH for 8 minutes, then strain. Complete step 3.

To Freeze

Cool, pack in usable quantities in polythene bag lined containers. Freeze until solid, then lift out of the containers. Freeze for up to 3 months.

To Thaw and Serve

Leave overnight in the refrigerator and reheat in a saucepan. Or gently reheat from frozen in a bowl over a pan of boiling water, stirring as the block thaws. Alternatively, transfer the solid block to a medium bowl. Microwave on HIGH for about 3–4 minutes for 300ml (½ pint), about 4–5 minutes for 450ml (¾ pint), breaking up the block as it thaws. Use as required.

NEAPOLITAN TOMATO SAUCE

SERVES 4

700g (1½lb) tomatoes, skinned and roughly chopped, or 397g (14oz) and 226g (8oz) can tomatoes, with their juice

1 garlic clove, skinned and crushed

75ml (5 tbsp) olive oil

1 sprig oregano, marjoram, basil or parsley, or 2.5ml (½ tsp) dried

2.5ml (½ tsp) sugar

salt and pepper

1 Place all the ingredients in a large saucepan and bring to the boil.

2 Lower the heat and simmer, uncovered, for about 10 minutes or until the oil has separated from the tomatoes. Stir frequently.

3 Taste and adjust seasoning. Serve with freshly cooked pasta.

To Microwave

Place all the ingredients in a large bowl and microwave on HIGH for 10 minutes or until the sauce has reduced and thickened, and the oil has separated from the tomatoes. Stir frequently. Taste and adjust seasoning before serving.

To Freeze

Cool, pack in useable quantities in polythene bag lined containers. Freeze until solid, then lift out of the containers. Freeze for up to 12 months.

To Thaw and Serve

Leave overnight in the refrigerator and reheat in a saucepan. Or gently reheat from frozen in a bowl over a pan of boiling water, stirring as the block thaws. Alternatively, transfer the solid block to a medium bowl. Microwave on HIGH for about 4–5 minutes or until hot, breaking up the block as it thaws.

MILD CURRY SAUCE

MAKES 450ML (¾ PINT)

50g (2oz) butter

1 medium onion, skinned and finely chopped

15–20ml (3–4 tsp) mild curry powder

45ml (3 tbsp) plain flour

450ml (¾ pint) milk or half stock and half milk

30ml (2 tbsp) mango or apple chutney, roughly chopped

salt and pepper

1 Melt the butter in a saucepan and fry the onion until golden. Stir in the curry powder and cook for 3–4 minutes. Add the flour and cook gently for 2–3 minutes.

2 Remove the pan from the heat and gradually stir in the milk. Bring to the boil slowly and continue cooking, stirring all the time, until the sauce thickens.

3 Add the chutney and seasoning. Reheat gently before serving. Use for vegetables such as marrow and cabbage wedges, hard-boiled eggs or combining with pieces of cooked fish, chicken or meat.

Note: Curry sauce is useful when you want to make a curry in a hurry, and makes good use of left-overs of meat, poultry and fish.

To Microwave

Place the butter in a bowl and microwave on HIGH for 2–3 minutes until melted. Add the onion and microwave on HIGH for 5–7 minutes or until softened. Stir in the curry powder and microwave on HIGH for 1 minute, stirring once. Blend in the flour and milk, whisking together. Microwave on HIGH for 5–6 minutes or until the sauce has boiled and thickened, whisking frequently. Add the chutney and seasoning. Microwave on HIGH for 1–2 minutes or until hot.

To Freeze

Cool, pack in usable quantities in polythene bag lined containers. Freeze until solid, then lift out of the containers. Freeze for up to 3 months.

To Thaw and Serve

Leave overnight in the refrigerator and reheat in a saucepan. Or gently reheat from frozen in a bowl over a pan of boiling water, stirring as the block thaws. Alternatively, transfer the solid block to a medium bowl. Microwave on HIGH for about 4–5 minutes, breaking up the block as it thaws. Microwave on HIGH for 1–2 minutes or until hot.

MUSTARD CREAM SAUCE

MAKES 450ML (¾ PINT)

40g (1½oz) butter

45ml (3 tbsp) plain flour

450ml (¾ pint) milk

30ml (2 tbsp) mustard powder

20ml (4 tsp) malt vinegar

salt and pepper

30ml (2 tbsp) single cream

1 Melt the butter in a saucepan, stir in the flour and cook gently for 1 minute, stirring.

2 Remove the pan from the heat and gradually stir in the milk. Bring to the boil slowly and continue cooking, stirring all the time, until the sauce boils and thickens. Simmer for about 5 minutes.

3 Blend the mustard powder with the vinegar and whisk into the sauce, then season. Stir in the cream. Reheat but do not boil. Use for carrots, celery hearts, herring, mackerel, cheese, ham or bacon dishes.

Variations

To vary the flavour, use different mustards, such as whole grain, Dijon or herb flavoured mustards, such as tarragon or chive.

To Microwave

Put the butter, flour and milk in a medium bowl and whisk together. Microwave on HIGH for 5–6 minutes or until the sauce has boiled and thickened, whisking frequently. Complete step 3.

To Freeze

Cool, pack in usable quantities in polythene bag lined containers without the cream. Freeze until solid, then lift out of containers. Freeze for up to 6 months.

To Thaw and Serve

Leave overnight in the refrigerator and reheat in a saucepan. Or gently reheat from frozen in a bowl over a pan of boiling water, stirring as the block thaws. Alternatively, transfer the solid block to a medium bowl. Microwave on HIGH for about 4–5 minutes, breaking up the block as it thaws. Add the cream, reheat and serve.

RICH CHOCOLATE SAUCE

MAKES ABOUT 300ML (½ PINT)

15ml (1 tbsp) cornflour
300ml (½ pint) milk
5ml (1 tsp) vanilla essence
50g (2oz) plain chocolate, broken into pieces
25g (1oz) butter, diced

1 Blend the cornflour with a little of the milk to make a smooth paste. Pour the remaining milk into a saucepan and stir in the cornflour and vanilla.
2 Bring to the boil over a gentle heat, stirring until thickened.
3 Place the chocolate in a small bowl over a pan of simmering water. Stir frequently until melted. Remove from the heat and beat in the butter. Add the chocolate mixture to the sauce and stir until blended. Serve with profiteroles (see page 205).

To Microwave

Place all the ingredients into a large jug and whisk together. Microwave on HIGH for 3½–4 minutes, or until smooth and blended, whisking frequently.

To Freeze

Cool, pack in usable quantities in a polythene bag lined containers. Freeze until solid, then lift out of the containers. Freeze for up to 6 months.

To Thaw and Serve

Leave overnight in the refrigerator and reheat in a saucepan. Or gently reheat from frozen in a bowl over a pan of boiling water, stirring as the block thaws. Alternatively, transfer the solid block to a medium bowl. Microwave on HIGH for about 4–5 minutes, breaking up the block as it thaws.

APPLE SAUCE

SERVES 4

450g (1lb) cooking apples, peeled, cored and sliced
25g (1oz) butter
little caster sugar

1 Put the apples in a saucepan with 30–45ml (2–3 tbsp) water and cook gently, uncovered, for about 10 minutes until soft and thick.
2 Beat to a pulp with a wooden spoon or potato masher, then, if liked, sieve or purée.
3 Stir in the butter and add a little sugar if the apples are very tart. Serve with pork or goose.

To Microwave

Put the apples and sugar into a bowl. Cover and microwave on HIGH for 5–6 minutes or until soft, stirring frequently. Complete steps 2 and 3.

To Freeze

Cool, pack in usable quantities in polythene bag lined containers. Freeze until solid, then lift out of the containers. Freeze for up to 12 months.

To Thaw and Serve

Leave overnight in the refrigerator and reheat in a saucepan. Or gently reheat from frozen in a bowl over a pan of boiling water. Alternatively, transfer to a bowl. Microwave on HIGH for about 4–5 minutes, breaking up the block.

GOOSEBERRY SAUCE

SERVES 4

350g (12oz) gooseberries
25g (1oz) butter
25g (1oz) sugar
1.25ml (¼ tsp) grated nutmeg
salt and pepper

1 Put the gooseberries in a saucepan with 150ml (¼ pint) water and cook for 4–5 minutes or until tender and pulped. Drain and rub through a sieve or purée in a blender or food processor.
2 Add the butter, sugar, nutmeg and seasoning. Reheat and serve. Serve with oily fish.

To Microwave

Place all the ingredients in a large bowl with 90ml (6 tbsp) water. Cover and microwave on HIGH for 5–6 minutes or until tender and pulped. Drain off any excess liquid, rub through a sieve or purée. Microwave on HIGH for 1 minute to reheat.

To Freeze

Cool, pack in usable quantities in polythene bag lined containers. Freeze until solid, then lift out of the containers. Freeze for up to 12 months.

To Thaw and Serve

Leave overnight in the refrigerator and reheat in a saucepan. Or gently reheat from frozen in a bowl over a pan of boiling water. Alternatively, transfer to a bowl. Microwave on HIGH for about 4–5 minutes, breaking up the block.

SWEET WHITE SAUCE

MAKES 300ML (½ PINT)

25ml (5 tsp) cornflour

300ml (½ pint) milk

about 25ml (5 tsp) sugar

1 Place the cornflour in a bowl and blend with 15–30ml (1–2 tbsp) of the milk to a smooth paste.

2 Heat the remaining milk in a saucepan until boiling. Pour on the blended mixture, stirring.

3 Return the mixture to the pan and bring to the boil, stirring continuously, until thickened. Cook for 1–2 minutes to make a white, glossy sauce. Add sugar to taste.

Note: For a thicker sauce, increase the quantity of cornflour to 30ml (2 tbsp). This will be necessary if adding cream, rum or any other form of liquid when the sauce has been made.

Variations

Flavour with any of the following when the sauce has thickened:

5ml (1 tsp) ground mixed spice or grated nutmeg

30ml (2 tbsp) jam

grated rind of ½ orange or lemon

15–30ml (1–2 tbsp) rum

1 egg yolk (must be reheated but not re-boiled)

Use 15ml (1 tbsp) cocoa powder for cornflour.

To Microwave

Blend the cornflour and sugar with a little of the milk in a medium bowl. Stir in the remaining milk. Microwave on HIGH for 3–4 minutes or until the sauce has thickened, stirring every minute. Stir well.

To Freeze

Cool, pack in useable quantities in polythene bag lined containers. Freeze until solid, then lift out of the containers. Freeze for up to 6 months.

To Thaw and Serve

Leave overnight in the refrigerator and reheat in a saucepan. Or gently reheat from frozen in a bowl over a pan of boiling water, stirring as the block thaws. Alternatively, transfer the solid block to a medium bowl. Microwave on HIGH for about 4–5 minutes, breaking up the block as it thaws.

CHESTNUT SAUCE

SERVES 4

225g (8oz) chestnuts, peeled

300ml (½ pint) chicken stock (see page 186)

1 small piece of onion, skinned

1 small piece of carrot, peeled

40g (1½oz) butter

45ml (3 tbsp) plain flour

salt and pepper

30–45ml (2–3 tbsp) single cream or milk

1 Place the chestnuts in a saucepan with the stock and vegetables. Cover and simmer for 20 minutes or until soft. Mash, sieve or purée in a blender or food processor.

2 Melt the butter in a pan, stir in the flour, cook gently for 1 minute, stirring. Remove pan from the heat and gradually stir in the chestnut purée. Bring to the boil, stirring – the sauce should be thick, but it may be necessary at this point to add a little milk or extra stock.

3 Season to taste, remove from the heat and stir in the cream. Heat without boiling and serve at once. Rich and satisfying with turkey or other poultry.

To Microwave

Place the chestnuts in a large bowl with the stock and vegetables. Microwave on HIGH for 15–20 minutes or until soft. Mash, sieve or purée in a blender or food processor. Place the butter in a bowl and microwave on HIGH for 1 minute. Stir in the flour and microwave on HIGH for 30 seconds. Gradually stir in the chestnut purée. Microwave on HIGH for 2–3 minutes or until boiling and thickened, whisking frequently. Season to taste and stir in the cream. Microwave on HIGH for 30–45 seconds to reheat.

To Freeze

Cool, pack in usable quantities in polythene bag lined containers without the cream. Freeze until solid, then lift out of the containers. Freezer for up to 3 months.

To Thaw and Serve

Leave overnight in the refrigerator and reheat in a saucepan. Or gently reheat from frozen in a bowl over a pan of boiling water, stirring as the block thaws. Alternatively, transfer the solid block to a medium bowl. Microwave on HIGH for about 4–5 minutes, breaking up the block as it thaws. Add the cream, reheat and serve.

DESSERTS

AUTUMN PUDDING

SERVES 6

700g (1½lb) mixed fruits, such as apples, blackberries, plums
25g (1oz) sugar
100–175g (4–6oz) white bread, thinly sliced
fresh fruit and mint sprigs, to decorate

1 Core and slice the apples. Quarter and stone the plums. Hull the blackberries. Place the fruits in a colander and wash under cold running water.
2 Stir 30ml (2 tbsp) hot water and the sugar together in a pan and bring slowly to the boil. Add the fruits and stew gently for 5–10 minutes or until soft but retain their shape.
3 Cut the crusts from the bread and line the base and sides of a 1.1 litre (2 pint) pudding basin with the slices, so that there are no spaces between them.
4 Pour in the fruit and completely cover with more slices of bread. Place a saucer with a weight on it on top of the pudding and refrigerate overnight. To serve, turn out on to a flat plate and decorate with fruit and mint. Serve with whipped cream.

To Microwave
Complete step 1. Stir the water and sugar together in a bowl and microwave on HIGH for 1–2 minutes or until boiling. Add the fruits and microwave on HIGH for 4–5 minutes or until soft but still retain their shape. Complete steps 3 and 4.

To Freeze
Pack in the pudding basin, overwrap and freeze for up to 6 months.

To Thaw
Leave overnight in the refrigerator.

To Serve
Turn out on to a flat plate and serve with whipped cream.

COFFEE AND CHOCOLATE MOUSSE

SERVES 8

150g (5oz) plain chocolate, broken into pieces
15ml (1 tbsp) coffee granules
4 eggs, separated
75g (3oz) soft light brown sugar
150ml (¼ pint) double cream
150ml (¼ pint) natural yogurt
15ml (1 tbsp) powdered gelatine
milk chocolate curls, to decorate (see page 211)

1 Melt the chocolate in a bowl with the coffee and 45ml (3 tbsp) water over a pan of hot water. Cool.
2 Beat the egg yolks and sugar together until thick and creamy. In a separate bowl, whisk the cream and yogurt until the mixture just holds its shape.
3 Sprinkle the gelatine over 45ml (3 tbsp) water in a bowl. Soak until spongy. Dissolve the gelatine by placing the bowl over a pan of simmering water.
4 Whisk the egg whites until they just hold their shape. Stir the cool chocolate into the egg mixture with the dissolved gelatine. Fold in the cream mixture with the egg whites.
5 Spoon the mousse into a serving dish. Cover and chill for about 3 hours until set. Decorate.

To Microwave
Place the chocolate in a bowl with the coffee granules and 45ml (3 tbsp) water. Microwave on HIGH for 1–2 minutes or until melted, stirring occasionally. Cool. Complete step 2. Sprinkle the gelatine over 45ml (3 tbsp) water in a bowl. Allow to soak until spongy. Microwave on HIGH for about 1 minute. Do not boil. Complete steps 4 and 5.

To Freeze
At step 5, spoon the mousse, undecorated, into a freezerproof dish. Overwrap and freeze for up to 3 months.

To Thaw and Serve
Leave overnight in the refrigerator. Decorate.

FRUIT AND RUM SAVARIN

SERVES 6

15g (½oz) fresh yeast
45ml (3 tbsp) lukewarm milk
100g (4oz) strong plain flour, sifted with a pinch of salt
30ml (2 tbsp) caster sugar
2 eggs, beaten
50g (2oz) unsalted butter, softened
225g (8oz) granulated sugar
120ml (8 tbsp) dark rum
2 bananas, peeled and sliced
450g (1lb) black grapes, halved and seeded
2 kiwi fruit, peeled and sliced
2 small oranges, skinned and segmented

1 Put the yeast in a warmed small bowl, add the milk and cream together. Add 25g (1oz) of the flour and beat well with a fork. Leave in a warm place for 10–15 minutes until frothy.

2 Put the remaining flour in a warmed large bowl with 5ml (1 tsp) of the caster sugar and the eggs. Add the frothy yeast mixture, then beat until an elastic dough is formed. Cover with a floured tea towel and leave in a warm place until doubled in size.

3 Beat the softened butter into the dough, a little at a time, until all is evenly incorporated.

4 Put the dough in a buttered and floured 1.1 litre (2 pint) savarin or ring mould. Cover with a floured tea towel and leave to prove in a warm place until it has risen to the top of the mould.

5 Uncover the mould. Bake in the oven at 200°C (400°F) mark 6 for 25–30 minutes or until risen and golden brown.

6 Meanwhile, make the rum sugar syrup. Put the granulated sugar and 200ml (7fl oz) water in a heavy-based saucepan and heat gently until the sugar has dissolved. Bring to the boil and boil steadily, without stirring, for 5 minutes until syrupy. Remove from the heat and stir in 90ml (6 tbsp) of the rum.

7 Turn the savarin out on to a wire rack placed over a large plate or tray. Prick all over the savarin with a fine skewer, then slowly spoon over the warm syrup. Collect any syrup that drips on to the plate or tray and spoon it back over the savarin. Leave until completely cold.

8 Toss the prepared fruits together with the remaining caster sugar and rum. Place the savarin on a serving plate and pile the fruits in the centre. Serve immediately with chilled single cream.

To Microwave

Complete steps 1–5. Put the granulated sugar in a heatproof bowl and pour over 200ml (7fl oz) boiling water, stir until dissolved. Microwave on HIGH for 2–3 minutes, without stirring, until syrupy. Cool slightly and stir in 90ml (6 tbsp) of the rum. Complete steps 7 and 8.

To Freeze

Open freeze on a tray at the end of step 7 and overwrap. Freeze for up to 4 months.

To Thaw and Serve

Leave at room temperature for 4–6 hours. Complete step 8.

TIPSY COFFEE AND PRALINE RING

SERVES 6

50g (2oz) whole unblanched almonds
225g (8oz) caster sugar
4 eggs
100g (4oz) plain flour
60ml (4 tbsp) strong black coffee
75ml (5 tbsp) brandy
300ml (½ pint) whipping cream

1 Place the almonds and 50g (2oz) of the sugar in a small pan. Heat gently, shaking the pan occasionally and gently prodding the sugar until it dissolves. Cook to a rich nut brown.

2 Turn the mixture on to an oiled baking sheet and leave until cold. Roughly crush half the praline and reserve. Finely crush the remainder.

3 Place the eggs and 100g (4oz) sugar in a bowl and, using an electric whisk, whisk until very thick and pale in colour – the mixture should leave a trail when the beaters are lifted from the bowl.

4 Using a metal spoon, carefully fold in the flour, finely crushed praline and 15ml (1 tbsp) of the coffee. Gently pour the mixture into a greased 1.6–1.7 litre (2¾–3 pint) ring mould.

5 Bake in the oven at 190°C (375°F) mark 5 for about 30–40 minutes or until well risen and just firm to the touch.

6 Meanwhile, prepare the brandy syrup. Pour 350ml (12fl oz) water into a saucepan, add the remaining sugar and heat gently until the sugar dissolves. Bring to the boil, then boil for 1 minute. Cool slightly and add 60ml (4 tbsp) of the brandy with the remaining coffee.

7 Remove the cake from the oven and prick the surface with a fine skewer. Spoon over half the syrup and leave to soak for about 20 minutes. Invert a ring on to a plate and spoon over the remaining syrup. Leave to cool.

8 Lightly whip the cream, stir in the remaining brandy and spoon into the centre of the ring. Decorate the cake as liked with the roughly crushed praline.

To Microwave

Put the almonds and 50g (2oz) of the sugar in a small heatproof bowl and microwave on HIGH for 2–3 minutes or until nut brown and caramelized. Complete steps 2–5. To prepare the brandy syrup, pour 350ml (12fl oz) boiling water over the remaining sugar, stir well. Microwave on HIGH for 1 minute. Cool slightly and add 60ml (4 tbsp) of the brandy with the remaining coffee. Complete steps 7 and 8.

To Freeze

Cool, pack in a rigid container at the end of step 7 and freeze for up to 3 months.

To Thaw and Serve

Leave overnight, wrapped, at cool room temperature. Complete step 8.

GOOSEBERRY CHARLOTTE

SERVES 6

450g (1lb) gooseberries, topped and tailed
75g (3oz) caster sugar
10ml (2 tsp) powdered gelatine
2 egg yolks
300ml (½ pint) milk
300ml (½ pint) double cream
angelica, to decorate
20 langue de chat biscuits, trimmed to size

1 Place the gooseberries in a small saucepan with 60ml (4 tbsp) water. Cover and simmer for about 10 minutes or until the fruit softens to a pulpy consistency.

2 Purée in a blender or food processor, then sieve to remove the pips. Stir in 50g (2oz) of the sugar. Place 30ml (2 tbsp) water into a bowl and sprinkle over the gelatine. Leave the gelatine to soak until spongy.

3 Meanwhile, make the custard. Beat the egg yolks with the remaining sugar in a bowl until light

in colour. In a small saucepan, warm the milk, then pour over the eggs and sugar, stirring until blended.

4 Return to the pan and cook over low heat, stirring all the time, until the custard thickens sufficiently to thinly coat the back of the spoon – do not boil.

5 Take off the heat and immediately add the soaked gelatine; stir until dissolved. Pour the custard out into a large bowl and mix in the gooseberry purée. Leave to cool for 45 minutes.

6 Lightly whip the cream. When the gooseberry mixture is cold, but not set, stir in half the cream until evenly blended.

7 Oil and base line a 15cm (6 inch) soufflé type non-metal straight sided dish and pour in the gooseberry mixture. Chill for 1–2 hours to set. When firm, turn out on to a flat serving plate.

8 Spread a thin covering of the remaining cream around the edge of the charlotte.

9 Spoon the rest of the cream into a piping bag fitted with a 1cm (½ inch) large star nozzle. Pipe the cream around the top edge. Decorate with angelica. Just before serving, arrange the biscuits carefully around the outside.

To Microwave

Put the gooseberries in a bowl with 60ml (4 tbsp) water, cover and microwave on HIGH for 6–8 minutes or until soft and pulpy. Complete step 2. To make the custard, beat the egg yolks with the remaining sugar until light in colour. Place the milk in a bowl and microwave on HIGH for 2 minutes. Pour the heated milk into the egg mixture and mix well. Microwave on HIGH for 1 minute, then microwave on LOW for 4–5 minutes or until the custard thinly coats the back of a spoon. Whisk several times during cooking. Immediately add the soaked gelatine, whisk until dissolved. Complete steps 5–9.

To Freeze

Cover with plastic wrap at the end of step 7 and overwrap. Freeze for up to 6 months.

To Thaw and Serve

Leave overnight in the refrigerator. Complete steps 8 to 9.

POACHED PEARS WITH POMEGRANATE

SERVES 4

4 pomegranates

4 firm pears

40g (1½oz) demerara sugar

1 Halve the pomegranates and extract the juice using a lemon squeezer. Strain.

2 Peel and halve the pears lengthways, scoop out the cores and place the pears in a single layer in a 2.3 litre (4 pint) ovenproof dish. Sprinkle over the sugar, pomegranate juice, there should be about 300ml (½ pint), and add 300ml (½ pint) water. Cover the dish tightly.

3 Cook in the oven at 190°C (375°F) mark 5 for about 1 hour or until the pears are tender.

4 Remove the pears and place in a serving dish, keep warm. Boil the cooking liquid until reduced by half. Spoon over the pears. Serve hot or cold.

To Microwave
Complete steps 1 and 2. Microwave on HIGH for 8–10 minutes or until tender. Complete step 4.

To Freeze
Cool, pack in a rigid container and freeze for up to 6 months.

To Thaw and Serve
Leave overnight at cool room temperature. Alternatively, microwave on HIGH for 2–3 minutes.

PINEAPPLE CHEESECAKE

SERVES 6

50g (2oz) digestive biscuits

15g (½oz) butter

4 eggs, separated

225g (8oz) caster sugar

450g (1lb) full fat soft cheese

40g (1½oz) plain flour, sifted

30ml (2 tbsp) lemon juice

300ml (½ pint) soured cream

432g (14½oz) can pineapple slices

20ml (4 tsp) arrowroot

90g (3½oz) walnut halves

300ml (½ pint) double cream

1 Put the biscuits in a strong polythene bag and crush them with a rolling pin. Lightly grease a 19cm (7½ inch) round loose-based cake tin and set aside.

2 Melt the butter and stir in the biscuit crumbs. Press this mixture over the base of the tin. Chill for 30 minutes to set.

3 Whisk the egg yolks with the sugar in a bowl until thick and creamy. In a separate bowl, beat the cheese lightly. Add the whisked mixture to the cheese and mix until smooth. Stir in the flour, lemon juice and soured cream.

4 Whisk the egg whites until stiff and fold into the cheese and lemon mixture. Pour into the cake tin and level the surface.

5 Bake in the oven at 130°C (250°F) mark ½ for 1½ hours. Turn off the heat and leave in the oven for 2 hours without opening the door. Remove from the oven and leave for 2 hours to cool in the tin. When cool, carefully remove cheesecake from the tin.

6 Drain the pineapple, reserving 150ml (¼ pint) syrup, and arrange over the top of the cheesecake.

7 Blend the arrowroot with a little of the syrup. Bring the remaining syrup to the boil. Add the arrowroot and, stirring all the time, cook for a few minutes until thickened. Cool slightly, then spoon the syrup over the pineapple on top of the cheesecake.

8 Finely chop the walnuts, reserving 12 halves. Whip the cream until stiff and spread a little over the sides of the cheesecake, reserving a little for decoration.

9 Press the chopped walnuts around the sides. Pipe the remaining cream on top and decorate with walnut halves.

To Microwave
Complete step 1. Place the butter in a small bowl and microwave on HIGH for 30 seconds. Complete steps 2–6. Blend the arrowroot with a little of the syrup. Place the remaining syrup in a bowl and microwave on HIGH for 1–2 minutes or until boiling. Add the arrowroot, stir well and microwave on HIGH for 1–2 minutes or until thickened, stirring frequently. Cool slightly, then spoon the syrup over the pineapple on top of the cheesecake. Complete steps 8 and 9.

To Freeze
Pack in a rigid container without the topping. Freeze for up to 1 month.

To Thaw and Serve
Leave overnight in the refrigerator. Add the topping and decorate.

CITRUS CURD FLAN

SERVES 8

3 eggs
175g (6oz) plain flour
45ml (3 tbsp) icing sugar
150ml (5oz) butter
225g (8oz) soft citrus fruits, such as tangerines or satsumas
100g (4oz) caster sugar
15ml (1 tbsp) lemon juice
icing sugar and tangerine segments, to decorate

1 Separate one of the eggs. Beat the remaining two eggs together. Sift the flour and icing sugar into a bowl. Using a fork, cut in 75g (3oz) of the butter until the mixture resembles fine breadcrumbs. Bind to a dough with the egg yolk and 15–30ml (1–2 tbsp) water. Knead the dough lightly, then wrap and chill for about 30 minutes.
2 Roll out the pastry and use to line a 20.5cm (8 inch) loose based fluted flan tin. Chill again for about 30 minutes. Bake blind in the oven at 190°C (375°F) mark 5 until set but not browned.
3 Cut the fruit into about eight chunks, discarding the pips. Place the peel, pith and flesh in a processor or blender and work until finely minced.
4 Pour the minced mixture into a bowl and add the sugar, lemon juice, remaining butter and the beaten eggs. Place the bowl over a pan of simmering water and stir gently for about 20 minutes until the mixture thickens slightly.
5 Pour the curd into the flan case. Bake in the oven at 180°C (350°F) mark 4 for about 30 minutes or until set and golden.
6 Serve warm or chilled, dusted with sifted icing sugar and decorated with fruit segments.

To Microwave
Complete steps 1–3. Place the minced mixture into a bowl and add the sugar and remaining butter. Mix the lemon juice and eggs together and strain into the bowl. Microwave on HIGH for 5–6 minutes or until the curd is thick, whisking well every minute. Complete steps 5 and 6.

To Freeze
Cool, pack the baked pastry case and citrus curd separately. Freeze the pastry case for up to 6 months, curd for up to 3 months.

To Thaw and Serve
Leave overnight at cool room temperature. Stir the curd well, then complete steps 5 and 6.

MARRON MERINGUES

SERVES 6–8

2 egg whites
100g (4oz) caster sugar
150ml (¼ pint) double cream
5ml (1 tsp) milk
100g (4oz) sweetened chestnut purée
chocolate powder, to dredge

1 Line two baking sheets with baking parchment.
2 Whisk the egg whites in a medium bowl until stiff. Whisk in half the sugar, then fold in the rest. Fill a piping bag fitted with a 1cm (½ inch) plain nozzle and pipe 4cm (1½ inch) rounds on the prepared baking sheets.
3 Bake in the oven at 130°C (250°F) mark ½ for 3½–4 hours or until completely dry. Leave to cool. Carefully peel the meringues off the lining paper.
4 Whip the cream and milk in a medium bowl until it just holds its shape. Fold in the chestnut purée. Fill a piping bag fitted with a 1cm (½ inch) star nozzle and pipe the filling on to half of the meringues. Sandwich together with the remaining meringues.
5 Dredge the meringues with chocolate powder.

To Microwave
A meringue mixture cooked by microwave differs slightly from the conventional recipe, but the results are perfect and ready in minutes rather than hours. Lightly beat ½ egg white with a fork in a medium bowl. Sift 175g (6oz) icing sugar and gradually mix into the egg white to form a smooth, stiff mixture. Knead the mixture well on a surface lightly dusted with icing sugar. Cut into pieces each the size of a hazelnut and roll into balls. Place six balls at a time on a sheet of baking parchment. Microwave on HIGH for 1–1¼ minutes or until risen and crisp. Repeat with the remaining mixture. Complete steps 4 and 5, filling just before serving.

To Freeze
Open freeze the filled meringues at the end of step 4, pack in a rigid container and freeze for up to 3 months. Open freeze the unfilled microwave meringues, pack in a polythene bag and freeze for up to 3 months.

To Thaw and Serve
Arrange the meringues on a serving dish and leave at room temperature for 1–1¼ hours. Dredge with chocolate powder. Serve chilled.

CHOCOLATE ROULADE

SERVES 6

150g (5oz) plain chocolate, broken into pieces

4 eggs, separated

caster sugar

400g (14oz) can apricot halves in natural juices

1cm (½ inch) piece of fresh root ginger, peeled

20ml (4 tsp) lemon juice

30ml (2 tbsp) whisky

5ml (1 tsp) powdered gelatine

150ml (¼ pint) double cream

150ml (¼ pint) natural yogurt

milk and white chocolate curls, to decorate (see page 211)

1 Cut out two large sheets of non-stick paper, 33 × 30.5cm (13 × 12 inches). Place the papers on top of each other and fold up 2.5cm (1 inch) all round. Snip the corners, then secure the edges with paperclips to form a stiff paper case. Place on a baking sheet.

2 Place the chocolate in a small bowl. Melt over a pan of hot water, then cool slightly. Whisk the egg yolks and 100g (4oz) caster sugar together until very thick. Stir in the cooled chocolate. Whisk the whites until stiff but not dry and fold through the chocolate mixture.

3 Pour the mixture into the prepared case. Bake in the oven at 180°C (350°F) mark 4 for about 17 minutes or until just firm to the touch. Remove from the oven, immediately cover with a damp tea towel and leave overnight.

4 Purée the apricots and juices, ginger and lemon juice in a blender or food processor until smooth. Cover and chill.

5 The next day, place 15ml (1 tbsp) of the whisky in a bowl and sprinkle over the gelatine. Leave to soak for about 10 minutes, then dissolve over a pan of simmering water.

6 Whisk the cream with the remaining whisky until it holds its shape. Add the yogurt and whisk again. Stir in the dissolved gelatine.

7 Remove the tea towel, then flip the roulade over on to sugared greaseproof paper. Peel off the paper case and spread the cream over the surface. Roll up the roulade as you would a Swiss roll using the greaseproof paper as a support.

8 Place on a serving dish. Serve chilled, decorated with chocolate curls and accompanied by the sauce.

To Microwave

Complete step 1. Place the chocolate in a small bowl and microwave on HIGH for 1 minute or until just melted. Complete steps 2–4. Sprinkle the gelatine over 15ml (1 tbsp) whisky in a bowl and leave to soak for about 10 minutes. Microwave on HIGH for 1 minute. Do not boil. Complete steps 6–8.

To Freeze

Open freeze the completed, undecorated roulade, then pack in a rigid container. Freeze the sauce separately in a rigid container. Freeze the roulade for up to 3 months, sauce for up to 6 months.

To Thaw and Serve

Unwrap the roulade and place on a serving plate. Leave at cool room temperature for about 4 hours. Leave the sauce at cool room temperature for 3 hours. Chill and decorate.

CHOCOLATE CHERRY TRIFLE

SERVES 6

4 trifle sponges

60ml (4 tbsp) cherry conserve

two 400g (14oz) cans stoned black cherries

45ml (3 tbsp) kirsch

30ml (2 tbsp) caster sugar

30ml (2 tbsp) cornflour

2 egg yolks, beaten

300ml (½ pint) milk

15g (½oz) butter

2.5ml (½ tsp) vanilla essence

50g (2oz) plain chocolate, broken into pieces

300ml (½ pint) double cream

grated chocolate, to decorate

1 Split the trifle sponges and sandwich together with the cherry conserve. Arrange in the base of a large glass serving dish.

2 Drain the syrup from one can of cherries, reserving 45ml (3 tbsp), and mix with the kirsch. Pour over the sponges with the cherries. Drain the second can of cherries, discard the syrup, and add cherries to the dish. Set aside.

3 Whisk the sugar, cornflour and egg yolks together in a medium bowl until pale. Heat the milk in a medium saucepan until scalding, then whisk into the egg yolk mixture. Return the custard to the saucepan. Whisk in the butter and vanilla essence. Heat the custard gently until it reaches coating consistency, stirring continuously.

4 Melt the chocolate in a small bowl over a saucepan of simmering water. Stir into the custard.

Allow to cool slightly, then pour over the sponge and cherries. Cool completely.

5 Whip the cream in a medium bowl until it just holds its shape. Spread over the set chocolate custard and decorate with the chocolate. Chill.

To Microwave

Complete steps 1 and 2. Whisk the sugar, cornflour and egg yolks together in a medium bowl. Place the milk in a jug or bowl and microwave on HIGH for 1½ –2 minutes. Whisk into the egg mixture. Microwave on MEDIUM for 4 minutes, whisking several times during cooking. Whisk in the butter, chocolate and vanilla essence and microwave on MEDIUM for a further 2½–3 minutes. Allow to cool slightly, then pour over the sponge and cherries. Cool completely. Complete step 5.

To Freeze

Make the trifle in a freezerproof serving dish and open freeze at the end of step 4. Wrap in plastic wrap, then in foil. Freeze for up to 3 months.

To Thaw and Serve

Leave overnight in the refrigerator. Alternatively, unwrap and microwave on LOW for about 15–20 minutes. Stand for 40–50 minutes at room temperature. Complete step 5.

LEMON ROULADE WITH RASPBERRY COULIS

SERVES 6

3 eggs, separated
100g (4oz) caster sugar
grated rind and juice of 1 lemon
50g (2oz) fine semolina
15ml (1 tbsp) ground almonds
300ml (½ pint) double cream
finely grated rind of ½ lemon
225g (8oz) frozen raspberries, thawed
30ml (2 tbsp) icing sugar
finely grated lemon rind, to decorate

1 Grease and line a 23 × 30.5cm (9 × 12 inch) Swiss roll tin with baking parchment. Grease the paper.

2 Place the egg yolks in a large bowl with the sugar. Place over a pan of simmering water and whisk with an electric whisk until thick and pale. Whisk in the lemon rind and juice. Stir in the semolina and almonds.

3 Whisk the egg whites until stiff. Fold into the egg yolk mixture. Turn the mixture into the prepared tin. Bake in the oven at 180°C (350°F) mark 4 for 15–20 minutes or until springy to the touch and pale golden in colour. Place on a wire rack and cover with a damp cloth. Cool completely.

4 Whisk the cream and lemon rind together until it just holds its shape. Turn the roulade out on to a sheet of greaseproof paper sprinkled with caster sugar. Trim the edges then spread with the cream, reserving some for decoration. Roll up and transfer to a serving dish.

5 Reserve a few raspberries for decoration. Place the remaining raspberries and icing sugar in a small saucepan. Heat gently for 5 minutes, stirring frequently. Cool. Press the raspberry mixture through a nylon sieve and discard the seeds. To decorate the roulade, pipe with the remaining lemon cream, and arrange the reserved raspberries on top. Sprinkle over the finely grated lemon rind and serve with the raspberry coulis. Serve chilled.

To Microwave

Complete steps 1 to 4. Reserve a few raspberries for decoration. Place the remaining raspberries and icing sugar in a medium bowl and cook on HIGH for 1–1½ minutes. Cool. Press the raspberry mixture through a nylon sieve and discard the seeds. To decorate the roulade, pipe with the remaining cream and arrange the reserved raspberries on top. Sprinkle over the finely grated lemon rind and serve with the raspberry coulis.

To Freeze

Wrap the roulade without the decoration in greaseproof paper, then in foil and place in a rigid container. Freeze for up to 3 months.

To Thaw

Unwrap the roulade and place on a serving dish. Leave in the refrigerator for 3–4 hours.

To Serve

Whisk 150ml (¼ pint) double cream with the grated rind of ½ lemon until it just holds it shape. Use to pipe decoratively on the roulade. Sprinkle with crystallized lemon rind if wished.

FLORENTINE TIPSY CAKE

SERVES 6

50g (2oz) blanched almonds
50g (2oz) hazelnuts
45ml (3 tbsp) brandy
30ml (2 tbsp) orange-flavoured liqueur
30ml (2 tbsp) cherry or almond-flavoured liqueur
350g (12oz) trifle sponges or Madeira cake
150g (5oz) plain chocolate
450ml (¾ pint) double cream
150g (5oz) icing sugar, sifted
25g (1oz) cocoa powder, sifted, to decorate

1 Spread out the almonds and hazelnuts separately on a baking sheet. Toast in the oven at 200°C (400°F) mark 6 for 5 minutes or until golden.
2 Transfer the hazelnuts to a clean tea towel and rub off the skins while still warm. Spread all the nuts out to cool for 5 minutes, then roughly chop.
3 Line a 1.4 litre (2½ pint) pudding basin or round-based bowl with damp muslin.
4 In a separate bowl, mix the brandy and liqueurs together and set aside.
5 Split the trifle sponges in half through the middle (if using Madeira cake, cut into 1cm (½ inch) slices). Sprinkle with the brandy and liqueur mixture.
6 Line the basin with the moistened split sponges, reserving enough to cover the top.
7 Using a sharp knife, chop 75g (3oz) of the chocolate into small pieces and set aside.
8 In a separate bowl, whip the cream with 100g (4oz) of the icing sugar until stiff and fold in the chopped chocolate and nuts.
9 Divide this mixture in two and use one half to spread over the sponge lining in an even layer.
10 Melt the remaining chocolate in a bowl over a pan of hot water. Cool slightly, then fold into the remaining cream mixture. Use this to fill the centre of the pudding.
11 Level the top of the pudding and cover with the remaining moistened sponge. Trim the edges. Cover and chill for at least 12 hours.
12 To serve, uncover, invert a flat serving plate over the basin and turn upside down. Lift off the bowl, and carefully remove the muslin. Serve cold, dusted with the remaining sifted icing sugar and cocoa powder.

To Microwave

Evenly spread out the nuts on a large plate and microwave on HIGH for 8–10 minutes, stirring frequently. Complete steps 2–9. Break the remaining chocolate into a bowl and microwave on HIGH for 1 minute or until melted. Cool slightly, then fold into the remaining cream mixture. Fill the centre of the pudding. Complete steps 11 and 12.

To Freeze

Pack in a rigid container at the end of step 11 and freeze for up to 4 months.

To Thaw and Serve

Leave overnight in the refrigerator. Complete step 12.

INDIVIDUAL APPLE SOUFFLÉS

SERVES 6

350g (12oz) cooking apples, peeled, quartered, cored and roughly chopped
butter
25g (1oz) caster sugar
30ml (2 tbsp) plain flour
150ml (¼ pint) milk
3 eggs, separated
30ml (2 tbsp) apple brandy
icing sugar
apple slices, to decorate (optional)

1 Place the apples in a small saucepan with 25g (1oz) butter and the caster sugar. Cover tightly and cook gently until the apples are very soft.
2 Uncover and cook over moderate heat, stirring frequently, until all excess moisture has evaporated. Mash or beat until smooth. Cool slightly.
3 Melt 25g (1oz) butter in a saucepan, stir in the flour and cook for 2 minutes, stirring. Remove from the heat and gradually add the milk. Bring to the boil and simmer for 2–3 minutes until thick and smooth, stirring continuously. Take off the heat, cool slightly, then stir in the apple purée and egg yolks. Gently mix in the apple brandy.
4 Lightly grease six 150ml (¼ pint) ramekin dishes. Dust them out with icing sugar. Whisk the egg whites until stiff but not dry. Stir one large spoonful into the apple mixture, then gently fold in the remaining egg whites. Divide between the ramekin dishes so that each is three-quarters full.
5 Bake in the oven at 180°C (350°F) mark 4 for about 30 minutes or until just set and golden brown. Dust quickly with icing sugar and decorate with apple slices, if liked. Serve immediately.

To Microwave

Place the apples in a medium bowl with 25g (1oz) butter and the caster sugar. Cover and microwave on HIGH for 5–6 minutes or until the apples are soft, stirring frequently. Mash or beat until smooth. Cool slightly. Place 25g (1oz) butter in a bowl with the flour and milk. Microwave on HIGH for 2–3 minutes until smooth and thick, whisking frequently. Stir in the apple purée and egg yolks. Gently mix in the brandy. Complete steps 4 and 5.

To Freeze

Overwrap the soufflés at the end of step 4 and freeze for a few days only.

To Thaw and Serve

Uncover and bake from frozen in the oven at 180°C (350°F) mark 4 for 35–40 minutes or until just set.

PEACHES AND ROSE CREAM

SERVES 6

100g (4oz) granulated sugar

triple-distilled rose-water

6 ripe peaches, halved and skinned

225g (8oz) strawberries

150ml (¼ pint) whipping cream or thick yogurt

1 Dissolve the sugar in 450ml (¾ pint) water in a saucepan, simmer the syrup for 5 minutes. Add 5ml (1 tsp) rose-water and the peaches. Cover and cook very gently for 10–15 minutes.

2 Remove the peaches. Stone and cool.

3 Purée the strawberries with 30–45ml (2–3 tbsp) syrup. Rub through a nylon sieve.

4 Sandwich the peaches together or top each half with whipped cream or yogurt. Top with sauce.

To Microwave

Dissolve the sugar in 450ml (¾ pint) boiling water in a large bowl. Microwave on HIGH for about 3–4 minutes or until slightly thickened. Add 5ml (1 tsp) rose-water and peaches. Microwave on HIGH for 3–5 minutes until tender. Complete steps 2–4.

To Freeze

Cool, pack the poached peaches in the syrup in a rigid container and freeze for up to 3 months.

To Thaw and Serve

Leave at cool room temperature for about 6 hours. Complete steps 3 and 4.

PROFITEROLES

MAKES 20

CHOUX PASTRY

50g (2oz) butter

65g (2½oz) plain flour

2 eggs

SAUCE

225g (8oz) plain chocolate, broken into pieces

50g (2oz) unsalted butter

60ml (4 tbsp) milk

30ml (2 tbsp) rum

300ml (½ pint) double cream, whipped, to fill

1 For the choux pastry, melt the butter in 150ml (¼ pint) water in a saucepan and bring to the boil. Remove from the heat and add the flour all at once. Beat until the paste is smooth and forms a ball in the centre of the pan. (Do not overbeat.)

2 Allow to cool slightly, then beat in the eggs gradually, adding just enough to give a smooth mixture of piping consistency. Using a large plain nozzle, pipe the paste on to greased baking sheets in small dots.

3 Bake in the oven at 220°C (425°F) mark 7 for about 20–25 minutes. Allow to cool and make a small hole for steam to escape.

4 For the sauce, place the chocolate in a bowl over a pan of hot water. Add the butter and milk. Stir occasionally until glossy and smooth. Stir in rum.

5 Make a small hole in each bun and fill with the whipped cream. Pile into a pyramid on a serving plate and spoon over a little chocolate sauce. Serve the remaining sauce separately.

To Microwave

Complete steps 1–3. For the sauce, place the chocolate in a medium bowl and add the butter and milk. Microwave on HIGH for 2–3 minutes or until just melted, stirring occasionally. Beat well with a wooden spoon until glossy and smooth. Stir in the rum. Complete step 5.

To Freeze

Open freeze the unfilled buns on baking sheets, then remove carefully and pack in polythene bags. Cool, pack the sauce into a rigid container. Freeze the choux buns and sauce for up to 6 months.

To Thaw and Serve

Gently heat the sauce in a heavy-based saucepan. Place the frozen buns on baking sheets. Bake in the oven at 180°C (350°F) mark 4 for 10 minutes or until crisp. Cool. Complete step 5.

CITRUS SYRUP PUDDING

SERVES 4–6

100g (4oz) butter

100g (4oz) caster sugar

2 eggs, beaten

100g (4oz) self raising flour

pinch of salt

grated rind and juice of 1 small orange

grated rind and juice of 1 small lemon

45ml (3 tbsp) golden syrup

orange and lemon slices, to decorate

1 Cream the butter and sugar together in a large bowl until light and fluffy. Beat in the eggs with 45ml (3 tbsp) of the flour and the salt.

2 Stir in the fruit rinds and juices, then fold in the remaining flour. Grease and line the base of a 900ml (1½ pint) pudding basin and add the syrup.

3 Spoon the sponge mixture into the basin. Cover loosely with buttered foil. Stand the basin in a saucepan with boiling water coming one-third of the way up the sides.

4 Steam for 1½–2 hours or until the top is springy to the touch and knife inserted into the centre comes out clean. Turn out to a warmed dish and spoon any remaining sauce over. Decorate.

To Microwave

Complete steps 1 and 2. Spoon the sponge mixture into the basin, cover loosely with absorbent kitchen paper and place on an inverted saucer. Microwave on HIGH for 5½–6 minutes or until the top is springy but still moist and a knife inserted into the centre comes out clean, turning occasionally. Stand for 3 minutes. Turn out and spoon over any remaining sauce. Decorate.

To Freeze

Cool, wrap in plastic wrap, then overwrap with foil and freeze for up to 3 months.

To Thaw

Leave overnight at room temperature. Alternatively, cover and microwave on LOW for about 10–15 minutes, turning the dish occasionally. Stand for 10–20 minutes.

To Serve

Cover and steam for 20–30 minutes. Alternatively, cover and microwave on HIGH for 3½–4 minutes or until piping hot. Turn out on to a warmed dish and spoon over any remaining sauce. Decorate.

APRICOT AND ORANGE CHEESECAKE

SERVES 6

175g (6oz) wholemeal digestive biscuits

50g (2oz) butter, melted

400g (14oz) can apricot halves in natural juice, drained

225g (8oz) full fat soft cheese

225g (8oz) cottage cheese

60ml (4 tbsp) caster sugar

5ml (1 tsp) vanilla essence

grated rind and juice of 1 orange

11g sachet powdered gelatine

300ml (½ pint) double cream

1 orange, peeled and sliced

60ml (4 tbsp) apricot jam, sieved

1 Crush the biscuits in a polythene bag with a rolling pin or in a food processor. Combine the biscuit crumbs with the melted butter in a medium bowl. Grease and line a 20.5cm (8 inch) loose-based cake tin. Press the biscuit mixture evenly over the base. Bake in the oven at 170°C (325°F) mark 3 for 10–12 minutes. Leave to cool.

2 Reserve a few apricot halves for decoration. Purée the remainder in a blender or food processor until smooth.

3 Beat the cheeses, sugar, vanilla essence, rind and juice of the orange and the apricot purée together in a large bowl.

4 Sprinkle the gelatine over 45ml (3 tbsp) apricot juice in a small bowl. Leave to soak for 5 minutes. Place over a pan of simmering water until dissolved. Allow to cool slightly, then beat into the cheese mixture.

5 Whip the cream in a medium bowl until it just holds its shape. Fold into the cheese mixture, then pour over the base. Chill for 3–4 hours until set.

6 Remove the cheesecake from the tin and place on a serving plate. Use the reserved apricot halves and orange slices to decorate the top of the cheesecake. Warm the apricot jam and spoon or brush over the fruit to glaze. Serve chilled.

To Microwave

Dice the butter into a small bowl and microwave on HIGH for 1 minute. Complete steps 1–3. Place 60ml (4 tbsp) apricot juice in a small bowl and sprinkle over the gelatine. Leave to soak for 5 minutes. Microwave on HIGH for 30–35 seconds or until the gelatine has dissolved, stirring frequently. Do not boil. Allow to cool slightly, then beat into the cheese mixture. Complete steps 5 and 6.

To Freeze

Open freeze the cheesecake without the decoration and wrap in plastic wrap, then foil. Freeze for up to 1 month.

To Thaw and Serve

Leave overnight in the refrigerator. Alternatively, unwrap and remove from the tin. Place on a serving plate and microwave on LOW for about 8–10 minutes, rotating the cheesecake once during thawing. Stand for 40–50 minutes. Decorate and glaze.

ICED ORANGE SABAYON

SERVES 6

6 egg yolks

175g (6oz) demerara sugar

90ml (6 tbsp) orange-flavoured liqueur

200ml (7fl oz) unsweetened orange juice

glacé cherries and candied peel, to decorate

1 Put the egg yolks and sugar in a bowl and whisk together until pale and creamy. Stir in the liqueur and orange juice.

2 Pour the mixture into a medium heavy-based saucepan. Stir over low heat until the mixture thickens and just coats the back of the spoon. Do not boil.

3 Pour the mixture into six individual soufflé dishes or ramekins and cool for at least 30 minutes. Freeze for 3–4 hours until firm. Wrap in plastic wrap and return to the freezer.

4 Serve straight from the freezer, decorated with cherries and peel.

To Microwave

Complete step 1. Pour the mixture into a medium bowl and microwave on LOW for 2 minutes or until the mixture starts to thicken around the edges, whisking occasionally. Complete steps 3 and 4.

To Freeze

Overwrap the dishes in plastic wrap. Freeze for up to 3 months.

To Thaw and Serve

As step 4. Alternatively, microwave on LOW for about 1½ minutes to soften slightly. Serve immediately.

LEMON SORBET

SERVES 4

100g (4oz) sugar

pared rind and juice of 3 lemons

1 egg white

1 Gently heat the sugar and 300ml (½ pint) water in a saucepan until dissolved. Add the lemon rind, bring to the boil and boil for about 10 minutes. Cool completely.

2 Stir in the lemon juice and strain into a shallow freezer container. Cover and freeze until mushy, about 3 hours.

3 Turn the sorbet into a bowl and beat gently to break down the ice crystals. Stiffly whisk the egg white and fold in. Freeze for at least 4 hours or until firm.

4 To serve, transfer the sorbet to the refrigerator to soften slightly for about 40 minutes.

Variations

MANGO SORBET

Omit the lemons. Peel 2 large ripe mangoes and remove the flesh from the stones. Purée in a blender or food processor, then push through a sieve. Mix with the syrup and juice of 1 large lime. Freeze as for lemon sorbet, adding the egg white. Serve straight from the freezer. Serves 8.

RASPBERRY SORBET

Omit the lemons. Purée 450g (1lb) raspberries with 30ml (2 tbsp) lemon juice and 30ml (2 tbsp) Kirsch. Push through a nylon sieve. Add to the syrup. Freeze as for lemon sorbet, adding an extra egg white. Serves about 6.

To Microwave

Pour the water into a large jug and microwave on HIGH for 2 minutes until boiling. Add the sugar and stir well to dissolve. Microwave on HIGH for 3–4 minutes or until syrupy. Cool completely. Complete steps 2 and 3.

To Freeze

Freeze for up to 3 months.

To Thaw and Serve

As step 4. Alternatively, microwave on LOW for about 1–2 minutes to soften slightly.

ICED STRAWBERRY SOUFFLÉ

SERVES 6

225g (8oz) strawberries, hulled

60ml (4 tbsp) almond-flavoured liqueur

30ml (2 tbsp) lemon juice

15ml (1 tbsp) icing sugar

450ml (¾ pint) double cream

15ml (1 tbsp) powdered gelatine

4 eggs, separated

175g (6oz) caster sugar

225g (8oz) strawberries

25g (1oz) small ratafias or macaroons

1 Put the strawberries in a bowl and stir in the liqueur, lemon juice and icing sugar. Cover and leave to marinate for 30 minutes.

2 Put the strawberries in a blender or food processor and work to a purée. Sieve to remove the seeds.

3 Tie a double band of greaseproof paper around the edge of a 1.1 litre (2 pint) soufflé dish to form a 5cm (2 inch) collar. Stand a straight-sided 450g (1lb) jam jar in the centre.

4 Lightly whip 300ml (½ pint) of the cream until it just holds its shape.

5 Put 45ml (3 tbsp) water into a small bowl and sprinkle over the gelatine. Leave to soak for about 5 minutes until spongy. Dissolve over a pan of simmering water.

6 Put the egg yolks and caster sugar in a bowl and whisk with an electric whisk until very light and creamy. Fold in the strawberry purée, whipped cream and dissolved gelatine.

7 Whisk the egg whites until stiff but not dry and fold into the strawberry mixture.

8 Pour the mixture into the prepared dish, keeping the jam jar in the centre. Chill for 1–2 hours until set. Transfer to the freezer for at least 3 hours until firm.

9 Remove the soufflé from the freezer and fill the jam jar with hot water. Twist gently to remove it. Fill the centre with the strawberries. Finely crush the ratafias or macaroons. Ease off the paper collar and coat the sides of the soufflé with crushed ratafias. Whip the remaining cream and use to decorate the soufflé.

10 Transfer the soufflé to the refrigerator for about 2 hours to soften before serving.

To Microwave

Complete steps 1–4. Sprinkle the gelatine over 45ml (3 tbsp) water in a bowl and soak for 5 minutes until spongy. Microwave on HIGH for 1 minute or until dissolved. Do not boil. Stir briskly. Complete steps 6–10.

To Freeze

Cover with plastic wrap at the end of step 8 and overwrap. Freeze for up to 3 months.

To Thaw and Serve

Leave at cool room temperature for 3–4 hours or until just soft. Alternatively, microwave on LOW for about 1½ minutes or until just soft. Complete steps 9 and 10.

VANILLA ICE CREAM

SERVES 4–6

300ml (½ pint) milk

3 egg yolks

50–75g (2–3oz) caster sugar

300ml (½ pint) double cream

1.25ml (¼ tsp) vanilla essence

1 Heat the milk in a saucepan until almost boiling. Beat the egg yolks and sugar in a bowl until well blended. Pour over the milk. Return to the pan and cook over a gentle heat, stirring all the time, until the custard thickens very slightly. It is very important not to let the custard boil or it will curdle. Pour into a bowl and leave to cool.

2 Whisk the cream into the cold custard mixture with the vanilla essence. Freeze for 2 hours or until ice crystals form around the edge of the ice cream.

3 Turn the ice cream into a bowl and beat well to break up the ice crystals. Refreeze for at least 4 hours, preferably overnight.

4 To serve, transfer the ice cream to the refrigerator for 30 minutes to soften slightly, then scoop into individual glasses. Serve immediately.

Variations

STRAWBERRY ICE CREAM

Slice 450g (1lb) strawberries. Sprinkle over 30ml (2 tbsp) icing sugar with 30ml (2 tbsp) lemon juice. Cover and macerate for about 1 hour. Purée in a blender or food processor, then push through a nylon sieve. Complete as for vanilla ice cream, omitting the vanilla essence and adding the strawberry purée with the cream. Serves 6–8.

DOUBLE CHOCOLATE ICE CREAM

Put the milk in a saucepan with 100g (4oz) plain chocolate and heat gently until the chocolate melts, then heat until almost boiling. Complete as for vanilla ice cream, stirring in 50g (2oz) dark chocolate drops at step 3. Serves 4–6.

PEANUT AND TOFFEE ICE CREAM

Put the milk in a saucepan with 75ml (3 tbsp) golden syrup and 30ml (2 tbsp) soft dark brown sugar. Heat gently until the sugar has dissolved, stirring occasionally. Complete the custard as before, then stir in 75ml (3 tbsp) crunchy peanut butter. Serve straight from the freezer. Serves 4–6.

To Microwave

Pour the milk into a large bowl and microwave on HIGH for 3 minutes or until almost boiling. Beat the egg yolks and sugar until well blended, pour over the milk and return to the large bowl. Microwave on LOW for 12–15 minutes or until slightly thickened, stirring frequently. Do not boil or the custard will curdle. Leave to cool. Complete steps 2–4.

To Freeze

Freeze for up to 3 months.

To Thaw and Serve

As step 4. Alternatively, microwave on LOW for about 1–2 minutes to soften slightly. Serve immediately.

CHRISTMAS PUDDING ICE CREAM

SERVES 4–6

100g (4oz) mixed no-soak dried fruit
25g (1oz) glacé cherries, halved
90ml (6 tbsp) port
grated rind and juice of 1 orange
450ml (15 fl oz) single cream
3 eggs
100g (4oz) caster sugar
150ml (¼ pint) whipping cream

1 Place the mixed dried fruit and glacé cherries in a bowl and spoon over the port and orange rind and juice. Cover and leave to soak overnight.
2 Heat the single cream in a saucepan until almost boiling. Beat the eggs with the sugar in a bowl until well mixed. Pour on the milk, return to the pan and cook over a gentle heat, without boiling, until the custard coats the back of the spoon. Strain, then cool for 30 minutes.
3 Whip the cream until stiff and mix into the custard with the fruit and port mixture.
4 Turn into a large bowl and freeze for 2 hours until mushy. Mix well and pack into a 1.1 litre (2 pint) pudding basin base-lined with non-stick paper. Freeze for 2–3 hours until firm.
5 To serve, remove from the freezer approximately 20 minutes before serving. Turn out onto a cold plate. Serve immediately.

To Microwave

Complete step 1. Pour the single cream into a bowl and microwave on HIGH for 2–3 minutes until hot. Beat the eggs with the sugar until well mixed. Pour on the milk, return to the bowl and microwave on HIGH for 1 minute, then on LOW for 6 minutes or until the custard thinly coats the back of a spoon, whisking frequently. Strain, then cool for 30 minutes. Complete steps 3–5.

To Freeze

Overwrap and freeze for up to 3 months.

To Thaw and Serve

As step 5. Alternatively, microwave on LOW for about 2–3 minutes. Turn out, then serve.

BAKING

ECCLES CAKES

MAKES 8

25g (1oz) butter
100g (4oz) currants
25g (1oz) chopped mixed peel
50g (2oz) demerara sugar
2.5ml (½ tsp) ground mixed spice
212g (7½oz) packet frozen puff pastry, thawed
1 egg white
caster sugar, for sprinkling

1 Melt the butter in a saucepan, then stir in the currants, peel, sugar and spice. Mix thoroughly.
2 On a lightly floured surface, roll out the pastry very thinly. Cut out eight 12.5cm (5 inch) rounds, using a saucer as a guide. Divide the fruit mixture between the rounds, damp the edges of the pastry and draw them to the centre, sealing well together.
3 Turn the cakes over and roll gently into rounds with a rolling pin. Brush with egg white and sprinkle with caster sugar. Make three diagonal cuts across the top of each. Place on dampened baking sheets.
4 Bake in the oven at 220°C (425°F) mark 7 for about 15 minutes or until light golden brown. Eccles cakes are best eaten slightly warm.

To Microwave
Dice the butter into a bowl and microwave on HIGH for 45 seconds. Stir in the currants, peel, sugar and spice. Mix thoroughly together. Complete steps 2–4.

To Freeze
Cool, pack in a rigid container and freeze for up to 3 months.

To Thaw and Serve
Unwrap and leave at cool room temperature for 4–6 hours. Alternatively, place four cakes at a time on absorbent kitchen paper on a rack. Microwave on LOW for about 25–35 seconds. Test and turn after 30 seconds. Stand for 10 minutes.

PEANUT COOKIES

MAKES ABOUT 20

50g (2oz) butter
75g (3oz) crunchy peanut butter
50g (2oz) soft light brown sugar
1 egg
150g (5oz) plain wholemeal flour
2.5ml (½ tsp) baking powder
50g (2oz) unsalted peanuts, roughly chopped

1 Beat the butter, peanut butter, sugar and egg together in a bowl until evenly blended. Stir in the flour and baking powder.
2 Roll a little of the mixture (about the size of a walnut) in your hands until smooth. Place well apart on baking sheets and flatten lightly with a fork. Chill for about 15 minutes.
3 Sprinkle peanuts over each biscuit.
4 Bake in the oven at 190°C (375°F) mark 5 for about 12 minutes or until pale golden.
5 Cool for about 5 minutes to firm up slightly, then transfer to a wire rack to cool completely.

To Microwave
Complete steps 1–3, arranging five of the biscuits, well apart in a circle, on a piece of baking parchment on the floor of the microwave. Microwave on HIGH for 2–2½ minutes or until the surface of the biscuits are dry. Stand for 5 minutes, then transfer to a wire rack to cool completely. Repeat with the remaining biscuits in batches of five.

To Freeze
Cool, pack in a rigid container and freeze for up to 6 months.

To Thaw and Serve
Leave overnight at cool room temperature. Alternatively, arrange five cookies at a time in a circle on a piece of baking parchment on the floor of the microwave. Microwave on HIGH for about 1½– 2 minutes. Stand for 5 minutes.

CHOCOLATE BRAZIL CAKE

SERVES 8–10

175g (6oz) Brazil nuts
300g (11oz) plain chocolate
butter
100g (4oz) caster sugar
4 eggs, separated
30ml (2 tbsp) cornflour
100g (4oz) icing sugar
plain and milk chocolate curls, to decorate (see Note)

1 Grease a 1.7 litre (3 pint) ring tin. Dust with flour and shake out the excess. Grind the Brazil nuts in a food processor.

2 Break 200g (7oz) of the chocolate into a small bowl and add 30ml (2 tbsp) water. Place over a saucepan of gently simmering water until melted. Remove from the heat and stir until smooth.

3 Cream 100g (4oz) butter with the caster sugar in a bowl until very pale and fluffy. Gradually beat in the egg yolks and cornflour. Fold in the cooled chocolate and Brazil nuts.

4 Whisk the egg whites until stiff but not dry. Stir one spoonful of egg white into the mixture to loosen it. Gently fold in the remainder. Spoon into the prepared tin.

5 Bake in the oven at 170°C (325°F) mark 3 for about 1 hour 20 minutes or until a skewer inserted into the centre comes out clean. Leave to cool in the tin for 5 minutes. Turn out on to a wire rack to cool completely.

6 Place the remaining chocolate in a bowl with a knob of butter and 60ml (4 tbsp) water. Melt over a saucepan of simmering water as in step 2. Beat in the sifted icing sugar until smooth. Cool, then refrigerate until the consistency of lightly whipped cream for about 15 minutes.

7 Place the cake on its rack over a baking sheet. Spread over the chocolate icing until thinly coated. Decorate with curls of chocolate. Leave to set for about 30 minutes before using.

Note: To make chocolate curls, allow a bar of chocolate to come to room temperature. Over a sheet of foil or greaseproof paper, draw a swivel potato peeler across the smooth surface of the bar to form small curls.

To Microwave

Complete step 1. Break 200g (7oz) of the chocolate into a small bowl and add 30ml (2 tbsp) water. Microwave on HIGH for 1 minute or until melted. Stir well until smooth. Complete steps 3–5. Place the remaining chocolate in a bowl with a knob of butter and 60ml (4 tbsp) water. Microwave on HIGH for 1 minute. Stir well, then beat in the sifted icing sugar until smooth. Complete steps 6 and 7.

To Freeze

Open freeze at the end of step 7, overwrap in foil, greaseproof paper or plastic wrap and seal in a polythene bag. Freeze for up to 4 months.

To Thaw and Serve

Leave unwrapped on a wire rack at cool room temperature for 4 hours. Alternatively, unwrap and carefully place the cake on kitchen paper on a rack. Microwave on LOW for about 1–1½ minutes. Test and turn after 1 minute. Stand for 5 minutes.

BANANA ROCK CAKES

MAKES ABOUT 10

200g (7oz) plain wheatmeal flour
7.5ml (1½ tsp) baking powder
75g (3oz) butter
15ml (1 tbsp) soft light brown sugar
50g (2oz) sultanas
225g (8oz) bananas
5ml (1 tsp) lemon juice
1 egg, lightly beaten

1 Place the flour and baking powder in a bowl. Using a fork, cut in the butter until the mixture resembles breadcrumbs. Stir in the sugar and sultanas, then make a well in the centre.

2 Mash the bananas with the lemon juice and stir in the egg. Pour this mixture into the dry ingredients and beat until well mixed.

3 Spoon the mixture into about 10 mounds on a baking sheet, allowing room for spreading.

4 Bake in the oven at 200°C (400°F) mark 6 for about 15 minutes or until the cakes are well risen and golden brown. Transfer to a wire rack to cool.

To Freeze

Cool, pack in a rigid container and freeze for up to 4 months.

To Thaw and Serve

Unwrap and leave at cool room temperature for 3–4 hours. Alternatively, arrange four cakes at a time on absorbent kitchen paper on a rack. Microwave on LOW for about 1–1½ minutes. Stand for 5 minutes.

MARBLED CHOCOLATE TEABREAD

SERVES 8–10

225g (8oz) butter

225g (8oz) caster sugar

4 eggs, beaten

225g (8oz) self-raising flour

finely grated rind of 1 large orange

15ml (1 tbsp) orange juice

few drops orange flower water (optional)

75g (3oz) plain chocolate

15ml (1 tbsp) cocoa powder

1 Grease a 900ml (2 pint) loaf tin and line the base and sides with greaseproof paper.

2 Cream the butter and sugar together until pale and fluffy, then gradually beat in the eggs, beating well after each addition. Fold in the flour.

3 Transfer half the mixture to another bowl and fold in rind, juice and orange water, if using.

4 Break the chocolate into pieces, put into a small bowl and place over a pan of simmering water. Stir until chocolate melts. Cool slightly, before folding into the plain cake mixture with the cocoa powder.

5 Put alternate spoonfuls of the two mixtures into the prepared tin. Use a palette knife to swirl through the mixture to make a marbled effect, then level the surface.

6 Bake at 180°C (350°F) mark 4 for 1¼–1½ hours, until well risen and firm to the touch. Turn out on to a wire rack to cool.

To Microwave

Grease a 1.7 litre (3 pint) ring mould. Complete steps 2 and 3, adding an extra 30ml (2 tbsp) milk. Break the chocolate into a small bowl and microwave on LOW for 2–3 minutes, until melted. Complete the remainder of step 4, adding 15ml (1 tbsp) milk, and step 5. Cover with kitchen paper, stand on a roasting rack and microwave on HIGH for 8–10 minutes, until well risen and firm.

To Freeze

Cool, overwrap in foil, greaseproof paper or plastic wrap and seal in a polythene bag. Freeze for up to 4 months.

To Thaw and Serve

Leave at cool at room temperature for 4–6 hours or overnight. Alternatively, place the cake on absorbent kitchen paper on a rack. Microwave on LOW for about 3½–4½ minutes. Test and turn after 2 minutes. Stand for 15 minutes.

CHELSEA BUNS

MAKES 12

15g (½oz) fresh yeast or 7.5ml (1½ tsp) dried

100ml (4fl oz) warm milk

225g (8oz) strong white flour

2.5ml (½ tsp) salt

40g (1½oz) butter, diced

1 egg, beaten

100g (4oz) mixed dried fruit

50g (2oz) light soft brown sugar

clear honey, to glaze

1 Grease a 18cm (7 inch) square tin.

2 Blend the fresh yeast with the milk. If using dried yeast, sprinkle it into the milk and leave in a warm place for 15 minutes until frothy.

3 Put the flour and salt in a bowl, then rub in 25g (1oz) of the butter until the mixture resembles fine breadcrumbs. Make a well in the centre, pour in the yeast liquid and the egg. Beat until mixture forms a dough that leaves sides of bowl clean.

4 Turn out on to a lightly floured surface and knead well for 10 minutes until smooth and elastic. Cover with a clean tea towel and leave in a warm place for about 1 hour until doubled in size.

5 Turn out the dough on to a floured surface and knead lightly, then roll out to a large rectangle, measuring about 30.5 × 23cm (12 × 9 inches). Mix the dried fruit and sugar together. Melt the remaining butter, then brush over the dough. Scatter with the fruit mixture, leaving a 2.5cm (1 inch) border around the edges.

6 Roll the dough up tightly like a Swiss roll, starting at a long edge. Press the edges together to seal them, then cut the roll into 12 slices. Place the rolls, cut side uppermost, in the prepared tin. Cover and leave in a warm place for about 30 minutes until doubled in size.

7 Bake in the oven at 190°C (375°F) mark 5 for 30 minutes or until well risen and golden brown. Brush with the honey while hot. Leave to cool slightly in the tin. Transfer to a wire rack; serve warm.

To Microwave

Complete steps 2–6, placing the rolls in a greased 20.5cm (8 inch) round dish. Complete the remainder of step 6. Stand the dish on a rack. Microwave on HIGH for 6–8 minutes or until well risen and firm to the touch. Stand for 10 minutes. Turn out, brush all over with the honey and brown under a hot grill. Serve warm.

To Freeze

Cool, overwrap in foil, greaseproof paper or plastic wrap and seal in a polythene bag. Freeze for up to 3 months.

To Thaw and Serve

Unwrap and leave at cool room temperature for 3–4 hours. Alternatively, place four buns at a time on absorbent kitchen paper on a rack. Microwave on LOW for about 25–35 seconds. Test and turn after 30 seconds. Stand for 2–3 minutes.

CHERRY AND ALMOND CAKE

SERVES ABOUT 12

275g (10oz) glacé cherries
225g (8oz) butter, softened
225g (8oz) caster sugar
6 eggs, beaten
65g (2½oz) self raising flour
pinch of salt
175g (6oz) ground almonds
2.5ml (½ tsp) almond flavouring
icing sugar, to decorate

1 Grease a deep 23cm (9 inch) loose-based round cake tin and line the base and sides with greaseproof paper. Grease the paper.
2 Arrange the cherries in the bottom of the tin.
3 Cream the butter and sugar together in a bowl until pale and fluffy. Beat in eggs a little at a time, adding flour if the mixture shows signs of curdling.
4 Sift in the remaining flour and salt, then add the ground almonds and almond flavouring. Turn the mixture into the prepared tin.
5 Bake at 180°C (350°F) mark 4 for 1 hour or until firm to the touch. Cover with greaseproof paper if browning too quickly. Cool in the tin.
6 When the cake is cold, remove from the tin and dredge the top with icing sugar to decorate.

To Freeze

Cool, overwrap in foil, greaseproof paper or plastic wrap and seal in a polythene bag without dredging with icing sugar. Freeze for up to 4 months.

To Thaw and Serve

Leave unwrapped on a wire rack at cool room temperature for 3–4 hours. Alternatively, unwrap and place the cake on absorbent kitchen paper on a rack. Microwave on LOW for about 1–1½ minutes, turning after 1 minute. Stand for 5 minutes.

CHOCOLATE AND ORANGE CAKE

SERVES 6–8

100g (4oz) butter
100g (4oz) sugar
1 egg, beaten
175g (6oz) self raising flour
30ml (2 tbsp) cocoa powder, sifted
5ml (1 tsp) bicarbonate of soda
175ml (6fl oz) milk
300ml (½ pint) whipping cream
10ml (2 tsp) orange-flavoured liqueur
grated rind and segments of 1 orange

1 Lightly grease two 15cm (6 inch) cake tins.
2 Melt the butter and sugar in a saucepan over a low heat. Leave to cool for 2 minutes. Add the egg and beat well. Fold in the flour and cocoa powder. Mix the bicarbonate of soda and milk together, then add slowly to the mixture. Pour into the prepared tins.
3 Bake in the oven at 180°C (350°F) mark 4 for 25 minutes or until cooked and risen.
4 Leave in the tins for 2 minutes, then turn out on to a wire rack to cool completely.
5 Whip the cream stiffly. Fold in the liqueur and most of the orange rind. Use to sandwich the cakes together, reserving a little for the top. Decorate with the remaining cream mixture and orange.

To Microwave

Place the butter and sugar in a large bowl and microwave on HIGH for 3 minutes until melted. Cool for 2 minutes. Complete step 2, pouring the mixture into a deep 18cm (7 inch) cake dish, base lined with greaseproof paper. Microwave on HIGH for 6–7 minutes or until the cake looks risen but still looks slightly moist on the surface. Stand for 10 minutes. Complete step 4. Cut the cake in half, then complete step 5.

To Freeze

Cool, overwrap in foil, greaseproof paper or plastic wrap and seal in a polythene bag at the end of step 4. Freeze for up to 3 months.

To Thaw and Serve

Leave unwrapped on a wire rack at cool room temperature for 3–4 hours. Alternatively, unwrap and place the cake on absorbent kitchen paper on a rack. Microwave on LOW for about 1–1½ minutes. Test and turn after 1 minute. Stand for 5 minutes. Complete step 5.

SPICED FRUIT CAKE

SERVES 12–14

250g (9oz) prunes, stoned

175g (6oz) glacé cherries, roughly chopped

250g (9oz) sultanas

40g (1½oz) cut mixed peel

30ml (2 tbsp) whisky

450g (1lb) plain wholemeal flour

20ml (4 tsp) baking powder

10ml (2 tsp) ground mixed spice

175g (6oz) soft dark brown sugar

300ml (½ pint) grapeseed oil

4 eggs, lightly beaten

60ml (4 tbsp) milk

1 Snip the prunes into small pieces. Place the prunes and cherries in a bowl with the sultanas and mixed peel. Stir in the whisky, cover and leave to stand in a cool place overnight.

2 Grease and line the base and sides of a 20.5cm (8 inch) square cake tin.

3 Place the flour, baking powder, spice and sugar in a bowl. Make a well in the centre and add the oil, eggs and milk. Beat well for about 3 minutes until very smooth. Stir in the fruit and spoon into the prepared tin.

4 Bake in the oven at 170°C (325°F) mark 3 for 1 hour, reduce the heat to 150°C (300°F) mark 2 and bake for a further 1¼ hours or until the cake is cooked. (Cover lightly with foil if necessary.) A skewer inserted into the centre of the cake should come out clean.

5 Leave the cake in the tin to cool. Turn out, then wrap in greaseproof paper and foil. Leave for 2–3 days to mature.

To Freeze

Overwrap in foil, greaseproof paper or plastic wrap and seal in a polythene bag after maturing. Freeze for up to 4 months. The cake will become more crumbly after freezing.

To Thaw and Serve

Leave wrapped overnight at cool room temperature. Alternatively, unwrap and place the cake on absorbent kitchen paper on a rack. Microwave on LOW for about 1–1½ minutes. Test and turn after 1 minute. Stand for 5 minutes.

APRICOT CRUNCH

MAKES 16 WEDGES

75g (3oz) dried apricots

100g (4oz) butter

100g (4oz) demerara sugar

75ml (5 tbsp) golden syrup

200g (7oz) crunchy toasted muesli cereal

150g (5oz) rolled oats

2.5ml (½ tsp) ground mixed spice

10ml (2 tsp) lemon juice

1 Line the bases of two 18cm (7 inch) round sandwich tins with non-stick paper.

2 Simmer the apricots gently in 200ml (⅓ pint) water for about 10 minutes or until softened. Press through a sieve or purée in a blender and food processor until smooth. Cool for 1 hour.

3 Slowly melt the butter, sugar and syrup in a saucepan. Stir in the cereal and oats and continue stirring until thoroughly combined. Add the puréed apricots, mixed spice and lemon juice. Mix well.

4 Divide the mixture between the prepared tins and spread evenly over the base. Press down well to level the surface.

5 Bake in the oven at 180°C (350°F) mark 4 for about 35 minutes. Cut each round into eight wedges. Cool in the tin for 30 minutes until firm. Carefully ease the wedges out of the tin.

To Microwave

Line the bases of two 18cm (7 inch) non-metallic round sandwich tins with non-stick paper. Put the apricots and 200ml (⅓ pint) water into a bowl. Part cover and microwave on HIGH for 6–8 minutes or until softened. Push through a sieve or purée in a blender or food processor until smooth. Cool for 1 hour. Place the butter, sugar and syrup in a bowl and microwave on HIGH for 2–3 minutes or until the sugar has dissolved, stirring once. Complete steps 3–5.

To Freeze

Cool, overwrap in foil, greaseproof paper or plastic wrap and seal in a polythene bag. Freeze for up to 4 months.

To Thaw and Serve

Unwrap and leave at cool room temperature for 3–4 hours. Alternatively, arrange four wedges at a time on a sheet of absorbent kitchen paper on a rack. Microwave on LOW for about 30–60 seconds. Stand for 10 minutes.

GINGERBREAD SQUARES

MAKES ONE 18CM (7 INCH) CAKE

175g (6oz) golden syrup
50g (2oz) black treacle
45ml (3 tbsp) orange marmalade
225g (8oz) butter
250g (9oz) plain wholemeal flour
3.75ml (¾ tsp) bicarbonate of soda
30ml (2 tbsp) ground ginger
5ml (1 tsp) ground cinnamon
50g (2oz) soft dark brown sugar
finely grated rind and juice of 1 lemon
150ml (¼ pint) milk
2 eggs

1 Grease and line the base of an 18cm (7 inch) square cake tin.
2 Weigh the syrup and treacle into a saucepan, add the marmalade and butter and heat, stirring gently, until the mixture is evenly blended. Cool.
3 Place the flour, bicarbonate of soda, spices and sugar together in a bowl. Add the finely grated rind of the lemon, then make a well in the centre.
4 Whisk the milk and eggs, stir in 15ml (1 tbsp) lemon juice. Pour into the well with the syrup and marmalade. Gradually beat in the flour.
5 Beat the mixture thoroughly (it should be very runny), then pour it into the prepared tin.
6 Bake in the oven at 140°C (275°F) mark 1 for about 2¼ hours or until the gingerbread is well risen and just firm to the touch.
7 Cool slightly in the tin, then turn out on to a wire rack to cool completely. Wrap the cold cake in greaseproof paper, then overwrap in foil and store in a cool place for at least 3 days. Cut into squares.

To Microwave
Complete step 1. Weigh the syrup and treacle into a large bowl, then add the marmalade and butter. Microwave on HIGH for 1 minute. Stir well until evenly blended. Complete steps 3–7.

To Freeze
Pack in a rigid container after maturing and freeze for up to 4 months.

To Thaw and Serve
Leave unwrapped at cool room temperature for 4–6 hours or overnight. Alternatively, unwrap and place the squares on absorbent kitchen paper on a rack. Microwave on LOW for about 1–1½ minutes. Test and turn after 1 minute. Stand for 5 minutes.

COCONUT CHOCOLATE COOKIES

MAKES ABOUT 20

175g (6oz) self raising flour
15g (½oz) cocoa powder
100g (4oz) butter
100g (4oz) caster sugar
25g (1oz) desiccated coconut
50g (2oz) plain chocolate chips
pinch of salt
1 egg, lightly beaten
5ml (1 tsp) vanilla essence

1 Grease and line two baking sheets.
2 Sift the flour and cocoa powder into a bowl. Rub in the butter until the mixture resembles fine breadcrumbs. Stir in the sugar, salt, desiccated coconut and chocolate chips.
3 Stir in the beaten egg and vanilla essence to form a smooth, stiff mixture. Knead lightly on a floured surface. Divide into about 24 pieces and roll into walnut-size balls.
4 Arrange the biscuits on the prepared baking sheets, leaving space between each one. Press each biscuit with a fork dipped in cold water to flatten slightly.
5 Bake in the oven at 200°C (400°F) mark 6 for 10–15 minutes or until dry on top. Leave for 5 minutes, then transfer to a wire rack to cool completely.

To Microwave
Complete steps 1–3. Arrange five of the biscuits in a circle on a piece of baking parchment on the floor of the microwave. Press each biscuit with a fork to flatten slightly. Microwave on HIGH for 2–2½ minutes or until the surface of the biscuits are dry. Stand for 5 minutes. Transfer to a wire rack to cool completely. Repeat with the remaining biscuits in batches of five.

To Freeze
Open freeze at the end of step 4, pack in a polythene bag and freeze for up to 6 months.

To Thaw and Serve
Place the biscuits on two greased and lined baking sheets. Bake in the oven at 190°C (375°F) mark 5 for about 15–20 minutes. Alternatively, arrange six biscuits in a circle on a piece of baking parchment on the floor of the microwave. Microwave on HIGH for 1–2 minutes. Stand for 5 minutes. Transfer to a wire rack to cool completely.

CARROT CAKE

SERVES 8

225g (8oz) butter

225g (8oz) light soft brown sugar

4 eggs, separated

finely grated rind of ½ orange

20ml (4 tsp) lemon juice

175g (6oz) self raising flour

5ml (1 tsp) baking powder

50g (2oz) ground almonds

150g (5oz) walnut pieces, chopped

225g (8oz) carrots, peeled and grated

225g (8oz) full fat soft cheese

10ml (2 tsp) clear honey

1 Grease and line a deep 20.5cm (8 inch) round cake tin.

2 Cream the butter and sugar together in a bowl until pale and fluffy. Beat in the egg yolks, then stir in the orange rind and 15ml (1 tbsp) of the lemon juice.

3 Sift in the flour and baking powder, then stir in the ground almonds, 100g (4oz) of the walnuts and the carrots.

4 Whisk the egg whites until stiff, then fold into the cake mixture. Pour into the prepared tin and hollow the centre slightly.

5 Bake in the oven at 180°C (350°F) mark 4 for about 1½ hours. Cover the top with foil after 1 hour if it starts to brown.

6 Leave to cool slightly. Turn out on to a wire rack and remove the lining paper. Leave to cool.

7 To make the topping, beat the cheese, honey and remaining lemon juice together and spread over the top of the cake. Sprinkle the topping with the remaining walnuts.

To Microwave

Grease a 1.6 litre (2¾ pint) ring mould. Complete steps 2–4, stirring in 30ml (2 tbsp) milk. Stand the mould on a roasting rack and microwave on HIGH for 10–12 minutes or until risen, firm, but still looking slightly moist on the surface. Stand for 10 minutes. Complete steps 6 and 7.

To Freeze

Cool, overwrap in foil, greaseproof paper or plastic wrap and seal in a polythene bag at the end of step 5. Freeze for up to 4 months.

To Thaw and Serve

Leave unwrapped at cool room temperature for 4–6 hours or overnight. Alternatively, unwrap and place the cake on absorbent kitchen paper on rack. Microwave on LOW for about 1½–2 minutes. Test and turn after 1 minute. Stand for 5 minutes. Complete steps 6 and 7.

APRICOT ALMOND CAKE

SERVES 8–10

butter

175g (6oz) caster sugar

3 eggs

225g (8oz) self raising white flour

225g (8oz) no-soak dried apricots, roughly chopped

50g (2oz) ground almonds

grated rind of 1 orange

about 30ml (2 tbsp) milk

50g (2oz) plain flour

50g (2oz) light soft brown sugar

50g (2oz) flaked almonds, chopped

pinch of grated nutmeg

1 Grease a deep 20.5cm (8 inch) round cake tin and line with greaseproof paper.

2 Cream 175g (6oz) butter with the caster sugar together in a bowl until pale and fluffy. Gradually beat in the eggs. Fold in the self raising flour, apricots, ground almonds and orange rind. Add enough milk to give a soft dropping consistency. Spoon into the prepared tin and level the surface.

3 Rub 25g (1oz) butter into the plain flour until the mixture resembles breadcrumbs. Stir in the brown sugar, flaked almonds and nutmeg. Sprinkle over the mixture.

4 Bake in the oven at 170°C (325°F) mark 3 for about 1½ hours or until a skewer inserted into the centre comes out clean. Cool in the tin for 5 minutes. Turn out on to a wire rack. Remove the lining paper.

To Freeze

Cool, overwrap in foil, greaseproof paper or plastic wrap and seal in a polythene bag. Freeze for up to 4 months.

To Thaw and Serve

Leave unwrapped at cool room temperature for 3–4 hours. Alternatively, unwrap and place the cake on absorbent kitchen paper on a rack. Microwave on LOW for about 1–1½ minutes. Stand for 5 minutes.

MARMALADE TEABREAD

SERVES 8–10

200g (7oz) plain flour
5ml (1 tsp) ground ginger
5ml (t tsp) baking powder
50g (2oz) butter, diced
50g (2oz) light soft brown sugar
60ml (4 tbsp) orange marmalade
1 egg, beaten
75ml (3 tbsp) milk
25g (1oz) candied orange peel, chopped

1 Grease a 750ml (1½ pint) loaf tin, then line the base with greaseproof paper and grease the paper.
2 Put the flour, ginger and baking powder in a bowl and rub in the butter until the mixture resembles fine breadcrumbs. Stir in the sugar.
3 Mix together the marmalade, egg and most of the milk. Stir into the prepared tin, level the surface and press the candied orange peel on top. Bake at 170°C (325°F) mark 3 for about 1¼ hours or until golden brown. Turn out on to a wire rack to cool. Serve spread with butter.

To Freeze
Cool, overwrap in foil, greaseproof paper or plastic wrap and seal in a polythene bag. Freeze for up to 4 months.

To Thaw and Serve
Leave at cool room temperature for 4–6 hours or overnight. Alternatively place the cake on absorbent kitchen paper on a rack. Microwave on LOW for about 2½–3½ minutes. Test and turn after 1 minute. Stand for 15 minutes.

HONEY CAKE

MAKES 12–16 squares

225ml (8fl oz) clear honey plus 45ml (3 tbsp)
75g (3oz) butter
350g (12oz) plain wholemeal flour
pinch of salt
5ml (1 tsp) ground mixed spice
5ml (1 tsp) bicarbonate of soda
50g (2oz) glacé cherries, halved
50g (2oz) chopped mixed peel
3 eggs
45ml (3 tbsp) milk
grated rind of 1 large lemon
25g (1oz) flaked almonds

1 Grease a 20.5cm (8 inch) square cake tin and line the base and sides with greaseproof paper.
2 Pour 225ml (8fl oz) honey into a saucepan, add the butter and heat gently, stirring, until blended. Sift the flour, salt, spice, and bicarbonate of soda into a large bowl, stirring in any bran left in the sieve. Add the cherries and peel.
3 Beat the eggs and the milk together and stir into the honey mixture with the lemon rind. Pour gradually onto the dry ingredients, beating well after each addition, until well blended.
4 Turn the mixture into the prepared tin and sprinkle with flaked almonds. Bake at 170°C (325°F) mark 3 for about 1¼ hours, until the cake is firm to the touch or a skewer inserted into the centre of the cake comes out clean.
5 Using a skewer, prick the top of the cake and spoon over the remaining honey. Turn out and leave to cool on a wire rack. Do not remove from the lining paper until the cake is cold.

To Microwave
Complete step 1. Put 225ml (8fl oz) honey and the butter in a medium bowl and microwave on HIGH for 2 minutes or until the butter has melted. Complete the recipe.

To Freeze
Overwrap in foil, greaseproof or plastic wrap and seal in a polythene bag. Freeze for up to 4 months.

To Thaw and Serve
Leave unwrapped at cool room temperature for 4–6 hours or overnight. Alternatively unwrap, and place on a sheet of absorbent kitchen paper on a rack. Microwave on LOW for about 3½–4½ minutes. Test and turn after 2 minutes. Stand for 15 minutes.

SPICED PECAN AND APPLE LOAF

SERVES 8–10

unsalted butter
2 eggs
few drops of vanilla essence
225g (8oz) caster sugar
100g (4oz) self raising white flour
100g (4oz) self raising wholemeal flour
pinch of salt
450g (1lb) cooking apples
75g (3oz) pecan nuts, chopped
10ml (2 tsp) ground ginger
25g (1oz) demerara sugar
45ml (3 tbsp) clear honey

1 Grease two 900ml (1½ pint) loaf tins and line with greaseproof paper.
2 Melt 150g (5oz) butter. Cool. With an electric whisk, beat the eggs, vanilla essence and caster sugar in a bowl until thick and pale. Whisk in the melted butter. With a large metal spoon, fold in the flours and salt.
3 Spoon a quarter of the mixture into each tin. Level the surfaces. Peel, core and thinly slice two-thirds of the apples. Divide between tins. Sprinkle 25g (1oz) of the pecan nuts and 2.5ml (½ tsp) of the ginger over each tin. Finish each tin with the remaining cake mixture.
4 Thinly slice the remaining apple into a small bowl. Add remaining nuts, 25g (1oz) melted butter, remaining ginger, demerara sugar and mix together. Arrange half the apple mixture over the surface of each cake.
5 Bake in the oven at 180°C (350°F) mark 4 for about 1 hour 20 minutes or until a skewer inserted into the centre comes out clean. Leave in the tins to cool for about 10 minutes. Turn out on to a wire rack. Remove the lining paper. Brush with honey.

To Freeze
Cool, overwrap in foil, greaseproof paper or plastic wrap and seal in a polythene bag. Freeze for up to 4 months.

To Thaw and Serve
Leave unwrapped at cool room temperature for about 3–4 hours. Alternatively, unwrap and stand each cake on absorbent kitchen paper on a rack. Microwave separately on LOW for about 1–1½ minutes. Test and turn after 1 minute. Stand for 5 minutes.

HOT MUSTARD LOAF

SERVES 6–8

175g (6oz) butter, softened
30ml (2 tbsp) wholegrain mustard
salt and pepper
1 large French loaf

1 Beat the butter, mustard and seasoning together in a bowl.
2 Slice the loaf into 1cm (½ inch) slices. Spread both sides of each slice with the mustard butter, then sandwich together again. Wrap in foil, in one or two parcels, depending on the size of the oven.
3 Bake in the oven at 220°C (425°F) mark 7 for 20 minutes or until crisp and piping hot. Serve at once.

Variations
HOT GARLIC BREAD
Follow the recipe above, omitting the mustard and adding 2 cloves crushed garlic and 45ml (3 tbsp) chopped fresh parsley.

HOT HERB BREAD
Follow the recipe above, omitting the mustard and adding 45ml (3 tbsp) chopped fresh herbs, such as parsley, chives and thyme.

To Microwave
Dice the butter into a bowl and microwave on HIGH for 30–40 seconds or until just soft enough to spread. Beat in the flavouring and season to taste. Cut the loaf into 1cm (½ inch) slices. Spread both sides of each slice with the flavoured butter, then sandwich together again. Wrap in greaseproof paper and microwave on HIGH for 1–2 minutes or until the bread is hot. Unwrap and stand for 1–2 minutes before serving.

To Freeze
Cool, overwrap in foil, greaseproof paper or plastic wrap and seal in a polythene bag. Freeze for up to 1 month.

To Thaw and Serve
Leave wrapped at cool room temperature for 4–6 hours. Alternatively, stand the loaf on absorbent kitchen paper and microwave on LOW for about 6–8 minutes, turning over during cooking. Stand for 5–15 minutes. Refresh in a hot oven for 5–10 minutes.

ONION LOAF

SERVES 8–10

15g (1/2oz) fresh yeast or 7.5ml (1½ tsp) dried and 5ml (1 tsp) sugar
225ml (8fl oz) tepid milk
350g (12oz) strong plain white flour
5ml (1 tsp) salt
pinch of cayenne
25g (1oz) butter
15ml (1 tbsp) vegetable oil
175g (6oz) onions, skinned and thinly sliced
1 egg yolk, lightly beaten

1 Blend the fresh yeast with the milk. If using dried yeast, sprinkle it into the milk with the sugar and leave in a warm place until frothy.

2 Place the flour, salt and cayenne in a bowl, then 'cut' the butter through the flour using a fork. Make a well in the centre of the flour and pour in the yeast liquid. Mix to a soft dough. Turn out on to a lightly floured surface and knead until smooth and no longer sticky – about 7 minutes.

3 Place the dough in a lightly oiled bowl, cover with a clean tea towel and leave in a warm place for about 1 hour or until doubled in size.

4 Knock back the dough and knead, then shape into a flat round, about 18cm (7 inch) in diameter. Place on a floured baking sheet and, with a sharp knife, slash the dough deeply into six wedges. Cover in a warm place for about 30 minutes until doubled in size.

5 Meanwhile, heat the oil in a frying pan and cook the onions, covered, until they are beginning to soften but not colour. Drain well.

6 Uncover the dough, brush with the egg yolk and spoon over the onions. Bake in the oven at 220°C (425°F) mark 7 for 15–20 minutes then reduce the temperature to 200°C (400°F) mark 6 and bake for 15–20 minutes or until risen, hollow-sounding when tapped on the base and the onions are golden. Cover with foil if necessary. Serve warm.

To Freeze

Cool, overwrap and seal in a polythene bag. Freeze for up to 1 month.

To Thaw and Serve

Leave wrapped at cool room temperature for 4–6 hours. Alternatively, stand the loaf on absorbent kitchen paper and microwave on LOW for about 4–6 minutes, turning over during cooking. Stand for 5–15 minutes. Refresh in a hot oven for 5–10 minutes.

PARSNIP BREAD

SERVES 8

450g (1lb) parsnips, peeled and cut into chunks
25g (1oz) butter
15g (1/2oz) fresh yeast or 7.5ml (1½ tsp) dried and 5ml (1 tsp) sugar
milk
450g (1lb) granary flour
5ml (1 tsp) salt
30ml (2 tbsp) cracked wheat

1 Lightly grease a baking sheet.

2 Cook the parsnips in a saucepan of boiling salted water for about 20 minutes or until tender. Drain well. Mash until smooth, adding the butter.

3 Blend the fresh yeast with 225ml (8fl oz) milk. If using dried yeast, sprinkle it into the milk with the sugar and leave in a warm place until frothy.

4 Place the flour and salt in a bowl and stir in the parsnip purée. Make a well in the centre and pour in the yeast liquid. Mix to a soft dough. Turn out on to a lightly floured surface and knead until smooth and no longer sticky – about 7 minutes.

5 Place the dough in a lightly oiled bowl. Cover with a clean tea towel and leave in a warm place for about 1 hour or until doubled in size.

6 Knock back the dough and divide into three. Knead and roll out each piece into a 35.5cm (14 inch) long sausage shape. Place the strips on the baking sheet, pinching them at one end to join. Without stretching the dough, plait the loaf. Make sure that the bottom edges are sealed.

7 Brush dough with milk and sprinkle over wheat. Leave in a warm place until doubled in size.

8 Bake in the oven at 200°C (400°F) mark 6 for 30 minutes until golden and sounds hollow when tapped on the base. Cover with foil if necessary.

To Microwave

Complete steps 1–7. Place the loaf on a roasting rack and microwave on HIGH for 6–8 minutes or until well risen and firm to the touch. Stand for 10 minutes. Turn out and grill until brown.

To Freeze

Cool, overwrap and seal in a polythene bag. Freeze for up to 1 month.

To Thaw and Serve

Leave wrapped at cool room temperature for 4–6 hours. Alternatively, wrap and place the bread on absorbent kitchen paper. Microwave on LOW for about 6–8 minutes, turn over. Stand for 5–15 minutes. Refresh in a hot oven for 5–10 minutes.

CHEESE AND MUSHROOM BRIOCHES

MAKES 8 BRIOCHES

275g (10oz) strong white flour, sifted

2.5ml (½ tsp) salt

15ml (1 tbsp) milk

5ml (1 tsp) caster sugar

15ml (1 tbsp) dried yeast

75g (3oz) unsalted butter

150g (5oz) button mushrooms, chopped

2 eggs, beaten

75g (3oz) Gruyère cheese, grated

beaten egg, to glaze

1 Grease eight individual brioche moulds.

2 Sift the flour and salt into a large bowl. Make well in the centre and set aside.

3 In a small bowl, beat the milk, sugar and yeast together. Leave in a warm place until frothy.

4 Meanwhile, melt 15g (½oz) of the butter in a pan and fry the mushrooms for 1½–2 minutes. Drain and cool completely.

5 Melt the remaining butter and stir into the flour mixture with the yeast mixture and eggs. Mix well to form a smooth dough. Add the mushrooms and cheese. Knead the dough for 10 minutes until smooth and elastic. Return the dough to the bowl, cover with a clean tea towel and leave in a warm place for 30 minutes until doubled in size.

6 Divide two-thirds of the dough into eight pieces and knead into balls. Place in the prepared moulds, then using the floured handle of a wooden spoon, make a small hole on top of each.

7 Divide the remaining third of the dough into six smaller balls and place on top. Indent the centre of each brioche again with the floured handle of a wooden spoon. Cover and leave in a warm place for about 30 minutes until doubled in size.

8 Carefully brush each brioche with beaten egg to glaze. Place on a baking sheet. Bake in the oven at 220°C (425°F) mark 7 for 25–30 minutes. Turn out on to a wire rack to cool completely.

To Microwave

Complete steps 1–3. Place the butter and mushrooms in a medium bowl, cover and microwave on HIGH for 2–3 minutes. Drain and cool completely. Complete steps 5–8.

To Freeze

Cool, open freeze, then pack into polythene bags. Freeze for up to 3 months.

To Thaw and Serve

Place the frozen brioches on a baking sheet and cover with foil. Bake in the oven at 200°C (400°F) mark 6 for 20–30 minutes or until warmed through. Alternatively, place the brioches in a circle on a sheet of absorbent kitchen paper on the floor of the microwave. Microwave on LOW for about 8–10 minutes or until warmed through, re-arranging.

COTTAGE LOAF ROLLS

MAKES 6 ROLLS

15g (½oz) fresh yeast or 7.5ml (1½ tsp) dried

300ml (½ pint) warm milk

450g (1lb) malted brown, strong wholemeal or white flour

5ml (1 tsp) salt

beaten egg, to glaze

1 Grease a baking sheet.

2 Blend the fresh yeast with the milk. If using dried yeast, sprinkle it into the milk and leave in a warm place for 15 minutes until frothy.

3 Put the flour and salt in a bowl. Make a well in the centre, then pour in the yeast liquid. Beat until the dough leaves the sides of the bowl clean.

4 Turn out on to a lightly floured surface and knead for about 10 minutes until smooth and elastic. Place in a clean bowl. Cover and leave in a warm place for about 1 hour until doubled in size.

5 Turn out the dough and knead lightly. Divide the dough into six, then cut off one third of each piece. Shape the dough into rounds. Place the larger rounds on to the baking sheet and brush with a little water. Place the smaller rounds on top.

6 Push the lightly floured handle of a wooden spoon down through the centre of the rolls right to the bottom. Cover and leave in a warm place for about 30 minutes until doubled in size.

7 Brush with egg to glaze and sprinkle with poppy or sesame seeds, if liked. Bake in the oven at 230°C (450°F) mark 8 for 10 minutes or until the rolls sound hollow when tapped on the bottom.

To Freeze

Cool, overwrap and seal in a polythene bag. Freeze for up to 3 months.

To Thaw and Serve

Leave to cool room temperature for 2–3 hours. Alternatively, place two rolls at a time on absorbent kitchen paper on a rack. Microwave on LOW for about 15–20 seconds. Stand for 2–3 minutes.

INDEX